PENGUIN EDUCATION

THE DEFERENTIAL WORKER

Geoff Murugham

1980

The Deferential Worker

A STUDY OF FARM WORKERS
IN EAST ANGLIA

Howard Newby

PENGUIN BOOKS

Penguin Books Ltd, Harmondsworth, Middlesex, England
Penguin Books, 625 Madison Avenue, New York, New York 10022, U.S.A.
Penguin Books Australia Ltd, Ringwood, Victoria, Australia
Penguin Books Canada Ltd, 2801 John Street, Markham, Ontario, Canada L3R 1B4
Penguin Books (N.Z.) Ltd, 182–190 Wairau Road, Auckland 10, New Zealand

—

First published by Allen Lane 1977
Published in Penguin Education 1979

—

Copyright © Howard Newby 1977
All rights reserved

—

Made and printed in Great Britain by
Richard Clay (The Chaucer Press) Ltd,
Bungay, Suffolk
Set in Monotype Bembo

Contents

Acknowledgements

One of the more pleasurable tasks of writing a book is to thank those who made it possible, and, such has been the period of gestation, the list is a large one. It must begin with my academic friends and colleagues whose practical assistance or intellectual stimulation I have preyed upon over the years. I owe an enormous debt to my colleagues in the Department of Sociology at the University of Essex for their constant support and encouragement. Parts of my argument owe a great deal to conversations with Leonore Davidoff, David Lockwood and Michael Mann. My thanks are also due to Terry Tostevin of the Essex University library staff and to Phil Holden for his computing assistance. Elsewhere I have benefited from the advice of Ada Cavazzani, George Ewart Evans, Geoffrey Hawthorn and Martin Whitby; and without David Reynolds my interest in farm workers would probably never have been aroused in the first place. Ruth Gasson will not agree with everything in this book, but her assistance over a number of years – not least in reading and commenting on the manuscript – has been immense. My greatest debt, however, must be to Colin Bell, whose encouragement, guidance and friendship has been invaluable. Without his help over nearly eight years this book would probably not have been written.

The fieldwork on which this book is based was eased by the generosity of a number of people. In the NUAAW I must particularly thank John Lumsden of Head Office for his friendly co-operation and interest and John Stewart for his kind attention and for sparing me so much of his time from his onerous duties as Suffolk District Organizer. Peter Shearer of the Suffolk NFU, now with COPA, was also most helpful. To those farmers and farm workers whom I interviewed, and who must perforce remain anonymous, I offer my sincere thanks. Almost invariably I met with more help and friendliness than I probably deserved. That my period in Suffolk was such a pleasant experience was mainly owing to Fred, Margaret, Gillian and Jean, in whose tied house I was living for six months. I was not only made to feel utterly at home, but they were wonderful key inform-ants. What more could a sociologist ask? My special thanks are due to them.

Linda Peachey, Alison Stephenson, Kathleen Butterfield, Gilly Burrell and Mary Girling all struggled bravely with my handwriting to produce a typescript. The help of Michael Shaw and Frances Kelly is also gratefully acknowledged. Jill Norman at Penguin Books has also helped to improve the final version with her editorial suggestions.

Finally my thanks to the players of Derby County for making me realize that there are finer things in life than sociology. And to my wife Janet for putting up with it all with such forbearance.

Howard Newby

Great Bentley, Essex
February 1976

Prologue: Peace, Rusticity and Happy Poverty

Agricultural workers are a group of whom most people have little knowledge or understanding. Scattered in small numbers across the countryside, often living in isolation from even local centres of population, their existence is only occasionally acknowledged. For the vast urban majority of Britain they remain mere figures in a landscape, fleetingly glimpsed from the nearest road or railway line. The social invisibility of the farm worker has made him an easy prey to caricature – 'Hodge', 'yokel', 'country bumpkin', 'clodhopper' – and even today he finds it difficult to shake off the derogatory term 'labourer', with its implication of unskilled toil and low status. The caricature of rural idiocy has enabled the general ignorance about his condition to remain unchallenged. 'Down on the farm' there may be poor pay, bad housing, inferior social facilities at every level, but out in the sticks they know no better and they seem happy enough, so why worry? There is an underlying comparison with contented cows – happiness abetted by a bovine intelligence. At most points of contact with the consciousness of the urban Englishman the agricultural worker is even denied his own identity: it is the farmer – not the farm worker – who produces Britain's food and to whom we owe our gratitude for British agriculture's startling productivity record; it is the farmer who holds up the traffic with his machinery or livestock; it is the farmer who is inside that tractor cab briefly discerned across the field as we speed by. The agricultural worker, on the other hand, retains his social invisibility, alternately ignored and caricatured in the public consciousness.

There is a marked contrast between the prevailing English attitude towards the plight of the agricultural worker and the attention lavished on the English countryside and the 'rural way of life'. Ever since England became a predominantly urban country, rural England has been regarded as the principal repository of quintessential English values. Culturally English society has never adapted itself to urban living, has never adopted an urban way of life. *Real* England has never been represented by the town, but by the village, and the English countryside has been converted into a vast arcadian rural idyll in the mind of the average Englishman. The theme of the rural idyll is thus a central element of our culture, yet it has never really benefited the agricultural worker – indeed it has hindered the general improvement of his conditions, since there has been a refusal to recognize the problem of rural poverty in the midst of this splendidly bucolic existence. The admission of the 'poor laborious natives of the place' would be to threaten the idyllic portrayal of the English countryside, and as such this strong cultural theme has been both a cause and a consequence of the agricultural worker's social invisibility.

Much of the fieldwork for this study was carried out in Suffolk, which is often regarded as the quintessence of the English countryside, attracting those images of idyllic existence so often conjured up by the words 'rural England'. The writer of a sociological study set in Suffolk, particularly one that concerns the agricultural worker, is therefore faced with a conventional taken-for-granted wisdom about the area which has to be dispelled at the outset. Suffolk has indeed attracted a huge and varied literature, a detailed reading of which gives, with only a few exceptions, a completely misleading picture of the social relationships to be found there and in the remainder of East Anglia. Its reputation as the epitome of England's green and pleasant land has been aided by thousands of Constable paintings hung in department stores up and down the country. The result is a transformation of much of the detail of rural life, a life which is represented in terms of peace, natural order, independence and mild eccentricity and from which the prevailing characteristics of the farm worker's history – poverty, exploitation, submission to authority – are largely omitted. The sentimental view of the English countryside is an easy prey to the parody of *Cold Comfort Farm*, yet the vision of the English village as an 'organic community' set in the midst of a rural idyll continues to dominate any consideration of rural society and the situation of the agricultural worker within it. It is therefore necessary to confront this idyllic portrayal at the very beginning.

The core of this tradition can be stated quite simply. Life in the countryside is viewed as one of harmony and virtue. The town is disorganized; the countryside is settled. The town is bad; the countryside is good. Social relationships in the town are superficial and alienating; relationships in the countryside are deep and fulfilling. The images

combine when the countryside is regarded as 'natural', the town as
'unnatural'. The English village has come to be regarded as the ideal
community, a tradition that prizes 'the thatched cottage and the half-
timbered house as the proper place for proper Englishmen to dwell
in'.[1] It is a tradition that has penetrated large areas of our culture,
including our literature, our aesthetics, our ideas about community,
our architecture and town and country planning, and even our social
science. Such a tradition acts not so much as a pair of blinkers as a
filter through which the reality of rural life for those who live in it is
constantly being reinterpreted by the rest of society until the stage has
been reached where an entirely misleading account of the nature of
rural social relationships is believed, not only by those on the outside,
but by those who experience them at first hand. In other words, the
tradition of the rural idyll is important to understand, not only because
it will otherwise hinder the interpretation of this book, but because it
has affected the agricultural worker's interpretation of his own situation, for a general cultural approval of the rural way of life is something that an otherwise low-paid, low-status group of workers is
grateful to adhere to with understandable enthusiasm. To analyse this
tradition, in both a national and a local context, is thus to begin an
analysis of the consciousness of the agricultural worker.

If the Good Life is to be set in a rural environment, of what does
this Good Life consist? The first essential element is one of unchanging
continuity. The English village is seen as a timeless institution of
immemorial antiquity, despite being in its essentials a product of
relatively recent developments. As W. E. Tate has shown[2] it arose out
of the Georgian enclosures and the Agricultural Revolution only a
short space of time before the Industrial Revolution transformed urban
Britain. In its social structure, in its economic base and even to a great
extent in the mere physical form it only just preceded the 'unnatural'
city; nevertheless the tradition insists that it is the town that lacks
'roots' while the village lends the weight of perpetuity to its social
structure. The sheer continuity of experience is supposed to render
relationships more meaningful and more real: 'The townsman envies
the villager his certainties and, in Britain, has always regarded urban
life as just a temporary necessity. One day he will find a cottage on the
green and "real values".'[3]

Another characteristic of the rural idyll is the so-called 'Golden
Age' syndrome. Since, historically, migration has occurred from the

countryside to the towns, rural life is susceptible to a more straightforward kind of nostalgia – the notion of the 'good old days'. One of
the best examples can be seen in works of Cobbett. In his critique of
industrialism he used the opportunity to conjure up a rural arcadia
peopled by merrie rustics and sturdy beef-eating yeomanry. The
repression and privations of old England were forgotten in a welter of
nostalgia for the mythical, lost paternalistic community. Succeeding
authors repeated Cobbett's vision of the ideal rural society, a society
which consisted, in the words of his biographer, of 'a benificent
landowner, a sturdy peasantry, a village community self-supporting
and static'.[4] It was a picture repeated by Coleridge – 'a healthful
callous-handed, but high and warm-hearted tenantry';[5] by Engels,
by the Hammonds and by a multitude of commentators and historians concerned with rural England. Cobbett indeed has spawned a
peculiarly English literary genre on the boundaries of history, sociology, natural history and biography – a retrospective documentary
approach to the chronicling of rural life.[6] Its monument is the Country
Book Club, but its practitioners are very numerous and the quality of
writing is extremely varied. It is a genre that encompasses such writers
as Richard Jefferies, W. H. Hudson, George Bourne, Flora Thompson,
H. J. Massingham and a host of local and regional authors, so that the
echoes of Cobbett's voice continue to roll through the pages of many
books on English rural life today. He was responsible for the popular-
ization during the nineteenth century of an idealization of rural life
that emerged out of the critique of urban industrialism but which has
since been consolidated into a tradition of its own.

The idyllic view of English rural life has thus encompassed all
shades of political opinion. Its very pervasiveness has led to what Ruth
Glass has called 'a lengthy, thorough course of indoctrination, to
which all of us, everywhere, have at some time or other been subjected . . . and to many of us the adjective "rural" has pleasant, reassuring connotations – beauty, order, simplicity, rest, grass-roots democracy, peacefulness, *Gemeinschaft*'.[7] Embedded deep in English culture
there is now a strong belief that work on the land has some intrinsic
value which renders it more morally beneficial and that to dwell in an
English village is to be more attuned to traditional realities. It is hardly
a view which has benefited the agricultural worker, for, as a result, he
has received little attention from those who have established a tradition of concern for the urban poor. For the agricultural worker more

metaphysical rewards have been deemed to be adequate compensation for his labour: 'Nevertheless, in spite of hard and ill-paid work and few of the recreations and distractions which we think essential to our existence, it would be a mistake to imagine that the average farm worker, even when elderly, poverty-stricken and ailing, fails to enjoy life and achieve a fair measure of happiness. Frequently he is a fine exemplification of the fundamental aphorism of Scripture, that "man's life consisteth not in the abundance of the things which he possesseth". He retains a keen interest in life, with the endless petty details of what to us would be a wearisome monotony, and his quiet humour and steadfast cheerfulness can be unfailing, and put to shame the grumbles of those endowed with far more material blessings. He can find contentment in the bare indispensables of life, and peace in the narrow circle of an unchanging daily round.'[8] It hardly needs to be added that such a passage could only be written by someone who was not himself 'elderly, poverty-stricken and ailing' but who had reached the level of material comfort to appreciate the less material advantages of a rural environment. There are echoes of the poet Gray's comment on Grasmere – 'This little unsuspected paradise, where all is peace, rusticity and happy poverty.'

The agricultural worker, then, is *not* deprived, according to this view, not because he possesses a high standard of living, but because a high standard of living *does not matter*. This point exemplifies much of the ambivalence that Blythe exhibits in *Akenfield*, a book which achieves a good deal in exposing the past degradations of the agricultural worker's life, but in which one also comes across passages such as the following: 'There is, in the bony quiet of their faces, not insularity or an absence of response, but a rational notion of "first things first" as they say. The peculiarly English social revolution which began immediately after the war has dramatically changed the countryman's life, though not nearly so dramatically as his cousin's life in the towns. He has his 1960s comforts and luxuries, as well as a fair inkling of popular sixties culture, but these things, though grabbed for by one who has a long memory of bleakness, are apt to be regarded as trimmings. The earth itself has its latest drugs and fertilizers poured into it to make it rich and yielding, but it is still the "old clay". In both its and his reality, the elemental quality remains uppermost.'[9] This passage illustrates Blythe's concern for continuity of experience and culture in the English village. It is echoed in a general concern that forms one of the themes of *Akenfield*, that in coming to terms with the changing exigencies of contemporary East Anglian life the community should not cut its 'atavistic thread' with the past. It is an attitude common among the new non-agricultural rural population and the readers of that thoroughly urban journal, *Country Life*.[10] They are the new rural *afficionados*, aware of country customs and respectful of the knowledge and wisdom of long-standing rural inhabitants. They are appreciative of the skill of the modern farm worker and would never denigrate him by the use of the old epithets. Indeed, rather than a clodhopper he is now regarded as the archetypal salt-of-the-earth figure. *Akenfield* exactly conforms to the expectations of these *afficionados*: it does not gloss over the harshness and depravity of the old authoritarian system, and it reminds the reader that agricultural workers are still low-paid and deserving of better treatment. Nevertheless Akenfield is presented as a community more attuned to the realities of living: a population of individual characters rather than bland conformists; a stable, integrated, but now threatened, community life; a commune with the soil, the 'elemental quality' that remains uppermost. Blythe's book, lyrically written and full of the most acute insights, nevertheless remains in the mainstream of the English literary tradition of rural retrospect: nostalgia with a dash of realism, but still nostalgic for an era that appears to be ending. On the reality of this situation, however, the agricultural workers in *Akenfield* remain suspiciously silent.

There has been, then, a customary elision between the aesthetic and the social – a belief that an environment that meets with our aesthetic approval must be capable of supporting a socially beneficial way of life for all its members, just as an aesthetically devalued appearance must accompany social deprivation. The 'little boxes' of suburbia are supposed to contain a way of life of dreary self-containment and crushing conformity. The huge conurbations support a lonely, conflictual, alienated, individualistic existence which reflects the 'inhuman' scale of city buildings. The rural equivalent is the 'organic community', a social structure that complements the admired aesthetic qualities of the English countryside.[11] The use of the word 'organic' emphasizes the elision between the aesthetic and the ecological on the one hand and the social on the other. It obviously derives in part from its connotations with the land and fertility. Yet it also emphasizes a prescribed form of social structure that was very common among nineteenth-century social thinkers, including important figures in the history of sociological thought, like Spencer and Durkheim. The rural way of life is alleged to consist of a structure of 'mutual dependencies' analogous to a human organism, with each part supporting the correct functioning of the system as a whole. It is a view which stresses the stability and harmony of village society, for just as conflict between two parts of the human organism is unusual, if not pathological, so rural society possesses a fundamental equilibrium which is only occasionally disturbed. This is because in the organic community there can be no conflict of interest between individual members, merely a 'natural order' in which each 'knows his place'.[12]

It may be argued that this debunking of the idealized portrayal of English country life is unnecessary. Indeed it has become rather fashionable in the academic literature on countryside planning to underline the conventionally sentimental vision of the rural village held by the vast non-agricultural majority in this country.[13] However, there are no indications whatever that the 'national village cult' is abating. There is a direct continuity between this cult and the recent fashionable concern for the environment, largely (though not entirely) regarded as an attempt to resist urban encroachments on a pristine English countryside. In the accompanying movement for the conservation – mostly expressed in fact as the preservation – of rural England can be discerned many of the familiar themes of rural retrospect. Moreover, recent realization that changes in the rural community are also being wrought from within as well as from outside has even brought upon the indigenous agricultural population the wrath of the preservationist lobby.[14] The rural idyll, then, remains a deeply engrained theme in English cultural life, already being transformed into another idiom to encompass contemporary changes. 'It is difficult,' writes Raymond Williams 'to overestimate the importance of this myth, in modern social thought.'[15]

Only Raymond Williams has examined in any detail the progression of this myth as it has appeared in English literature. He is concerned with what he calls 'the persistence and historicity' of the concepts of the country and the city, or, more precisely, 'what kind of experience do the ideas appear to interpret, and why do certain forms occur or recur at this period or at that?'[16] Williams then traces the various clusters of ideas that the English countryside has encompassed – harmony, settlement, virtue, retreat, community, innocence,

identity, retrospect – and links these (together with a parallel cluster
of ideas about the city) to the development of the capitalist mode of
production in England since the Middle Ages. He argues that ideas
about the countryside and the city have represented, over the centuries, an idiom in which those who have experienced the fundamental
economic and social transformations wrought by capitalism have
been able to express these experiences. 'Clearly,' he writes, 'ideas of
the country and the city have specific contents and histories, but just
as clearly, at times, they are forms of isolation and identification of
more general processes. People have often said "the city" when they
meant capitalism or bureaucracy or centralized power, while "the
country" . . . has at times meant everything from independence to
deprivation, and from the powers of an active imagination to a form
of release from consciousness. At every point we need to put these
ideas to the historical realities: at times to be confirmed, at times
denied. But also, as we see the whole process, we need to put the
historical realities to the ideas, for at times these express, not only in
disguise and displacement but in effective mediation or in offered and
sometimes effective transcendence, human interests and purposes for
which there is no other immediately available vocabulary. It is not
only an absence or distance of more specific terms and concepts; it
is that in country and city, physically present and substantial, the
experience finds material which gives body to the thought.'[17]

One specific example may illustrate this point – the persistent theme
of rural retrospect, the idea that the 'real' countryside was the countryside of yesterday and that an era in which 'real' country predominated
stretched back in unbroken continuity until a recent transformation
had overthrown it. Just as today one hears how an ancient rural
culture has since the war been destroyed by the effects of the internal
combustion engine on both the farm and the village, so, before the
war, one finds an equally widespread belief that traditional rural
England had been destroyed by the break-up of the large landed
estates since the First World War. However, at the turn of the century,
when George Bourne (Sturt) had written in *Change in the Village* of a
rural England that 'is dying out now', there was a similar belief that
the indigenous rural culture had been eliminated by rural depopulation since the middle of the nineteenth century – at which time it was
complained that the real village community had been destroyed by
enclosure and the Poor Law since the eighteenth century. And so

further back one goes in the search for this lost rural community, back to the time when Goldsmith was writing in *The Deserted Village* that

> E'en now, methinks, as pondering here I stand
> I see the rural virtues leave the land.

Back and back one goes until, one supposes, Domesday and even the ultimate rural idyll – the Garden of Eden.[18] This lost rural England is a myth, but nevertheless a myth that has been widely held and sincerely believed in, just as it has corresponded to certain real experiences in the development of agricultural production in this country.

Raymond Williams relates the persistence of this myth to one of the important contradictions in unfettered capitalist development – its ability to increase real wealth in an unprecedented manner, but its simultaneous tendency to distribute it unevenly.[19] This created recurrent problems of maintenance of social stability in rural England and produced a series of mainly social and political controls that, given the enormous disparities in economic reward, were extraordinarily successful in stifling any concerted attack upon the system. Ostensibly, this may seem all the more remarkable, since the disparities in wealth and power that capitalism created were all the more visible in the small-scale, particularistic social system of the rural village. In most rural areas the necessary transformations in social and economic relationships were conducted, not by impersonal, absentee institutions, but by knowable, all-too-present individuals – the local landowners. However, it was precisely because they were present and because social control could be carried out on a personal, face-to-face basis that they were able to dissociate themselves from the consequences of their own actions. They, too, were led to regret the contemporary demise of rural society, to ameliorate with charity the conditions of those whom the new economic system had displaced. They, too, regretted the breakdown of a traditional way of life. The myth of rural retrospect thus became, consciously or unconsciously, an agent of social control.[20] Williams summarizes this process as follows: 'Of course to the extent that the new social system was itself becoming more successful, more pervasive and more confidently aggressive, there was always likely to be a local basis for some kind of retrospective regret. In this place and that, different ways, different times, could be actually remembered. But under the pressure of the general contradictions of the system this realistic local observation grew to a general historical outline, and then to a myth. The English land-owning class, which had changed itself in changing the world, was idealized and displaced into an historical contrast with its own real activities. In its actual inhumanity, it could be recognized only with difficulty by men linked to and dependent on it, and the great majority of the poor and oppressed were without a connecting voice to make clear the recognition which was their daily experience. Thus a humane instinct was separated from society; it became a sympathy and a pity, *after* the decisive social events. The real ruling class could not be put in question, so they were seen as temporarily absent, or as the good old people succeeded by the bad new people – themselves succeeding themselves. We have heard this sad song for many centuries now: a seductive song, turning protest into retrospect until we die of time.'[21]

The tradition of rural retrospect is far from dead today. Anyone with even the most cursory acquaintance with agricultural workers will know that they constantly refer to the past when analysing their contemporary experiences. Their view of this past is ambiguous. When discussing wages and working conditions, they are regarded as 'the bad old days', probably a result of the considerable absolute (though not necessarily relative) rise in their standard of living. However, the past becomes 'the good old days' when they begin to consider changes in the life of the village. Many agricultural workers have seen their village overrun, as they regard it, by an alien, urban, over-whelmingly middle-class population, variously labelled as new-comers, immigrants, outsiders or, simply, 'furriners', who are viewed as having destroyed a distinctive rural way of life and a close-knit community in which 'everybody knew everybody else'. In the same breath they idealize their lost 'organic' community and produce a hostile response towards the urban newcomers whom they feel have been responsible for its demise. In reality, however, the appearance in the village of a large non-agricultural population has been due in no small part to changes within agriculture itself, notably the diminution in the demand for labour that has resulted from mechanization and the consequent outflow of the rural population in search of employ-ment in the towns. The process described by Raymond Williams is therefore repeating itself. Today many farmers share with their employees a quite sincere regret for a state of affairs that they them-selves, in responding to market factors, have brought about. Farmer and farm worker *together* retain an insular response towards a social group who are merely the outward manifestation of social changes wrought by the continuing economic development of agriculture. It is the new urbanites, not the rural employers, who are blamed for the declining rural way of life. Thus, changes in the social composition of the English village have not resulted in any increasing conflict between farmer and farm worker. Indeed their shared response to these changes may well have brought them closer together.

One may conclude, then, that the traditional English approach to life in the countryside is far from being an irrelevancy to the understanding of how contemporary agricultural workers perceive their social situation. From almost every possible cultural source and personal acquaintance they are presented with a particular interpretation of rural society and its recent changes that, not surprisingly, has eventually gained their widespread adherence. It is also apparent that if agricultural workers represent a group whose present behaviour is highly conditioned by their perceptions of the past, then it is necessary to be aware of what this past contains. For their view of the past *is* ambiguous. While many agricultural workers view past village life with affectionate nostalgia, they equally adhere to a view, fuelled by an entirely different set of experiences and cultural traditions, which recalls bitter exploitation over pay and working conditions.

1. P. Laslett, *The World We Have Lost*, Methuen, 1965, p. 25.
2. W. E. Tate, *The English Village Community*, Gollancz, 1967, Ch. 1.
3. R. Blythe, *Akenfield: Portrait of an English Village*, Allen Lane, 1969, pp. 5–6. Echoes of Blythe's comment abound elsewhere. For example: 'The countryman stands for the real England, changing only with the seasons, adapting only according to need ... When the Englishman is abroad, he does not think of home as the Balance-of-Payments situation, the white hot heat of technological competition, but recalls the annual point-to-point, the village green, the local pub, the cricket team, the sound of church bells. East Anglia still represents these realities.' These 'realities' belong to R. Booth in his essay 'The Rich Land' in M. Watkins (ed.), *The East Anglian Book*, East Anglian Magazine Ltd, Ipswich, 1971, p. 101.
4. W. B. Pemberton, *William Cobbett*, Penguin Books, 1949, p. 139.
5. Quoted by R. Williams, in *Culture and Society, 1780–1950*, Penguin Books, 1961, p. 34.
6. See the collection of extracts in E. W. Martin (ed.), *Country Life in England*, Macdonald, 1966.
7. R. Glass, 'Conflict in Cities', in the CIBA Foundation symposium *Conflict in Society*, Churchill, 1966, p. 142.

8. H. Batsford and G. Fry, *The English Cottage*, Batsford, 1938, p. 99.

9. Blythe, op. cit., pp. 14–15. See also C. H. Warren, *Corn Country*, Batsford, 1940, p. 104; and the same author's *Content With What I Have*, Bles, 1967, pp. 37, 39.

10. N. Fairbrother, *New Lives, New Landscapes*, Penguin Books, 1972, p. 101.

11. See Martin (ed.), op. cit., pp. 180–93.

12. The organic approach to English rural society has been clearly set out by H. J. Massingham: 'There are three anatomical essentials in every genuine English parish – the church, the houses, and the fields, corresponding to the three ultimates: God–Man–Earth. This indivisible trinity is a hierarchy of separate entities, the fields being subordinated to the houses, the house to the church. Every authentic village recognizes this triune order by its siting. Translate this arrangement into human terms and, broadly speaking, it represents folk–food–faith . . . The fold were subdivided into five main types – the peasant, the yeoman, the craftsman, the squire, and the priest or parson, represented by the cottage, the farmstead, the workshop, the manor, and the rectory or priest's house by the church. This was the fundamental pattern of the village from Anglo-Saxon times up to the nineteenth century. Now look at these five types as they are today, and it is obvious that each one is suffering from functional disturbance . . . That is to say the structural equilibrium has been thrown out of relation and out of gear; the functional working has been dislocated. What is more important, nothing of any organic reality has taken its place.' See Martin (ed.), op. cit., p. 191.

13. W. Petersen, 'The Ideological Origins of Britain's New Towns', *American Institute of Planners' Journal*, vol. XXXIV, No. 2, May 1968, pp. 160–70; R. J. Green, *Country Planning: The Future of the Rural Regions*, Manchester University Press, 1971, Ch. 1; Glass, op. cit.; Fairbrother, op. cit.

14. For example, the high-priest of the preservationist lobby, Sir Colin Buchanan, has accused farmers of being 'the most ruthless section of the business community. The planners and the road engineers have had a good bashing, but they have learnt their lesson. The real danger to the countryside now lies with the agricultural community' (speech to the Council for the Preservation of Rural England, reported in *Farmers Weekly*, 1 June 1973, p. 47).

15. R. Williams, *The Country and the City*, Chatto and Windus, 1973, p. 96. This chapter relies a good deal upon Williams's analysis. The gist of his argument was expressed in two radio broadcasts reprinted in *The Listener*: 'Literature and Rural Society', 16 November 1967; and 'Literature and the City', 23 November 1967.

16. Williams (1973), op. cit., pp. 289–90.

17. ibid., p. 291.

18. ibid., Ch. 2.

19. ibid., p. 82.

20. ibid., pp. 82–3.

21. ibid.

CHAPTER ONE
The Historical Context

One suspects that for most people the history of the agricultural worker means the Tolpuddle Martyrs, but, while they have guaranteed the agricultural worker a special place in the history of British trade-unionism, their significance is almost entirely symbolic. The characteristic response of the agricultural worker to his social and economic position has not been one which has placed him in the vanguard of the labour movement. The very strong and frequently overlooked tradition of rural protest and class conflict has taken other, more individual, covert and subtle forms of action, not always amenable to conventional methods of historical investigation. Because the organized labour movement has always been weak among agricultural workers, the attention paid to them by labour historians has shown a progressive decline the more one moves from the Captain Swing riots in the 1830s to the present day and, though there are now some encouraging signs of a revival of interest, the history of the agricultural worker badly needs to be rewritten in the light of contemporary concerns and issues. Hobsbawm and Rudé have accomplished this for the Swing era,[1] but there is little to show for the remainder of the nineteenth century, apart from a few isolated examples on the 1870s, and even less on the early part of the twentieth century. Predictably, the recent trend towards a more sociological approach to the history of the working class has concentrated on urban history, while no one has systematically investigated the history of the rural working class in the manner that, say, F. M. L. Thompson has for their upper-class counterparts.[2] One could almost repeat *verbatim* Sidney Webb's despairing Preface to Hasbach's *A History of the English Agricultural Labourer*, including his comment that, 'In spite of the fact that the materials for such a history were abundant and easily accessible, and that the subject has for thirty or forty years been one of social and political interest, none of the schools of history of our universities has produced a student with the necessary zeal and capacity to do the work that lay to hand.'[3]

It is certainly not the purpose of this chapter even to attempt such a task. But equally any study of the contemporary social situation of agricultural workers cannot ignore their history, particularly as it is a history to which they themselves, however imperfectly, constantly refer. In what is really, then, a mere historical introduction, this chapter will analyse certain themes in the agricultural workers' past, otherwise it becomes impossible to comprehend their current attitudes and behaviour.

The Work

Until very recently the rural village and the society which it contained was organized first and foremost around a particular kind of *work*. Agriculture was the *raison d'être*, indeed the defining characteristic, of all rural areas and, whatever the extent of other extractive or small manufacturing industries, virtually every inhabitant of the rural village was engaged in, or dependent on, farming for a livelihood. For this reason, accidents of climate and topography have conferred on certain rural areas particular configurations of social structure and this has always made generalization about British agriculture a somewhat hazardous exercise; hence generalizations about rural society can be fraught with difficulty. The physical environment, however, may still impose certain constraints on farming practice and so one broad generalization that may still be made with some degree of truth is the importance of the distinction between the predominantly pastoral, upland areas of the north and west and the mainly arable, lowland areas of the south and east.[4] The growing of crops entails an altogether different cycle of production, rhythm of work and, most importantly, deployment of land, labour and capital resources from the tending and grazing of animals. This is not, however, to argue for an ecological determinism of the rural social structure, for, whatever the nature of the husbandry, the land itself can be held in quite different ways. Thus, while it is true to say that in general land was, and is, divided into small units of production in the pastoral areas and into much larger units in the lowland, arable areas, there are numerous exceptions in each case. Extensive farming – 'ranching' – in the upland areas could produce very large units (as around Westrigg), just as in the Isle of Axholme in Lincolnshire a holding of forty acres of land was considered large.[5]

In each case variations in the agricultural system produce different social structures. In Britain there are many local and regional variations in agriculture that are reflected in the structure of local social systems, and it is important that these should not be obscured by generalizations that can become too sweeping.

On the other hand, it is not necessary to retreat into a belief in the unique qualities of each and every rural village and the impossibility of any summarization. Generally speaking the pastoral/arable distinction remains an important one and its geographical line of demarcation remains roughly where Caird placed it.[6] It is certainly important not to conflate the two areas when discussing their respective social structures and the location of hired agricultural workers within them. Broadly, in the pastoral areas farms are smaller in size, family labour predominates and little hired labour is used. Most hired workers have kinship links with farmers and many can confidently await their inheritance of the family farm. Settlements tend to be more scattered and the distinctions in life-style between farmer and farm worker are less marked than in the lowland, arable areas. It is this kind of agricultural area that has been most extensively studied by sociologists and anthropologists, and there are some excellent descriptions of the work-cycle of this type of agriculture in the sociological literature.[7] Some aspects of this literature are discussed in the next chapter. The pastoral farming areas of the Highland Zone require a quite separate analysis and possess a quite separate history. It is not intended that the analysis of this chapter, or indeed the rest of this book, should apply to them.

In the lowland, arable areas of the south and east, and especially in East Anglia, the nature of arable farming, with its lengthy cycle of production and the necessity to regiment a large labour force for certain specific periods of intense activity, like seed-time and harvest, made for a rigid and hierarchical social structure.[8] The sheer size of the labour force created a reasonably complex division of labour on many farms, particularly in East Anglia, where the farms were bigger and employed more labour. In 1851, for example, there were at least eighty-three farmers in Suffolk employing thirty or more men and nearly one-fifth of Suffolk farmers were employing ten or more, a figure which, as Hobsbawm and Rudé point out, 'was by no means unimpressive even by contemporary non-agricultural standards'.[9]

Unlike his counterparts in livestock farming areas, therefore, the Suffolk farmer needed to have no particular skill or expertise in crop

Table 1 Number of labourers employed on farms in England and Wales and in Suffolk, 1851

| | England and Wales | | Suffolk | |
Labourers No.	Farmers No.	%	Farmers No.	%
0	68,348	23·8	748	14·7
1	45,809	16·0	686	13·5
2	36,259	12·6	650	12·8
3	27,902	9·7	482	9·5
4	22,260	7·8	468	9·2
5	17,488	6·1	321	6·3
6	17,743	6·2	268	5·3
7	12,344	4·3	194	3·8
8	10,893	3·8	170	3·3
9	9,292	3·2	160	3·1
10–14	8,208	2·9	489	9·6
15–19	4,033	1·4	186	3·7
20–24	2,465	0·9	136	2·7
25–29	1,367	0·5	39	0·8
30–34	930	0·3	44	0·9
35–39	546	0·2	11	0·2
40–44	413	0·1	7	0·1
45–49	266	0·09	7	0·1
50–54	201	0·07	5	0·1
55–59	128	0·04	1	0·02
60 and over	98	0·03	8	0·1

Source: J. Glyde, *Suffolk in the Nineteenth Century* ..., 1856

husbandry, still less a capability to perform manual labour on the farm. His importance lay in the provision of capital, the management of labour and careful planning in the timing of essential farming tasks. Since it cost as much to produce a bad arable crop as a good one, profit was determined essentially by yield, which in turn depended upon the farmer's entrepreneurial skill in mitigating the possible adverse effects of soil and weather conditions. Therefore, as a succession of immigrant Celts and foreign observers throughout the nineteenth century were to discover to their amazement, the East Anglian farmers did not work: 'They supervised and gave the proverbial pig the proverbial prod while leaning over the proverbial gate. Economically their importance was capital.'[10] To the capitalist agricultural entrepreneurs of East Anglia labour was just one more resource to be manipulated. By the end of the century Wilson Fox was to observe laconically: 'In the two Eastern counties, Norfolk and Suffolk ... [there] is the tendency for relations between employers and employed to become confined solely to business matters, there being no identity of interest after each has during the working hours fulfilled his part of the contract, that is the one to work for pay and the other to pay for work.'[11]

Arable farming in East Anglia had become consolidated as a thoroughgoing capitalist enterprise in the period during and immediately after the Napoleonic Wars, and what came to be regarded as the traditional tri-partite socio-economic structure of the English countryside was established during this period. Landlord, tenant-farmer and agricultural labourer represented the three 'natural orders' upon which rural society was based. Their emergence stemmed from the increasing market-orientation of agriculture and its most renowned accoutrement–enclosure. The precise chronology of the enclosure movement is a matter of some debate, but by 1850 the effect was clear enough: the English peasantry had disappeared to be replaced by a rural working class of agricultural labourers on the one hand and a prosperous tenantry on the other. This process of proletarianization of the mass of the English peasantry had occurred fitfully and unevenly, both in time and in location. In the eastern extremities of East Anglia, for example, the land had been enclosed since Saxon times, but elsewhere in arable England enclosure had been given little impetus until the eighteenth-century growth of the urban population and the artificially induced monopoly during the revolutionary and Napoleonic Wars, preserved after the war by the Corn Laws.

By the time of their repeal in 1846, farmers were quite clearly a qualitatively different group from their employees, a degree of social distance which had originated in the growing abandonment of in-service and the progressive proletarianization of the labour force over the previous hundred years. Such social distinctions were reinforced by the era of prosperity which the repeal of the Corn Laws (spuriously) opened; indeed the distinctions of wealth, income and life-style were considerably exacerbated during this period. Arable England was embarking upon the period of 'high farming' which was to be nostalgically recalled as the 'Golden Age' during the later years of depression after 1873.[12] There is a good deal of evidence to show that farmer and worker became a great deal more remote from each other, socially and culturally, and that the apparent peace and tranquillity which descended on rural England after the Captain Swing disturbances were almost everywhere superficial and ephemeral. It is probably from this period that a distinctive rural working-class subculture was born, a culture which, allowing for the constraints of a scattered and isolated rural population, was not dissimilar to that which emerged in the towns. It was a culture that contained elements of both conservative deference and radical resistance, but was probably most marked by fatalistic acceptance, an accommodation to a situation which the agricultural worker was powerless to alter and to which he reacted for the most part by silence, taciturnity and a withdrawal into a close-knit and for the most part impenetrable circle of fellow workers. From this he would emerge to behave to his 'betters' with the appropriately servile and 'deferential' demeanour that was expected of him. For the appellation of 'high farming' carried a number of social as well as agricultural connotations. High farming also represented the desire of many tenant farmers – and their wives – to become 'gentleman' farmers, and a corollary of this was a demand to be treated with the proper respect to which they were becoming accustomed.

The basis of the high-farming, arable/livestock system was the Norfolk four-course rotation, 'perhaps the most perfectly balanced rotation in farming history', as one survey of British farming practice has called it.[13] This was the rotation which established the reputation of the eighteenth-century agricultural improvers, most notably 'Turnip' Townshend. The rotation consisted of red clover–winter wheat–turnips–spring barley. 'The beauty of the system,' write the Donaldsons, 'was that each crop contributed to the welfare of the next: the build-up of weeds, disease and pests was avoided because susceptible crops were followed by non-susceptible, and the orderly sequence of winter and spring planting balanced the work throughout the year'.[14] The end-products of the system were cereals – wheat and barley – and sheep, which were grazed on the grass and 'folded' on the turnips, in each case returning fertility to the soil which was to be extracted by the cropping of cereals. As long as cereals and sheep *together* remained profitable, the system was maintained. Not until the final quarter of the century was the profitability of the rotation endangered; then the combined threats of poor seasons, cheap imports of grain from North America and the importation of New Zealand lamb produced a crisis in the high-farming system from which it never recovered.[15]

Since sheep were so important to high farming, shepherds were common in East Anglia, juxtaposed in the farm work-force with the ploughmen – 'horsemen' in East Anglia – who were the mainstay of the arable farm.[16] This division of labour was also often a status division, for shepherds traditionally regarded themselves as something of a race apart from the horsemen. By the nature of their job, shepherds usually worked alone. They were subject neither to the close supervision of employers nor to the informal norms of the horsemen, who tended much more to work together as a group and take their breaks together. Shepherds therefore had much more discretion and control over their own activities than the average horseman. The shepherd also maintained the kind of aloof independence from his employer that Littlejohn noted much more recently in the Scottish borders.[17] This was no doubt aided by the strong market situation of the shepherd – both farmers and shepherds knew that the key to the profitability of the flock was the employment of a skilled and trustworthy shepherd. As in Westrigg, esteemed farmers and shepherds sought each other out and competition for shepherds with an established reputation could be fierce. This was reflected not only in their autonomy but also in their payment being above that of the horseman and in their having a yearly contract rather than the daily one of the ordinary farm labourer.

The separation of the shepherd from his fellow workers was also emphasized by the different timing of periods of peak activity. Lambing is 'the shepherd's harvest' but it occurs at a time of the year when work on the arable side is at its slackest. Early lambs were born at the end of December and lambing was largely completed by seed-time. Shearing was carried out in June, and, since this normally coincided with haysel (the hay harvest), was performed by a 'company' (itinerant gang) of shearers. Flocks of sheep were often moved around the district to be folded on the root crops of different farms and in the summer were moved to the marshes and water-meadows around the East Anglian coast and river estuaries. All these factors

meant that, like any stockman, the shepherd had to be in constant close
contact with the animals in his charge, but the devotion of shepherds
in particular is notorious and has even entered the area of metaphor
and cliché in the English language. Ketteridge and Mays, for example,
describe the work of a shepherd on the Essex–Cambridgeshire border:
'Riley was the simplest of men and illiterate; he had done nothing in
life except tend his flock, and this he did lovingly seven days a week
throughout each year without a holiday ... From a flock of 300 a
good half will lamb in a fortnight, and several within a few minutes
of each other. During this important season Riley went home only
to "fetch a mite more wittels", when he was really ravenous. It is
doubtful whether he ever spent Christmas at home with his wife and
daughter during his "precious time", as he called it. Most of his early
lambs were born at the end of December, and he would divide
Christmas time between the lambing pens and his four-wheeled van,
drawn up close to hand in the nearest field. He would not take off his
clothes for ten days and slept only in snatches in the hut, in which the
tiny stove would often go out and if the cold did not wake him the
first bleat of one of his charges would. His new lambs were the first
and last thing in his life ... He never complained.'[18]

It is not, then, difficult to envisage the degree of separation between
the shepherd and the other agricultural workers on his farm. Their
situation is summarized by Robert Savage, a retired shepherd and one
of Evans' respondents in *Ask the Fellows Who Cut the Hay*. 'Us
shepherds had to be serious chaps. The farmer would let us git on by
ourselves. You were independent and you had to think forrard. You
can't say with sheep: "I'll do this now and maybe I'll do that tomorrow." You got to wait and do everything in its turn. You got to
think forrard. And you can't break into something different when you
a-shepherding. I couldn't give any hid [head] to anything else until
after I'd given up sheep. Though you got plenty of time to think
when you are with the sheep, cos shepherding is a lonely life. You got
no one to talk to. For the whole fore part of the day, when you took
them up to the walks you wouldn't see a soul.'[19]

The same could hardly be said of the horsemen. They were much
more gregarious, working together in the care and management of
the horses in the stables as well as frequently ploughing together in the
same field out on the land. This gregariousness created and maintained
a particular occupational subculture, with its own set of norms and

values and with its own status distinctions. The main division was between the horsemen and the 'day-men', who were farm labourers in the literal sense of that term and whose conditions of employment were inferior to those of the horsemen. Day-men, as the term suggests, worked by the day, whereas horsemen were on a fixed weekly wage. Day-men were therefore likely to be laid off on wet days and on other occasions when the land could not be worked – principally during the winter. In many respects day-men represented a pool of reserve labour frequently living on the margin between employment and poor relief. Horsemen were more secure in their employment; they were not sent home on wet days, or, even if they were, they did not lose their wages for the days they lost. The horsemen were entitled to more perquisites and were generally more skilled – their ability to plough a straight furrow or drill an immaculate seed-bed was one that was recognized by farmer and fellow employees alike. Within the ranks of the horsemen, however, there was an order of precedence that was rigidly adhered to. This was celebrated twice a day in the order in which the horsemen departed for the fields and in the order in which they returned. Evans describes well the quasi-ritual atmosphere in which they turned out: 'The head horsemen or first baiter went first; then came the first baiter's mate; then the second baiter who was followed by his mate. If a horseman, either through perversity or absent-mindedness, took his team out of the stable before his turn in the ordered procession, there was a true disturbance. The erring groom was rated with a peremptory, "Don't you know where your place is?" The same precedence was carefully observed at the end of the day when the teams had completed their work in the field. If a second horseman, for instance, happened to finish ploughing somewhere near the gate, it would not do for him to proceed out. He had to "hold to one side", draw his horses away from the gate until the first horseman and his mate had passed through. Only then could he move his team into the procession that both horses and men had looked forward to, at least during the latter hours of their long task in the field.'[20]

Both the timing and the rhythm of the work was vastly different from those of the mechanized agriculture of today. The horseman was up at 4 a.m. to feed the horses, and, after having returned home for breakfast, would turn out to plough at 6.30 (7 a.m. in the winter). The horseman would then be out working on the land continuously until

around 2.30 p.m., with a twenty-minute break for 'elevenses', eaten
out in the field. The customary amount of ploughing for a day's work
was one acre, although it could be slightly more or less according to
the condition of the land. This alone involved the horseman walking
eleven miles by the time he had completed his stint. Having returned
the teams to the stables, the horsemen went home for dinner, returning at 3.30 p.m. to feed, clean and groom their horses until they
finished their days work at 5.30 p.m. This daily routine occurred on
six days of the week, though the intensity of the work would vary
during the year. Seed-time and harvest were the periods of most
intense activity, particularly harvest. The horsemen were, however,
kept fully employed at other times of the year, carting hay, muck-
spreading, autumn ploughing and, during the winter, on threshing or
hedging and ditching. Both Evans and Ketteridge and Mays[21] have
given extended descriptions of the work-cycle of arable agriculture in
the latter part of the nineteenth century, and they indicate the degree
of variety which the changing of the seasons introduces into work on
the land and which has not, of course, been removed by wholesale
mechanization.

Sociologically there are a number of points of significance that arise
from the work situation of the East Anglian agricultural worker in
these years. Partly because of the larger size of the labour force and the
nature of arable cultivation, the employer was a much more remote
and authoritarian figure: he did not for the most part work alongside
his employees and his personal contact with his workers was often
limited to the issuing of orders and the payment of wages – and even
these tasks could be mediated through the foreman or head horseman.[22] The larger number of workers also entailed some degree of
hierarchical organization among them: authority over everyday
matters had to be delegated for the farm to run smoothly. This in
itself accounts for a certain amount of the status distinctions within
the agricultural work-force – they derive from the occupational
division of labour. However, these status distinctions were maintained and reinforced in a number of ways.

Positions of responsibility in the farm labour force were obtained
by establishing a reputation for skill at work. Skill was therefore an
important attribute of status both on an individual basis among the
workers on a particular farm and between different farms in the same
locality. It is hardly surprising that skill should determine status in

what was after all an occupational community and there is plenty of evidence of its importance to the farming population. Evans writes that, 'So great was the interest in ploughing a well-finished stretch with mathematically straight furrows, or in the faultless drilling of a seed-bed and so keen was the rivalry between various horsemen that, even after they had spent most of an autumn day ploughing an acre or so in the field, they would spend the rest of it ploughing the land over once again in the cosiness of the inn bar. And on a Sunday morning they walked round the parish inspecting their neighbours' week of ploughing to see if it measured up to the high claims that had been made for it during the detailed preliminary examination at the four-ale bar.'[23] This kind of prestige-seeking was institutionalized in ploughing matches and championships which were regular occurrences in East Anglia. For the stockmen, the equivalent arenas for status were the markets and the agricultural show.[24] In all cases the bases of prestige allocation were very public: in the case of the ploughman they could remain a feature of the rural landscape for six months or more. A botched job was visible to all – both to the horseman's neighbours and to the casual passer-by. Here farmer and farm worker found a common cause in wishing the work to be as correct as possible, for the 'loss of face' resulting from a badly ploughed field brought odium upon the whole farm. Responsibility particularly fell on the head horseman, for he had to bear the full brunt of the farmer's criticism if things went wrong. Because of this, and because he was the most skilled of the men, he would usually draw the first furrow from which the remaining furrows would perforce take their cue. If he bent it, then, as Evans notes, 'the mistake would soon be recorded in every farm and public house in the parish'.[25] Pride in his job, which has often been regarded as the hallmark of the rural worker, therefore often derived from something less than sheer altruism.

The allocation of status in this way had important effects on the individual agricultural worker's perceptions of his own situation. Society at large placed the agricultural worker at the very bottom of the status ladder. No fine distinctions were made between horsemen and day-men – all farm workers were considered as agricultural *labourers*, with the connotations of unskilled toil which the term carries. Within his own locality, however, an individual worker's status could be extremely high and his skill highly valued. Because of the isolation and stability of this local social system and because its values were reinforced both at work and in the village at large, it was his status in the locality which was more meaningful to the agricultural worker. He might be aware that outside the village he could be considered an unskilled yokel, but it was less significant to him and hardly led him to question the system of values that consigned him to such a lowly status position.[26]

The evaluative consensus that such a status system required was reinforced both at work and in the community. The community structure will be dealt with below, but at this point it is important to note how the organization of work on the farm fostered the kind of continuous interaction between fellow workers which was conducive to the formation of a sub-culture which often opposed the 'official' values of farmer and landowner. Farm workers, with the exception of shepherds, worked together in groups far more than is the case today. While ploughing the field it was customary to break for short 'breathers' every hour or so, during which gossip and chat would be freely exchanged. Meal-breaks were often taken together out in the fields, particularly in the summer. The kind of workplace camaraderie which supported informal work values and norms easily developed under such conditions, and ostracism was thus a powerful weapon in enforcing these norms, particularly when it could easily be extended beyond work to activities in the village. In particular it was possible to maintain some degree of usually covert antagonism to the injustices of employers. The nature of farmer–worker relationships, often rigid, formal and authoritarian, meant that the antagonisms of class conflict would be more easily maintained under these conditions than under those that have pertained more recently. Because interaction between farmer and worker was on the whole less extensive than it is today, while interaction among fellow workers was much greater, farmer–worker relationships tended to be viewed much more as antagonistic, in terms of 'us' and 'them' – us, the workers, *versus* them, the bosses.[27]

Earnings and Conditions

By any criterion, nineteenth-century agricultural workers were often cruelly exploited. Their pay, particularly in East Anglia, where there were few non-agricultural employment opportunities, was abysmal.

Weekly agricultural wage rates were barely half of weekly industrial wage rates, while on the whole agricultural workers worked longer hours. Thus, although their standard of living rose appreciably during the latter half of the nineteenth century, agricultural workers remained decisively at the foot of the wages league.[28] Generations of grinding poverty in the English countryside have therefore established agricultural workers as traditionally the poorest section of the labour force. (See Table 2.)

Table 2 Agricultural and industrial wage rates, 1850–1914

| | Weekly wage rates | | Ratio, agriculture: industry | |
	Agricultural	Industrial	Unadjusted	Adjusted for retail price difference
	s. d.	s. d.	%	%
1850–57	10 0	22 10	44	49
1858–66	11 0	23 7	47	52
1867–73	12 2	25 11	47	52
1874–8	13 9	27 11	49	55
1879–83	13 7	27 0	50	56
1884–96	13 8	27 9	49	55
1897–1910	15 0	31 4	48	53
1911–14	16 2	32 11	49	54

Source: J. R. Bellerby, *Agriculture and Industry: Relative Income*, 1956

During the nineteenth century, however, there were long-standing regional variations in wage rates attributable to competition for labour from local extractive or manufacturing industries. Thus wages were traditionally higher in the northern industrial counties and in Kent and Surrey, while the low-wage areas were the most agricultural: the eastern counties and the south-west. In these regions average agricultural wages were only between 35 and 38 per cent of the average industrial wage rates throughout England and Wales as a whole.[29] Before the increasing standardization of wages after the First World War, therefore, there existed two main categories of agricultural labour in England.[30] In areas where labour was relatively scarce, wages were higher, sufficiently high, indeed, to be above subsistence level; thus productivity was little affected by nutrition levels. On the other hand, where labour was more abundant and where there was little competition wages were low and productivity was low. In these areas surplus population was disguised by under-employment and the peak harvest demand. The existence of this temporary labour shortage for a few months of the year in turn retarded migration on a scale sufficient to create a labour surplus and wages therefore remained low, depressed often to bare subsistence levels. As Burnett has shown, 'this was a population existing permanently on the verge of starvation'.[31]

East Anglia was predominantly a low-wage area, and Suffolk notoriously so. In 1850, Suffolk wages were half of those prevailing in Yorkshire, and, although after 1870 the gap began to narrow somewhat, wage rates in Suffolk remained consistently well behind those in the north (see Table 3). These rates can be deceptive, however. For

Table 3 Average weekly wage rates of agricultural labourers in selected counties

	1850–51		1860		1870		1881		1892	
	s.	d.	s.	d.	s.	d.	s.	d.	s.	d.
Surrey	9	6	12	8	13	9	15	0	15	0
Essex	8	0	11	3	11	4	12	6	11	6
Suffolk	7	0	10	7	10	10	12	6	12	0
Norfolk	8	6	10	7	10	5	12	6	12	0
Dorset	7	6	9	4	9	4	11	0	10	0
Wiltshire	7	0	9	6	10	7	12	0	10	0
Lancashire	13	6	–		14	8	17	6	18	0
Warwickshire	8	6	10	9	12	0	14	0	11	6
Derbyshire	–		12	0	13	9	16	6	16	0
Yorkshire, W.	14	0	13	6	15	10	16	6	16	0
Durham	11	0	14	3	16	2	17	8	–	
Northumberland	11	0	14	0	15	8	16	6	17	0
Average for England and Wales	9	7	11	7	12	3	14	2	13	5

Source: W. Hasbach, *A History of the English Agricultural Labourer*, 1966

example, although the hours worked were less in the arable areas than in the pastoral areas, in the latter hirings were on a yearly basis. This was only true for the elite horsemen and shepherds in East Anglia; otherwise hiring was weekly, or even daily. Piecework was most available in counties where weekly wage rates were lowest. However, the availability of piecework depended greatly on the type of soil and crops grown and therefore varied considerably from farm to farm. In the arable areas, therefore, wages were altogether more variable over any specified period, either because of fluctuation in wage rates or because of the continuing fluctuation in employment opportunities which led workers to be laid off at short notice. It is impossible to measure accurately the effects of this, although on the eve of the First World War the unofficial Liberal 'Land Enquiry Committee' found that reductions in wages due to wet or frosty weather were prevalent in only 18·7 per cent of the parishes in the northern counties, compared with 67·5 per cent of the parishes in the east.[32]

Table 4 Proportion of agricultural workers to total occupied males in English rural districts, 1901

	%
Northern counties	14·1
Midland counties	20·0
Southern and south-western counties	24·1
Eastern counties	39·9
Suffolk	43·1
Norfolk	40·8
Cambridgeshire	43·0
Essex	34·3
England and Wales	22·4

Source: *Second Report by Mr Wilson Fox . . .*, Cd 2376, 1905

The general situation was summarized by Wilson Fox in three reports on agricultural labour written at the change of the century.[33] Fox showed how pressure on the rural labour market was remarkably low: agricultural employers in East Anglia had retained a position of supreme strength in the hiring of labour, to the extent that wages

corresponded quite closely to movements in the price of grain. Such
was the lack of competition for labour that throughout Suffolk this
method of calculating wages was customary in the nineteenth century.
Many agricultural labourers were, then, kept literally and metaphori-
cally on the bread line.[34]

Housing

Throughout the latter half of the nineteenth century, therefore, rural
Suffolk was one of the poorest areas in England. A vast rural proletariat existed on the margin of employment and even when work
was available there was little escape from an unremitting poverty,
except by emigration to the north or to the colonies. The housing
conditions of the agricultural labourer were of little relief. Housing
was a crucial resource in rural areas, not only for its intrinsic qualities,
but because the decision to erect new cottages had important consequences for the local labour market. As Best has pointed out,
'Ownership of cottages was a cardinal point in the grand scheme of
subordination.'[35] Since the Act of Settlement the most important
regulator of the rural housing situation had been the structure of local
landholding. Where a resident squire owned most of the land in the
parish, or where a few very large farmers owned the land between
them, they had an incentive to limit, if not diminish, the housing
stock and thus avoid attracting additional families of labourers who
might later become a charge on the poor rates. Villages where there
were a large number of freeholders, however – the so-called 'open'
villages – attracted labour without any hindrance, encouraged very
often by local tradesmen and smallholders who became petty landlords by letting damp, insanitary, semi-derelict dwellings to local
labourers. These villages formed reservoirs of surplus labour for the
surrounding farms (including the near-by 'closed' villages) and their
housing was generally regarded as being much inferior.[36]

Suffolk suffered particularly badly from poor housing because,
since Saxon times, Suffolk had contained a high proportion of freeholders. Inquiring journalists and Royal Commissioners made the
condition of farm labourers' cottages in Suffolk a national scandal.[37]
They were quick to point out the vicious nature of the circle of deprivation within which the farm labourer was caught. The biggest

landowners who could best afford to erect new dwellings had least incentive to do so. In the open villages, however, surplus labour depressed wage levels, making it impossible for the agricultural labourer to pay a rent which would render housing improvements profitable. A few large landowners were stirred by their social obligations to construct model cottages and villages, such as the Helmingham estate of Lord Tollemache.[38] For the most part, however, as a succession of government Blue Books chronicled with depressing consistency, the labourer was consigned to a damp, insanitary over-crowded hovel.

As the century progressed the conditions in these open villages became a matter of deep concern to many liberal-minded onlookers. Health inspectors worried about sanitation risks; clergymen were concerned about the moral consequences of overcrowding; and many employers began to view with alarm the potential that open villages presented as hotbeds of political agitation. Each had some cause for complaint. The Blue Books on the 'Sanitary Condition of the Labouring Population of England' presented a vivid, if not lurid, account of conditions. For example the *Seventh Report* of 1861 recounted that in 821 country parishes the population had increased from 305,567 in 1851 to 322,064, while the number of houses had *fallen* from 69,225 to 66,109. In the sample of 5,375 'typical cottages' the average number of persons per house had risen from 4·41 to 4·87; in 8,805 bedrooms slept 13,432 adults (persons over thirteen) *plus* 11,338 children. Only 250 of the cottages had more than two bed-rooms. The roofs were often warped, the houses were badly aired, the floors were often rotten or full of holes and the rooms were often damp, dark, cold and smoky.[39] In 1874 a reporter for *The Times* described conditions in Exning, Suffolk, an 'open' village where a lock-out had begun in this year, as follows:

'Many cottages have but one bedroom. I visited one such cottage in which father, mother, and six children were compelled to herd together – one a grown-up daughter ... In another case the woman said they had put the children upstairs, and she and her husband had slept in a bed on the brick floor below until the bottom board of the bed had fallen to pieces from damp, and then they had to go among the children again. The sanitary inspector visits these dwellings occa-sionally to prevent overcrowding, but the difficulty is for the poor to find other cottages, even when they are inclined to pay more rent. Some of the worst of these cottages belong to small occupiers; some are mortgaged up to the hilt, and the owners often can afford neither to rebuild nor repair. It is a hard thing, again, for the sanitary inspector to pronounce a cottage unfit for human habitation, when no better – perhaps literally no other – can be had for the family.'[40]

'Open' villages were not only feared because of their conduciveness to epidemics of disease or incest, however. They were also believed to maintain and promote a deviant working-class sub-culture – 'a sort of penal colony for men of bad character from the whole neighbourhood', in Hasbach's phrase.[41] 'The arrangement,' wrote Wilson Fox in 1893, 'creates a community among whom there is a constant exchange of ideas, one consequence of which is the frequency of early marriages, involving a hard struggle for existence on the part of young couples who have scarcely reached manhood or womanhood. Another is the facility for organization by means of unions.'[42] Certainly some 'open' villages were centres of a lively rural working-class counter-culture of, in varying mixes, poaching, beer-drinking, nonconformity and trade-unionism. Often literally out of sight of the local employers, they became the most vigorous examples of rural occupational communities and of their associated sub-cultural norms and values.

'Closed' villages covered their peaks of labour demand, principally harvest, by using the gang system of labour organization.[43] The system fell into disrepute during the 1860s, however, culminating in the Gangs Act of 1867, which brought the system under control, restricting the employment of women and children and introducing a licensing system. Gangs were regarded as sources of cheap labour, but the Act eliminated many of the economic advantages of employing a semi-permanent 'casual' labour force while many large farmers were coming to believe that the work was often done hastily and badly. Farmers, therefore, sought to secure their own gangs and began to build cottages near their farms. Changes in the administration of the Poor Law following the Union Chargeability Act of 1865 also encouraged this. Cottages rented directly from the farmer in this way were known as 'tied' cottages, as opposed to 'free' cottages which were held direct from the landowner. Tied cottages could be rented only for the duration of employment on that farm. Because of the short period of hire they were not prevalent in East Anglia but, as the hiring of agricultural labour was placed on a more regular basis, the tied cottage was to assume much greater significance. At this stage, however, it is probably only necessary to note that its origins lay in the desire by farmers to control the supply of their labour force and to restrict its mobility. Even after the disappearance of the gang system and the Poor Law these motives were to retain the tied-cottage system in existence.

Poor Relief

Low wages, underemployment and insanitary, damp housing frequently propelled the agricultural labourer in one direction – towards pauperism. Pauperism was endemic to rural East Anglia, even after the Act of 1834. Certainly one mid-century observer of Suffolk was in no doubt as to its prevalence:

'Pauperism! what a theme! What a brood of evils are engendered by this one! The extent of moral and social evil flowing from this social malady, as well as the pecuniary loss that is incurred, it is difficult to determine. It is the plague spot of this country; a social cancer preying upon the vitals of the community, and festering away the self-respect, independence, and industry of almost every class of our working population. Our permanent and hereditary paupers are a very numerous class. At the census in 1851 it was found that 65 in every 10,000 persons in Great Britain were paupers. In Suffolk the paupers numbered 153 in every 10,000 persons enumerated. On the average of the five years ending March 1853, no less than 26,582 persons have annually received parochial relief. One out of every 12 of our population is a pauper, and the cost of supporting what Thomas Carlyle aptly designates "this army of paupers", has, during the five years ending March 1852, averaged £142,688 per annum.'[44]

For centuries the Poor Law had represented the idiom in which rural class relationships were expressed, for the Poor Laws were not 'simply a matter of relief, but in fact they raised fundamental questions of social policy'.[45] Since 1601 overseers of the poor (who in rural areas were almost invariably farmers) had levied a poor rate for the relief of the sick, the aged and the unemployed. Eighteenth-century enclosures and the effect on food prices of the Napoleonic Wars, however, produced an unprecedented rise in the number of poor applying for relief and a commensurate rise in poor rates. The Speenhamland system, introduced throughout the south and east of England after 1795, effectively pauperized almost the entire rural working class by subsidizing their low wages out of poor rates. In 1834 the Poor Law Amendment Act had set out to remedy this by severely controlling outdoor relief and by forcing all other recipients to enter the local workhouse.

For the agricultural worker the new Poor Law represented a complete break with customary practice. Paupers were to be relieved only in the workhouse, where families were separated, and in addition the parish no longer had a duty to find them work, paying an allowance to make up for inadequate wages. This represented a denial of the paternalism embodied in the Speenhamland system, and now, more than ever before, it became essential for the agricultural worker to keep on good terms with his employer. In this respect the new Poor Law did little to diminish the power of local landowners and farmers, particularly as they usually composed the Board of Guardians who were responsible for operating the new system locally. The Poor Law remained as it always had been: a paternal, custodial, coercive and primitive system of labour control.[46]

The Poor Law co-existed in rural areas with a more informal, unofficial and personal form of poor relief – charity. Charity was an integral part of the relationship between the agricultural worker and his social superiors and provided a substitute for the deficiences of the Poor Law at the local level: 'The relief of destitution by means of charity (whether private or institutional) went along with the relief of it through the Poor Law, and so closely were the two sides of the operation connected in the Victorians' minds that it could be difficult to say that the latter held a more "official" or "mandatory" character than the former.'[47] Indeed charity and patronage complemented the Poor Law as a means of social control: charity was the carrot while the Poor Law represented the stick which was to engender harmonious class relations.

For several centuries the rural English upper classes had cultivated a tradition of what Best has called 'prudential charity',[48] using repeated doles of food, clothing, almshouses, hospitals, schools and so on as a sedative to tide the poor – particularly the 'deserving' poor – over periods of social distress. In the English countryside such charity was particularly prevalent since it was most effective in the relatively small, face-to-face social structure of the English village – hence the tradition of Lady Bountiful. Certainly the role of charity was recognized by many of its nineteenth-century exponents. Lady Stradbroke, in a letter to *The Times* during the 1874 lock-out, enumerated the 'many Benefit Clubs, clothing, coal and shoe clubs, etc. subscribed to unanimously and chiefly supported by their employers; their cottage garden shows and prizes; their dinners and treats at Christmas and harvest; schools for their children, which until the passing of the late Act, were kept up entirely, and many are still, by their employers and landlords. All these are benefits and comforts which are not thought of, and would not be feasible in large manufacturing districts, but which add materially to the happiness and unity of the two classes – employers and labourers.'[49]

This was one of the problems which so exercised the Victorian middle and upper classes – how to translate this extremely effective use of charity as a form of social control from its customary milieu of the rural village to the huge urban conglomerations that threatened to undermine social order. The problem, as Simey has pointed out, was that 'The system of local responsibility for local distress required as its foundation a stable society with a clear conception of the rights and duties of its various members.'[50] In the cities it was 'an impossible hope', although this does not mean that it was not tried.[51] The growth of urban-industrial society presented a crisis to philanthropy with which an attempt was made to come to terms, a crisis which enabled the rationale for charity to become clearly articulated. For all its apparently Christian motivations, altruism was, as Harrison has noted, clearly not the entire story.[52] One of the aims of the Metropolitan Visiting and Relief Association was 'to promote kindly feelings between those classes of society which are kept so far asunder by the difference of their wordly conditions', while for the Houseless Poor Society it was 'by calling forth the most unprecedented exertions for the relief of the poor, effectually recall them to a knowledge of their real benefactors'.[53] It is noticeable how, during the nineteenth century, periods of social unrest were followed by a quickening of the pace of philanthropy.[54]

The contrast between the effectiveness of charity in the city and in

the countryside was summarized by Thomas Chalmers. 'In a pro-
vincial capital,' he wrote in his treatise on voluntary assistance, 'the
great mass of the population are retained in kindly and immediate
dependence on the wealthy residents of the place ... This brings the
two extreme orders of society into the sort of relationship which is
highly favourable to the general blandness and tranquillity of the
whole population. In a manufacturing town, on the other hand, the
poor and the wealthy stand more disjoined from each other. It is true
that they often meet, but they meet more in the area of contest than in
a field where the patronage and custom of the party are met by the
gratitude and goodwill of the other.'[55] In the village, then, local
landowners and employers could be seen to be protectors and benefactors of their communities. F. M. L. Thompson has demonstrated
that this 'central core of benevolence' was well maintained until 1914.
It represented the 'sinews of attachment of a community to its lord',
and to be truly effective it had to be on a personal, face-to-face basis
and to be a voluntary and uninstitutionalized relationship between
giver and receiver.[56] Correctly handled charity was not only a social
sedative but contributed towards the identification of the rural poor
with a system that had consigned them to poverty. A paternalistic
concern for the village's welfare, generosity in the endowment of
local institutions and societies, and frequent visits to the sick and needy
could produce feelings of deference and gratitude which conferred
stability on a very arbitrary and oppressive society.[57] 'If the squire and
his lady,' writes Flora Thompson, 'were charitable to the poor,
affable to the tradesmen, and generous when writing out a cheque
for some local improvement, they were supposed to have justified the
existence of their class.'[58]

Rural philanthropy was, however, a very patchy affair. By no means
all agricultural workers were in receipt of the patronage of a local
'big house'. Nor were the effects of charity always those that were
intended. What Owen calls 'undue condescension and immoderate
nosiness' could produce results entirely contrary to those desired. 'Let
it never be forgotten,' wrote one nineteenth-century adviser on these
matters, 'that the lower classes are extremely sensitive to the *spirit* in
which they are treated, and that the moral influence of charity depends
infinitely more upon the manner of the donor than upon the value of
the gift.'[59] It was always possible for the rural poor to be servile rather
than grateful, to become professional mendicants, or, like the inhabit-

ants of Tysoe, to accept charity cynically while withholding their goodwill.[60] It was easy for the exercise of charity to become ritualized, as in rural Northamptonshire in the 1860s, where 'Women and girls dropped low curtsies, men and boys touched their caps and pulled their forelocks at the sight of any of the quality. Doles of warm clothing, boots and shoes, flannel and calico, sheets and blankets were distributed in the great hall every Christmas. A fat ox was killed and joints of beef were given to labourers and tenants. But of the real existence of their poorer neighbours and dependents, of their habits and thoughts and ways of living, the inmates of the big house knew nothing.'[61]

There were many villagers who held themselves at arm's length from the circle of benevolence, dependence and obedience, just as there were others who held the local squire and his lady in the deepest affection. In any case, the English village was a higly particularistic society and conditions could vary wildly – and notoriously – from one parish to the next. Burn sums up the situation in his typically elegant way: 'The shadow of the Big House loomed over a society which was becoming more and more hierarchical; yet it was, almost certainly, a misfortune for the labouring man if there was no Big House in the parish, if there was no one, squire or parson or maiden lady, to cushion him in time of need. One can only guess at the proportion of cases in which benevolence demanded the reward of obedience or conformity.'[62]

The Village Community

It is now possible to draw together the aspects of the agricultural worker's existence that have so far been considered in this chapter by locating his position within the set of social relationships which went to make up the village community. Immediately, however, it is necessary to note that the community had a dual existence – as an ideology and as a local social system. It is necessary to keep these two facets carefully separated.

As has already been noted, the village community *as a social system*[63] was, from the standpoint of the agricultural worker, a hierarchical and authoritarian occupational community. In East Anglia, where nucleated settlements predominated, most workers did not live on the farm itself, following the decline of farm service at the beginning of the nineteenth century, but in a village which, whether 'open' or 'closed', consisted mainly of the dwellings of fellow agricultural workers. The employers, on the other hand, were scattered around the periphery of the village on the farmers' own holdings of land. This ecological pattern tended to be reflected in the pattern of social relationships in the local social system. In a very real sense the village represented a dual community; there was a communal solidarity to which the employers, whether farmers or landlords, did not belong, what Hobsbawm and Rudé rather melodramatically call 'the dark village' in contrast to 'the official village' within which landowners, farmers, clergy and professional people were included.[64] The 'dark' village was no more than a locally based working-class sub-culture, which contained its 'criminal' underworld aspects but which also exhibited familiar patterns of working-class neighbourly association. That is to say there was a strong sense of group identity based upon geographical isolation, a common occupation, kinship links and an overlapping of work and non-work roles.[65] It represented a 'mutality of the oppressed'[66] (which is in no way intended to overlook the gossip and petty strife which was also a prevalent feature of village life) in the sense that co-operation in times of family crisis – childbirth, illness, death, unemployment – was an accepted code of behaviour which reinforced communal identity and involvement among a population which constantly lived under the shadow of poverty. As an occupational community it was not surprising that skill at work was, as we have seen, an important attribute of status. The group identity of a common occupation manifested itself in the tendency of farm workers to socialize together outside working hours, to 'talk shop' even during leisure time and to derive standards of behaviour and conduct from those which pertained at work. Ostracism was thus an effective weapon in maintaining sub-cultural norms and values.

There are few adequate descriptions of the agricultural worker's communal existence which are not tainted by nostalgia or a vicarious quaintness. Few agricultural workers have written down their experiences and, as was indicated in the previous chapter, middle-class accounts must be treated with the deepest scepticism. The work of George Ewart Evans has helped to salvage a certain amount of mostly oral material from rural inhabitants who lived through the period when the village was an occupational community, and there are some authentic treatments by Flora Thompson, Margaret Ashby and Fred Archer. From these accounts it seems that the rural working-class sub-culture would best be described as accommodative rather than antagonistic. Expressions of resistance to their position took on a variety of covert rather than overt forms: poaching, 'the horseman's word', rick-burning, or the solidarity of the tap room, where subversion could be propagated and discussed – though rarely acted upon.[67] This integration into a sub-cultural milieu often meant, however, that alternative definitions and interpretations of the agricultural worker's social situation to those fostered by the local employers were available as part of a rural working-class tradition and could be sustained. For this reason class conflict was never far from the surface in many villages in East Anglia during the nineteenth century; occasionally it would burst out in sporadic, often localized expressions of discontent, but more often it was channelled into the gamut of rural underworld activities, about which we still know very little in any detail.

Interaction with farmers and landowners formed the other dimension of relationships in the village community. These were, of course, relationships with authority. Almost by definition in a rural area they possessed a near monopoly over employment opportunities, a degree of power reinforced by their control of housing. Therefore farmers and landlords, whatever their internal differences of opinion, formed from the point of view of the agricultural worker a coherent, identifiable ruling class – 'them' – counterposed to the equally coherent group solidarity of 'us'. The authority of farmers and/or landlords – from the point of view of the farm worker it made little difference – in the local social system was confirmed by their multiple occupancy of authoritarian roles – they were not only employers, but also magistrates, councillors, landlords and school governors. This gave farmers and landowners as a group, and occasionally individuals, considerable power in the community against which farm workers were relatively powerless. It was for this reason – on the whole a very realistic assessment of the chances of success rather than simple fatalism – that class conflict was rarely open. For the most part agricultural workers bit their tongues and busily developed their notorious taciturnity and ability somewhat sullenly to 'keep themselves to themselves'.

For most of the nineteenth century, therefore, the agricultural worker was never left in any doubt as to where the power in his village lay. But he could also recognize that this power could be used in different – legitimate and illegitimate – ways, and it was how this power was interpreted to and by the agricultural worker which is most important in understanding his response to it. What legitimacy conferred on the relationship between master and man was *stability*, and this quest for stability is the key to understanding the nature of rural class relationships in the nineteenth century (and in many respects remains so today).[68] Economically, stable employer–employee relationships were necessary for the performance of many complex and arduous farming operations like harvest. Socially, stability alone ensured the long-term maintenance of a system of power and privileges upon which the rural ruling class could continue to draw. It was recognized, consciously or unconsciously, that the use of physical coercion *alone* was a potentially unstable basis for social relations – it was economically disruptive and counterproductive, wasteful of resources and no guarantee that discontent would not be renewed in the future. In both the 1830s and the 1870s the rural ruling class showed that it was prepared to act savagely if necessary to put down any threat to its dominance, but, as the century wore on, more enlightened employers realized that a labour force that *identified* with them and their work was in the long run more reliable and more efficient than a group of workers who gave their grudging consent under the threat of sanctions, and it was around this point that a heated and celebrated correspondence took place in *The Times* during the 1874 lock-out.[69] A number of (largely unconscious) strategies were evolved by which it was hoped that such an identification – and hence social stability – could become established.

Before examining these strategies, however, we must look at the social structure of the nineteenth-century rural village in some degree of abstraction. Village society, like any social hierarchy, was best stabilized by persuading those in subordinate positions to subscribe to the system which endorsed their own inferiority. This is the kind of attitude which many historians have referred to as 'deference'.[70] The origins of deference lay in the processes of legitimation whereby factual matters of power become imbued with evaluative overtones – not only *did* the squire rule the village but it was believed that he *ought* to do so. Now power relations do not automatically become moral ones, though clearly those in power do have an interest in cultivating this conversion if they wish to establish a stable system of legitimate authority. What legitimizes power is the ability to promote and maintain a set of values which confer status honour on those in dominant positions: 'An order which is adhered to from motives of pure expediency is generally much less stable than one upheld on a purely customary basis through the fact that the corresponding behaviour has become habitual. The latter is much the most common type of subjective attitude. But even this type of order is in turn much less stable than an order which enjoys the prestige of being considered binding, or, as it may be expressed, of "legitimacy".'[71] In other words, the conversion of the local employers' power into prestige could ensure stability, for, if the agricultural worker could be persuaded to defer to the farmer rather than be commanded to obey him, conflict was much less likely to arise.[72]

Throughout the nineteenth century farmers typically legitimated their authority by tradition: that is, by conforming to expectations of their behaviour that were handed down from the past. This was what F. M. L. Thompson has called 'the principle of inherited authority' which underpinned rural society up until the First World War despite, by the beginning of the century, having come under increasing attack.[73] The beauty of traditional authority was that it was the most stable of all forms of legitimation, since deference was granted to both the tradition itself and to the *person* holding the position of authority. In terms of personal behaviour this gave holders of traditional authority considerable room to manoeuvre.[74] The idiom in which this personal form of authority was expressed was the ethic of the 'gentlemen'. It was a marvellously flexible instrument which, by virtue of its personal and particularistic nature, enabled a long line of rural gentlemen to indulge their notorious eccentricities without disturbing their legitimacy one iota. Because of the flexibility of the gentlemanly ethic, an agricultural worker believed he could recognize a 'real' gentleman whenever he saw one, but exactly what constituted a gentleman was by no means clear. A set of gentlemanly possessions, such as wealth, an estate or a family tree, obviously helped, but in themselves they were not sufficient, for to be a gentleman also involved a set of rules of individual conduct and behaviour, a strict code of what was 'done' and 'not done'. A paternalistic concern for the affairs of the village was also a consideration to be taken into account, but it was certainly *not* necessary for the gentleman to possess a particular brand of technical expertise in each of his many leadership roles. The very elasticity of the gentlemanly ethic was, indeed, a prerequisite of its continuation if the traditional rural elite were to survive the changing social and economic circumstances of eighteenth-century rural England. If the gentlemanly ethic was to involve, in Burn's phrase, the 'annexation of morals' which enabled an unassailable moral superiority to be retained, it was necessary from time to time to alter the *content* of these morals in response to potential changes in rural society which threatened the legitimacy of gentlemanly rule.[75] Paradoxically, it was the very variability – some would say mystification – of the gentlemanly ethic which ensured the stability of traditional authority in many areas of rural England; by blurring the criteria of gentility it was possible to alter them, to render them, for example, more subtle and more personalized as the nineteenth century progressed.

In the village, the whole system of recognition was based, of necessity, on *personal* knowledge and contact. The agricultural worker tended to pride himself on his ability to distinguish between the 'real' gentleman and some aspirant who was not quite the genuine article. Any 'real' gentleman could be distinguished by his 'bearing', an attribute which, it was believed, could be acquired only through breeding or lengthy practice. In the close-knit, face-to-face world of village society the importance of demeanour in personal relationships across class boundaries was therefore considerable. Correct demeanour was at a premium because of the degree of precision required in conveying exactly the expected mixture of intimacy and distance – of identification and differentiation – in relationships: it did not do for the gentleman to be either too convivial or too aloof if he wished to retain the deference of those beneath him. Such considerations presented something of a dilemma and an intuitive grasp of how to cope with these contradictory elements was essential. Differences in rank demanded a degree of social distance, for 'Aristocratic society maintains itself by an insistence on social distinctions and differences. The obeisances, condescensions and ceremonial taboos which characterize a highly stratified society exist for the express purpose of enforcing the reserves and social distances upon which social and political hierarchy rests.'[76] This distance–within–intimacy dilemma was obviated by the enforcement of a number of petty rituals which acted as social distancing mechanisms in situations of close personal contact. Touching the forelock was perhaps the most widespread and notorious, but although the gesture became habitual and unthinking it was not entirely meaningless. It was taken as the signal of recognition of social rank and as such introduced the symbolism of social hierarchy into even the most trivial of acquaintanceships.[77] These nuances of interaction could be decisive in reaffirming social legitimacy, but they were also of a most particularistic kind, a mode of conduct that required no written set of rules, but which betrayed itself 'quietly in glances, in topics, in the set of shoulders, the folding of hands, and in the serene assumption of certain standards and particular values as common to all'.[78]

To be a gentleman carried with it certain rights, but also certain obligations. The agricultural worker might be willing to defer to those who ruled over him, but he would expect in return for his deference a paternalistic concern for his own welfare. The gentleman, therefore, accrued to himself certain rights but also certain obligations. In order to obtain the legitimate right to rule the village he was also expected to shoulder the responsibility of being its protector, of generally 'knowing what was best' for its inhabitants and acting accordingly. Legitimacy therefore depended upon a consensus over the desired 'rate of exchange' of rights and obligations between ruler and ruled – *which* rights were to be exchanged for *which* obligations. The 'going rate' was likely to be normatively prescribed, and there is no doubt that in many nineteenth-century villages the ruling ideas about this exchange were, to paraphrase Marx, those of the ruling class. The way in which definitions of equivalence in the exchange of rights and obligations were interpreted to the agricultural worker was, therefore, central to retaining his identification with the system in which he found himself. There were, however, certain prerequisites for the effectiveness of this control of ideas, the distribution of which may help to explain the occurrence, both temporal and geographical, of their rejection.

Paternalism, as the term itself implies, is most effective on the basis of personal contact. Any landowner, great or small, wrote Lord Percy, 'could manage men with whom he could talk'.[79] Deference to traditional authority will be most marked, therefore, among those individuals who directly experience the social influences and judgements of traditional elite members. This is because a crucial element in this process is the provision of a consistent and coherent set of ideas which reinforce legitimacy, particularly in the area of defining rights and obligations. Where the agricultural worker was in a social situation in which he was constantly provided with interpretations of his own position that were commensurate with those of his 'betters', then, as Lord Percy's dictum indicates, it was more likely that these interpretations would come to be shared by him. The efficacy of personal contact in inculcating these elite definitions of the situation – and changes in the situation – placed a premium on certain types of social organization. In particular a degree of *totality* in the situation of the agricultural worker was necessary. Where the agricultural worker's subordination was a *total* one, across all his many roles, he would 'know his place', because the pressures of personal dependency would be ubiquitous. Any possible doubt as to his 'place', any possible ambiguity deriving from his multiplicity of social roles as to their normative regulation, could be extinguished and from none of his social relationships would he be able to 'learn to question the appropriateness of his exchange of deference for paternalism'.[80] What this would amount to would be complete ideological hegemony: the leadership of farmers and landowners in the village would be regarded as entirely 'natural', for literally no alternatives were capable of being considered, let alone evaluated, and their interpretations of the situation would be taken automatically and unthinkingly to be 'correct' interpretations. Wherever possible they busily tried to create the conditions conducive to such patriarchal rule.[81]

Consequently there was during the nineteenth century a strong adherence in rural areas to a particular form of territoriality – localism. The encouragement of localism enabled identification with the social system to prevail by emphasizing a common adherence to territory, a solidarity of place, encompassing both elite and subordinates alike. The traditional English landowning class placed an ideological gloss on their monopoly of power within the locality through the concept of 'community'.[82] 'Community' *as an ideology* became superimposed onto the reality of the village community *as a social system*, so that it becomes very difficult to disentangle the two. Some aspects of the village 'community' as an ideology have already been dealt with. In terms of social relationships the ideologically prescribed 'community' involved notions of stability, harmony and social order; but community also involved the *spatial* framework within which these orderly and harmonious relationships were played out. The community therefore also represented a geographical area, usually the parish, with which all inhabitants identified. Lastly, community also contained a visual, aesthetic aspect – it was a landscape which gave its inhabitants a sense of place. Ideally (and this was no doubt a somewhat rare occurrence) all three aspects would run together: here the village consisted of clearly defined 'natural orders' who rarely ventured beyond the parish boundaries (apart from their upper-class emissaries who were the representatives of the village to the outside world) and who lived among the picturesque surroundings of green fields, manor house, church tower and quaint cottages.

There were many English landowners who tried assiduously to cultivate this idealized 'community' in their own locality; some were brought up in the midst of it, and, safely cocooned by wealth and residential separation, actually believed in it without realizing the less congenial reality that lay behind – they may even have been reasonably successful in transmitting their view to those below them. Here there would be, in Best's words, 'a beautiful and profitable contrivance, fashioned and kept in smooth working order by that happily undoubting class to whom the way of life it made possible seemed the best the world could offer'.[83] The village itself would become a 'little kingdom', the undisputed sphere of influence of the local squire, geographically isolated, ideologically self-supporting and sharply delineated from its neighbours. The solidarity of 'community' at this level was a different matter from the unavoidable communality of the poor referred to earlier in this chapter, though doubtless the two overlapped and were somewhat complementary. The 'organic community' existed almost entirely at the level of symbolism – in such rituals as 'beating the bounds', in village fairs and festivals, in the pursuit of sports as diverse as fox-hunting and cricket. In each case, it could be pointed out how all the village came together as equals and how a profound and meaningful sense of 'community' reigned, and in many cases, no doubt, this symbolism could override the more mundane, everyday exploitation of work on the land which continued to underpin this idealized view.[84]

This sense of 'community' was also reflected in the physical layout of the village. Views from the 'big house' were carefully designed by landscape gardeners so as to produce 'pleasing prospects' which were themselves the product of a particular social perspective. For example, the social assumptions which underlie the views of John Loudon, a celebrated mid-nineteenth-century architect, are obvious: 'To me nothing is more cheerless than that exclusive solitary grandeur so much affected in the present day, which forbids the poor even to set foot within the precincts of greatness. As the most beautiful landscape is incomplete without figures, so the general affect of a park is always lonely, unless it have a footpath frequented by the picturesque figures of the labouring classes, and giving life and interest to the scene ... The approach to a residence is commonly one of the most important features about the place. A villa should always form part of a village, and be placed, if possible, on rather higher ground, that it may appear to be a sort of head and protector of the surrounding dwellings of the poor, as it ever was formerly ... Supposing, then, that the estate is bounded on one side by the great public road, about a mile from the house; I would form a good parish road from the most convenient point in the public road, through a pretty enclosed country, watered by the stream from the park, which I should cross by a bridge of one or two arches, near the parish mill, and thence ascend to the village, passing among the scattered farm houses and cottages, with their pretty gardens and orchards, crossing the village green, on which should stand the school-house shaded by lofty trees, to the other extremity of the village, where a handsome arched gateway should form the entrance to the park. Passing through the gateway into an open glade of oaks, the church will be seen at a little distance among the trees, through which the road is continued with a gentle ascent, till the house suddenly presents itself, stables and offices, backed by a woody eminence; and sweeping across the plain in front, through some scattered trees and hollies, you at length reach the steps of the porch.'[85] What member of the 'labouring classes' could fail to be impressed and overawed by such a prospect? And yet how closely Loudon's vision conforms to the English vision of the ideal community. It can be seen from Loudon's *beau idéal* of the English village how regarding the leadership of the community as 'natural' combined all kinds of aesthetic, social, moral and even agricultural overtones which reflected the ideology in which the term was embedded.

Where conditions allowed, therefore, this vision of 'community' defined the agricultural worker's situation for him. It was reinforced in hundreds of trivial ways each day, both substantively and symbolically, and, unless he could cling to an alternative definition of the village community, this was the image that was likely to predomin-ate. By their ideological alchemy local rulers were able to convert the exercise of their power into 'service' to those over whom they ruled and to transmute a rigid and arbitrarily controlled hierarchy into an 'organic' community of 'mutual dependency' in which they exercised their obligations through assuming the responsibilities of leadership and through their periodic doles of charity and patronage. Implicitly the ideology of 'community' became a means of social control. By cultivating an identification with the locality, and then by defining the relationships within the locality as those of social harmony, amity and affection, it was possible to use the 'limited horizons' of the village dweller to protect him from the possibly corrupting influences of alternative definitions of the situation from outside.[86]

How far is this model of ideological hegemony an accurate reflection of the situation of the East Anglian agricultural worker up until the end of the century? Complete hegemony was obviously unlikely, since it was difficult, even in the conditions pertaining in the nineteenth century, to isolate the agricultural worker entirely from alternative definitions of his situation. This was particularly the case where he was a member of an occupational community, with its own thriving rural working-class sub-culture and its associated set of norms and values. Few rural villages were completely isolated and, ideologically speaking, closed. Trips to markets provided an opportunity to mix with other workers from further afield, and most villages contained a number of craftsmen and tradesmen whose 'horizons' were by no means limited by the parish boundary, who were literate and articulate and who possessed a consummate amount of economic and political independence. Most important, however, was the fact that in East Anglia the structure of landholding, the nature of the work situation and the community structure, especially in the 'open' villages, enabled alternative definitions of the situation to those encompassed by the dominant value system to be available and be sustained. In terms of the values of this sub-culture, the individual agricultural worker could deny the status of the landowning class and instead substitute those of his own – skill at work, for example. The 'us/them' view of the village social system was capable of predominating over a more deferential view in which no conflicts of interest were perceived or admitted. On the other hand, the cohesion of the traditional, landowning class rendered their control very extensive. Each landowner's interpretation of the village social system and its institutional supports was likely to be fundamentally the same as his neighbours', for the patterns of upper-class and middle-class sociability enabled them to retain a considerable coherence and consistency in the legitimation of their dominance, despite their geographical dispersal.[87]

Undoubtedly there were local variations which corresponded to different configurations of local social structure; in any case, without detailed local historical investigations it would be impossible to assess the predominance of differing interpretations among agricultural workers of their situation in different areas at different times. These interpretations would range from the profoundly deferential, through varying degrees of accommodation and ambivalence to outright rejection and a desire for radical change.[88] However, it is not without significance that trade-unionism was more prevalent among the large labour-intensive farms and occupational communities of East Anglia, while elsewhere – where farm and community structures were very different – the 'limited horizons' of the agricultural worker that were a consequence of somewhat closer contact with his 'betters' prevented its widespread growth. Without any further historical evidence, however, it is impossible to say little more beyond these broad generalizations, except perhaps on one point. There is one area in which ideological hegemony seemed to prevail, even in East Anglia, and this was in the inability of agricultural workers to comprehend any alternative system to the one which they experienced, despite the antagonistic nature of class relationships. In this sense horizons were very definitely limited and, moreover, structurally determined. Flora Thompson reflects this accurately in her observation of the village pub: '. . . the landlord,' she wrote, 'standing back to the fireplace with legs astride, would say with the authority of one in his own house, "It's no good you chaps think'n you're goin' against the gentry. They've got the land and they've got the money, *an'* they'll keep it. Where'd *you* be without them to give you work and pay your wages, I'd like to know?" and this, as yet, unanswerable question would cast a chill over the company.'[89] The question was unanswerable for many farm workers because the social structure within which they were located rendered alternative conceptions unavailable. The structural basis of their social ignorance was not, however, static. Changes in the structure provided a constant threat to social order of rural society with which rural landowners and farmers constantly had to come to terms.

Structural Change

Structural change in nineteenth-century rural society cannot be considered without reference to the relationship between agriculture during this period and the development of capitalism in British society as a whole. This may seem trite, if not a truism, but must remain the starting-point nonetheless. The relationship between a farmer and his workers was not an isolated and unique phenomenon, whatever the desire of individual farmers and landowners to make it appear so. It did not exist in a social vacuum, but was derived from a system of social stratification whose basis was essentially economic. The fundamental stimulus to this relationship was the necessities of economic production, and in this respect the farmer was not, any more than the farm worker, an entirely voluntaristic actor. The exigencies of the market for agricultural products, over which the individual farmer could have no control, in turn provided a set of limiting conditions by constraining the resources available to him in managing his relationships with his employees. Farmers and landowners throughout the nineteenth century were therefore concerned with how far the developments in agrarian and industrial capitalism threatened to undermine the structural conditions which were conducive to social stability in rural society.

The problems of instability are particularly acute in agriculture, for in certain respects markets in agricultural commodities correspond fairly closely to perfect competition, with very high supply elasticities coupled to relatively low demand elasticities. These can result in extreme price fluctuations – the 'cobweb' cycles beloved of economics textbooks – while the enterprise structure of agriculture renders control of the market by oligarchical or monopolistic combination impossible without the imposition of institutional superstructures like co-operatives. The economic stability of an agriculture left to free-market forces is therefore highly questionable, and yet it is this stability for which individual agricultural entrepreneurs crave, both from the point of view of planning their economic enterprises and for creating conditions within which labour relations can be fixed. At the beginning of the nineteenth century the English landowning class attempted to introduce stability to the market through the device of the Corn Laws and stability to their labour relations through the institution of the Speenhamland system of poor relief. By the middle of the nineteenth century, however, both had disappeared, opening up the possibility of chronic instability once more. Attempts to control the market remained a political impossibility (and here, of course, the political struggle between 'the agricultural interest' and 'the manufacturing interest' is of paramount importance) until the artificially created conditions of the First World War. The patriarchal ethic embodied in the Speenhamland system remained, however; as we have seen, such traditionalism was the necessary adjunct of the quest for immutably harmonious relationships between capital and labour in agriculture for much of the nineteenth century.

It is therefore possible to see after the repeal of the Corn Laws two contradictory sets of relationships which somehow had to be reconciled: the (to paraphrase Genovese) patriarchalism of the village community, and the commercial and capitalistic exploitation demanded by the exigencies of the world market.[90] Raymond Williams also recognizes the centrality of this: 'Yet there was always a contradiction in English agrarian capitalism: its economics were those of a market order; its politics were those of a self-styled aristocracy and squirearchy, exerting quite different and "traditional" disciplines and controls.'[91] As the nineteenth century progressed, this traditionalism was squeezed from both sides at once – through the actions of the market in agriculture and through the progressive penetration of the 'closed', isolated, self-contained village society by a series of alien and potentially subversive ideas and institutions.

The nineteenth century saw widespread changes in ideas about legitimation that stemmed largely from the growth of industrial capitalism – what Perkin has termed the triumph of the 'entrepreneurial ideal' over the 'aristocratic ideal' of the countryside.[92] The industrialization of Britain, with its ever-increasing technological innovation, led to a much greater complexity that permeated all spheres of society. This growth in complexity was perforce accompanied by a growth in specialization, with the result that an ever-increasing premium was placed on specialized knowledge and technical expertise. Tradition, patronage, the cult of the gentlemanly amateur, was overtaken by efficiency, competition, independence and professionalism. Slowly this general cultural change began to invade the village, where it threatened to overthrow the authority of employers and landlords, hitherto unquestioned simply because that was the way it had always been in the past. Cobden was one of the principle spokesmen of the attack on patriarchalism: 'Mine is the masculine species of charity which would lead me to inculcate in the minds of the labouring classes the love of independence, the privilege of self-interest, the disdain of being patronized or petted, the desire to accumulate and the ambition to rise.'[93] This was a far cry from the 'natural orders' of traditional rural society.

The nineteenth century witnessed the enactment of a whole series of measures which reflected the triumph of this ideal, whose consequence was to reduce the 'closed' nature of village society and to dilute the absolute autocracy of the local squire. They ranged from the Poor Law Amendment Act of 1834 to the Local Government Acts of 1888 and 1894 and step by step they marked the curtailment of the power of landownership in society as a whole.[94] Slowly, haltingly and with various setbacks and vicissitudes, it was to be through these measures that the agricultural worker was to gain some minimal 'citizenship' rights – health, education, the franchise and so on.[95] Rural areas were also to become less geographically isolated – they were, of course, never completely so – under the impact of industrialism through the onset of the railway, and later, in some ways no less significantly, of the bicycle. All these developments represented the invasion of the village community by a set of influences whose genesis was outside, and they all in their various ways undermined the localism upon which traditional authority over the farm worker depended for its success. As the village became more integrated into a national (which, after the 1840s, meant urban and industrial) system, so it became increasingly difficult for the rural ruling class to apply its distinctively parochial and patriarchal rule within a self-contained and static traditional world. During this period, as Saville points out, 'no statistical balance of advantages and disadvantages can hope to catch the changing attitudes of the agricultural labourer which followed the slow widening of his horizons. There is no doubt that in the second half of the century many labourers were beginning to recognize the backwardness of rural life, and this not only in economic terms.'[96]

The growth of industrialism also wrought changes in the economic basis of agriculture, however, so that stable class relationships also became threatened from *within* rural society. As Britain industrialized and moved away from being an agrarian, subsistence-based economy, so the proportion of national income spent on food declined. From the middle of the nineteenth century onwards, therefore, returns to agriculture began to fall steadily behind the returns to capital invested in trade and manufacturing industry, particularly in the arable areas. Those landowners who did not invest in industrial expansion began slowly to pay for the privilege. 'Particularly in bad years, but also in good times, landlords' outlays were increased, and the rewards they received were generally diminished. In this way the landowners bore a good part of the cost of the ascendancy of commerce and industry and the secondary position to which agriculture was being relegated. Behind the façade of the "Golden Age of English Agriculture", which is said to have lasted for the twenty years after the outbreak of the Crimean War, a distinct weakening in the economic position of agricultural landowners can be detected.'[97]

The repercussions of this long-term trend were enormous. In the final quarter of the nineteenth century, during the long period of agricultural decline that marked the Great Depression, the deficiencies of capital investment in agriculture began to take their toll on social relationships, leading to 'the decay of that essential pillar of the landed interest, the deferential tenant'.[98] Cracks began publicly to appear in the relationships between landlord and tenant, who, whatever their domestic differences of opinion, had always previously maintained a united front to the outside world, including their own servants and workers. Now, however, the law intervened in their supposedly voluntary economic arrangements, decisively altering the balance of power over, in particular, security of tenure. By the 1880s it was becoming apparent, even to the loyal agricultural worker, that the 'organic community' was beginning to fall apart under the impact of depression. Land reform became a burning political issue, tenant farmers were exerting greater economic and political independence, and the customary definition of relationships between the 'natural orders' of rural society was becoming increasingly questioned.[99]

The effects of economic decline within the landowning class expressed themselves in other, more direct ways to the agricultural worker, however. The ability of landowners to adopt a leisured lifestyle of lavish and conspicuous consumption became undermined; reduced circumstances in many cases rendered only a somewhat less-than-authentically aristocratic way of living possible. This had effects on the extent of local philanthropy, landowners being forced to withdraw from their role as visible protectors and benefactors of the village community, although they were still able to retain, in Thompson's words, 'a central core of benevolence, shorn of some of its extraneous extremities' up until the end of the nineteenth century. 'Indeed,' he writes, 'nowhere before 1914 did local communities altogether repudiate their traditional leadership or throw off their traditional respect, but the means by which deference was secured had everywhere been weakened by the passage of a century and the final onslaught of falling landed incomes.'[100]

Table 5 Decrease in agricultural workers in England and Wales, 1851–1901

Year	'Shepherds' and 'Agricultural labourers, farm servants'	Decrease No.	%	Percentage of males aged ten and over engaged in agriculture
1851	1,110,311	–	–	23·5
1861	1,098,261	12,050	1·1	21·2
1871	923,332	174,929	15·9	16·8
1881	830,452	92,880	10·1	13·8
1891	756,557	73,895	8·9	11·6
1901	609,105	147,452	19·5	9·5

Source: Population Census

For much of the nineteenth century the principal recipient of the burden of declining returns to agriculture was the agricultural worker. His powerlessness in the local labour market meant that the gap between returns to industry and returns to agriculture was expressed in terms of the gap between industrial wage rates and agricultural wages.[101] This gap in earnings, together with the insatiable demands of industry for more labour, began to draw the agricultural worker away from the land and propel him towards the factories, a movement facilitated by the new railways. This was the most prevalent, the most widespread and the most silent protest by agricultural workers about their conditions over the whole period. The precise configuration of factors leading to this rural exodus could vary from place to place and from time to time, but the economic factor remained paramount, as a whole series of government inquiries were to establish.[102] Although the reasons came to be conceptualized in terms of the 'push' of mechanization and the 'pull' of higher industrial wages, the arguments were as unilluminating as those of 'was he pushed, or did he fall?'. The 'drift from the land' prevailed both during periods of agricultural prosperity *and* depression, so that neither 'push' nor 'pull' may be said to have predominated overall, in the context of national trends, though no doubt there were local variations.

The effects of the drift from the land on the social structure of rural society are no less difficult to evaluate. The nature of mechanization introduced in the latter half of the century did not fundamentally alter the agricultural worker's work situation. On the other hand there was a tightening-up of the rural labour market from the late 1860s onwards which enabled him to maintain and even improve his standard of living during the Great Depression.[103] But this exodus on its own hardly altered the nature of the relationships between the agricultural worker and those above him in the village social hierarchy. It was believed by most rural observers that those who left the land were the young, the energetic and the intelligent, leaving behind them a residual sediment of the old and the unskilled. By the end of the nineteenth century the age structure of rural and urban areas was indeed markedly different, but it is not without significance that the conventional wisdom of the towns was the exact opposite: *they* believed they were receiving the drifters, the shiftless and the work-shy, the unattached flotsam of agricultural change. Without any clear evidence for a *socially* selective basis to rural emigration, the role of rural depopulation must be seen to be symptomatic of imminent changes in the rural social structure rather than a direct cause of them.[104]

The contradictions between the patriarchalism of rural society and the exigencies of the market showed themselves most decisively, therefore, not so much in the relationship between employer and employee – notwithstanding the events of the 1870s – but in changing relationships *within* the employing class. The Great Depression of the last quarter of the nineteenth century for the first time admitted tenant farmers to a 'proprietary interest' in the running of agriculture through the Agricultural Holdings Acts, and their attachment to their landlords began slowly to wane as the contradictions between commercial farming and the patriarchal rule of hereditary landlordism began to exert themselves.[105] When landlords were no longer capable of providing a buffer against economic distress they were to abdicate their rule, both locally and nationally, to a new breed of owner-occupying farmers.

This movement began before the First World War under the impact of Lloyd George's budgetary measures. In 1910 'a flood of land sales started, continuing through to the outbreak of war in 1914'.[106] After the war the flood became a deluge: in 1921 the *Estates Gazette* concluded that one-quarter of England had changed hands in the previous four years. 'Such an enormous and rapid transfer of land,' writes Thompson, 'had not been seen since the confiscations and sequestrations of the Civil War, such a permanent transfer not since the dissolution of the monastries in the sixteenth century. Indeed a transfer on this scale and in such a short space of time had probably not been equalled since the Norman Conquest. The transfers also marked a startling social revolution in the countryside, nothing less than the dissolution of a large part of the great estate system and the formation of a new race of yeoman.'[107] In many areas, owner-occupying farmers assumed the mantle of leadership of rural society – though not universally, for it is possible to exaggerate the extent of this change: by 1927 still only 36 per cent of land was owner-occupied. Nevertheless the *landed* interest was replaced irrevocably by the *farming* interest as the architects of rural society and this transformation was to be accompanied in some areas by new criteria of status, of legitimacy and of authority.

What had transformed the traditional structure of rural society was not, then, a struggle between capital and labour: the orderly chain of deference and paternalism or of power and subordination down the social scale had been snapped at the link between landlord and tenant farmer, not at the link with the agricultural worker. This is not to say that the agricultural worker was supine over this period, however. For the last quarter of the century which had seen the assertion of tenant right also witnessed the renewed assertion of the right of combination via the more impersonal solidarities of class.

Resistance and Struggle

It has been customary to regard the struggle of the agricultural worker against his powerlessness and poverty during the nineteenth century in terms of two great 'explosions' of rural unrest with a period of tranquillity in between. There is some plausibility to this view, but between the demise of Captain Swing in the 1830s and the 'Revolt of the Field' in the 1870s resistance took a more subterranean form which has not attracted the interest of historians of social movements. Up until the 1850s rural incendiarism continued to be endemic; in Suffolk, for instance over the period 1848 to 1852, 38 per cent of rural prisoners in the gaols at Ipswich and Bury were there for arson.[108] Poaching also took on the countenance of a kind of guerrilla class warfare, culminating in the Prevention of Poaching Act of 1862 and its associated 'game laws' which, uniquely, granted totally arbitrary powers of search on the public highway. The values implicit in these individual and collective acts of resistance could be sustained by the strength of the sub-culture of the village community and the camaraderie of the work situation. The skilled poacher or arsonist could be an admired and respected member of the working-class community, a 'craftsman' whose workmanship was able to obtain high status. It is not too fantastic to suggest that symbolically he represented the village working class itself, for the game laws were narrowly class-based legislation designed to protect the recreational tastes of the upper class against the vast majority of rural inhabitants.[109]

The values of 'us versus them' did not simply disappear over this period, therefore, to be miraculously resurrected in the 1870s. However, there is no doubt that the means of expressing these values *did* alter considerably. One only has to compare the 'primitive', in Hobsbawm's use of this word, rebellion of the Swing riots with the more 'modern' expression of trade-union activity forty years later to see this transition. The movement of the 1870s did not, by and large, express itself in incendiarism, machine-breaking and mysterious leadership but in strikes, centralized organization, and a recognized national champion. The 'Revolt of the Field' still contained its primitive elements, however, especially its strong millennial overtones and the expectations of rapid success. One can agree with Dunbabin that it represented a transitional stage in the collective action of the agricultural worker, exhibiting a combination of both modern trade-unionism and the earlier, primitive types of protest.[110] In its mix of millennialism and organization it reflected the more passive expression of class antagonism that characterized the intervening years – the rise of Nonconformity, particularly Primitive Methodism.

Nonconformity underwent an explosive growth, especially in East

Anglia, in the years after Swing. Primitive Methodism in particular captured the imagination of thousands of agricultural workers and between 1829 and 1835 the number of adherents had multiplied four times. After this membership levelled off, but the 1860s saw a further rapid expansion prior to the onset of trade-unionism.[111] Methodism – Primitive or Wesleyan – expressed an alienation from the established social and religious order of the countryside. It was thus capable of breaking down the ostensible unity of the rural parish and destroying the sense of an ideal community which, as has been pointed out above, was one of the prerequisites of social order and deference to traditional authority. Everitt has concluded from his study of the pattern of rural dissent in the nineteenth century that it was most likely to be established in villages where, for one reason or another, conditions already rendered the ideological hegemony of the rural ruling class weak – for example, 'open' villages, nucleated settlements or villages 'situated well away from the nearest parish church and in many cases far from any manor-house'.[112] It seems likely, therefore, that Nonconformity was the vehicle through which any pre-existing rural working-class tradition of class antagonism was transmitted during this period rather than the creator of such a tradition, though in so doing it moulded this tradition in its own image.

Nonconformity, for example, contributed a new sobriety to rural working-class behaviour. It is, as Hobsbawm and Rudé point out, 'quite incredible that the newly saved village Baptist or Primitive Methodist, with his hatred of liquor, pubs and sports, should have taken part in the rick-burning and cattle-maiming so patently associated with the bold, hard-drinking and hard-playing poachers and their circles'.[113] Their respectability was at first to split the unamimity of rural working-class culture and they must also have contributed to the plausibility of the settled and harmonious view of relationships between employers and workers which swept England after 1850. Other aspects of Nonconformity were rather more subversive, however. It was a powerful educative force, contributing to a more articulate and more socially aware agricultural worker through the institution of day and Sunday schools and through the provision of opportunities for agricultural workers to meet, discuss and organize in a formal and systematic manner. In many respects the organization of Nonconformist religion provided a model for the structure of trade-unionism, and it is therefore not surprising that so many union leaders and officials were to be supplied by the Methodist movement. Recent research by Scotland has confirmed the traditionally accepted belief that most of the local trade-union leaders of the 1870s were Methodists, and that the presence of a Methodist chapel could be decisive in the founding of a local union branch by providing a place for union meetings.[114]

Perhaps the most subversive aspect of Methodism, however, was that it furnished the agricultural worker with a sense of justice – or more precisely, in respect of his worldly lot, injustice – through the prevailing tenets of Methodist biblicism. It has been outlined already in this chapter how the legitimation of the rural social hierarchy rested upon the ability to define the equivalence of elite rights and obligations which would continue a stable domination. Methodism threatened to upset this system of legitimacy by generating alternative views of what was right and proper, what was fair and just, in the exercise of authority. Consequently later union meetings were often virtually indistinguishable from Primitive Methodist gatherings (including hymns, prayers and sermons), while union demands were frequently expressed in the idiom of biblical analogy. Nonconformity therefore presented the agricultural worker with alternative definitions of his situation to those fostered by landlord, farmer and parson, with alternative conceptions of what constituted status, legitimate authority and a gentlemanly ethic. It also fired a somewhat cowed and dispirited population, following on their experiences of the 1830s, with a new passion and zeal for improvement – they were becoming, in the words of a contemporary Lincolnshire newspaper, 'rather "bold" in asserting their rights and claims'.[115] Some of these aspects of the link between Methodism and the union movement of the 1870s are highlighted in Selley's account of the first national congress at Leamington in 1872: 'The "National" Committee put on record this following resolution: "The Committee believe in the justice and righteousness of their cause, and have the firmest faith that Divine blessing will rest upon it." The Congress was marked by unbounded enthusiasm, and had all the characteristics of a religious revival. This is largely explained by the fact that many delegates were Methodist preachers. At times the conference bore a strong resemblance to a Methodist "love feast". In homely language, these rough, unlettered men told of their sufferings, their struggles and their aspirations. The speeches were punctuated with cries of "Amen", "Praise Him" and other devout utterances. The gentlemen on the platform were variously referred to as "Honnered sirs", "These yer worthy gents", "These rual genlmen", etc. The audience was alternately moved to laughter and tears. One delegate said: "Sir, this be a blessed day: this ere Union be the Moses to lead us poor men up out o' Egypt"; and another delegate commenced his speech with this explanation given in a confidential tone: "Genelmen and b'luv'd Crissen friends, I's a man, I is, as goes about wi' a oss." Another informed the assembly that "King Daavid sed as ow the 'usbandman as labourers must be the first partaker o' the fruit," adding, "and now he's mo'astly th' last, and loicke enuff gets none at all." Yet another, descanting on the ways of Providence, remarked that "little things was often chus to du graat ones, and when e sa' the poor labrin' man comin' furru in this ere movement, and a bringin' o' the faarmers to terms, he were remoinded o' many things in th' Scripters, more perticular o' th' ram's horns that blew down the walls o' Jericho, and frightened Pharaoh, King of Egypt." '[116]

Other, more secular, developments were eroding the placid exterior of mid-century rural life. Essentially local village benefit clubs and friendly societies were being replaced by the establishment of local branches of national organizations, like the Oddfellows and the Ancient Order of Foresters – their growth was particularly marked in the decade after 1858.[117] As with Methodism they provided the agricultural worker with administrative experience and an organizational model: friendly society benefits were to be a major feature of succeeding agricultural unions. In addition, they marked the penetration of the isolated village by national institutions that had their centres of operations outside the locality, integrating the farm worker into a wider set of relationships or at least making him come to terms with the outside world.

The years between 1850 and 1870 were also marked by a widening of the social and economic gap between the agricultural worker and his employer. The dynamics of capitalist agriculture during these years of 'high farming' was characteristically to distribute income disproportionately in favour of the farmer rather than the farm worker. The economic circumstances and social status of the tenant farmer rose considerably over this period and this increasing social distance between employer and employee was reflected in their domestic separation – many Victorian farmhouses were rebuilt

outside the village and in the lowland south and east the proportion
of farm servants declined dramatically (in Suffolk the ratio of 'indoor'
to 'outdoor' servants rose from 1:15·1 in 1851 to 1:194·5 in 1871).[118]
If the traditional, patriarchal quality of farmer–worker relationships
depended upon maintaining a balance between social differentiation
and social identification, then this trend, which derived from the
underlying forces of economic production, was pregnant with disturbing possibilities.

The tightening of the labour market during the 1860s and the
passage of the Master and Servant Act of 1867 (before which farm
workers were frequently imprisoned for breach of employment
contract if they left their work) stretched the tensions of farmer–
worker relationships to breaking point. In the late 1860s there was
sporadic unrest in the Midlands and in many southern counties. An
attempt to form a national union was made in the spring of 1868
under the aegis of Canon Girdlestone, who had been active in organizing the migration of hundreds of his parishioners at Halberton in
Devon to the north. Despite support from other middle-class radicals
and urban trade-union leaders, the campaign failed to establish itself
at grass-roots level. In 1871 more spontaneous union movement again
manifested itself, most notably in Herefordshire, where Thomas
Strange, a Primitive Methodist schoolteacher, formed a union designed to promote emigration, but which disavowed strikes. At its
height it spread across six counties and achieved an estimated membership of 30,000.

In 1872, the villages finally 'took the flame'.[119] The first sparks flew
in Warwickshire, where a meeting was held at Harbury on 29 January
and a further one at Charlcote a week later. The Charlcote workers –
eleven in all – formed a club and enlisted the help of a local champion
hedgecutter and Primitive Methodist lay preacher, Joseph Arch.
Within a week Arch was addressing over a thousand workers at
Wellesbourne, where it was agreed to form a union; two weeks later
the union handled its first strike after the Wellesbourne men had
demanded sixteen shillings a week. By the end of March, the union
had 5,000 members in sixty-four branches and a meeting at Leamington established the Warwickshire Agricultural Labourers' Union.
Within two months, Arch was back at Leamington, this time presid-
ing over the first National Congress of Agricultural Labourers at
which was founded the National Agricultural Labourers' Union

(NALU). Nor was Arch's union the only organization – indeed the characteristic pattern of the movement was the spontaneous formation of extremely local unions which only later either appealed to or came to the notice of the national organizations with whom they then merged. Most counties south of the Trent experienced this sudden explosion of unrest from which innumerable little local unions emerged, eventually to coalesce around three more general ones: the NALU; the Eastern Counties Union, led by James Flaxman, a Primitive Methodist schoolteacher, which had its headquarters at Fakenham and was particularly strong in Norfolk; and the Amalgamated Labour League, led by William Banks, a Radical journalist, with a membership centred around Lincolnshire. A meeting called in March 1873 in London to promote the formation of a single union broke down owing to the intransigence of Arch, and thereafter the movement remained split between the NALU, a highly centralized organization based at Leamington, and the much looser Federal Union of Labourers, which allowed local unions a fair amount of autonomy. Despite this setback the year 1873 was one of heady triumph for agricultural trade-unionism; between them the unions could muster around 120,000 members, and wages had been raised by two shillings a week all round, and as much as four shillings (25 per cent) in some places, through the largely successful pursuit of countless local wage demands and strikes.

Narrative accounts of agricultural trade-unionism's exhilarating advance up to the spring of 1874 are not hard to come by,[120] but systematic analysis of the movement has been rather more scanty. The first point that needs to be made is that the movement would never have been so successful if it had been forced to rely entirely on its own resources. Unlike the Swing uprising, the 'Revolt of the Field' was communicated to a wider national audience through the medium of the national press with the help of two relatively recent Victorian innovations, the railways and the penny post.[121] This was a movement in which wider influences – which the employers were soon to perceive and denounce – were at work. Arch's union received national attention through the reporting of the *Royal Leamington Chronicle* and its sympathetic editor, J. E. Matthew Vincent, was to become the treasurer of the NALU and editor of the union's own newspaper, the *Labourers' Union Chronicle*. The *Daily News* sent its war correspondent, Archibald Forbes, to cover the Wellesbourne strike, and later, in 1874, Frederick Clifford's reports to *The Times* on the East Anglian lock-out created considerable national controversy. It was through the press that Arch was able to appeal for national support, particularly in the early days when Arch was a shrewd exponent of publicity; during the first rash of strikes the union was rescued from virtual penury by appeals to urban trade unions and Radical M.P.s that produced a flood of donations.

In this respect the unionism of the 1870s was typical of rural protest movements in being heavily dependent on external sources of support. Arch was indeed fortunate in being so close to the geographical centre of Radical Liberalism, and Chamberlainite M.P.s were not slow to seize the opportunity of making political capital out of unrest in the Tory heartlands of rural England. The NALU – and Arch personally – were grossly exploited by the Liberal Party, particularly after the extension of the franchise to many agricultural workers in 1885. A gaggle of Liberal M.P.s were on the platform of the Leamington Congress in 1872, after which the farm worker was increasingly wooed by the Liberal Party. The demands of the unions for land, principally smallholdings and allotments, were zealously taken up by Chamberlain himself – 'three acres and a cow' – and fitted in well with the much wider pursuit of land reform by the Liberals in the 1880s.[122] This sponsorship was not without its rewards – the extension of the franchise, a limited establishment of smallholdings, local government reform – but the more politically embarrassing demands – land nationalization, disestablishmentarianism – were ignored and the conduct of many strikes owed more to political considerations than to the interests of the members. In addition to the Liberal Party, urban trade unions also took a hand, hoping to lessen the threat to wage levels in the towns by improving conditions in the countryside.

The fact remains, however, that despite the increasingly national character of the movement's formal organization and political aspirations, its centre of gravity remained stubbornly local.[123] The distribution of union membership was extremely patchy, with enormous fluctuations across very small geographical areas. This was an aspect of the movement that perplexed contemporary observers and mortified the early union pioneers. 'It was curious, also,' wrote Clifford, 'to find strong union developments in one village, and none, or next to none, in the next.'[124] This suggests that explanations of the distribution of trade-union activity have to be sought in the configuration of local social structures rather than in broader, regional patterns. Dunbabin, for example, has demonstrated the limited explanatory power of regional variations in wage levels, housing conditions and access to smallholdings and allotments in accounting for the incidence of the movement, 'for such variations were more visible, and therefore probably more influential, at the village rather than the regional level'.[125]

Dunbabin's assessment of the relevant village-level factors is somewhat inconclusive, though the data-collection problems are formidable. Nevertheless the limited conclusions that he draws are commensurate with the orientation outlined earlier in this chapter: an undermining of the conditions conducive to traditional, patriarchal authority and a failure to limit the expectations of the agricultural worker to those defined by this system – 'one must regard it,' writes Dunbabin, 'as a revolution of rising expectations'.[126] Patriarchal authority was capable of being maintained where personal contact between employer and employee was most prevalent; thus Dunbabin has discovered a high degree of association between the prevalence of farm service and the lack of unionization, together with the converse relationship, high unionization and a high concentration of hired labour. Although farm service declined in the south between 1851 and 1871, it actually increased in the north, where the associated institution of the hiring fair provided a means of testing the labour market without resort of collective action: 'Where hiring fairs really flourished, a high proportion of the farm workers were unmarried, and boarded in the farmhouses. And this certainly militated against the development of formal trade unions. For a strike must have been difficult to organize when one was actually living in a farmer's house; and close social relations were universally believed to make for an identification of the farmer's and labourers' interests.'[127] On the other hand trade-unionism and industrial action tended to occur on large farms with 'outdoor' labour. Clifford reported that around Woodbridge in Suffolk industrial action began against 'twelve large farmers . . . employing altogether about 170 men'.[128]

Trade unionism also tended to take hold in nucleated villages away from the embracing influence of the 'big house', where a vigorous working-class subculture had been maintained. More than likely there were strong associations with the local distribution of Nonconformity, although Dunbabin regrettably does not explore this connection, beyond noting 'the incidence of unionism and that of Nonconformist places of worship' in Dorset.[129] Even in these villages, however, the traditional accoutrements of paternalism could provide an effective prophylactic against unrest, and it was an accusation made by more enlightened observers that the unrest was directly attributable to the attenuation of traditional relationships by the lapsing of charities and benefit clubs, the decrease of payments in kind and perquisites and the discontinuation of many club feasts, harvest dinners and 'other occasions for local conviviality'.[130] There were many suggestions that farmers were abrogating their social responsibilities in the pursuit of profit maximization and there were some belated attempts at rectification. The Duke of Rutland, in a circular to the workers on his Cheveley estate, reflected this view. 'The relation of the farmer to the labourer,' he wrote, 'must rest on one of two principles – either on that of the mercantile or the confidential. Hitherto it has been on the latter, and I hope you will allow it to remain so. The one treats the labourer as a man whose family and children are to be cared for and protected; the other treats him as a machine out of whom the greatest amount of work is to be obtained at the lowest cost. It may be that the mercantile would be the best principle for the farmer's pocket, though I doubt it; but I am sure no paltry saving of money could compensate for the loss of kindly feelings and friendly relations existing between the different classes here.'[131] Even Clifford, a generally sympathetic and detached observer of the conflict, was moved to write: 'It was unfortunate, I think, that other men of influence in the country – the natural leaders, one may say of the two classes at issue – held aloof from the meetings of labourers, instead of trying to guide them aright and to counteract any mischief which might arise among them from evil counsel and ignorance.'[132] The very personal exercise of influence that was demanded probably accounts for the movement's bewilderingly variable distribution from village to village and for the difficulties in generalizing over causal factors. Again apparently trivial differences could be decisive: the Duke of Rutland, who *wrote* to his workers, failed to stem the unrest, but Sir Edward Kerrison, who *attended* a labourers' meeting, was entirely successful.[133]

In general, the initial reaction of farmers and landlords to the growth of trade-unionism in the countryside was one of complete surprise. Given their view of the village community, it seemed as though a serenely harmonious and stable world had suddenly erupted

into a maelstrom of bitterness, hatred and class antagonism. The sud-
denness of the union's growth led to a belief in a small band of
'agitators' who were busily involved in fermenting trouble from
outside, the nationwide character of the movement giving this more
than a modicum of plausibility. Appeals were made to workers to
ignore these 'outsiders' and to remember the repeated acts of kindness and benevolence of those who had their best interests at heart.
This paternalism infuriated union leaders like Arch, who replied in
turn with more and more extreme statements, thus increasing the
bitterness of the conflict. There were countless acts of petty oppression
from employers. The Duke of Marlborough deliberately made over
the cottages and allotments on his estate to the tenant farmers so that
they could evict union members. At Ascot-under-Wychwood in
Oxfordshire, six women were sentenced to between seven and ten
days' hard labour for giving blackleg labour 'rough music' – a case
which attracted the wrath of *The Times*. All over the south of England
union members were threatened with eviction from tied cottages and
from their allotments; elsewhere charity was withheld from them –
in Hampshire a man was refused a coffin for his child. In north
Oxfordshire a farmer literally flogged his middle-aged labourer
because he had joined the union.[134] The bitterness with which the
farm workers' mainly modest and politely worded requests were met
indicates that more was at stake than an improvement in their material
conditions – in many cases what was perceived to be at issue was none
other than the continued existence of a benevolently paternalistic
social structure in the English countryside. Instinctively this seemed
infinitely more worthwhile fighting for than the concession of
another few pence a week or a Saturday half-day.

This conclusion is prompted by a consideration of the East Anglian
lock-out which began in 1874. It was the climax of the 'Revolt of the
Field' and it effectively broke the movement. Like many crises it also
led affected parties to articulate their underlying, and usually unstated,
social principles and to urge the restoration of harmonious relationships through a pursuit of them. The dispute began at Exning, an
'open' village near Newmarket, where as early as September 1872
local farmers had received a petition signed by seventeen men asking
for an extra shilling a week. The local farmers formed a defensive
alliance, the Newmarket Agricultural Association, and decided
to ignore the latter. The request was repeated in February 1874,

whereupon, having given a week's notice, the men proceeded to strike. This time the farmers' reply was to decide that 'all union men be locked out after giving one week's notice' and later resolving that 'the members of this association shall not in future employ any men to work for them who are members of the union'.[135] On 21 March 1,600 men were locked out for refusing to leave the union. The lockout quickly spread into the surrounding counties, so that at its height 10,000 men were thrown out of their jobs across most of East Anglia and even as far afield as Dorset and Gloucestershire.

It was immediately apparent that the dispute was over something much more significant than an extra shilling a week, or even the principle of combination *per se*. What the employers were defending was the very structural principle upon which the effectiveness of their control was based, namely localism. At the first public meeting of the Newmarket Farmers Association, the chairman succintly summarized their aim: 'This is not a struggle for a paltry rise of one shilling in wages,' he stated. 'It is not a question of wages at all. The question is, Are these delegates to rule over us?' According to Clifford, 'the demand of 14s. . . . would have been readily conceded by the majority of the masters if it had come straight from the Exning men, and not from delegates behind them. Thus the question of wages was not really the issue between the combatants. The farmers felt that, with unionists in their employ, they were never safe.'[136] Perceived from the farmers' point of view, they were undoubtedly correct, for, as Orwin and Whetham point out, 'the idea of labourers listening to people outside the village instead of to their natural leaders within it seemed to them to cut at the roots of rural society'.[137] And so it did. Once agricultural workers were no longer amenable to their definition of the situation, to what was 'natural', right, proper and equitable, there was no telling where it would end or how the continuation of a stable social hierarchy was to be ensured. Farmers and landowners therefore set about defending their local spheres of influence with every weapon – coercive, economic and ideological – that was available to them.

The prevailing tenor of the battle for the workers' minds was to combine the exercise of gentlemanly paternalism with the stigmatization of union leaders. Thus the Duke of Rutland, in the circular referred to above, admonished as follows: 'Now, with respect to the union, the question is, not whether it is lawful to belong to it, of which I think there can be no doubt, but whether it is a good thing, in the interests of the employed and the employer, that you should do so. I am strongly of opinion that it is not a good thing, as those who advocate it are generally entire strangers, who do not live among you, and who know little of your position, or wants, or necessities.'[138] Other farmers from around Woodbridge told Clifford: 'We could not forget that the union had destroyed the peace of our villages, and we determined not to recognize in any way a combination so conducted. If our men had anything to say to us on their own account we were ready to hear them, but we were also determined to ignore concerted demands made by an anonymous committee, and showing the cloven hoof of the Union.'[139] Meanwhile Lord Walsingham believed that 'it was as ridiculous that disputes between farmers and labourers should be settled by Mr Morley or Mr Dixon, as it would be if any farmers ... interposed between the Manchester cotton-spinners and their "hands" to decide upon the hours of labour'.[140] Arguments like these were, according to Clifford, 'the farmers' *tu quoque*, and in some form or other you heard it wherever you went. It was this "interference" by strangers, whether philanthropists or paid delegates, which the farmers so violently resented.'[141]

This probably explains the bitterness which characterized the lock-out and which to the outsider could seem out of proportion with the ostensible issues involved. It was the apparently unnecessary ferocity of the conflict which prompted the Bishop of Manchester to begin a lively correspondence in *The Times*.[142] 'Are the farmers of England going mad?' he asked. 'Can they suppose that this suicidal lock-out, which has already thrown 4,000 labourers on the fund of the Agricultural Union, will stave off for any appreciable time the solution of the inevitable question, what is the equitable wage to pay the men? The most frightful thing that could happen for English Society would be a peasant's war. Yet, that is what we are driving to, if insane counsels of mutual exasperation prevail.' It was this letter which moved Lady Stradbroke to make her itinerary of local charity by way of reply, adding, 'Our labourers have hitherto been a content, peaceable, honest set of men. Delegates have now been sent down from districts like your own, where class has been fighting class for a quarter of a century, and have sown the first seeds of unhappiness ... Come down and judge for yourself if the agricultural labourers in this east of England will act wisely in throwing themselves into antagonism with their employers and benefactors. Far from blaming the farmers and calling them mad for resisting the spread of the union, you would, I am sure, counsel the men to have nothing to do with it, to trust those who have supported them in sickness and distress, and who in self-interest, even putting aside all higher motives, will never trample upon a class whom they have been taught from their growth up to regard as fellow workmen.' Lady Stradbroke's reply resulted in further controversy, with the bishop referring to her picture of Suffolk as too 'idyllic'. Part of the argument centred around the ability to achieve lasting social stability through confrontation and an enforced return to patriarchal rule or whether the principles of legitimacy had to be altered to meet changing economic circumstances. For example, her near-neighbour, Sir Edward Kerrison, generally considered among the most enlightened of Suffolk landowners and an assistant Commissioner on the 1867 inquiry into the employment of women and children in agriculture, proposed an end to what he called 'the internecine war now raging in the Eastern Counties' through arbitration. He also recognized the more deeply rooted nature of the conflict and the inevitability of structural change: 'The whole labour question as now existing must be divested of all those benevolent or charitable adjuncts which with the most praiseworthy but most mistaken views are imported into it; they only divert the real question at issue, that of wages, which of necessity must henceforth be based upon commercial principles.'

Such realism was lost on those East Anglian farmers bent of winning their war of attrition. Somewhat to their own surprise they were able to cope with the essential tasks of the farming calendar, using imported blackleg labour, their own families, and the help of neighbours, and even having a spell at long-unaccustomed work on the land themselves. For five months the workers also remained solid, aided by the social mores of the occupational community – 'labourers who did not join the union and remained at work throughout the lock-out district had a bad time of it'.[143] What finally broke the men's resistance was the ability of the farmers to gather that year's harvest without the help of the locked-out men. By the end of July 1874 between six and seven thousand men were still locked out and the harvest was manifestly not being hindered. Moreover, the financial support of the men was driving the unions to the brink of bankruptcy – over five months the executive of the NALU authorized payments of nearly

£15,000 to the Newmarket district alone. On 27 July the NALU executive met at Leamington and stated, 'That in the face of the harsh and prolonged lock-out in the Eastern Counties, this committee cannot feel justified in supporting the labourers in enforced idleness indefinitely; nor can they seek public support continually while the harvest is waiting to be gathered in.' They resolved to promote migration instead. Two days later the Federal Union followed suit.[144]

Whatever gloss union leaders and sympathetic observers could place on these events, the lock-out ended in capitulation and the unions were broken, both financially and spiritually. The membership departed in droves, the leadership descended into a round of petty recriminations, feuds and real or imagined financial scandals. The NALU struggled on as a benefit society mainly in the eastern counties while Arch was increasingly patronized and incorporated by the Liberal Party.[145] The onset of prolonged depression in agriculture, especially in the arable areas, hardly created the conditions which facilitated trade-unionism. There was a brief revival in 1890 under the influence of the New Unionism in the towns, and largely promoted by them. The 1889 dock strike had been successful only because it coincided with harvest and thus escaped the influx of blackleg labour from the countryside. The urban unions therefore set about converting the agricultural worker once more, adding to the 'rainbow series of missionary vans' which brightened many English villages in the early 1890s.[146] Even this brief revival was, however, killed off by a poor harvest and a severe winter in 1893. By 1896 the agricultural worker was, in the words of F. E. Green, 'left destitute of any kind of trade-union organization . . . Rural trade-unionism was now at its lowest ebb since 1872'.[147]

In the aftermath of the lock-out there was no shortage of post-mortems. The immediate blame was laid on the organization of the movements concerned: the overbearing character of Arch, the inability to join forces into a single union, the financial chaos. This disillusionment was in itself a reaction to the exaggerated expectations of unionism, fostered by the leadership's analogies with the children of Israel and the Promised Land. In so far as the 'Revolt of the Field' was a semi-primitive, mercurial movement, it was especially liable to be cast down by a major defeat, such as was inflicted in 1874, and wither away. Moreover the unions could not afford, tactically or financially, to become involved in a long-drawn-out battle. The production cycle being what it is in agriculture, employers could happily afford to spend five months watching the crops grow while their locked-out employees were forced to exist on a pittance from their union. There also loomed the prospect of eviction from tied housing: 'Undeniably,' writes Dunbabin, 'the control of cottages was a useful weapon, and the events of 1874 led many East Anglian landlords to strengthen it by

Table 6 Membership of the NALU, 1873–96

Year	Membership	Year	Membership
1873	71,835	1885	10,700
1874	86,214	1886	10,366
1875	40,000	1887	5,300
1876	55,000	1888	4,660
1877	30,000	1889	4,254
1878	24,000	1890	8,500
1879	20,000	1891	15,000
1880	20,000	1892	15,000
1881	15,000	1893	14,746
1882	15,000	1894	1,100
1883	15,000	1895	None given
1884	18,000	1896	Dissolved

Source: P. L. R. Horn, *Joseph Arch*, Kineton, 1971

letting their cottages no longer directly to the labourers, but indirectly through the farmers.'[148] The most effective action remained short, sharp strikes at certain critical periods – seed-time and harvest – yet the prospects of this receded as first the feasibility of collective industrial action and then that of trade-unionism itself became increasingly called into question.

The 'Revolt of the Field' thus tested the patriarchalism of the English countryside but it did not destroy it. Despite the national attention which the movement received, and in spite of its undoubted symbolic importance, the movement was still only a minority one. There were over 980,000 agricultural workers in England and Wales in the 1870s, and at no stage did the unions attract much more than a 12 per cent density of membership. Clifford calculated that in Suffolk no more than 25 per cent ever joined the unions and of the 4,654 'farmers and graziers' in the county only 650 belonged to the defence associations, 'and it was a material fact that even during the heat of the late struggle, about one-half the union labourers in Suffolk were kept in work by their masters'.[149] In a paradoxical way, the 'Revolt of the Field', while demonstrating the continued tenacity of the tradition of rural resistance and protest, also illustrated the continued strength of patriarchalism. The two continued to co-exist side by side according to whatever the nature of the local social structure allowed, up until the First World War, though exactly in what proportions it is impossible to say.

To equate the disappearance of trade-unionism with the absence of any change in the structure of rural society would, however, be a mistake. The last quarter of the nineteenth century saw considerable changes under the impact of depression, although for the most part the agricultural worker was a passive participant in these developments rather than an active agent in fermenting them. Numerous official reports during the 1890s viewed the period as one of uneasy transition from high farming to an agriculture more attuned to the realities of world markets. In consequence there was a similar commercialization of employer–employee relationships particularly, as Wilson Fox pointed out, in the harvest-hit cereal-growing areas of eastern England. The Royal Commission on Labour also noted in 1892 that 'The familiar and quasi-patriarchal terms upon which farmers used to live with their men are fast giving way to mere contractual relations.'[150] When agricultural trade-unionism was to re-emerge, therefore, in 1906 its leaders were to find a much firmer structural basis for collective action.

The Agricultural Worker in the Twentieth Century

Few would deny the extent to which the social situation of the agricultural worker has changed since 1900, although, bearing in mind the observations of Raymond Williams, these changes should not always be regarded as particularly cataclysmic nor even novel. It is not the purpose of this brief concluding section to examine these changes in any detail, since this is the function of later chapters in this book: Chapter 3, on pay and conditions; Chapter 4, on trade-unionism;

Chapter 5, on the work situation; and Chapter 6, on changes in the rural community. Nevertheless some general points can be made at this stage.

Without wishing to advocate any crude technological determinism, one can say without doubt that some of the most fundamental changes in the agricultural worker's social situation have been wrought by the introduction of the internal combustion engine. Its adoption, both on the farm and in society as a whole, has profoundly affected the everyday life of the farm worker possibly more than any other single factor. On the farm the introduction of tractors and combine harvesters has, along with other technological innovations, accelerated the long-standing trend in the outflow of labour from agriculture. Up until 1939, their rate of introduction was slow and followed the pattern set by mechanization in the nineteenth century by not making any fundamental qualitative changes in the nature of the agricultural worker's work. Although the introduction of tractors began before the First World War, there were still less than 5,000 in the U.K. by 1925, and 55,000 by 1939. Then, however, mechanization was more rapid under the stimulus of wartime state control and there were 200,000 tractors in use by 1945 and over 480,000 by the mid-1950s. Combine harvesters showed a similarly startling increase: there were only 940 in England and Wales in 1942, but nearly 5,000 in 1948, almost 40,000 by 1958 and over 60,000 by the end of the 1960s.[151] This wholesale mechanization since the war has become known as the 'second agricultural revolution' and this appellation is probably justified. As with its eighteenth-century predecessor it has not only brought about a rapid outflow of labour from agriculture but has had a profound effect on those who have remained.

In general the agricultural worker has, as a result of this 'revolution', become more isolated from his fellow workers while at work. Not only are there fewer workers on each farm, but driving farm machinery involves a considerably greater degree of isolation from other workers than walking behind a plough. Working on a farm can now be a very lonely occupation. The effect on the village community has also, in most cases, been no less dramatic. As the job opportunities in rural areas have decreased so the rural working population has moved out. The internal combustion engine has allowed them to be replaced by a set of car-owning, predominantly urban, middle-class inhabitants who have no connection with agriculture. Today the bulk of the population of most of our rural villages no longer live *and* work in the village. The occupational community has thus disintegrated.

The ramifications of these changes are extremely complex and must be connected to a wider cultural change briefly referred to earlier in this chapter. It was noted how farmers have been caught up in a general cultural development that has depreciated the traditional

Table 7 Numbers of agricultural workers in Great Britain, 1921–70 (thousands)

Year	Full-time workers	Total	Percentage change in full-time workers
1921	789	996	–
1926	757	921	−4·1
1931	714	829	−5·7
1936	643	751	−9·9
1941	602	759	−6·4
1946	739	889	+22·8
1951	642	812	−13·1
1956	528	700	−17·8
1961	449	617	−15·0
1966	342	488	−23·8
1970	217	352	−36·5

Source: MAFF

authority of the gentlemanly amateur and seen a more professional ethic of economic rationality overtake agriculture. This general reorientation in British society towards justifying authority in terms of efficiency and knowledge has meant that unless agricultural workers have been culturally isolated from the mainstream of British society it is unlikely that they will continue to accept unquestioningly the authority of their employer simply because that is the way it has always been in the past. The changes in the structure of rural society have not been so potentially destructive of patriarchalism as it at first might seem, however. Many agricultural workers remain cut off socially and geographically from other sections of society, often because of, rather than in spite of, the technological innovations of the twentieth century. As the village has been invaded by an alien population so the worker in many cases has followed the nineteenth-century retreat of the farmer out to the farm, where he once again can come under the pervasive social influences and judgements of his employer. This illustrates that the farmer may continue to have considerable *choice* as to the form of authority that he wishes to exercise, though perhaps 'choice' is the wrong word since the process is rarely as conscious as this implies. Nevertheless, where the agricultural worker has become increasingly farm-centred, so the structural underpinnings of traditional authority have, ironically, been restored.[152] Those farmers who prefer to embrace a gentlemanly ethic rather than a professional one may be able to carry it off quite successfully. A much fuller analysis of this issue, however, must await later chapters in this book; at this point it is necessary merely to indicate that changes in the agricultural worker's social situation are not nearly so unilinear as is sometimes supposed.

In this century there is no doubt that the material conditions of the farm worker have undergone an unprecedented improvement. The advent of two world wars has fostered a universal (which is to say, urban) awareness of the importance of agricultural production and of the duty of the state to support it, and the agricultural worker has undoubtedly benefited from this in conjunction with the industry as a whole. He has also acquired his full citizenship rights through the enactment of universal welfare legislation and as a by-product of the gains made by better-organized industrial workers. Wholesale changes in the technology of agricultural production have also removed much of the dirty, routine drudgery of work on the land, and allowed the farm worker to obtain the skills that are given high prestige in modern society. Today the farm worker is better educated, better fed, better clothed and better housed than ever.

It thus seems easy and plausible to view the twentieth century as having marked the emancipation of the agricultural worker from the old ties of dependency and poverty. Indeed the agricultural worker, looking back to the 'old days', will usually make such a comparison. The experience of the nineteenth century, and indeed the period of this century up until the Second World War, form a vaguely defined 'then' to be contrasted with 'now'. In retrospect, the issues of what was right and wrong seemed more clearly defined 'then' than they do today: near-starvation wages, wretched housing, benevolent paternalism or authoritarian despotism, anti-trade-union oppression. It seems difficult to believe that, despite the amelioration of his circumstances, in *relative* terms the position of the agricultural worker has remained substantially the same. The agricultural worker remains for the most part powerless to increase the flow of rewards to him as compared to other sections of society and the constraints that surround him continue to ensure that his life-chances remain severely curtailed. These two facets of his situation, the absolute improvement but the relative inertia, create confusion and ambiguity in the minds of many agricultural workers, their situation seemingly less clear-cut than it was, yet still subject to influences beyond their control. Agricultural workers may have contributed the Tolpuddle Martyrs to trade-union history, but they have still to find their 'place in the sun'[153] and profit from the sacrifice themselves.[154]

1. E. J. Hobsbawm and G. Rudé, *Captain Swing*, Lawrence and Wishart, 1969.
2. F. M. L. Thompson, *English Landed Society in the Nineteenth Century*, Routledge and Kegan Paul, 1963.
3. S. Webb, Preface in W. Hasbach, *A History of the English Agricultural Labourer*, Cass, 1966; orig. 1908, p. vii.
4. J. L. Coppock, *An Agricultural Geography of Great Britain*, Bell, 1971, and *An Agricultural Atlas of England and Wales*, Faber and Faber, 1964; D. B. Grigg, 'Small and Large Farms in England and Wales, Their Size and Distribution', *Geography*, vol. XLVIII, No. 3, July 1963, pp. 268–79.
5. J. Littlejohn, *Westrigg*, Routledge and Kegan Paul, 1963.
6. See the map reproduced in Hobsbawm and Rudé, op. cit., p. 25.
7. For example, C. A. Arensberg and S. T. Kimball, *Family and Community in Ireland*, Harvard University Press, Cambridge, Mass., 1968; A. Rees, *Life in a Welsh Countryside*, University of Wales Press, 1950; W. M. Williams, *The Sociology of an English Village*, Routledge and Kegan Paul, 1956, and *A West Country Village: Ashworthy*, Routledge and Kegan Paul, 1964; Littlejohn, op. cit.; J. Nalson, *The Mobility of Farm Families*, Manchester University Press, 1968; D. Jenkins, *The Agricultural Community in South West Wales*, University of Wales Press, 1971.
8. G. E. Evans, *Pattern under the Plough*, Faber, 1966, p. 152.
9. Hobsbawm and Rudé, op. cit., p. 33.
10. ibid.
11. Royal Commission on Labour (C.6894), *The Agricultural Labourer*, Vol. I, part III, *Reports by Mr Arthur Wilson Fox upon Certain Selected Districts in the Counties of Cumberland, Lancashire, Norfolk, Northumberland and Suffolk*, HMSO, 1893, p. 6.

12. For details, see C. S. Orwin and E. H. Whetham, *History of British Agriculture, 1846–1914*, Longman, 1964; J. H. Clapham, *An Economic History of Modern Britain*, CUP, 1930, 1932, 1936, 1938; E. L. Jones, 'The Changing Basis of English Agricultural Prosperity, 1853–1873', *Agricultural History Review*, vol. 10, No. 2, 1963, pp. 102–19.

13. J. G. S. and F. Donaldson, in association with D. Barber, *Farming in Britain Today*, Penguin Books, 1972, p. 163.

14. ibid.

15. For details see P. J. Perry, *British Farming in the Great Depression, 1870–1914*, David and Charles, 1974, and the collection of papers in P. J. Perry (ed.), *British Agriculture, 1870–1914*, Methuen, 1974.

16. See G. E. Evans, *Ask the Fellow Who Cut the Hay*, Faber, 1956, Ch. 1.

17. Littlejohn, op. cit., pp. 27–36.

18. C. Ketteridge and S. Mays, *Five Miles from Bunkum*, Eyre Methuen, 1972, pp. 64–5.

19. Evans (1956), op. cit., p. 28.

20. G. E. Evans, *The Horse in the Furrow*, Faber, 1960, p. 28. See also his *Where Beards Wag All*, Faber, 1970, Ch. 6.

21. Evans (1960), op. cit.; Ketteridge and Mays, op. cit., Ch. 6.

22. H. Barrett, *Early To Rise, A Suffolk Morning*, Faber, 1967, pp. 36–7; Evans (1966), op. cit., p. 152; R. Blythe, *Akenfield*, Allen Lane, 1968, Ch. 1, passim, and pp. 84–90; Royal Commission on Labour, op. cit., p. 6.

23. Evans (1970), op. cit., p. 64. Also F. Kitchen, *Brother to the Ox*, Dent, 1940, p. 71, and S. G. Kendal, *Farming Memoirs of a West Country Yeoman*, Faber, 1944, p. 174.

24. Littlejohn, op. cit., pp. 34–6.

25. Evans (1960), op. cit., p. 34.

26. This point is developed in H. Newby, 'Agricultural Workers in the Class Structure', *Sociological Review*, vol. 20, No. 3, August 1972, pp. 413–39.

27. There are extensive descriptions of this sub-culture in the work of Evans (see the references to his work above). See also Kitchen, op. cit.; F. Thompson, *From Lark Rise to Candleford*, Penguin Books, 1973; orig. 1939; M. K. Ashby, *Joseph Ashby of Tysoe, 1859–1919*, CUP, 1961.

28. For historical data on agricultural workers' earnings, see J. R. Bellerby, 'The Distribution of Farm Income in the U.K., 1867–1939' in W. Minchinton (ed.), *Essays in Agrarian History*, vol. II, David and Charles, 1968, pp. 259–80 and *Agriculture and Industry: Relative Income*, Macmillan, 1956; Hasbach, op. cit., passim.

29. Bellerby (1956), op. cit., p. 162.

30. See E. H. Hunt, 'Labour Productivity in English Agriculture, 1850–1914', *Economic History Review*, second series, vol. 20, 1967, pp. 280–92; Royal Commission on Labour, op. cit.

31. J. Burnett, *Plenty and Want*, Penguin Books, 1966, p. 28.

32. A. H. D. Acland, *The Land. Report of the Land Enquiry Committee, Volume One: Rural*, Hodder and Stoughton, 1913, p. 21.

33. Royal Commission on Labour, op. cit.; Board of Trade, Labour Department, *Report by Mr Wilson Fox on the Wages and Earnings of Agricultural*

Labourers in the United Kingdom, Cd 46, HMSO, 1960; and *Second Report . . .*, Cd 2376, HMSO, 1905.

34. See the account of the dietary standards of the agricultural worker in H. Perkin, *The Origins of Modern English Society, 1780–1880*, Routledge and Kegan Paul, 1969, pp. 147–8. The most comprehensive account was by B. S. Rowntree and M. Kendall, *How the Labourer Lives*, Nelson, 1913. Using Rowntree's famous nutritional measures, they concluded that 'the wage paid by farmers to agricultural labourers is, in the vast majority of cases, insufficient to maintain a family of average size in a state of merely physical efficiency' (p. 31). The idea of linking wages to the price of corn had a lengthy ancestry: it was commended as early as 1847. See H. Raynbird, 'On the Farming of Suffolk', *Journal of the Royal Agricultural Society of England*, vol. 8, 1847, pp. 261–329.

35. G. Best, *Mid-Victorian Britain, 1851–75*, Panther, 1973, p. 87.

36. See Hobsbawm and Rudé, op. cit., Ch. 3.

37. Details in J. Thirsk and J. Imray, *Suffolk Farming in the Nineteenth Century*, Suffolk Records Society, Ipswich, 1958.

38. ibid., p. 32; also Evans (1970), op. cit., Chs. 11, 12.

39. For a concise summary of rural housing conditions, see Best, op. cit., pp. 88–9; Hasbach, op. cit., Appendix V, pp. 397–403.

40. F. Clifford, *The Agricultural Lock-Out of 1874*, William Blackwood, 1875, p. 33; reprinted in Thirsk and Imray, op. cit., p. 150.

41. Hasbach, op. cit., p. 400.

42. Royal Commission on Labour, op. cit., p. 6.

43. On the gang system and its relationship to housing, see Hasbach, op. cit., pp. 192–204, 268–9.

44. J. Glyde, *Suffolk in the Nineteenth Century: Physical, Social, Moral, Religious and Industrial*, Simpkin, Marshall, 1856, p. 161.

45. J. F. C. Harrison, *The Early Victorians, 1832–51*, Panther, 1973, p. 106.

46. See J. ten Broek, 'California's Dual System of Family Law: Its Origin Development and Present Status', part I, *Stanford Law Review*, vol. 16, No. 2, 1964, pp. 251–81. On the wider implications of Poor Law reform, see A. Sinfield, 'Poor Laws and Poor History: A Suitable Case for Retreatment', paper presented to the Social Administration Association annual conference, Nottingham, 1972; Perkin, op. cit., pp. 329 ff.; and Harrison, op. cit., pp. 106–12.

47. Best, op. cit., p. 158.

48. ibid., p. 153. The importance of charity in the maintenance of traditional authority is elaborated in H. Newby, 'The Deferential Dialectic', *Comparative Studies in Society and History*, vol. 17, No. 2, April 1975, pp. 139–64.

49. Reprinted in Thirsk and Imray, op. cit., p. 143.

50. M. B. Simey, *Charitable Effort in Liverpool in the Nineteenth Century*, University of Liverpool Press, 1951.

51. The phrase is from D. Owen, *English Philanthropy, 1660–1960*, Harvard University Press, 1965, p. 138. Owen places considerable emphasis on the sedative effect of charity. See also, G. Stedman Jones, *Outcast London*,

Clarendon Press, 1971, especially part III; E. C. P. Lascelles, 'Charity', in G. M. Young (ed.), *Early Victorian England, 1830–1865*, vol. II, OUP, 1934, pp. 319–22; and Brian Harrison's important summary article, 'Philanthropy and the Victorians', *Victorian Studies*, vol. 9, 1965–6, pp. 353–74.

52. ibid., p. 358.

53. Cited by Owen, op. cit., pp. 141, 143.

54. Lascelles, op. cit., p. 322; Owen, op. cit., pp. 477–8.

55. Cited by Lascelles, op. cit., p. 337.

56. Thompson, op. cit., pp. 211, 210. On the importance of such patronage see Perkin, op. cit., pp. 38–62.

57. For the significance of 'the gift', see M. Mauss, *The Gift*, Cohen and West, 1970, and other references cited in Newby (1975), op. cit.

58. Thompson, op. cit., p. 417.

59. Owen, op. cit., p. 140.

60. Ashby, op. cit.

61. Cited by W. L. Burn, *The Age of Equipoise*, Allen and Unwin, 1968, p. 239–40.

62. ibid., p. 241.

63. For a discussion of this concept, see C. Bell and H. Newby, *Community Studies*, Allen and Unwin, 1971, Ch. 2; and the same authors' 'The Sources of Variation in Agricultural Workers Images of Society', *Sociological Review*, vol. 21, No. 2, May 1973, pp. 229–53. For the sake of parsimony the word 'community' is retained, despite reservations about its usage.

64. Hobsbawm and Rudé, op. cit., p. 62. This was according to Burn (op. cit., p. 240) 'the thorny, intractable side which the most benevolent squire or parson could never reach'. See also Williams (1973), op. cit., p. 104.

65. cf. the descriptions of other occupational communities by D. Lockwood, 'The Sources of Variation in Working-Class Images of Society', *Sociological Review*, vol. 14, no. 2, 1966, pp. 249–67.

66. Williams (1973), op. cit., p. 104.

67. On poaching see G. Christian (ed.), *James Hawker's Journal: A Victorian Poacher*, OUP, 1961; E. W. Martin, *The Secret People*, Phoenix House, 1955, Ch. 7; on 'the horseman's word', see Evans (1960), op. cit.; I. Carter, 'Class and Culture Among Farm Servants in the North East of Scotland', in A. Maclaren (ed.), *Social Class in Scottish Society*, Routledge and Kegan Paul, forthcoming; on the solidarity of the tap room, see Thompson, op. cit., Ch. IV.

68. See Newby (1975), op. cit., for an elaborated discussion of this point. Also L. Davidoff, J. L'Esperance and H. Newby, 'Landscape with Figures: Home and Community in English Society', in J. Mitchell and A. Oakley, *The Rights and Wrongs of Women*, Penguin Books, 1976.

69. See Thirsk and Imray, op. cit.

70. For example, Burn, op. cit.; Best, op. cit.; Harrison, op. cit.; H. Perkin, op. cit.; Thompson, op. cit.; and A. P. Thornton, *The Habit of Authority*, Allen and Unwin, 1966. This is not, however, perhaps the best way of

utilizing this concept – see Newby (1975), op. cit., and below, Chs. 2 and 8.

71. M. Weber, *The Theory of Social and Economic Organization*, The Free Press, Glencoe, Ill., 1964, p. 125 (my emphasis). For a broader theoretical discussion of the relationship between power, legitimacy, status and authority, see Newby (1975), op. cit.

72. See ibid.

73. Thompson, op. cit., p. 184.

74. Weber, op. cit., pp. 341–2.

75. W. L. Burn, op. cit., p. 264. On the metamorphosis of the gentlemanly ethic, see in addition A. Livingston, 'Theory of a Gentleman', *Encyclopaedia of the Social Sciences*, vol. VI; Harrison, op. cit., pp. 121 ff.; D. C. Coleman, 'Gentleman and Players', *Economic History Review*, vol. XXVI, vol. I, 1973, pp. 92–116; R. H. Wilkinson, 'The Gentlemanly Ideal and the Maintenance of a Political Elite', in P. W. Musgrave (ed.), *Sociology, History and Education*, Methuen, 1970, pp. 126–42; L. Davidoff, *The Best Circles: 'Society', Etiquette and the Season*, Croome Helm, 1973, Ch. 3; Best, op. cit., pp. 245–63; Thompson, op. cit., passim. For a contemporary account, see R. Perrott, *The Aristocrats*, Weidenfeld and Nicolson, 1968.

76. R. E. Park, *Race and Culture*, The Free Press, Glencoe, Ill., 1950, p. 258.

77. This line of inquiry has been brilliantly explored by Erving Goffman. See his paper, 'The Nature of Deference and Demeanour' in *Interaction Ritual*, Penguin University Books, 1972, pp. 47–96. Also J. M. Beshers, E. H. Mizruchi and R. Perrucci, 'Social Distance Strategies and Status Symbols: An Approach to the Study of Social Structure', *Sociological Quarterly*, vol. 4, 1963, pp. 311–24. There is some evidence that subordinates use similar strategies to reduce the impact of their symbolically affirmed inferiority – for instance M. Tumin, *Social Class and Social Change in Puerto Rico*, Princeton University Press, 1961, p. 480; J. Dolland, *Caste and Class in a Southern Town*, Doubleday, New York, 1957; O. Patterson, *The Sociology of Slavery*, Routledge and Kegan Paul, 1957.

78. V. Sackville-West, *The Edwardians*, cited by Perrott, op. cit., p. 159.

79. E. Percy, *Some Memories*, Eyre and Spottiswoode, 1958, cited by D. Spring, 'Some Reflections on Social History in the Nineteenth Century', *Victorian Studies*, vol. IV, 1960–61, p. 58.

80. Lockwood, op. cit., p. 254. Also Bell and Newby (1973), op. cit.; Perkin, op. cit., p. 37, and F. Parkin, *Class, Inequality and Political Order*, MacGibbon and Kee, 1971, pp. 82–4.

81. See Davidoff *et al.*, op. cit.

82. *ibid.* See also Bell and Newby (1971), op. cit.

83. Best, op. cit., p. 85.

84. See Harrison, op. cit., p. 121 – 'As a social institution foxhunting was an effective assertion of gentlemanly leadership and the bonds of deference.' Also Williams (1973), op. cit., Chs. 12, 16; Thompson, op. cit., passim.

85. J. C. Loudon, *An Encyclopaedia of Cottage, Farm and Villa Architecture . . .*, London, 1853, pp. 791–2. See also Davidoff *et al.*, op. cit., and Williams (1973), op. cit., Ch. 12.

86. See Newby (1975), op. cit.

87. Thompson, op. cit., p. 87.

88. See Bell and Newby (1973), op. cit., for a heuristic model.

89. Thompson, op. cit., p. 66.

90. E. D. Genovese, *The World the Slaveholders Made*, Allen Lane, 1970, p. 98.

91. Williams (1973), op. cit., p. 182; Hobsbawm and Rudé, op. cit., p. 47.

92. Perkin, op. cit.

93. Cited ibid., p. 225.

94. On the importance attached to the undermining of localism, see Best, op. cit., pp. 53–61; Burn, op. cit., Ch. 4, passim. Of course, in many areas the changes could be more nominal than real. 'Here and there,' wrote Green, 'there was a show of democracy. The landowner and the vicar, the landowner's coachman, the landowner's gamekeeper, his head-gardener, and his brother would sit, though of separate classes, as one happy family party, along with the blacksmith who shod the landowner's carriage horses, and the saddler who supplied the harness. But reform, as might be imagined under these circumstances, had to be warily suggested by anyone but the chairman' (F. E. Green, *A History of the English Agricultural Labourer*, P. S. King and Son, 1927, p. 124).

95. Education, in particular, was feared by many farmers. It was seen to 'raise a man above his work'. On the debate of the Education Bill of 1870, Lord Onslow trusted that 'there would be no attempt to establish a very high class of education in our rural schools, as over-education would have the effect of driving away manual labour from the country'. See O. J. Dunlop, *The Farm Labourer: The History of a Modern Problem*, Fisher Unwin, 1913, pp. 130–32.

96. J. Saville, *Rural Depopulation in England and Wales 1851–1951*, Routledge and Kegan Paul, 1957, p. 19. For the impact of the bicycle see Thompson, op. cit., Ch. XXXIX, and P. J. Perry, 'Working Class Isolation and Mobility in Rural Dorset, 1837–1936', *Institute of British Geographers Transactions and Papers*, Vol. 46, 1969, pp. 121–42. On the impact of the railways see Best, op. cit., pp. 88–92, and Thompson, op. cit., pp. 256–63.

97. Thompson, op. cit., p. 240 ff. The economic mechanism whereby returns to total factors in agriculture tend to fall behind returns to other industries in industrial economies are described in Bellerby, op. cit.; D. Metcalf, *The Economics of Agriculture*, Penguin Books, 1969; and M. Capstick, *The Economics of Agriculture*, Allen and Unwin, 1971.

98. Thompson, op. cit., p. 196.

99. The profound ramifications of declining capital returns are well documented by Thompson. See also Perry (1974), op. cit.; and H. Perkin, 'Land Reform and Class Conflict in Victorian Britain', in J. Butt and I. F. Clark, *The Victorians and Social Protest*, David and Charles, 1973, pp. 177–217.

100. Thompson, op. cit., p. 211.

101. Bellerby, op. cit.; H. Newby, 'The Low Earnings of Agricultural Workers: A Sociological Approach', *Journal of Agricultural Economics*, vol. XXIII, No. 1, 1972, pp. 15–24.

102. Evidence is summarized in Saville, op. cit.

103. See Perry (1974), op. cit., Ch. 6.

104. The most comprehensive review of the literature on the degree of selectivity in rural depopulation is B. S. Bosanquet, 'The Quality of the Rural Population', *Eugenius Review*, vol. XLII, No. 2, July 1950, pp. 75–92.

105. As Thompson points out (p. 291), 'There was no escape from the dilemma of wealth and status. Without land, they would no longer be a landed aristocracy. With land, only those whose estates were fortunate enough to benefit from industrial values were wealthy enough to remain dominant.' Perry also sees the hallmark of the transfer of rural leadership as the growing tendency for the landowner to become an acceptor rather than an originator of change. See Perry (1974), op. cit., p. 87.

106. Thompson, op. cit., p. 322.

107. ibid., pp. 332–3. See also S. G. Sturmey, 'Owner-Farming in England and Wales, 1900–50', *Manchester School*, vol. XXIII, 1955, pp. 246–68.

108. Hobsbawm and Rudé, op. cit., p. 285.

109. Howkins, op. cit.

110. J. P. D. Dunbabin, 'The "Revolt of the Field": The Agricultural Labourers' Movement in the 1870s', *Past and Present*, No. 26, 1963, pp. 68–97. On the use of 'primitive' in this context, see E. J. Hobsbawm, *Primitive Rebels*, Manchester University Press, 1968.

111. Hobsbawm and Rudé, op. cit., pp. 288–91; J. P. D. Dunbabin, 'Labourers and Farmers in the Late Nineteenth Century – Some Changes', *Bulletin of the Society for Labour History*, vol. 11, 1965, pp. 6–9.

112. A. Everitt, *The Pattern of Rural Dissent: the Nineteenth Century*, Leicester University Press, 1972, p. 44.

113. Hobsbawm and Rudé, op. cit., p. 281; also Dunbabin (1965), op. cit.

114. N. A. D. Scotland, 'The Role of Methodism in the Revolt of the Field in Norfolk, Suffolk and Lincolnshire, 1872–1895', paper presented to University of Aberdeen Sociology of Religion Conference, February 1974.

115. Cited by R. C. Russell, *The 'Revolt of the Field' in Lincs*, NUAW Lincs. County Committee, 1956, p. 17.

116. E. Selley, *Village Trade Unions in Two Centuries*, Allen and Unwin, 1919, p. 47. Arch even went as far as to suggest at an anniversary meeting held at Wellesbourne in 1873 that 'the labourers might set up a free and independent church of their own'. P. L. R. Horn, *Agricultural Labourers' Trade Unionism in Four Midland Counties (1860–1900)*, University of Leicester Ph.D. thesis, 1968, p. 69.

117. P. H. J. H. Gosden, *The Friendly Societies in England, 1815–75*, Manchester University Press, 1961; Hobsbawm and Rudé, op. cit., pp. 294–6.

118. J. P. D. Dunbabin, 'The Incidence and Organization of Agricultural Trades Unionism in the 1870s', *Agricultural History Review*, vol. 16, 1968, pp. 114–41.

119. E. H. Phelps-Brown, *The Growth of British Industrial Relations*, Macmillan, 1960, p. 174.

120. See Hasbach, op. cit.; Green, op. cit.; Selley, op. cit.; Russell, op. cit.; Horn, op. cit. Also R. Groves, *Sharpen the Sickle!*, Porcupine Press, 1948; G. E. Fussell, *From Tolpuddle to T.U.C.*, Windsor Press, Slough, 1948; P. L. R. Horn, *Joseph Arch*, Roundwood Press, Kineton, 1971; and Arch's

own *Autobiography*, MacGibbon and Kee, 1957; orig., 1898. For accounts of the movement in Scotland, see G. Evans, 'Farm Servants' Unions in Aberdeenshire from 1870–1900', *Scottish History Review*, vol. XXI, 1952, pp. 29–40; Carter, op. cit. There is no evidence of any direct connection between the English and Scottish movements.

121. Dunbabin (1963), op. cit.; Horn (1971), op. cit., pp. 48–9.

122. Summarized in Perkin (1973), op. cit. On the connections with the Liberal Party, see Dunbabin (1963), op. cit., and (1965), op. cit., Horn (1971), op. cit., pp. 74–5, 178 and Ch. 11.

123. Dunbabin (1968), op. cit. 'Branches sprang up suddenly in out-of-the-way villages like mushrooms in the night; strikes were declared by little village communities who rarely saw an organizer or consulted a leader' (Green, op. cit., p. 96). Also Dunlop, op. cit., pp. 144 ff.

124. Clifford, op. cit., p. 69.

125. Dunbabin (1968), op. cit., p. 114.

126. Dunbabin (1965), op. cit., p. 6.

127. Dunbabin (1968), op. cit., p. 122.

128. Clifford, op. cit., p. 90.

129. Dunbabin (1968), op. cit., p. 129.

130. Royal Commission on Labour, op. cit., p. 154.

131. Cited by Clifford, op. cit., p. 81.

132. ibid., p. 101.

133. ibid., pp. 80–82, 101–7. The figure of Sir Edward Kerrison exemplifies the effectiveness of the traditional personal modes of control. When a local union meeting was called, he spoke to the men as follows: 'It would be odd indeed if a meeting should be held in the village close to my house, and I – who am constantly among you, who am to be seen in this village and in the surrounding villages almost every day among the labouring people, who speak to them, who live among them, and who know more about them than I do about any other class around me – should be un-willing, or anything but glad, to meet you.' Later, in the middle of the lock-out, he was invited to the annual dinner of the Hoxne branch of the NALU. There he delivered a speech (a local farmer presided and carved the joints) and a vote of thanks was carried with acclamation. Kerrison was, however, a 'progressive' landowner not averse to the principle of trade-unionism (see below, p. 76).

134. Details in Groves, op. cit., Ch. 3; Horn (1971), op. cit.; Dunlop, op. cit., pp. 151 ff.; Arch, op. cit., passim.

135. Groves, op. cit., p. 73.

136. Clifford, op. cit., pp. 42–3. Later (p. 79) Clifford wrote: 'I rarely heard a farmer utter an unkind word against his labourers, except, perhaps, in the way of complaint that some among them did not work up to the proper standard. It was the interference of an executive sitting in Leamington, Lincoln or London, which the farmers dreaded and could not bring themselves to brook.'

137. Orwin and Whetham, op. cit., p. 232.

138. Clifford, op. cit., p. 81.

139. ibid., p. 163.

140. ibid., p. 128 (Morley and Dixon were two Liberal M.P.s active in the hierarchy of the NALU).

141. ibid., p. 100.

142. Much of this correspondence is reprinted in Thirsk and Imray, op. cit., from which the following extracts are taken.

143. Clifford, op. cit., p. 52.

144. Groves, op. cit., pp. 78–9.

145. For details, see Horn (1971), op. cit.; Green, op. cit. Arch became an increasingly pathetic figure, prone to incipient alcoholism, devoutly respectful of royalty (Sandringham was part of his constituency during his brief spell in Parliament) and unsympathetic to Socialism. When Arch married for a second time in 1890, it was in his local parish church rather than a Methodist Chapel.

146. Ashby, op. cit., p. 147. The nineties are well described by Green, op. cit., Ch. 5. It is perhaps worth mentioning that the most vigorous farm workers' union during this period was the Eastern Counties Labour Federation, which in 1890 had a membership of 16,881, the 'greater proportion being in Suffolk'. Its headquarters were in Ipswich. Wilson Fox reported that the farmers in the area were 'forcing the labourers into rebellion' by reducing wages without accepting offers of arbitration. However, within a few years the Federation was defunct. See Royal Commission on Labour, op. cit., pp. 37, 55 and vol. 5, part 1 (*General Report*), pp. 146–56.

147. Green, op. cit., pp. 140–41.

148. Dunbabin (1963), op. cit., p. 88.

149. Clifford, op. cit., p. 169.

150. Royal Commission on Labour, op. cit., p. 146. See also Perry (1974), op. cit., and Thompson, op. cit., Chs. IX–XI.

151. Coppock (1971), op. cit., pp. 104–5.

152. See H. Newby, 'The Changing Sociological Environment of the Farm', *Journal of Farm Management*, vol. 2, No. 9, 1974, pp. 474–87.

153. Edwin Gooch's vision for the farm worker. See the *Land Worker*, January 1944, p. 6.

154. P. Self and H. Storing, *The State and the Farmer*, Allen and Unwin, 1962, p. 158.

CHAPTER TWO

The Sociological Context

The academic study of rural society can hardly be said to have been immune to the idealized view of rural life discussed at the beginning of this book. Indeed until very recently the Romantic view of the countryside dominated what passed for rural sociology in both Europe and the United States. The reasons for this are not too difficult to see: sociology as a separate academic discipline was itself forged in the nineteenth-century reaction to industrialization and urbanization of which the Romantic movement was a part. It therefore accepted uncritically the prevailing view of rural society as a system of stable and harmonious communities, more integrated and more attuned to the realities of life, but at the same time threatened by the powerful and potentially disintegrating forces of urban industrial advance. Rural society itself, therefore, was rarely seen as problematic – either socially or sociologically (which in the nineteenth century amounted to virtually the same thing). The problem was rather how to preserve the rural *status quo* against enfeeblement by alien social forces, to avert the disintegration of rural communities and the decline of the traditional rural way of life and to preserve the existence of a separate rural identity.

This doctrine emanated from the liberal conservative strands of the sociological tradition which have been fully described by Nisbet[1] and there are obvious affinities with the ideological view of 'community' outlined in the previous chapter, including the desire to retain order and social stability through traditional modes of control. It went without saying during the nineteenth century that 'real' communities could be found only in the countryside. However, this perspective on rural society was not only the preserve of the conservative elements in the sociological tradition – in its desire to elevate the supposed desirability of communal living it linked up with the utopian aspects of socialist thought. Here there was a tendency to equate capitalism with industrialism and the existence of a proletariat with urbanism. The countryside and its indigenous population was either, in Marx's famous phrase, 'non-existent, historically speaking', a residual element hardly deserving of serious analysis, or, as in Engels, William Morris, the Hammonds and the Fabians, the location for various utopian blueprints.

Rural society was not, therefore, ignored; rather its composition was taken for granted and rarely seriously examined. Instead much more attention was paid to urban industrialism and its attendant social problems and evils. Thus in Britain academic sociology developed out of the Booth and Rowntree tradition of urban poverty studies, while *rural* poverty was virtually ignored; thus today urban sociology is a flourishing area of the discipline, while rural sociology is almost non-existent. In the United States, on the other hand, concern to preserve the Jeffersonian values of community and grass-roots democracy led to active state sponsorship of rural sociology as a means of servicing the rural population in the retention of distinctively rural values and ways of life. Through the facility of the Land Grant, rural sociology became part of an explicit social policy aimed at preserving, as far as was possible, the peculiarly wholesome virtues of rural America.[2] Galpin, who was to establish rural sociology in the United States, was quite explicit about his commitment, fearing that the physical transition from rural to urban life would give rise to a society 'immuned in brick and stone, gaining its outlook, as it were, through periscopes'.[3] He embarked upon an ambitious programme of research and education aimed at fortifying an apparently jeopardized rural way of life. Thus, while in the United States rural sociology was nowhere near as moribund as in Great Britain, it was nevertheless the captive of a generally sentimental and nostalgic ideology which was to restrict its professional development.

There is little to be gained from combing the American literature in the hope of theoretical insights into the social situation of agricultural workers; indeed Rushing, in a recent survey of farm labour in Washington State, was forced to rely on the novels of John Steinbeck and the television documentaries of Ed Murrow.[4] In recent years the academic standards of American rural sociology have been subjected to a series of devastating attacks, though with little recognizable effect. In 1950, for example, Anderson wrote: 'As measured by formally allocated research time and personnel, rural sociologists have enjoyed a distinctively favourable position. Unfortunately, this support has entailed administrative and cultural restrictions that have hampered professional development of the field. Scholarly output has not improved in quality or in adaptation to the changing society commensurate with this institutionalized recognition. Indeed the interests of rural sociologists have changed little during the present century, a century that has seen major orientations in other areas of sociology ... In recent years, these contributions (to sociological theory) have diminished, and much of the work merits the impatient judgement it receives: "fact-finding".'[5] Olson has also attacked the American rural sociologist as one who 'never gets beyond the clichéd and subjective experiences of the people he is studying',[6] and more recently Haller has referred to the 'arid contemporaneity and parochial cast' of work in this area.[7] In fact, as Nolan and Galliher have pointed out, most of the recent theoretical contributions have come from those who are not themselves rural sociologists. These are indeed, as they observe, 'hard times' for conventional academic rural sociology.[8] These 'hard times' are largely of rural sociology's own making. Where, as in the United States and much of continental Europe, rural sociology has attracted the interest of a substantial number of scholars, its exponents have on the whole been only too willing to enter the embrace of governmental agencies whose motives have often deserved a healthy scepticism. Rural sociology has sadly become locked into a bureaucratic straitjacket – well described by both Anderson and Olson – which has utterly stifled any theoretical analysis, and in some respects one can be grateful that the lack of interest in Britain has never allowed this situation to arise here. However, conventional rural sociology has also lost its way because of a growing realization of the bankruptcy of the hitherto arcadian view of rural society and the associated embodiment of this view in a theoretical scheme that derives from Tönnies – the rural–urban continuum. Once the taken-for-grantedness of this scheme was questioned and the social structure of rural society examined rather more closely, instead of being taken as 'given', it was always likely that a different account might emerge. This is in fact what has occurred in the last decade.

Tönnies and the Rural–Urban Continuum

Ferdinand Tönnies might fairly be described as the founding father of rural sociology.[9] Certainly his twin concepts of *Gemeinschaft* ('community') and *Gesellschaft* (variously translated as 'society', 'organization' or 'association') have had an enormous influence, represented by Nisbet as one of the unit ideas of the sociological tradition.[10] It is, perhaps, necessary to state that Tönnies' concepts of *Gemeinschaft* and *Gesellschaft* originally referred to forms of association, not types of settlement. *Gemeinschaft* extended beyond the purely *local* community to include any set of relationships characterized by emotional cohesion, depth, continuity and fulfilment; *Gesellschaft*, on the other hand, referred to the impersonal, the contractual and the rational aspects of human association. What in retrospect can be seen as Tönnies' most mischievous legacy was to ground these types of relationships in particular patterns of settlement and in particular geographical locales. Adopting the prevailing idealized views of rural life, Tönnies believed the rural village to represent *Gemeinschaft* – 'it is stronger there and more alive'[11] – while the city was characterized by *Gesellschaft*. Thus *Gemeinschaft* and *Gesellschaft* were abandoned as concepts and became reified into actual groups of people 'out there' which could be observed and investigated. From being a typology of social relationships Tönnies' concepts became a taxonomy of settlement patterns, and such was their conduciveness to prevailing cultural views of urban and rural ways of life that it was the latter usage which became much the more strongly established, while the former was lost in the welter of similar 'linked antitheses' developed by other early sociologists to cope with exactly those fundamental changes in social organization that so interested Tönnies.[12]

There is no doubt that, correctly and imaginatively used, the concepts of *Gemeinschaft* and *Gesellschaft* could be valuable in understanding the nature and direction of social changes in both a rural *and* an urban setting.[13] Unfortunately, however, they were used largely to classify communities almost like so many butterflies, and contributed to the low-level fact-gathering tendencies of rural sociology, particularly American rural sociology. In addition, since the prevailing trend of society as a whole was regarded as being quite clearly from

Gemeinschaft to *Gesellschaft*, there was a reinforced tendency to look upon rural society as traditional, static and fighting a rearguard action to preserve itself against the encroaching and undesirable influences of urbanism. Tönnies therefore imported the prevailing cultural perspectives on rural life into academic sociological theory, thereby opening the door for a particular style of research which has continued until the present day. Once the broad categories of characteristic rural social traits had been derived by Tönnies, it merely remained for a myriad of locality studies to establish how *gemeinschaftlich* was community X (equals 'good', 'healthy', 'natural') and how *gesellschaftlich* was community Y (equals 'bad', 'alienating', 'unnatural'). Hence the lack of analysis of subsequent rural sociology and the endless descriptions of rural institutions and organizations. Literally hundreds of studies have followed Galpin's pioneering *Social Anatomy of an Agricultural Community*, each, as Olson has pointed out, being remarkably similar in format, subject matter, conceptual scheme and research style and each almost exclusively concerned with the same aspects: ecology (primarily settlement patterns), social organization (family, church, education, voluntary organizations, etc.) and social participation (mainly in local organizations). Most are attempts to gauge the 'health' of the individual communities concerned using criteria derived essentially from Tönnies (and the cultural tradition which he represents), while simultaneously upholding the virtues of rural life. Very few, however, have been used to examine the theoretical presuppositions themselves.[14]

Tönnies' *Gemeinschaft–Gesellschaft* typology became therefore a rural–urban continuum in the hands of Sorokin and Zimmerman and later the folk–urban continuum of Redfield. Sorokin and Zimmerman's aim was to establish 'the differential characteristics of the urban and rural community whose totality gives the type of each of these social aggregates'.[15] They did so by listing the differences between rural and urban society on a number of dimensions – occupation, environment, size, density, etc. Their approach to rural society is typical of this *genre* – at one point Sorokin conjures up a vision of happy peasants singing in the fields[16] – and it is perhaps worth quoting their conclusions at some length as a representative illustration of this approach:

'Up to recent times, at least for the bulk of the city population, the city environment, as such, has been much less natural and has given much less opportunity for the satisfaction of basic human needs and fundamental impulses than the rural environment. For a clarification of this idea, let us consider the situation of the urban proletariat, its work, its occupational environment, and the essentials of its mode of living. This group works in a closed factory or shop, which has been, especially in the past, often unhygienic, ugly, unaesthetical, and unattractive to eyes, or ears, or to the organs of smell or other perceptors. They are surrounded by the kingdom of dead machinery, steel, iron, coal and oil. Enormous noises, clangs, grinds, knocks, raps, clatters and taps of machinery and tools fill their ears. Dirt, summer heat, and winter cold assail them. Such has been and still is their occupational environment to a considerable degree. The work itself is also tiresome, monotonous, mechanical, half automatic. It furnishes little, if any, creative or interesting outlet for them. It goes on monotonously day in day out, for months and years ... Can such a city environment and manner of living satisfy these fundamental impulses and habit developed in quite a different situation and adapted to quite a different environment? The answer is no. Neither the impulses for creative activity; nor for orientation, curiosity, and novelty; nor the lust for variety and adventure; nor the physiological needs for fresh air; ... nor the physiological and psychological necessity for being in touch with nature; nor to enjoy with eyes the greenishness of the meadows, the beauties of the forest, the clear rivers, the waves of golden wheat in the fields; nor to hear the birds singing, the thunderstorm, or the mysterious calm of an evening amidst nature; these and thousands of similar phenomena have been taken from the urban man ... In spite of the enormous improvement of the conditions of the urban labour classes in these respects, the city still has a great deal of these elements of 'unnaturality' and through that stimulates dissatisfactions and disorders.

'The farmer–peasant environment, on the contrary, has been much more "natural" and much more identical with that to which man has been trained by thousands of years of preceding history. The basic impulses of man, as they have been shaped by the past, are to be satisfied much easier in the environment and by the occupational activity of the farmer. There is neither lack of nature, nor the killing monotony of work, nor extreme specialization, nor one-sidedness. His standard of living may be as low as that of a proletarian; his house or lodging may be as bad; and yet the whole character of his structure of living is quite different and healthier and more natural.'[17]

Sorokin's statement mirrors almost exactly the prevailing view of the English countryside considered in the prologue of this book. The basic components are all there, even down to the typical disregard of material standards for alleged metaphysical benefits, renewed through the elision of the aesthetic and the social aspects of rural life. While few would be so explicit, Sorokin is merely expressing the assumptions which underlay the whole approach to the rural–urban continuum which existed down to and including the work of Redfield. Redfield's famous paper 'The Folk Society',[18] though more sophisticated and more sociological than Sorokin's work, used much the same descriptions – small-scale, isolated, agricultural, non-literate, homogeneous and with a strong sense of group solidarity. Needless to say, urban society consisted of the opposite features.

The notion that ways of life could be linked to settlement patterns was first undermined by Oscar Lewis's restudy of Tepoztlan, the original 'folk society'. Whereas Redfield had discovered a homogeneous, smoothly functioning, well-integrated, contented, stable and harmonious community, Lewis emphasized 'the underlying individualism of Tepoztlan institutions and character, the lack of co-operation, the tensions between villages within the *municipio*, the schisms within the village, the pervading quality of fear, envy, and distrust, in interpersonal relations'.[19] This is a far cry from *Gemeinschaft*, but it was a view of rural society that was to be repeated in a number of attacks upon the 'misplaced polarities' of the rural–urban continuum during the 1960s.[20] The declining influence of the scheme was also hastened by the discovery of disconcertingly *gemeinschaftlich* communities in the centre of large urban conurbations, notably in the Bethnal Green studies in England and Gans' *The Urban Villagers* in the United States.[21] Gans in particular doubted the *sociological* relevance of the terms 'rural' and 'urban' in highly complex industrial societies: 'Ways of life,' he wrote, 'do not coincide with settlement types.'[22] It remained for Pahl finally to dismiss the utility of the rural–urban continuum in his important critical article which appeared in 1966.[23] In effect, Pahl considered the concepts of 'rural' and 'urban' not to be sociological variables at all, but merely a 'geographical expression'. He adduced evidence from recent community studies to show that, far from these being an exclusive continuum from *Gemeinschaft* to

Gesellschaft, relationships of both types could be found in the same localities, yet 'for sociologists, the association between "rural" and *Gemeinschaft* is so hard to break'.[24] He went on to argue: 'Any attempt to tie patterns of social relationships to specific geographical milieux is a singularly fruitless exercise,'[25] and that the mere cataloguing of demographic and economic differences between rural and urban settlements was a misleading substitute for an examination of their social structures. In particular Pahl drew attention to the confrontation between the local and the national and between the small-scale and the large-scale: 'it is the basic situation of conflict or stress that can be observed from the most highly urbanized metropolitan region to the most remote and isolated peasant village.'[26]

The implications of Pahl's arguments for the continuation of rural sociology as a viable intellectual discipline were indeed profound. At a stroke he had demolished the conceptual scheme upon which rural sociology had been based since Tönnies and Galpin, while at the same time demonstrating that rural sociology could no longer continue to consider the 'rural' sector in isolation from the rest of society. Eighty years after the publication of *Gemeinschaft und Gesellschaft*, Tönnies' tools of analysis had been restored to their correct ontological status and the misleading aspects of his contribution to sociological theory had been erased. However, a further consequence of Pahl's argument was to leave a theoretical vacuum in rural sociology which has never been filled. It is not therefore surprising that more sophisticated attempts to resurrect the rural–urban continuum continue to abound.[27] There is certainly a sense in which Pahl overstated his argument, for, in the limiting case, geographical milieux *may* define patterns of social relationships through the constraints which they apply to the local social structure, a point which Pahl has himself developed in his work on urban inequality.[28] In other words, if social relationships and institutions are constrained in such a way as to render them locality-based there *may* be a local social system – which for the sake of parsimony we might even call 'rural' – which is worthy of sociological attention.[29] It must be emphasized, however, that any causal connection between the nature of this local social system and its 'rurality' is purely spurious – it merely stems from the inability of the inhabitants to transcend the spatial constraints imposed upon them, this incapacity being linked to inequalities rooted in a wider system of social stratification rather than in a rural milieu *per se*.

Thus, to paraphrase Pahl, there is no rural population as such; rather there are specific populations which for various, but identifiable, reasons find themselves in rural areas.[30]

Only in this highly limited and spurious sense can the analysis of agricultural workers presented in this book be regarded as a piece of rural sociology. There is nothing in the social structure of the East Anglian countryside that could not be found in an urban setting, and nothing in the attitudes and behaviour of agricultural workers which could not be found among certain groups of urban, industrial workers. The analysis could be regarded as a piece of industrial sociology, the industry merely being agriculture, the plant size being small and the job satisfaction high. Alternatively it could be regarded as an investigation of certain relational and normative aspects of social stratification within a diffuse and particularistic social structure. Other examples of this could be found in the city, and even the problem of stratification being organized around the institution of property rather than occupation is not a peculiarly agricultural phenomenon. This is not to say, of course, that agricultural workers do not perceive vast and unbridgeable social differences between the countryside and the towns; on the contrary, this perception is an extraordinarily prevalent one, and the move out of agriculture is still regarded as a more distinctive and decisive move than out of any other occupation. Nevertheless, this belief can be seen to be based as much upon the traditional English cultural perspective of rural life as upon any hard evidence concerning a peculiarly rural social structure. Sociologically agricultural workers are 'rural' only because the constraints of the labour and housing markets mean that they must both live and work in the same locality.

Rural Sociology in Britain

As was pointed out at the beginning of this chapter, rural sociology in Britain has been a moribund area of the discipline, despite early flickers of concern from investigators like Mann, Rowntree and Davies.[31] Work which has been carried out in this area has more often than not been an adjunct of another discipline, usually social history, agricultural economics or social anthropology. Social anthropologists have been particularly active, especially in the Celtic fringe areas, where a fair amount of evidence has been gathered on the social structure of subsistence farming, and in particular the relationships between landholding and kinship. Unfortunately, these studies, with one notable exception, are not set in areas where there is a high concentration of hired labour. The anthropologically oriented studies of Arensberg and Kimball, Rees, Williams, Nalson, Jenkins, etc.[32] are all situated in areas of family farming which contain a completely different social structure from that of rural East Anglia. Interesting though many of these studies are, therefore, they can be used only as a contrast to the capitalist farming areas of lowland England, where many of the upland pastoral farms described in these studies could be set with ease on a single field of a medium-sized arable enterprise.

Most of these studies have also been set explicitly within the framework of rural *Gemeinschaft*. As Williams pointed out in the introduction to his study of Ashworthy, there has existed in rural British community studies the customary tendency to regard rural communities as stable and static, and on the verge of some irrevocable decline by succumbing to externally imposed social changes.[33] The absence of hired labour, and therefore readily identifiable class divisions, increased the plausibility of emphasizing the *gemeinschaftlich* qualities of the rural way of life. It was possible to suggest the existence of an internally homogeneous and consensual rural social system, based on self-help and mutual co-operation, which could be contrasted, often with thinly disguised approval, with its urban counterpart. Only Littlejohn, in his study of Westrigg, analysed a rural area in terms of social class and conflicts of interest, rather than through an inherently consensual set of rural norms and values, and this was in an area with a high concentration of hired labour, where the social relationships in agriculture were those of employer and employee rather than of kinship. Significantly, Littlejohn goes as far as to call the population of Westrigg 'industrial', even though the village is, geographically, very rural.[34] Elsewhere, however, Littlejohn's approach has not been repeated. It is now some time since Frankenberg regretted in *Communities in Britain* that there was no account of social life in 'the capitalist organized business farming areas' of lowland England. 'This,' he stated, 'is one of the most glaring gaps in the literature.'[35] For even those community studies of areas where agriculture had this industrialized countenance – like Pahl's study of the metropolitan fringe in Hertfordshire[36] – concerned themselves with other aspects of the local social structure than the relationships between farmers and agricultural workers. Thus while our knowledge of family farming has a fairly sound basis, non-family agricultural workers have been almost entirely overlooked. It need hardly be added that one of the initial aims of this study was to begin to fill this gap.

There is one further problem in using these studies as a source of data on agricultural workers, and that is that they are now rather dated. The fieldwork for the studies by Arensberg and Kimball and Rees was carried out in the 1930s and 1940s, while the studies by Littlejohn, Williams and Frankenberg were based on data gathered in the 1950s. Reading about the arrival of the first bread van in Gosforth[37] – the harbinger of urban penetration – now simply seems rather quaint. Even Littlejohn's account of Westrigg is coloured by the relatively short-lived atmosphere of post-war emancipation among farm workers. Only very recently have there been signs of a revival of interest in rural community studies, with Whitehead's study of a Herefordshire parish, Ambrose's book on Ringmer in Sussex, and the study of the Norfolk village of 'Hennage' by 'Clement Harris'.[38] Otherwise, one must depend upon Blythe's *Akenfield*, which, for all its faults, is certainly not lacking in intuitive insights.

The conclusions which can be drawn from a consideration of the major British rural community studies are therefore rather negative ones. There is, as has been indicated elsewhere,[39] a lack of almost any sociological data on how recent changes in the social structure of rural communities have affected the social situation of the agricultural worker, although it seems reasonable to suppose that these changes will be more complex than simple *Gemeinschaft–Gesellschaft* or rural–urban dichotomies suggest.[40] From the outset, it was one of the aims of this study to investigate the nature of these changes. While not intending to carry out a community study in the conventional sense, it was realized at an early stage that various configurations of local social structure would have to be covered in order to ascertain their impact on the overall situation of the agricultural worker and that the research design would need to incorporate an examination of more than one type of local social system. It seemed likely that the agricultural worker's perceptions of his own situation would be different in the kind of occupational community described in the previous chapter from those where he lived in a village overrun by mainly urban, middle-class newcomers. These aspects are examined in Chapter 6.

Agricultural Workers and the Class Structure

The main purpose of studying agricultural workers was, however, not to investigate problems that have arisen from conventional rural sociology, and only tangentially related to rural community studies. The problems to which this study was originally addressed were derived from certain issues involving the class structure of British society. The background therefore involved not a concern with rural sociology, but the debate on certain facets of the British working class.

The most striking aspect of sociological research into the working class during the 1960s was the overriding concern with the problems of class awareness and class consciousness. This was a measure of the increasing cross-fertilization between the occasionally Marxist-influenced sociology of conventional academic research into social stratification and the sociologically informed theoretical writing of orthodox Marxist pedigree, particularly among the 'New Left'.[41] The renewed attention which was paid to the problem of class consciousness undoubtedly stemmed from the third successive electoral victory, with moreover an increased majority, of the Conservative Party in 1959 and the subsequent disarray among the British Left. Old questions about the relationship between 'objective' class position and class consciousness were re-opened and re-examined, and within Marxist thought in Britain there was a self-proclaimed crisis and a re-appraisal of many of the fundamental tenets of Marxist doctrine, signified by the title of Perry Anderson's important paper, 'The Origins of the Present Crisis'.[42] There were signs of an increasing impatience with the crude economically deterministic interpretations of Marx's writing and an unwillingness to continue to take for granted the hitherto underexamined connection between class formation and class consciousness. In particular there was an increasing scepticism of the utility of the Marxist–Leninist formulations of 'true' and 'false' consciousness, except as ciphers, and a realization that the bases of 'false' consciousness and lack of revolutionary zeal among the British working class might be related to systematic variations in the structural features of different occupational or other groups *within* it.[43] There was thus opened up the whole question of the social bases of class consciousness, whether this be regarded as 'true' or 'false' in relation to expectations derived from Marxist theory.

Marxist writers were, then, willing to grant a much greater degree of causal autonomy to the realm of ideas in the fashioning of structural stability and change, while not denying the determinacy of the economic base in the last instance. Here the debate centred around Marx's famous dictum that 'the ideas of the ruling class are, in every age, the ruling ideas', although this was initially adapted into a simplistic formulation of brainwashing or conscious class-based indoctrination, an interpretation of Marxism as vulgar as the economically deterministic version that was being reacted against. In this sense Gramsci's detailed discussion on the problem of consciousness, which had been adopted with considerable enthusiasm, was almost too apposite: it was very tempting to consign the problem of consciousness to a crudely elaborated 'hegemony', which appeared all the more attractive in being either tautological or trivially true. Thus, to attribute the successful domination of the ruling class to their 'profound cultural supremacy'[44] was hardly an advance. Fortunately, however, a remarkable *tour de force* from E. P. Thompson corrected the worst excesses of these claims for a massive and all-pervading pall of false consciousness across the British working class.[45] Henceforward the 'old and crucial' Marxist question about the conversion – or non-conversion – of a class 'in itself' into a class 'for itself' was tackled with a much greater degree of sophistication, and, as Goldthorpe has pointed out, through a much closer *rapprochement* with social inquiry conducted in a more strictly academic style and context.[46]

The run of Conservative electoral successes and the growing belief in the alleged classlessness of British society during the 1950s also had its effect on conventional academic social science. Psephological post-mortems on the 1959 general election were quick to invest it with far-reaching significance. Butler and Rose, for example, argued that 'the swing to the Conservatives cannot be dismissed as an ephemeral veering of the electoral breeze. Long-term factors were also involved. Traditional working-class attitudes had been eroded by the steady growth of prosperity'.[47] This argument was also elaborated at greater length by Abrams and Rose in *Must Labour Lose?*.[48] In retrospect it can be seen that not only was research into social stratification and political sociology in Britain dominated by this problem for the next decade, but also that the terms in which it was to be considered were also set by these considerations. For example, the belief that there were a set of 'traditional working-class attitudes' which had somehow become eroded was widespread, yet there was little consideration of what these attitudes were, nor how prevalent beyond Bethnal Green and Hunslet.[49] Instead the traditional worker, cloth-capped and Labour-voting, became a kind of sociological caricature to contrast with two new stereotypes: the affluent worker and deference voter, who owned washing machines and voted Conservative.

Sociological research concentrated on the thesis of *embourgeoisement* and the affluent worker. Goldthorpe and Lockwood were able to expose some of the looser aspects of the *embourgeoisement* thesis by expertly dissecting it in 1963 before they had even begun to establish its empirical validity. By breaking down the concept of *embourgeoisement* into its economic, relational and normative aspects, they were able to demonstrate that there was 'little basis for the more ambitious thesis of *embourgeoisement* in the sense of the large-scale assimilation of manual workers and their families to middle-class life-styles and middle-class society in general. In particular, there is no firm evidence either that manual workers are consciously aspiring to middle-class society, or that this is becoming any more open to them'.[50] These conclusions were upheld by the subsequent 'affluent worker' study, although it also indicated a degree of what Goldthorpe and Lockwood called 'normative convergence' between certain sections of the working and middle classes over such issues as the instrumental collectivism of trade union and party political support and an increasing privatization of leisure activities. Most importantly, Goldthorpe and Lockwood warned that 'The link between "affluence" and "vote" is mediated by the social situation in which the affluent worker finds himself.'[51] There was here a brief allusion to the same problem that was at the centre of the Marxist debate: what were the social bases of political commitment and class-based identity? As Westergaard pointed out, if the working class was not becoming more bourgeois, neither was it seething with revolutionary fervour – 'If the conjunction of rising expectations and persistent inequalities indicates a potential from which a clear challenge to the established order could emerge, what circumstances account for the apparent repression or dissipation of that potential?'[52]

In a seminal paper published in 1966,[53] Lockwood attempted a bold and imaginative answer to these questions. He later called this paper 'an extended footnote to Chapter Five of Volume Three of *The Affluent Worker*',[54] but this hardly did justice to his attempt to draw together existing work on various working-class occupational groups and to relate their social imagery to the structure of their market, work and community relationships. Although in one sense Lockwood was merely trying to carry forward the insights of Elizabeth Bott into the relationship between structural variables and 'images of society', rather than class consciousness *tout court*, there also seems little doubt that the latter was a strong underlying theme. Lockwood had, after all, previously used this type of analysis in *The Blackcoated Worker*, the sub-title of which was 'A Study in Class Consciousness'. In addition, parallel attempts by Willener and Popitz were rather more explicitly concerned with the question of consciousness, and even Bott, in her classic statement of the problem, referred to 'class ideology'.[55] Operating, then, within a modified Weberian framework, Lockwood attempted to develop a typology of sources of variation in working-class images of society based upon his delineation of traditional proletarian, traditional deferential and privatized workers. 'The method,' he later wrote, 'was one of conflation, that is the assembly of a set of properties defining work and community structures which, together with certain sociological assumptions of a general kind, may be thought to constitute extreme or limiting cases of working-class *milieux*. The cases were of a limiting kind in the sense that all the relevant properties bearing upon the production of a given model of social consciousness were assumed to have values which are at a maximum or minimum so that all factors work together cumulatively in one direction to create a certain, and again, limiting image of society. Thus the types of work and community structure represent an imaginable but not necessarily a probable or even possible state of affairs.'[56] The value of these typologies was, therefore, essentially heuristic and, whatever the criticisms of Lockwood's original scheme, there can be little doubt that they have been extraordinarily successful in stimulating the empirical verification of theories of class consciousness among a wide variety of occupational groups.

The *Affluent Worker* study by Goldthorpe and his colleagues has an examination of one of these 'limiting cases' – the privatized worker. Ironically the original pretext for the study was removed by the result of the 1964, and then the 1966, general elections, thus vindicating Goldthorpe and Lockwood's earlier scepticism about the political consequences of working-class affluence. Moreover, the uninterrupted period of economic stagnation and retrenchment since 1963 has also killed the *embourgeoisement* thesis as a serious argument by contributing to a renewed heightening of social tension and intermittent conflict which have underlined the previously somewhat obscured realities of a capitalist British society. Nevertheless, Westergaard's assessment of the degree of class consciousness among British workers continues to apply and sociological theory remains less than adequate in its explanations of the social bases of class consciousness.

In political science, the investigation into the aftermath of the Conservative Party's electoral success took a different tack. Instead of seeking explanations in terms of the working class becoming more middle-class, political scientists sought to understand the phenomenon in terms of increased working-class 'deference'. A spate of studies during the 1960s attempted to assess the deferential component of English political culture, and Bagehot's ideas on the subject were enthusiastically resurrected. Once again there were links with the concurrent Marxist debate (the 'peculiarities of the English' is a phrase taken from Bagehot's *The English Constitution*), where the concept of deference was taken to mean false consciousness *par excellence*. Samuel's article 'The Deference Voter', published in the *New Left Review* in 1960, assumed that working-class deference was increasing: 'If their number has increased, it is partly because of what has happened to Britain in the fifties ... by the visible power of business, the celebration of consumer values, and the mood of frustrated nationalism. In the next five years the Conservatives are likely to appear even more "national" for they will be shaping the nation in their own image.'[57] Because of this underlying concern with false consciousness, deference was considered entirely as a working-class phenomenon; middle-class deference, apart from an occasional acknowledgement of its existence, was entirely ignored as an object of study. Essentially deference meant, within the context of this debate, working-class Conservative voting behaviour.[58]

This tendency to slide from deference, as indicated by working-class Toryism, to false consciousness and back again is well illustrated in Samuel's article. 'The aim of the working-class Tory,' he wrote, 'is not so much to draw nearer to his rulers in social status, but *to acknowledge the difference between them and himself, to defer* to them precisely *because* "they were born to rule"'. His Tory beliefs often include a lively sense of his own inferiority in matters of state and economy, together with a settled conviction that these are not proper matters for working people to decide. Ruling should be left to the ruling class.'[59] Why certain individuals should express these views and how, if at all, they are related to their position within the social structure is not considered by Samuel, nor was it by other contemporary political analysts who had broached the subject. The only insights to be gained were from the community studies of Banbury and Glossop,[60] and it was from these, together with some of the evidence on 'deference' voting contained in psephological studies like *Must Labour Lose?*, that Lockwood constructed his ideal-typical 'deferential traditionalist'. Direct evidence was therefore rather meagre and Lockwood's account was, by his own admission, 'wholly speculative'.[61]

Lockwood's conception of the traditional deferential worker is not, in fact, wholly dissimilar from that of Samuel. According to Lockwood, he 'does not identify himself with his superiors or strive to reach their status; he defers to them socially as well as politically. His recognition of authentic leadership is based on his belief in the intrinsic qualities of an ascriptive elite who exercise leadership paternalistically in the pursuit of "national" as opposed to "sectional" or "class" interests. Since he thinks in terms of "genuine" or "natural" leaders in both a local and a national context, it is likely that he thinks also of "spurious" leaders and, by implication, of "misguided" followers. Spurious leaders . . . lack the hereditary or quasi-hereditary credentials which the deferential worker recognizes as the true marks of legitimacy. Misguided followers are those . . . who refuse to acknowledge the objects of his deference, and who aid and abet the spurious leaders in usurping authority. If the deferential worker has an image of society as a status hierarchy, then the existence of "undeferential" workers is almost a necessary condition for the protection of his own sense of self-esteem. There are few instances of lower status groups who both accept the legitimacy of the status hierarchy and fail to discover groups with an even lower status than their own.' Lockwood also suggests that deferential workers share certain structural characteristics in their overall class situation. Typically, deferential traditionalists tend at work to be brought into persistent face-to-face contact with their employers and live in communities with established local status systems which allow contact between all strata. Thus those at the bottom of the social hierarchy continually experience the social evaluations and judgements of dominant class members: 'For the deferential traditionalist such a system of status has the function of placing his work orientations in a wider social context. The persons who exercise authority over him at the place of work may not be the same persons who stand at the apex of the local status system, but the structural principles of the two social orders are homological and from neither set of relationships does he learn to question the appropriateness of his exchange of deference for paternalism.'[62]

Whatever the absence of any sociological investigation of deference, however, 'a veritable army of scholars has seized on the deferential component' of English political culture.[63] Indeed the deference hypothesis has proved more durable than the *embourgeoisement* thesis as a plausible explanation of political changes during the 1960s, despite the fact that, as Kavanagh has shown, there is precious little data to support some of its more simplistic versions. In many respects, this resilience can be accounted for by the way in which the term 'deference' itself has been used in so many different ways. In addition to those already cited – working-class Conservative voting behaviour, false consciousness and a particular image of society – 'deference' has also been used to refer to certain forms of obsequious and/or ingratiating behaviour;[64] certain positive evaluations of ascriptive elites and/or symbols of traditional authority like the monarchy, House of Lords, etc.;[65] the stability and longevity of British political institutions;[66] subscription to and endorsement of the hierarchical nature of the British class structure;[67] and the dynamic, interactional aspect of social status.[68] Kavanagh has suggested that the ambiguities in the use of the term have rendered it almost meaningless and that furthermore the obsession of political scientists during the 1960s with the concept of deference has served to hinder a more realistic analysis of English political attitudes. Kavanagh, however, was implicitly concerned only with English political attitudes and political culture – indeed he found

Shils's sociological conceptualization of deference 'highly persuasive'.[69] Nevertheless much of Kavanagh's criticism could be applied to the sociological usage of deference with equal force; Martin and Fryer, for example, have noted that the major obstacle to a sociological examination of deference is a precise definition of it, and there remains, in Kavanagh's own words, 'a theory of deference in search of data'.[70]

Agricultural workers are deferential traditionalists in Lockwood's terms,[71] and indeed have customarily been regarded as the epitome of the deferential worker, together with servants. Bagehot, in his original discussion of deference, believed that the phenomenon was particularly prevalent among two groups, 'servants and rustics',[72] and a number of the voting studies carried out in the 1950s and 1960s appeared to confirm this impression by demonstrating the higher incidence of working-class Toryism in rural areas.[73] One of the original motives in studying agricultural workers was, therefore, to investigate the validity of the concept of deference. The strategy was similar to that used by Goldthorpe and Lockwood, namely to examine a 'limiting case' most favourable to the utility of the model and to ascertain whether or not it stood up to empirical examination.[74] Nevertheless, it must be apparent that the precise nature of the model is hardly unambiguous and therefore it is necessary to examine the concept of deference in more detail.

Deference and the Agricultural Worker

The most simplistic version of deference views it merely as a form of behaviour, whether it be voting for the Conservative Party or touching the forelock. Undoubtedly it is the observation of the past practice of certain kinds of behaviour defined as deferential – bowing, touching the forelock, etc. – which has led to agricultural workers being labelled 'deferential'. The problem here is to distinguish between powerlessness, or dependence, and deference. For it so happens that the structural conditions which are alleged to produce deference (however it may be defined) are also those which are likely to render the pressures of personal dependency ubiquitous.[75] From this point of view, therefore, deference is not so much an inadequate concept as a redundant one – a great deal of deferential behaviour can be under-

stood solely in terms of the social constraints which the actor per-
ceives as sanctioning any other type of behaviour. Deference is, under
these circumstances, merely the 'necessary pose of the powerless'.[76]

In many cases, therefore, what this behaviour signifies is submission
to certain rules of conduct laid down by those in power. However,
deference, whatever the ambiguities of definition, has always been
taken to mean something rather more than subservience or powerlessness, for, as once again the tenuous connections with the concept
of false consciousness show, there has been an underlying interest in
the degree of commitment of the actor to such behaviour. 'Deference' is generally reserved to explain at least this minimal commitment to 'deferential' forms of behaviour – otherwise 'quiescence'
would suffice. However, differentiating deference from quiescence is
far from easy, and not a problem to which sociologists have paid
much attention, preferring instead to take it for granted that power
relationships will, through some unexamined metamorphosis, automatically become moral ones over time.

These considerations have been highlighted by the work of Goffman to the extent that they cannot be ignored. Goffman has argued
that what is necessary for the possibility of social interaction is merely
an agreement on a definition of the situation which enables the parti-
cipants to select correctly from their total repertoire of status positions
and associated gestures and idioms. The process of maintaining this
agreement is one of skewed communication: over-communicating
those gestures, actions, etc. – what Goffman calls 'demeanour' –
which confirm the relevant status positions and under-communicating
those which are discrepant. Goffman describes this process as 'impression management', which occurs while an individual is 'on
stage'. However, when the role constraints are removed and the individual is 'off stage', only then can their identification with their 'on
stage' behaviour be assessed.[77] Undoubtedly a great deal of 'deference' can be explained away in this fashion – all too often onlookers
have been prepared to infer from observed behaviour a particular
meaning and a set of attitudes which they have felt, often mistakenly,
warrants labelling the actor 'deferential'. But behind the everyday
rituals of deferential behaviour there have frequently lain attitudes
and motives which are quite the opposite.

These aspects can be observed even in the political studies of voting
behaviour. Research into working-class Toryism by Nordlinger, and

particularly by McKenzie and Silver, has established that, far from indicating a deferential set of attitudes or image of society, many of the working class vote Conservative for purely calculative reasons. This has led, for example, McKenzie and Silver to divide deferential voters into 'real' deferentials and 'secular' deferentials,[78] a division brought about by their initially limited behavioural usage of deference and their eventual recognition that some of the individuals who behaved deferentially exhibited characteristics which they, in defining the nature of their problem, wished to regard as non-deferential. Similar analogies could be drawn with other apparently deferential actors – witness, for example, the behaviour of servants 'behind the green-baize door' or 'below stairs', or the notorious ability of agricultural workers to touch their forelocks while simultaneously raising two fingers behind their backs.[79]

Purely behavioural definitions of deference therefore invariably break down, and recourse is made to the meaning of the behaviour and the attitudes of the actor. It is worth pointing out that this is not, of course, a novel problem in sociology: the limitations of a positivist approach to watching and counting the social actions of people has long been recognized. It is also a problem which has been encountered in the study of an ostensibly deferential group in other social contexts than modern Britain. For example, much of the debate between Elkins and other American historians who have sought to understand the dynamics of the slaveholding system in the Deep South has been conducted over precisely this issue: to what extent can the docility of the Negro slave be accounted for by the development of a 'slavish' personality, that is deference, and how far can it be regarded solely as a result of the fearsome and all-embracing constraints on behaviour supplied by the plantation organization?[80] This question is in effect part of a much wider one which involves an understanding of the processes whereby interaction of the powerless with the powerful becomes identification of the powerless with the powerful, a point overlooked by Lockwood in his model of the deferential traditionalist in which he assumed that continuous and ubiquitous interaction between the powerless and the powerful would automatically lead to this identification. However, there is often, in Genovese's words, a 'broad belt of indeterminacy between playing a role and becoming the role you play',[81] and this process cannot be entirely taken for granted.

The study of slavery has raised these problems in an acute form. In order to demonstrate the mechanisms whereby a deferential slave personality – 'Sambo' – could emerge, Elkins employed analogies with other total institutions, notably the concentration camp. He also drew upon social–psychological explanations like Freud's theory of infantile regression and Sullivan's theory of 'significant others' in order to understand the processes whereby 'interaction with' becomes 'identification with'.[82] Genovese, however, has preferred to cut through this problem: 'We do not need an elaborate psychological theory to help us understand the emergence of the slaveholder as a father figure. As the source of all privileges, gifts and necessaries, he loomed as a great benefactor, even when he simultaneously functioned as a great oppressor. Slaves, forced into dependence on their master, viewed him with awe and identified their interests and even their wills with his.'[83] Genovese, significantly writing from a Marxist perspective, therefore dismisses the connection between deference and dependence as a non-problem, although, somewhat contradictorily, he does not deny the existence of 'Sambo'. Elkins' thesis is objectionable to him only 'because it proves too much and encompasses more forms of behaviour than can usefully be merged under a single rubric'.[84] Other commentators have gone even further, however, by suggesting that 'Sambo' himself is a myth, that Elkins and Genovese have both been duped, as were the slaveowners themselves, by the ability of the slaves to 'put Whitey on', to affect a degree of dissembling obsequiousness which hid their true feelings from their masters – and from subsequent academic investigators.

This is the simplest radical alternative to the equally simplistic behavioural application of deference. In order to support their assertion that 'Sambo' is a myth, a number of the historians of slavery have pointed to the sporadic outbreaks of slave rebellion, whether in Santo Domingo or the revolt led by Nat Turner, and to evidence of sporadic slave intransigence.[85] It seems likely that this view is as over-deterministic as that of Elkins. A more flexible model of the connections between the organizational parameters of the slave plantation and the attitudes and behaviour of individual slaves would seem to be required. Genovese has argued that Negro docility was too prevalent, even under conditions when sanctions were removed, for the phenomenon to be dismissed out of hand. Those slaves who took up arms to protect their masters and were prepared to kill fellow slaves in their defence were hardly 'putting Whitey on'.

Similar arguments to and fro could be constructed about the conduct of agricultural workers in British society. Certainly, labelling them 'deferential' appears less than satisfactory in the light of certain aspects of their history, described in the previous chapter. The Swing revolt, the growth of Primitive Methodism, the 'Revolt of the Field' and the continued existence of a rural underworld during the nineteenth century all suggest that agricultural workers were not entirely quiescent, let alone deferential. However, the very limited extent of unionization, the exasperation of union organizers in trying, often unsuccessfully, to prise farm workers away from an attachment to their 'betters' and the workers' appreciation of a 'real gentleman', even when a union member – all these factors give some credence to the deference hypothesis. In every caricature there is a grain of truth.

The question is really one of degree. Lockwood's readiness to allocate his ideal-typical constructs to particular occupational groups can, in retrospect, be seen as an over-simplification. There are likely to be variations in images of society *within* these occupational groups in so far as they are subject to differing market, work and status situations.[86] As far as deferential traditionalism is concerned, these differences then need to be related to a set of issues which have been succinctly summarized by Lemisch: 'First, how widespread was non-deferential conduct: do not historians and historical sources tend to minimize it? Second, when we find deferential conduct, how much does it reflect deferential attitudes and how much the necessary pose of the powerless ...? Third, if people are found to be genuinely deferential, how permanent is the malady: might they not become less deferential when the coercive factors which made them defer were removed or lessened?'[87] Ultimately these are empirical questions: we cannot establish the validity or redundancy of the concept of deference until we actually study an ostensibly deferential group of individuals.

There seems to be some minimal consensus among those commentators on the concept of deference that 'real' deference refers to a set of attitudes rather than a form of behaviour, most centrally a set of beliefs about the nature of society and an associated set of criteria for the 'evaluative classifications of self and other'.[88] Precisely what these criteria are, as has already been pointed out, is far from clear. Moreover, the assumption that workers share a coherent system of beliefs of any kind has, from recent empirical evidence, been called into some considerable doubt. Horton and Thompson, for example, concluded from a study of political attitudes that the consciousness of the powerless is 'founded less on accurate political knowledge than on an existential guess'.[89] Converse has also argued that as one moves down the social hierarchy 'the contextual grasp of "standard" political belief systems fades out very rapidly'. He continues: 'Instead of a few wide-ranging belief systems that organize large amounts of specific information, one would expect to find a proliferation of clusters of ideas among which little constraint is felt, even, quite often, in instances of sheer logical constraint. At the same time ... the character of the objects that are central in a belief system undergoes systematic changes. These objects shift from the remote, generic and abstract to the increasingly simple, concrete, or "close to home".'[90] Mann has developed these insights to argue that the more typical value-orientation to be found in the working class is a 'pragmatic acceptance' of the concrete and specific issues with which the individual is confronted in his everyday life rather than a consensus or dissensus with abstract beliefs and ideologies.[91] Parkin calls this facility 'accommodation', and he cites Hoggart's portrayal of this underlying theme of the subordinate value system as follows: 'When people feel that they cannot do much about the main elements in their situation, feel it not necessarily with despair or disappointment or resentment but surely as a fact of life, they adopt attitudes towards that situation which allow them to have a liveable life under its shadow, a life without a constant and pressing sense of the larger situation.'[92] The possibility that there is not one clearly articulated belief system, but that there is a set of situationally relevant beliefs, internally inconsistent though not necessarily perceived as incongruous, is something that threatens to undermine both the assumptions underlying the use of false consciousness, of deference or indeed of most existing approaches to the normative aspects of social stratification. However, Parkin does not suggest (nor for that matter do Converse and Mann) that pragmatism is universal, but that it is juxtaposed in a subordinate value- or meaning-system with deferential, aspirational and radical models. It remains important, however, to know how pragmatic acceptance is distributed throughout the population – in terms of the structural configurations employed by Lockwood – and if its location is in any-way systematic or noteworthy.

The issue of the acceptance, or non-acceptance, of inequality and the extent of perceptions concerning the inegalitarian nature of society is one that was raised some time ago by Runciman. 'All societies are inegalitarian,' he wrote. 'But what is the relation between the in-equalities in a society and the feelings of acquiescence or resentment to which they give rise?'[93] Runciman accounted for the relationship between social inequality and social grievance through the concept of 'relative deprivation', which related feelings of injustice to the various reference groups to which the individual belonged and/or compared his situation. He was able to show that a great many people at the bottom of the social scale thought there were no others better off than themselves, and, where workers *were* conscious of these dis-crepancies, they tended not to perceive them in class terms. The con-cept of relative deprivation seems tailor-made to explain the attitudes and behaviour of agricultural workers, whose reference groups, to use the terms adopted by Runciman, are undoubtedly restricted. At an early stage in the research, therefore, the utility of relative depriva-tion was appraised, but subsequently, on *a priori* grounds, it was dis-carded. This was for a number of reasons, including pragmatic ones – on a small-scale preliminary investigation of agricultural workers it was discovered to have little explanatory value and this verdict has been confirmed by a much more thorough survey of farmers' atti-tudes by Gasson.[94] However, the most obdurate difficulty was one recognized by Runciman himself: 'The most difficult question of all, however, is how far a person's reference group should be seen as the cause or the effect of his other aspirations or attitudes.'[95] Runciman dismisses the former on empirical grounds. Unfortunately the avail-able data – principally from *The American Soldier* study and experi-ments on American undergraduates – is, as Barry and Urry have demonstrated with some overwhelmingly persuasive arguments, not only open to other interpretations but does not show which way causality operates.[96] Among the devotees of relative deprivation it is apparent that this problem has not been systematically investigated and even among the papers in the well-known reader by Hyman and Singer, Patchers seems to argue both ways, while the paper by Form and Geschwender suggests that limited expectations are responsible for a low degree of grievance rather than a 'limited reference group' causing a lowering of expectations.[97] The problem is therefore to explain low aspirations rather than limited reference groups, which are a *result* of the low aspirations rather than a cause of them.

Barry and Urry have also criticized the concept on logical grounds not unassociated with these empirical problems. Runciman's general approach to the study of social stratification derives, as his debate with Ingham has shown, from what Macpherson calls the 'political theory of possessive individualism'.[98] Because of this Runciman's concern is with individuals rather than with groups – or at least it is with groups only in so far as they consist of individuals who may be members of a multiplicity of groups which have no overriding social–structural coherence other than purely contingent coalitions of interests. This leads to a concentration on the *attributes* of individuals rather than the *relationships* between them. Hence an individual's reference group is not derived from, nor does it operate through, the social structure. Its existence is only notional – indeed it need not be a 'group' at all – and one ascribes individuals to it only by virtue of this ascription. Patterns of 'reference-group membership' are thus not theoretical concepts but artifacts of research methodology: to reify them and use them as an *explanatory* variable to account for 'reference group behaviour' seems circular reasoning. It is not therefore surprising that 'reference group' has become such an amorphous term, 'a magic term', as one writer has put it, 'to explain anything and everything concerning group relations'.[99]

Runciman's approach means that he has a much greater affinity with the studies of deference carried out by political scientists than with the pattern of sociological research into changes in the class structure during the 1960s, since Runciman eschews a structural determinism in favour of a methodological individualism. Thus, he writes, 'Is it not possible that the social correlates, however consistent, of working-class Conservatism are less important than the notorious "deference" of the British electorate upon which Bagehot first remarked and which explains much of the persistent discrepancy between relative deprivation and inequality which working-class Conservatism implies?'[100] Runciman's approach is, indeed, the exact opposite to that adopted in this study, where, having established the extent to which the behaviour of agricultural workers can be understood by the concept of deference, an attempt is made to account for the existence of deference through structural variables. Deference is therefore regarded as being an outcome of the location of an individual or group of individuals within certain configurations of structured relationships. Although deference may account for the stability of this structure and for its maintenance, it cannot, according to this approach, explain its *origin*, a view directly contrary to that of Runciman, for whom the individual's attitudes are the independent variable.

There remains the problem of precisely what set of attitudes are to be regarded as 'deference'. The definition adopted is that suggested by Parkin – the subscription to a moral order which endorses the individual's own political, material and social subordination.[101] However, it is refined a little further in view of the absence in Parkin's definition of any criteria for this subordination. The criterion used is that of tradition. This seemed appropriate for two reasons. First it provided some continuity with the usage of the term by historians, who have emphasized, as has been demonstrated in the previous chapter, the fluctuations in what Thompson calls 'the principle of inherited authority' in rural England.[102] Secondly, it is apparent from Parkin's definition that the concept of deference applies to an area of sociological interest which, although akin to that of false consciousness, derives from a different paradigm, namely the Weberian concern with the *legitimacy* of social hierarchy. It is therefore important to be clear about the basis for the subordination implied in deference – in this case it has been taken to be 'the sanctity of the order and the attendant powers of control as they have been handed down from the past'.[103] This also follows Lockwood's typification of agricultural workers as deferential traditionalists, and the underlying concern of many of the political studies of deference with the alleged success of the traditional British elite in retaining the support of a substantial section of the working class.

It must be emphasized, however, that this definition was very much an operational one. It seemed to convey what most (though not all) writers had understood by the term and it was empirically verifiable or refutable. By the end of the research into an ostensibly deferential group, it was, however, apparent that even this definition was in need of drastic revision if the concept of deference (or at least the underlying concerns which the use of the concept implies) were to retain its utility in the analysis of social stratification. This, however, is the persistent and unavoidable dilemma of empirical research. A clearer appreciation of the problem is only available when the investigation has been completed; and if this could be gained at the outset there would be no point in carrying out the study. A reformulation of the concept of deference is therefore suggested in the final chapter.

Work Situation and the 'Size-Effect'

One of the structural variables to which particular attention is paid is the nature of the agricultural worker's work situation. In his study of blackcoated workers, Lockwood defined the work situation as 'the set of social relationships in which the individual is involved at work by virtue of his position in the division of labour'.[104] Later, however, in his paper 'The Sources of Variation in Working-Class Images of Society', the concept of work situation was expanded to include an 'orientation to work' variable which involved the notions of job satisfaction and job commitment. Now this conception of work situation is qualitatively different from the earlier one and neither is it the same kind of structural feature that is included in Lockwood's own characterization of status situation in the same paper. The nature of the work situation is, therefore, not entirely unambiguous. This is a problem more recently acknowledged by Lockwood himself: 'Another deficiency of the original scheme is that there is a glaring difference between the nature of the properties defining work situation and community structure. While the latter is characterized by reference to such structural elements as degree of occupational status differentiation and degree of interactional and attributional ranking, the definition of the work situation is in terms of the social psychological attributes of workers; that is, work involvement and degree of identification with employers and workmates. Now, quite obviously, job involvement is not something that can be considered independently of factors external to the work situation, and is in any case not a property of the industrial structure. Again the assumption that positive or negative identification with employers and workmates is directly related to degree of interaction is far too simple . . . In short, the structural properties of work organizations underlying these orientations . . . remain to be specified in a way comparable to the differentiation of the community structure.'[105]

These considerations become important in the study of agricultural workers, since the tendencies in their overall class situation are of a kind that render them a suitable test case for the relative importance of the work situation (defined provisionally in the original terms used in *The Blackcoated Worker*) as a feature of the total situation of deferential traditionalist workers.[106] *Prima facie* it can be argued that recent changes in agriculture and agricultural communities (to be considered in detail in subsequent chapters of this book) have affected the agricultural worker's market, work and status situations in different ways. While the market situation of agricultural workers has deteriorated in comparison with those of other manual workers, his status in the local community seems also to have declined. Both of these trends would, *ceteris paribus*, lead one to expect agricultural workers to express increasing dissatisfaction with their situation and to question any hitherto more optimistic interpretations of it. On the other hand, trends in the work situation have evinced a greater degree of contact between farmer and farm worker and a growing isolation and autonomy among employees. Moreover the community situation of agricultural workers has tended to become increasingly farm-centred (thus, incidentally, making the delineation of work situation and status situation increasingly difficult). The work situation thus appears – from aggregate trends and without prejudice to detailed examination – to be a particularly important area for investigation in the advent of any generalized tendencies towards the retention of deference among agricultural workers. This makes a clear exposition of the work situation an important necessity.

It is apparent that the work situation contains elements taken from both a worker's market and status situations. The market is the allocative mechanism whereby the worker is consigned to a particular position in the division of labour; on the other hand, in so far as workers form their own sub-cultural system at work, with its own peculiar set of norms and values and system of interactional status, the work situation is an important arena for the allocation of status, which may also arise out of the division of labour. Within agriculture, however, the division of labour has become, for the most part, rudimentary in the extreme and therefore most (though not all) workers share a basically similar market situation – certainly compared with the important craft and skill divisions prevalent in many other industries – and so status tends to be attributed on the grounds of other criteria than occupational rank, except for a relatively small proportion of supervisory workers and highly skilled and qualified specialists, mostly in livestock farming. Notwithstanding interactional status differences within the work-force, therefore, it can be argued that the most decisive distinguishing characteristic of the work situation in agriculture is the nature of the relationship between employer and employees. This is because, compared with industrial workers, agricultural workers enjoy a much greater degree of interaction with their employer, and, because they work predominantly on their own, a much lesser degree of interaction with fellow workers.

The work situation of agricultural workers will therefore be considered *primarily* in terms of the workplace relationships between farmer and farm worker, though, of course, interaction between workers cannot be entirely ignored. It is argued that the feature of the work situation that defines both the nature of employer–employee relationships *and* interaction between employees will be the mode of control operated by the farmer. Analytically, two modes may be distinguished. One is based on particularistic, diffuse, personal, 'gaffer-to-man', face-to-face relationships – *patriarchal* in the Weberian sense. The other mode of control is the opposite of this: impersonal, contractual, and mediated through the trappings of a formal code of rules and regulations – a *bureaucratic* administration similar to that found in many factories and other large organizations.[107] It is highly likely that these modes of control will be associated in some way with farm size; it is also highly likely, judging by the findings of a number of studies in industrial sociology, that the 'size-effect' will also affect the nature of the workers' images of society.

The phenomenon of the size-effect is, as Ingham has pointed out,[108] scarcely a recent discovery. Durkheim stated that 'small-scale industry where work is less divided displays a relative harmony between worker and employer. It is only in large-scale industry that these relations are in a sickly state.'[109] Marx also noted the size-effect on the growth of class consciousness: herding large numbers of workers into organizations with only minimal employer-employee interaction intensified the conflict between capital and labour.[110]

More recently Bendix has also located how large plants tend to break down traditional, personalized authority structures and a number of empirical studies have, as Ingham has shown, demonstrated an inverse relationship between plant size and worker attachment or commitment.[111] There is also some evidence that this traditionalism spills over into political attitudes and/or voting behaviour – for example, that offered by Lipset in *Political Man*, and by Nordlinger, Stacey and, more cautiously, by Ingham.[112] On the other hand, Hamilton's data on political attitudes in France shows that the small-plant workers are the most radical, together with those in very large plants, while medium-size-plant workers are the most conservative.[113]

Over the last few years there have been a number of studies which have shown correlations between plant size and a number of political attitudes. Unfortunately, as Ingham has pointed out, we have absolutely no *explanations* of these correlations in structural terms. After all, size is not a structural variable: 'In a sense there is nothing in plant size itself which suggests that these workers ought in small plants to be conservative deferentials, and that in large plants they ought to be revolutionaries.'[114] It is clear that size needs in some way to be related to some or other structural variable, and that the nineteenth-century observations on the phenomenon of the size-effect suggest that it should be the organizational control structure, and possibly the criteria of legitimate authority which workers bring with them 'through the factory gate'. Bureaucratization is related to size, and it seems likely that the decision to bureaucratize control of the work situation will involve a number of consequences in the *kind* of worker commitment that ensues. There is likely to be some sort of threshold involved in this: a certain size – determined by the means of production in the broadest sense – will impose a degree of bureaucracy, but below this threshold the employer will have considerable *choice* as to the mode of control which he employs. The outcome of this choice will, however, determine the nature of the response of the employees to their employer's authority.[115]

There is no reason to suppose, then, that the relationship between plant *size* and conservatism is a straightforward linear one. Nor for that matter is the converse relationship: that worker–employer separation fosters class consciousness and political radicalism. To return to an issue raised earlier in this chapter, the simplistic assumption that 'interaction with' automatically assumes 'identification with' can be discounted. Nevertheless, as far as agricultural workers are concerned, the nature of their work situation still remains a potentially fruitful area of investigation in understanding their overall perception of their class situation. The persistence or absence of traditionalism and its social correlates at work provides a method of entry into a search for a structural explanation of the size-effect.

Locale and Methodology

It has already been signified that the focus of the inquiry into the social situation of agricultural workers was the county of Suffolk, more precisely East Suffolk. Locating a study of farm workers is fraught with difficulties and some care was taken over the selection of the area upon which attention was concentrated. Regional variations in British agriculture are such that no one area can be regarded as 'typical' of the country as a whole and so no pretentious claims are made that this book is an attempt to portray the life of the 'typical' agricultural worker – indeed this would be somewhat irrelevant since the object of study is not a group of workers but a set of theoretical problems. It would be meretricious, and churlish, to deny that there was no personal interest in the plight of the agricultural worker, but methodologically they must be regarded merely as a source of data, and similarly the exploration of various theoretical issues must rest upon systematic variations *within* this data. Nevertheless it is important to place the sources of data within a broader social context, so that some limits can be placed on the potentialities of extrapolation to other areas.

In addition some indication of the research techniques employed is essential. The methodology was deliberately eclectic, involving the routine perusal of agricultural and population census statistics, a search of historical sources (both documentary and oral), participant observation and a survey investigation. Since many of the concerns of the study involve the interrelationships of farmers and farm workers and of farm workers with each other, it was apparent from the outset that a degree of participant observation would be necessary. However, the almost complete lack of any sociologically relevant data, even of a sociographic kind, made it desirable to conduct a survey. In effect the survey and the period of participant observation increasingly came to complement each other: insights gained from participant observation could be checked against survey data; on the other hand much of this data could often only become *meaningful* through the experiences gained from living with a farm worker and his family in a tied cottage for six months and gaining first-hand knowledge about the work and community situation. As the period of fieldwork continued, the participant observation became more and more important as many of the shortcomings of using interview material to obtain knowledge of relationships became apparent; nevertheless 'doing a survey' was a very good excuse for talking to farm workers and for prompting them to articulate their feelings about their own experiences which would otherwise have remained unstated. These interviews were carried out with seventy-one farmers and 233 farm workers within an area of forty-four parishes in central East Suffolk. A more detailed account of the methodological problems, including the derivation of this sample, can be found in Appendix I. The fieldwork was carried out between the first week of March and the third week of August 1972.

It was always intended that the study of agricultural workers should be set in East Anglia. The region is, after all, the area where the largest concentrations of agricultural workers may be found – in many areas of the north and west of England, and in Wales, hired workers are so few and far between that there would be considerable logistical difficulties involved in the investigation of them. Southern and eastern England is quite simply the area where the majority of farm workers are located. Additionally, one was mindful of Frankenberg's hitherto unanswered plea for research into the highly mechanized and 'industrialized' farming areas of lowland Britain,[116] of which East Anglia is one of the most typical examples. Ostensibly, though, East Anglia does not seem to be an area conducive to the study of deference. It has a reputation for a high degree of political radicalism for a predominantly rural area and it was the centre of the trade-union movement among agricultural workers both under Joseph Arch and the twentieth-century counterpart led by George Edwards. Closer inspection of this reputation, however, reveals that it is almost entirely limited to Norfolk and the Fens. Norfolk is indeed the centre of agricultural trade unionism, amounting in some areas almost to a closed shop, while, together with the adjacent fenland areas, it has been notorious among psephologists for 'doing different' at election time.[117] For this very reason, therefore, it was decided not to locate the study in Norfolk, particularly as it had been discovered, from past experience,[118] that it is extremely difficult to uncover non-union labour in Norfolk, a situation which clearly makes it highly atypical of even the lowland areas of England. Essex was eliminated because of the impact of London. There was no desire to turn the study simply into a repeat of Pahl's in Hertfordshire, and in Essex there seemed less likelihood of being able to obtain a heterogeneous range of community situations owing to the effects of urbanization. There are very few remaining agricultural occupational communities in Essex, except possibly in the north-western corner: the electrification of most of the county's railways has enabled the London commuter population to spread out across almost the entire county.

There remained Suffolk. *A priori* this looked a much more likely candidate. It was sufficiently far from London to deter all but a few hardy commuters to make the daily trek. Its antiquated minor road system had also preserved a number of villages from the influences of local centres of population like Ipswich and Lowestoft. There was, therefore, a sufficient heterogeneity of community structures and enough residual agricultural communities, though they were fast disappearing, for an exploration of the relationship between local status situation and the agricultural worker's image of society. Suffolk also seemed to be a much better locality to explore the nature of deference. On the admittedly crude index of trade-union membership it was reasonably typical of other lowland counties – indeed the density of membership in the survey sample was to be very similar to that estimated for the country as a whole – and thus neither especially over- nor under-representative of one of the few readily visible indicators (all that one was able to go on at this stage) of attachment to non-deferential views. Suffolk was therefore explored further – even literally, since to drive around rural Suffolk can lead to a fairly accurate appraisal of the extent of the non-agricultural inhabitation of its villages, such is the visibility of the accoutrements of urban, middle-class living.

Eventually an area of forty-four parishes in East Suffolk was chosen, principally on three criteria. First, they run in a north–south bloc from just outside Halesworth to the edges of the highly urbanized Ipswich–Woodbridge area of south-west Deben. This gave a range of communities, broadly speaking from the purely agricultural in the north, through a 'mixed' area, to villages in the south almost completely overrun by urban commuters. Secondly, there was a sufficiently wide range of agricultural work situations in this area, as

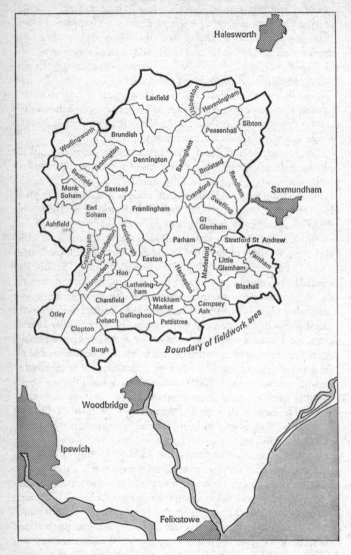

Location of fieldwork area in East Anglia

measured by the Ministry of Agriculture's 'standard-man-day' classification.[119] Comparative statistics are given in Table 8. These show that the size of holdings in the forty-four parishes is reasonably representative of that of Suffolk as a whole. Although the standard-man-day classification is a reasonably accurate way of calculating the scale of farming enterprises, however, it is less accurate as far as the

Table 8 Distribution of holdings by standard-man-day groups, 1972

Standard-man-day groups	England & Wales %	Eastern region %	Suffolk %	East Suffolk %	The 44 parishes %
1–274	42·5	40·8	34·8	35·6	33·8
275–599	23·2	20·2	21·0	20·8	19·6
600–1199	20·2	17·6	20·5	22·2	23·0
1200–2399	9·7	12·1	14·1	14·0	14·8
2400+	4·4	9·3	9·6	8·4	8·8

Source: MAFF Statistics

distribution of regular, whole-time workers is concerned. Hence, using the parish summaries of the Ministry of Agriculture's census data, a frequency distribution of whole-time male workers per holding (full- and part-time) was computed for each parish. Of the forty-four parishes, eleven were from each quartile of this distribution, thus ensuring as far as such aggregate data allowed (the Ministry refused to release individual returns or even select the sample) that the area contained a sufficiently varied distribution of work situations, although there was no way of avoiding the dangers of the ecological fallacy. The third criterion was the distribution of union branches and the strength of branch membership. The National Union of Agricultural and Allied Workers' year book was used to arrive at estimates, from the annual amount of contributions collected, of the size of each branch in East Suffolk. West Suffolk was eliminated because the TGWU organizes many agricultural workers in that area, and so NUAAW figures are not a very accurate estimate of overall unionization there. A frequency distribution of the 122 branch membership was calculated in terms of pounds per annum in members' subscriptions. The actual and expected distributions of the branches are shown in Table 9. Although in terms of the non-existence of union branches the forty-four parishes are completely representative, in terms of the distribution of branch size there is a notable bunching towards the medium-sized branch membership. However, attempts to rectify this by tinkering with the boundaries of the area merely made it less representative of East Suffolk on work-situation criteria.

Table 9 Actual and expected distribution of union branch strength in the fourty-four parishes, 1970

	Actual	Expected
No branch	26	26
Small branch	4	6
Medium-sized branch	10	6
Large branch	3	6

Eventually the decision was made to go ahead with this area regardless, and the desire for absolute representativeness was later dropped after further difficulties were encountered in drawing a sample of workers for interviewing (see Appendix I). Essentially the 233 workers interviewed, the seventy-one farmers, and the forty-four parishes are representative of nothing but themselves: they merely provide usable data for some explorations in theory.

The location of the forty-four parishes is shown in the map on p. 126 and some relevant sociographic data is presented in Table 10. The area is almost entirely agricultural and there are few alternative sources of employment for those unwilling to travel outside. Principally this means to Ipswich, with its engineering, chemical, milling and port industries; to the nuclear power station on the coast at Sizewell; to an engineering works at Leiston; and in the north to a recently established agricultural engineering factory at Halesworth. Otherwise, the only local alternatives to agriculture are the associated service, and contracting firms scattered around the area; the local shopping centres of Woodbridge, Saxmundham, Wickham Market and Framlingham; and the American air-force bases at Woodbridge and Bentwaters. In the Woodbridge Employment Exchange area, of which the forty-four parishes constitute roughly half, primary industries contribute just over 30 per cent of male employment, service industries over 58 per cent and manufacturing only 11 per cent. Although, in common with elsewhere in the country, employment in agriculture is declining, employment in agriculture-related industries is increasing rapidly (by 20 per cent between 1962 and 1966). The extent of local dependence upon agriculture for employment is, therefore, considerably understated by these statistics.[120]

The population of the area is distributed among mostly nucleated villages, with a few larger ones (Framlingham, Wickham Market) acting as local market, service and commercial centres. Some of the parishes – Ubbeston, Tannington, Hoo, Letheringham, Debach, Burgh – contain more scattered populations without a recognizable 'village', while Blaxhall has a recognizable centre, but neither is it particularly nucleated. From 1901 up until 1961, the area was generally one of declining population, drifting towards the south-west and the two industrial corridors between Ipswich and Woodbridge and Ipswich and Stowmarket. The population in the north-east, associated with the Lowestoft–Yarmouth area, and around some of the coastal towns, at Southwold and Aldeburgh, also increased. Since 1961, however, there has been a more general increase over the area which has, despite planning policies, been somewhat random.[121] This increase is undoubtedly attributable to the arrival of many urbanite immigrants to the rural villages of the area, including a number of retired newcomers, although they head mainly for the coastal resorts. However, the more remote villages continue to suffer a declining population, relatively and absolutely, so that the dominance of the larger towns and market centres is increasing at the expense of their more rural hinterlands.

The terrain is hardly mountainous, but on the other hand it is by no means as flat and monotonous as the reputation of Suffolk, or through-travellers on the A12, the A140 and the railway line to Norwich, would have it. Away from the sandy heaths east of the A12, the land is an elevated plateau intersected by shallow river valleys which give it a 'rolling' aspect. Much of the charm of the country lies in its property, however – in the villages rather than the surrounding open countryside. Suffolk's famous churches are a testament to the time (up until the Napoleonic Wars) when the county

Table 10 Sociographic features of the forty-four parishes (1972)

Parish	Holdings	Farmers	Regular whole-time male farm workers	Farm workers per farmer	Population	Percentage change in population	
					1966	1951–61	1961–6
Heveningham	14	11	3	0·3	180	−18·1	24·1
Peasenhall	20	16	16	1·0	630	−8·4	16·0
Sibton	17	16	14	0·9	240	−12·6	−13·4
Ubbeston	10	6	5	0·8	50	−18·7	−45·1
Ashfield	11	10	8	0·8	250	−12·7	39·5
Badingham	21	14	37	2·6	450	−18·7	22·0
Bedfield	13	9	15	1·7	270	−11·6	6·3
Brandeston	9	11	6	0·6	280	5·3	8·1
Bruisyard	9	7	12	1·7	140	−44·6	27·5
Cransford	5	6	6	1·0	170	8·7	−2·3
Cretingham	10	8	18	2·3	140	−3·5	−15·2
Dennington	13	10	21	2·1	510	−8·3	7·6
Earl Soham	13	12	1	0·1	440	−1·5	−6·0
Easton	5	6	26	4·3	350	6·2	21·1
Framlingham	28	20	35	1·8	2060	3·2	2·7
Great Glenham	4	3	11	3·7	190	−17·8	−16·3
Hoo	5	6	11	1·8	50	−21·4	−38·3
Kettleburgh	6	5	6	1·2	140	5·4	−34·6
Letheringham	6	10	28	2·8	80	−11·2	−8·0
Marlesford	6	5	10	2·0	250	−7·5	−12·3
Monewden	5	8	7	0·9	150	−6·6	31·6
Monk Soham	10	7	4	0·6	180	−3·7	−2·2
Parham	10	9	35	3·9	260	−15·9	−8·8
Rendham	11	10	18	1·8	290	7·0	−14·2
Saxstead	10	9	8	0·9	340	6·9	21·9
Stratford St Andrew	6	3	15	5·0	130	−10·8	−17·7
Swefling	5	5	1	0·2	260	0·4	14·0
Tannington	5	10	50	5·0	50	−1·7	−58·0
Brundish	11	9	34	3·8	190	3·2	−16·7
Laxfield	26	27	39	1·4	640	−3·3	−1·7

Table 10 – *continued*

Parish	Holdings	Farmers	Regular whole-time male farm workers	Farm workers per farmer	Population 1966	Percentage change in population 1951–61	1961–6
Worlingworth	28	25	31	1·2	470	−9·1	2·2
Blaxhall	6	4	9	2·3	270	−1·8	−19·6
Burgh	8	5	1	0·2	130	−10·3	−17·2
Campsea Ash	5	5	24	4·8	360	−2·6	5·9
Charsfield	17	11	19	1·7	330	−8·3	10·7
Clopton	11	16	6	0·4	410	−26·1	21·7
Dallinghoo	11	11	11	1·0	330	−15·6	56·4
Debach	4	5	92	18·4	60	−7·8	−27·7
Otley	23	25	15	0·6	560	−4·9	11·6
Pettistree	4	3	6	2·0	130	−3·1	−39·8
Wickham Market }	7	10	38	3·8 {	1360	9·9	6·0
Hacheston ⌡					430	6·0	10·5
Farnham }	5	6	10	1·7 {	180	−27·2	52·5
Little Glemham ⌡					220	−0·5	5·3

Sources: Population Census; MAFF Parish Summaries

was part of the most heavily populated, prosperous area of England – the nation's medieval industrial centre. The former thriving textile towns have now become sleepy villages, while Dunwich, at one time the largest port in the country outside London, has long since disappeared beneath the waves of the North Sea. Nevertheless there is a great deal of medieval architecture left to admire – and to attract affluent, putative thatched-cottage dwellers. Many villages in the forty-four parishes are consequently succumbing to an encroaching *embourgeoisement* – village stores have become delicatessens, antique shops abound, wine shops vie with bookshops, and thatchers and blacksmiths are rich men. This, however, is not the carnivorous

middle class of Barnet or Surbiton, but the herbivorous variety –
particularly artists, authors and media men.[122] Each village, it seems,
has its own resident 'celebrity'. It is perhaps significant that three of
the forty-four parishes are the subject of recent books – Peasenhall,
Blaxhall and 'Akenfield' – while a fourth, Helmingham, abuts on the
area in the south-west.[123]

The agriculture of Suffolk has been most meticulously and com-
prehensively described by Trist.[124] Its socio-economic characteristics
are those outlined by Frankenberg as typifying capitalist organized
business farming areas, namely little or no marginal land, a free
market in farm labour, competition rather than co-operation among
farmers and investment in and industrialization of agriculture by
entrepreneurs.[125] Within the forty-four parishes, the farming is
predominantly arable, although there is dairying along the Deben
valley, which flows eastwards from Debenham to the sea at Aldeburgh. The land is mostly heavy Suffolk clay, but east of the A12,
around Farnham, Blaxhall, Campsea Ash and parts of Pettistree, the
soils are light and sandy. Unlike other areas of Britain, East Suffolk
has no tradition of small peasant holdings, farmed by owner or
tenant: the predominant relationship on the land has always been one
of employer and employee. Even the tenanted farms were of a
sufficient size to require a large amount of hired labour, while landlords were never solely landlords, or even absentees, preferring instead
to farm some of their own land 'in hand'. There is, therefore, no
history of landlord–tenant conflict in East Anglia (except against the
Church, significantly both an absentee *and* a non-farmer) and today
the nature of cross-cutting ties between landowners and farmers is
considerable, nor is their relationship necessarily a hierarchical one.
As far as the agricultural worker is concerned tenurial status comes a
long way down the list of attributes which he regards as being significant in the evaluation of local farmers; indeed their tenurial status
is often unknown.[126]

The main crops grown in the area are winter and spring cereals,
mainly wheat and barley. They provide the fulcrum of agricultural
activity around which all the other commodities – collectively often
referred to as 'break' crops – rotate. Break crops include sugar beet,
broad beans, potatoes and rape. In addition, there are extensive
acreages of vegetables grown under contract for food-processing
firms, the most significant of which is Birds Eye. These include peas,

dwarf beans and more limited numbers of brussels sprouts. Stock are rarely seen out and about on farms in this area; although most arable farmers now have a pig unit which utilizes their own corn, these units are entirely under cover. Sheep have virtually disappeared apart from the odd isolated flock; cattle can be seen only on the poorer pasture land by the rivers; and poultry are hidden away in long, low barrack-like buildings with a large food-hopper at one end, often totally isolated (there is a smell problem from the manure) and given the occasional visit by peripatetic poultrymen driving Minivans and armed with a vaccine-gun from a chicken-processing factory some miles away. On the whole, the land is much too valuable to allow animals to roam all over it and the only creature which is consistently granted this privilege is the pheasant, in preparation for the annual shoot. Otherwise farming is a serious business of making money and bears little resemblance, either in its visual aspects or as a way of life, to the bucolic world of many books on farming and rural life, from which most urban Englishmen obtain their impressions.

1. R. Nisbet, *The Sociological Tradition*, Heinemann, 1966; also R. Glass, 'Conflict in Cities', in the CIBA Foundation symposium *Conflict in Society*, Churchill Press, 1966, pp. 141–83.

2. See P. J. Schmitt, *Back to Nature. The Arcadian Myth in Urban America*, OUP, New York, 1969, p. 180 ff.; P. Olson, 'Rural American Community Studies: The Survival of Public Ideology', *Human Organization*, vol. 10, 1965, pp. 342–50.

3. C. Galpin, *Rural Life*, Century, New York, 1918, p. 11.

4. W. A. Rushing, *Class, Culture and Alienation: A Study of Farmers and Farm Workers*, D. C. Heath, Lexington, Mass., 1972, p. 21.

5. C. A. Anderson, 'Trends in Rural Sociology', in R. K. Merton, L. Broom, and L. S. Cottrell, *Sociology Today*, Basic Books, New York, 1959, vol. 11, pp. 360, 362.

6. Olson, op. cit., p. 350.

7. A. Haller, Review of *Seventy Years of Rural Sociology in the United States* (ed. Alvin Bertrand), *Contemporary Sociology*, vol. 3, No. 2, 1974, p. 138.

8. M. F. Nolan and J. L. Galliher, 'Rural Sociological Research and Social Policy: Hard Data, Hard Times', *Rural Sociology*, vol. 38, No. 4, 1973, p. 491. See also H. Newby, B. Galjart and B. Benvenuti, 'The Current Status of Rural Sociology', *Sociologia Ruralis*, vol. xv, No. 1/2, 1975, pp. 1–22.

9. Just as elsewhere I have described him as the founding father of community studies – see C. Bell and H. Newby, *Community Studies*, Allen and Unwin, 1971, p. 23. But then, it has always been believed that *real* communities were to be found in the countryside.

10. Nisbet, op. cit., p. 6; F. Tönnies, *Gemeinschaft und Gesellschaft*, ed. C. P. Loomis, Harper, New York, 1957; Bell and Newby, op. cit., Ch. 2.

11. Tönnies, op. cit., p. 35.

12. For an extended discussion see Newby *et al.* (1975), op. cit.

13. See, for example, P. Allum, *Politics and Society in Post-War Naples*, CUP, 1973; T. Nairn, *The Left Against Europe*, Penguin Books, 1973.

14. See Olson, op. cit.

15. P. A. Sorokin and C. C. Zimmerman, *Principles of Rural-Urban Sociology*, Henry Bolt, New York, 1929; Kraus Reprint, 1969, p. 15.

16. ibid., p. 509.

17. ibid., pp. 466–7; cf. Schmitt, op. cit., passim; also L. Davidoff, J. L'Esperance and H. Newby, 'Landscape with Figures: Home and Community in English Society', in J. Mitchell and A. Oakley (eds.), *The Rights and Wrongs of Women*, Penguin Books, 1976. Sorokin is by no means unusual in his views – they were shared, as Schmitt shows, by all the founding fathers of American sociology, including Cooley, Park and the whole of the Chicago School. In *The City*, Park wrote: 'Our great cities, as those who have studied them have learned, are full of junk, much of it human.'

18. R. Redfield, 'The Folk Society', *American Journal of Sociology*, vol. 52, 1947, pp. 293–308.

19. O. Lewis, 'Controls and Experiments in Fieldwork', in A. R. Kroeber *et al.* (eds.), *Anthropology Today*, Chicago University Press, 1953, p. 123; also O. Lewis, *Life in a Mexican Village: Tepoztzan Restudied*, University of Illinois Press, 1951; see also Bell and Newby, op. cit., pp. 42–53 and Ch. 3.

20. J. Gusfield, 'Tradition and Modernity: Misplaced Polarities in the Study of Social Change', *American Journal of Sociology*, vol. 72, 1967, pp. 351–62; R. Dewey, 'The Rural-Urban Continuum: Real But Relatively Unimportant', *American Journal of Sociology*, vol. 66, No. 1, 1960, pp. 60–66; P. M. Hauser, 'Observations on the Urban-Folk and Urban-Rural Dichotomies as Forms of Western Ethnocentrism', in P. M. Hauser and L. Schnore, *The Study of Urbanization*, Wiley, 1965, pp. 503–18. R. E. Pahl, *Urbs in Rure*, Weidenfeld and Nicolson, 1965.

21. M. Young and P. Wilmott, *Family and Kinship in East London*, Routledge and Kegan Paul, 1957; H. Gans, *The Urban Villagers*, The Free Press, Glencoe, Ill., 1962.

22. H. Gans, 'Urbanism and Suburbanism as Ways of Life', in R. E. Pahl (ed.), *Readings in Urban Sociology*, Pergammon, 1970, p. 114.

23. R. E. Pahl, 'The Rural-Urban Continuum', *Sociologia Ruralis*, vol. VI, Nos. 3–4, 1966; reprinted in Pahl (ed.), op. cit., pp. 263–305.

24. R. E. Pahl, 'The Rural-Urban Continuum: A Reply to Eugen Lupri', *Sociologia Ruralis*, vol. VII, No. 1, 1967.

25. Pahl (1970), op. cit., p. 293.

26. ibid., p. 286.

27. For example, L. F. Schnore, 'The Rural-Urban Variable', *Rural Sociology*, vol. 31, 1966; G. A. Hillery, *Communal Organizations*, Chicago University Press, 1969; R. Frankenberg, 'British Community Studies: Problems of Synthesis', in M. Banton (ed.), *The Social Anthropology of Complex Societies*, Tavistock, 1966, pp. 123–54 and his *Communities in Britain*,

Penguin Books, 1966, part II; G. E. Jones, *Rural Life*, Longman, 1973; D. E. Poplin, *Communities*, Macmillan, New York, 1972.

28. See R. E. Pahl, *Whose City*, Longman, 1970.

29. cf. M. Stacey, 'The Myth of Community Studies', *British Journal of Sociology*, vol. 20, 1969, p. 139.

30. Pahl, op. cit. (1970), p. 105.

31. H. H. Mann, *The Social Framework of Agriculture*, Cass, 1967; orig. 1904; B. S. Rowntree and M. L. Kendall, *How the Labourer Lives*, Nelson, 1913; M. F. Davies, *Life in an English Village*, J. Fisher Unwin, 1909.

32. See Chapter 1, fn. 7, p. 83. The 'notable exception' is Littlejohn's study of Westrigg.

33. W. M. Williams, *A West Country Village: Ashworthy*, Routledge and Kegan Paul, 1964, pp. xiv–xxi; also 'Changing Functions of the Community', *Sociologia Ruralis*, vol. IV, Nos. 3–4, 1964, pp. 299–314.

34. J. Littlejohn, *Westrigg*, Routledge and Kegan Paul, 1963, p. 75.

35. Frankenberg, op. cit., 1966, p. 252.

36. Pahl (1965), op. cit.; also R. Crichton, *Commuter Village: A Study of Community and Commuting in a Berkshire Village*, David and Charles, 1964.

37. W. M. Williams, *The Sociology of an English Village*, Routledge and Kegan Paul, 1956, p. 32.

38. A. Whitehead, *Social Fields and Social Networks in an English Rural Area, with Special Reference to Stratification* (University of Wales Ph.D. thesis, 1971); P. Ambrose, *The Quiet Revolution*, Chatto and Windus for Sussex University Press, 1974; C. Harris (pseud.), *Hennage*, Holt, Reinhart and Winston, New York, 1974.

39. H. Newby, 'Agricultural Workers in the Class Structure', *Sociological Review*, vol. 20, No. 3, 1972, pp. 413–39.

40. For data on farmers, see D. C. Thorns, 'The Changing System of Rural Stratification', *Sociologia Ruralis*, vol. VIII, No. 2, 1968, pp. 161–78. Some of the social planning literature has skirted this problem – for example, G. D. Mitchell, 'The Relevance of Group Dynamics to Rural Planning Problems', *Sociological Review*, o.s., vol. 43, 1951, pp. 1–16; H. E. Bracey, *English Rural Life*, Routledge and Kegan Paul, 1959; J. Higgs (ed.), *People in the Countryside*, N.C.S.S., 1966.

41. J. H. Goldthorpe, 'Class, Status and Party in Modern Britain: Some Recent Interpretations, Marxist and Marxisant', *European Journal of Sociology*, vol. XIII, 1972, pp. 342–72.

42. In P. Anderson and R. Blackburn (eds.), *Towards Socialism*, Fontana, 1965.

43. Centred initially around discussions of the 'labour aristocracy', but later broadened out into a much more wide-ranging discussion. See H. Wolpe, 'Some Problems Concerning Revolutionary Consciousness', *Socialist Register*, 1970.

44. P. Anderson, op. cit.

45. E. P. Thompson, 'The Peculiarities of the English', *Socialist Register*, 1965.

46. J. Westergaard, 'The Rediscovery of the Cash Nexus', *Socialist Register*, 1970; Goldthorpe, op. cit. Also J. H. Goldthorpe, D. Lockwood, F. Bechhofer and J. Platt, *The Affluent Worker in the Class Structure*, CUP, 1969, Introduction.

47. D. E. Butler and R. Rose, *The British General Election of 1959*, Macmillan, 1960, p. 15.

48. M. Abrams and R. Rose, *Must Labour Lose?*, Penguin Books, 1960.

49. M. Young and P. Willmott, op. cit.; R. Hoggart, *The Uses of Literacy*, Penguin Books, 1960. See also D. Lockwood 'In Search of the Traditional Worker', in M. I. A. Bulmer (ed.), *Working-Class Images of Society*, Routledge and Kegan Paul, 1975.

50. J. H. Goldthorpe and D. Lockwood, 'Affluence and the British Class Structure', *Sociological Review*, vol. 11, No. 2, 1963, p. 155.

51. ibid., p. 156.

52. J. Westergaard, op. cit., p. 112.

53. D. Lockwood, 'The Sources of Variation in Working-Class Images of Society', *Sociological Review*, vol. 14, No. 3, 1966, pp. 249–63.

54. See Bulmer (ed.), op. cit., p. 11.

55. See R. Dahrendorf, *Class and Class Conflict in Industrial Society*, Routledge and Kegan Paul, 1959, pp. 280–89; E. Bott, *Family and Social Network*, Tavistock, 1957, p. 163. Lockwood has written, in Bulmer (ed.), op. cit., p. 448, that 'It was never part of the intention of the original essay to provide an account of working-class consciousness. It would be nonsensical to try to explain the formation of a societal and political ideology of their kind exclusively from the vantage point of work and community relations. The purpose was more limited: to show how certain forms of the latter sustained communal sociability and dichotomous class imagery.' These ideas of identity and opposition are, however, essential *parts* of a formation of class consciousness – see M. Mann, *Consciousness and Action in the Western Working Class*, Macmillan, 1973.

56. D. Lockwood, in Bulmer (ed.), op. cit., p. 239.

57. R. Samuel, 'The Deference Voter', *New Left Review*, 1960, p. 13.

58. In spite of Abrams and Rose's early insistence that 'Deference influences middle-class people too . . . some of whom seem as ready to defer to their "betters" as the least of domestic servants' (op. cit., p. 88).

59. Samuel, op. cit., p. 11.

60. M. Stacey, *Tradition and Change*, OUP, 1960; A. H. Birch, *Small Town Politics*, OUP, 1959.

61. Lockwood (1966), op. cit., p. 252.

62. ibid., pp. 252–4.

63. D. Kavanagh, 'The Deferential English: A Comparative Critique'. *Government and Opposition*, May 1971, p. 333.

64. The original conception by Walter Bagehot in *The English Constitution* first published in 1867; new edition with an introduction by R. H. S. Crossman, Fontana, 1963.

65. W. G. Runciman, *Relative Deprivation and Social Justice*, Routledge and Kegan Paul, 1966; E. A. Nordlinger, *The Working Class Tories*, MacGibbon and Kee, 1967; R. McKenzie and A. Silver, *Angels in Marble*, Heinemann, 1968; W. L. Guttsman, *The British Political Elite*, MacGibbon and Kee, 1963; H. J. Hanham, *Elections and Party Management*, Longman, 1959; J. M. Lee, *Social Leaders and Public Persons*, OUP, 1963; D. E. Butler and D. E. Stokes, *Political Change in Britain*, Macmillan,

1969; J. H. Goldthorpe, *et al.*, *The Affluent Worker: Political Attitudes and Behaviour*, CUP, 1968; F. Parkin, 'Working Class Conservatism: A Theory of Political Deviance', *British Journal of Sociology*, vol. XVIII, 1967, pp. 280–90.

Also the use of 'deference' by historians has tended to follow this definition. There are useful discussions in: W. L. Burn, *The Age of Equipoise*, Allen and Unwin, 1964; J. F. C. Harrison, *The Early Victorians, 1832–1851*, Panther, 1973; G. Best, *Mid-Victorian Britain, 1851–1875*, Panther, 1973; H. Perkin, *The Origins of Modern English Society, 1780–1880*, Routledge and Kegan Paul, 1969; F. M. L. Thompson, *English Landed Society in the Nineteenth Century*, Routledge and Kegan Paul, 1963; A. P. Thornton, *The Habit of Authority*, Allen and Unwin, 1966.

66. G. A. Almond and S. Verba, *The Civic Culture*, Princeton University Press, 1963; H. Eckstein, 'The British Political System', in S. H. Beer and A. Ulam (eds.), *Patterns of Government*, Random House, New York, 1965.

67. Lockwood (1966), op. cit.; F. Parkin, *Class, Inequality and Political Order*, MacGibbon and Kee, 1971; R. Martin and R. H. Fryer, *Redundancy and Paternalist Capitalism*, Allen and Unwin, 1973.

68. E. Shils, 'Deference', in J. A. Jackson (ed.), *Social Stratification*, CUP, 1968, pp. 104–32; P. S. and R. C. Taylor, *Socioeconomic Status and Residential Differentiation*, University of Kent, Centre for Research in the Social Sciences, 1971.

This list is intended to be illustrative rather than exhaustive. See, for further references, Kavanagh, op. cit.; and R. D. Jessop, 'Civility and Traditionalism in English Political Culture', *British Journal of Political Science*, vol. 1, No. 1, 1971, pp. 1–24.

69. Kavanagh, op. cit., p. 333.

70. ibid., p. 360.

71. Lockwood (1966), op. cit., p. 253.

72. W. Bagehot, op. cit., p. 248.

73. Runciman, op. cit.; Nordlinger, op. cit.; McKenzie and Silver, op. cit.; J. Blondel, *Voters, Parties and Leaders*, Penguin Books, 1963. Lockwood was, however, careful to distinguish deferential traditionalists from deferential voters.

74. J. H. Goldthorpe *et al.*, *The Affluent Worker: Industrial Attitudes and Behaviour*, CUP, 1968, p. 2.

75. See Lockwood (1966), op. cit., pp. 252–5.

76. J. Lemisch, 'The American Revolution Seen from the Bottom Up', in B. J. Bernstein (ed.), *Towards a New Past*, Chatto and Windus, 1970, p. 40, n. 90.

77. E. Goffman, *The Presentation of Self in Everyday Life*, Allen Lane, 1969, and 'The Nature of Deference and Demeanour', in *Interaction Ritual*, Penguin University Books, 1972, pp. 47–96. Also F. Barth, *Models of Social Organization*, Royal Anthropological Institute Occasional Paper No. 23, 1966.

78. McKenzie and Silver, op. cit.

79. On servants, see L. Davidoff, 'Mastered for Life: Servant, Wife and Mother in Victorian and Edwardian Britain', *Journal of Social History*,

forthcoming; for the evidence on the rural underworld see Ch. 1 of this book.

80. S. M. Elkins, *Slavery*, University of Chicago Press, second edition, 1968; A. Lane (ed.), *The Debate over Slavery*, University of Illinois Press, 1972.

81. E. D. Genovese, *In Red and Black*, Allen Lane, 1971, p. 93.

82. Elkins, op. cit.

83. Genovese, op. cit., p. 92.

84. ibid., p. 74.

85. See, for example, the contributions by Thorpe, Lewis and Frederickson and Lasch in Lane (ed.), op. cit.

86. See C. Bell and H. Newby, 'The Sources of Variation in Agricultural Workers' Images of Society', *Sociological Review*, vol. 21, No. 2, 1973, pp. 229–53, and below, Chs. 7 and 8.

87. Lemisch, op. cit., p. 40, n. 90.

88. Shils, op. cit., p. 116.

89. J. E. Horton and W. E. Thompson, 'Powerlessness and Political Negativism: A Study of Defeated Local Referendums', *American Journal of Sociology*, vol. 67, No. 5, 1962, p. 493.

90. P. E. Converse, 'The Nature of Belief Systems in Mass Publics', in D. E. Apter (ed.), *Ideology and Discontent*, The Free Press, Glencoe, Ill., 1964, p. 213.

91. M. Mann, 'The Social Cohesion of Liberal Democracy', *American Sociological Review*, vol. 35, No. 3, 1970, pp. 423–31.

92. Hoggart, op. cit., p. 92, cited in Parkin (1971) op. cit., p. 88.

93. Runciman, op. cit., p. 3.

94. R. Gasson, 'Relative Deprivation and Attachment to Farming', *Sociological Review*, vol. 19, No. 4, 1971, pp. 557–83.

95. Runciman, op. cit., p. 15.

96. B. Barry, 'The Roots of Social Injustice', *Oxford Review*, Michaelmas, 1966, pp. 33–46; J. Urry, 'Role Performances and Social Comparison Processes', in J. A. Jackson (ed.), *Role*, CUP, 1971, pp. 129–41, together with Runciman's 'Reply to Mr Urry', ibid., pp. 143–7; J. Urry, 'Some Notes on the Study of the Promotion Finding in "The American Soldier"', *European Journal of Sociology*, vol. XII, 1971, pp. 133–40. See also Tom Burns' review of *Relative Deprivation and Social Justice* in the *British Journal of Sociology*, vol. 18, 1967, pp. 430–34.

97. H. Hyman and E. Singer, *Readings in Reference Group Theory and Research*, Free Press, New York, 1968.

98. G. K. Ingham, 'Social Stratification: Individual Attributes and Social Relationships', *Sociology*, vol. 5, No. 1, 1970, pp. 105–13; W. G. Runciman, 'Social Stratification: A Rejoinder to Mr Ingham', *Sociology*, vol. 5, No. 2, 1970, pp. 246–8; C. B. Macpherson, *The Political Theory of Possessive Individualism*, OUP, 1964.

99. M. Sherif, 'The Concept of Reference Groups in Human Relations', in Hyman and Singer, op. cit.

100. Runciman (1966), op. cit., p. 144; Runciman has essayed an answer to his critics in a postscript to the second edition of *Relative Deprivation and Social Justice*, Penguin Books, 1971.

101. Parkin (1971), op. cit., p. 84.

102. Thompson, op. cit., p. 184.

103. M. Weber, *The Theory of Social and Economic Organization*, The Free Press, Glencoe, Ill., 1964, p. 341.

104. D. Lockwood, *The Blackcoated Worker*, Allen and Unwin, 1958, p. 15.

105. D. Lockwood, in Bulmer (ed.), op. cit., p. 240.

106. Newby, op. cit.

107. On the defining characteristics of patriarchalism and bureaucracy, see Weber, op. cit., pp. 324–57.

108. G. K. Ingham, 'Organizational Size, Orientation to Work and Industrial Behaviour', *Sociology*, vol. 1, No. 3, 1967, pp. 239–58.

109. E. Durkheim, *The Division of Labour in Society*, The Free Press, Glencoe, Ill., 1964, p. 356.

110. K. Marx, 'Germany: Revolution and Counter Revolution', in V. Adoratsky (ed.), *Selected Works of Karl Marx*, vol. 2, International Publishers Inc., New York, 1960, p. 470.

111. R. Bendix, *Work and Authority in Industry*, Harper and Row, New York, 1963; the literature is summarized in Ingham (1967), op. cit., and in his *Size of Industrial Organization and Worker Behaviour*, CUP, 1970. On the tensions between patriarchalism and bureaucracy as modes of control, see A. W. Gouldner, *Patterns of Industrial Bureaucracy*, The Free Press, Glencoe, Ill., 1954.

112. S. M. Lipset, *Political Man*, Heinemann, 1960; Nordlinger, op. cit.; Stacey, op. cit.; G. K. Ingham, 'Plant Size: Political Attitudes and Behaviour', *Sociological Review*, vol. 17, 1969, pp. 235–49.

113. R. F. Hamilton, *Affluence and the French Worker in the Fourth Republic*, Princeton University Press, 1967, pp. 205–28.

114. G. K. Ingham, in Bulmer (ed.), op. cit., p. 352.

115. Ingham (1967), op. cit.

116. Frankenberg (1966), op. cit., p. 252.

117. For an interesting exploration of this, R. Johnson, 'The Nationalisation of English Rural Politics: Norfolk S.W., 1945–70,' *Parliamentary Affairs*, vol. 26, 1973.

118. H. Newby, *From Conflict to Cohesion*, unpublished dissertation, University of Essex, Dept of Sociology, 1969. This is a small-scale study of the factors contributing to the unionization of agricultural workers in North Norfolk.

119. 'Standard-man-days' are a measure of the size of farming enterprise that obviates the use of acreages. One 'standard man' working on eight-hour day represents one standard-man-day; a holding capable of providing sufficient work for a full working year is said to consist of 275 s.m.d.s.

120. Statistics from *East Suffolk Administrative County Statistics*, East Suffolk C.C., Planning Dept, Ipswich, n.d.

121. See A. R. Emerson and R. Crompton, *Suffolk – Some Social Trends*, Report to the Suffolk Rural Community Council, University of East Anglia, 1968.

122. On the distinction between 'herbivores' and 'carnivores' see M. Frayn, 'Festival', in M. Sissons and P. French (eds.), *The Age of Austerity*, Hodder and Stoughton, 1963.

123. Respectively, R. J. White, *The Women of Peasenhall*, Macmillan, 1969;
     G. E, Evans, *Ask the Fellow Who Cut the Hay*, Faber, 1956; R. Blythe,
     Akenfield, Allen Lane, 1969; G. E. Evans, *Where Beards Wag All*, Faber,
     1971.
124. P. J. O. Trist, *A Survey of the Agriculture of Suffolk*, R.A.S.E., 1971.
125. Frankenberg (1966), op. cit., p. 253.
126. In the selection of the forty-four parishes, therefore, no check was made
     for tenure characteristics. Although there is no evidence that, from the
     point of view of agricultural workers, that it is an important aspect of the
     local social structure, it is worth pointing out that the area is highly aty-
     pical in consisting of a disproportionate percentage (73·9) of owner-
     occupiers compared with the remainder of Suffolk (64·8 per cent owner-
     occupied) and the UK (53 per cent).

CHAPTER THREE

The System of Constraints

In the previous chapter it was stated that agricultural workers could be regarded as 'rural' only to the extent that the constraints of the labour and housing markets meant that the majority must both live and work in the same locality. It is the purpose of this chapter to describe the nature of these constraints and to assess the extent of the agricultural worker's freedom to determine his own life-chances within the environment set by these constraints. A brief glance at the history of the social situation of agricultural workers will show that it is unpromising to adopt too voluntaristic a model of their behaviour: for the most part they have been relatively powerless to alter the flow of rewards accruing to them. Nevertheless the parameters of choice and the self-determination of life-chances need to be explored.

The Economics of Agriculture – An Introductory Note

At the outset it is necessary to give some consideration to the political economy of British agriculture, since it is from this system that a whole series of structural conditions arise which affect both farmer and farm worker alike. The use of the adjective 'political' is even more appropriate to agriculture than to many other industries in this country, since the British government, in common with most others around the world, has intervened decisively in the operation of the market in agricultural produce. The economics of British agriculture are, therefore, heavily politicized, a fact which is symbolized by the annual determination of prices and guarantees in Whitehall and by similar stints of hard bargaining in Brussels. There is no need, however, to consider these negotiations in any detail, since as far as the individual farm worker is concerned their *outcome* is what most concerns him, albeit often indirectly, while even his trade union is only cursorily consulted during the bargaining process. Hence, farm workers' representatives are only marginally involved in the decision-making procedures which accompany the formulation of agricultural policy, and agricultural workers, either individually or through their organizations, show little interest in, or understanding of, the complexities of modern agricultural policy. This is considered to be primarily the prerogative of their employers, in conjunction with the government of the day.[1]

Because of this the political economy of agriculture, using this term now in the nineteenth-century sense, is something that confronts agricultural workers as given. To a certain extent this is a view which is often shared by the individual farmer, and even, where the market is a global one, by successive governments. A great deal of government intervention is of a short-term nature and often *ex post facto* – reacting to particular alterations in market conditions rather than controlling the operation of the market itself. For a British government to control the market in many commodities is, in any case, an impossibility and there are therefore many aspects of market conditions from which British farmers are *not* shielded, particularly long-term changes affecting the structure of the industry, the relationship of agriculture to other industries, methods of production and the changing pattern of the required resource mix at farm level.[2] These are very complex and important issues which cannot be analysed in any detail here, particularly when one bears in mind the fact that the agricultural industry produces a whole range of commodities with widely differing market conditions and also that world agriculture during the early 1970s has been undergoing a number of changes which make it difficult to distinguish between relatively short-term alterations in, say, the supply price of many commodities and much more fundamental structural problems.[3] Nevertheless, when one is dealing with a particular market-oriented group of agricultural enterprises like East Anglian arable farms, it is necessary to consider, however briefly and crudely, some of the general economic influences on British agriculture.

The relative importance of agriculture in an economy depends most of all on the state of economic development of the nation concerned – indeed, according to some definitions of development this is so by definition. In the United Kingdom, agriculture contributes slightly less than 3 per cent of the Gross National Product, a proportion which has been steadily falling over the years. This pattern of

relatively declining returns to the agricultural sector among in-
dustrially developing economies is so well established that it has
become endowed with the status of an economic law – Engels's Law.
It is due to the tendency of the income elasticity of expenditure on
food to be very low and, indeed, itself to decline as development
proceeds. Because the capacity to consume food is limited, expenditure on food does not increase proportionally with increases in
income – it tends to be spent instead on manufactured goods and
services. In the UK, for example, for every 10 per cent increase in
incomes, the demand for food increases by only about 2 per cent and
even this proportion has been steadily falling. In addition, those increases in income which are spent on food tend to be on higher-
quality food and, in particular, on processed foods. Returns to agriculture therefore decline as a proportion of returns to the economy as
a whole, both because a smaller proportion of income is spent on food
and because an increasing proportion of what is expended goes to the
food processor rather than to the farmer. The only counteracting
factor is any increase in population.[4]

This is a necessary, though not sufficient, condition for the earnings
of individuals engaged in agriculture to undergo a similar comparative decline. The only way in which incomes could be maintained
would be by a decrease in the volume of employment in agriculture
but, as Johnson has pointed out, these movements would have to be
on such a massive scale in most cases that it is unrealistic to expect
them to occur.[5] Instead there has been a long-standing tendency for
incomes in agriculture also to fall behind those obtainable in other
sections of the economy. One of the major objectives of government
intervention has therefore been to support the income-levels of those
engaged in agriculture through the execution of various support
schemes – capital grants, deficiency payments, import quotas and
tariffs, etc. This has not been the only objective of government intervention, however, for one long-term solution to the low-income
problem of agriculture would be to allow the self-balancing mechanism of the market to divert resources to other sectors and to re-
establish a new equilibrium for agricultural prices. That successive
governments, since the war, have not allowed this is due to a combination of strategic, social and economic reasons. Two submarine
blockades of the British Isles during this century have provided sharp
reminders of the strategic importance of maximizing indigenous

agricultural production and of providing an equitable level of income to farmers which will both finance and provide an incentive for expansion. More recently, similar arguments have been used concerning the import-saving role of an expanded British agriculture and the consequent contribution to the balance of payments. Agricultural support has also been used to prevent the wholesale depopulation of certain rural areas, particularly hill-farming areas, where direct grants of government money have been used to maintain these farms in existence. Economically government support has also ironed out much of the violent short-term fluctuations in agricultural returns ('cobweb' and 'scissor' cycles) which are extremely damaging to the stability of the industry – thus inhibiting capital promotion, technological innovation and ultimately raising prices to the consumer. In other words, in promoting a measure of economic stability within agriculture, governments have attempted to increase the efficiency of the industry and maintain food prices at as low a level as possible.[6] These arguments have often been vociferously advocated by a superbly organized farmers' lobby whose (often overrated) voting strength in a number of constituencies has made all political parties attentive to their needs.[7]

Government intervention in agriculture has substantially altered the pattern of farm organization even at the most mundane level. With varying degrees of success, it has enabled the individual farmer to escape from a position whereby the more he increased his productivity in an attempt to raise his own income, the greater was the tendency for output to rise faster than demand, thus reducing prices and the farmer's gross income. Intervention has protected producers 'from the full effects of their collective achievements'[8] and has encouraged the adoption of new technological innovations which will substantially increase output without depressing prices. The situation has, therefore, been transformed into one where more output has meant a higher, not lower, gross income to the farmer. Thus the rate and level of technological development in a protected agriculture has been faster than that achieved in a free market. As Galbraith has pointed out, 'As a consequence ... of price security and associated ability to plan, there has been much increased investment by farmers in new capital and technology. The further result has been gains in productivity in recent years that have been considerably greater in agriculture than in industry.'[9]

Governmental regulation of prices has therefore altered the structure of the agricultural industry enormously. It has made possible – and encouraged – a wholesale substitution of capital for labour, and, owing to the different abilities to accumulate the necessary capital, increased the concentration of production on fewer larger farms. The number of agricultural workers has declined drastically while the use of farm machinery has shown a massive increase, with a consequently thoroughgoing alteration in the day-to-day work situation on the farm (see Chapter 5 below). This change in the nature of capital-labour mix at the farm level has altered the relationship between agriculture and its ancillary industries. There has been a growing dependence on non-farm inputs and a developing integration with a much wider set of industrial concerns involved in food production and processing. The government, in supporting the farmer, is now increasingly supporting in addition large sections of the engineering industry through the farmers' purchases of agricultural machinery, the chemical industry (fertilizers, pesticides, etc.) and a large part of the processing, packaging and distributive trades. Many of these firms are large, even multi-national corporations – for example, Ford's, Massey-Ferguson, ICI, Fison's, Shell, Unilever, Imperial Tobacco, etc.

Gradually the farming industry has been drawn more and more into a closer integration with this overall food-production complex. On the input side farmers' dealings have mostly been with the engineering and agro-chemical industries. Here farmers have been in a relatively weak bargaining position over the price of their inputs owing to the manufacturers' freedom to raise prices as they see fit, while the farmer can only hope to recoup these increases through the success of negotiations the following January with a Minister who also has one eye on both the price of food to the consumer and the level of public expenditure. In addition farm-gate prices for farm outputs have also been declining as a proportion of retail prices, owing to the farmers' weak marketing position *vis-à-vis* the large food-processing companies. This squeeze on both ends of the farming enterprise has led farmers to increase their efficiency where possible, albeit by selective encouragements and threats from the government, in order to retain their profitability.[10] This, in turn, has led to successive attempts to cut costs, which of course include the cost of farm labour.

For the foreseeable future it seems that these trends will continue in British agriculture. This means that the concentration of production on fewer, larger farms will continue, while these farms will be more capital-intensive and will employ fewer workers. This is a trend which is very familiar to the East Anglian agricultural worker and is one which has shaped the market for agricultural labour since the war. A falling supply of labour has chased a falling demand in an ever-decreasing spiral which has enabled agricultural wage rates to remain depressed. In many areas (though not all) the exigencies of the local labour market have allowed the farmer to pass on some of the pressure on his own returns by paying low wages.[11] It is perhaps ironical that governmental policy towards agriculture has, in attempting to alleviate the low-income problems of farmers, also created a set of conditions which have helped to perpetuate, and certainly done little to destroy, the low-income problems of agricultural workers.

The Nature of the Rural Labour Market

The use of a term like 'the rural labour market' suggests a unity which is often completely absent in practice.[12] Although it was the conclusion of a group of economists who had investigated the situation that 'agriculture approximates most closely to a perfectly competitive labour market',[13] this was by way of comparison with the situation elsewhere, which, by some accounts, is not saying very much.[14] Certainly at an aggregate level the market for agricultural labour conforms to none of the main tenets of the perfect competition model, like, for example, the consistently important role of excess demand for labour (represented by the agricultural unemployment rate) in determining upward wage movements. Nevertheless there are some dangers of committing ecological fallacies in drawing conclusions from aggregate data and applying them to the experiences of individual farmers and farm workers. In the real world the rural labour market and the agricultural labour market – and it is as well to maintain this distinction – are composed of a multiplicity of sub-markets, delineated by various criteria; in Kerr's terms they are balkanized.[15] Nevertheless certain aspects of the farm worker's market situation are determined nationally by employers' and employees' representatives – most notably pay and conditions – and these form a context within which the mostly localized labour-market situation in which the farm worker finds himself is placed. In addition nationally determined levels of economic activity have a substantial effect upon employment opportunities at the local level. It is, therefore, necessary to consider both national and local factors in making an assessment of the agricultural worker's market situation, though it is helpful to maintain an analytical distinction between the two.

Nationally the most important feature of the agricultural labour force has been its massive decline. There is little sign that this outflow is abating – indeed net migration from farms actually accelerated during the 1960s. This steadily downward trend – 'the drift from the land' – has not occurred uniformly, however, either structurally, geographically or chronologically. As Table 11 shows, although the total number of hired workers more than halved over the twenty-year period between 1948 and 1968, there was a substitution of female labour for male labour, and more particularly of part-time, seasonal and temporary female labour for regular labour, both male and female. Over this period labour use declined, on average, by 18,700 workers per year, though during the 1950s the rate was much lower than this and during the 1960s much higher – more than 20,000.[16] This decline is spread across all types of labour, though there are signs that the decline has been accompanied by a proportionately more rapid decline among arable workers. Similarly all counties in England and Wales have lost labour, though the rates of decline have varied considerably, with the greatest losses occurring around London and the south-east, the west Midlands, south Wales and, less understandably, in north and west Wales; that is, with the exception of the latter area, around some of the main centres of industrial population where job opportunities outside agriculture are greater.[17] The differences are, however, much greater at a more local level, where trends may cut across the overall regional pattern.

Agricultural economists have devoted considerable attention to understanding the dynamics of the drift from the land, particularly since the early 1960s, when, for almost the first occasion in peacetime, there appeared to be long-term shortages in some categories of labour, particularly those possessing a high degree of skill in certain sectors like stockbreeding. Two approaches have been used to investigate this problem. One has been to interview ex-farm workers (or sometimes their ex-employers by proxy) in order to ascertain their reasons

Table 11 Changes in agriculture's use of hired labour in England and Wales, 1948-68

| | Regular whole-time workers | | | | Regular part-time seasonal temporary | | | | Total hired workers | | | |
| | Male | | Female | | Male | | Female | | Male | | Female | |
	No.	% p.a. com-pound	No.	% p.a. com-pound	No.	% p.a. com-pound	No.	% p.a. com-pound	No.	% p.a. com-pound	No.	% p.a. com-pound
Total 1948	506·5		66·2		110·6*		58·2		617·1		124·4	
Average annual change												
1948–53	−6·4	−1·3	−4·1	−7·8	−1·3	−1·2	+0·1	+0·1	−7·6	−1·3	−2·5	−2·2
1953–8	−15·1	−3·4	−2·5	−6·7	−2·5	−2·6	+1·6	+2·6	−17·6	−3·2	−0·9	−0·9
1958–63	−13·5	−3·6	−1·6	−5·5	−2·5	−2·8	−1·1	−1·7	−14·0	−3·0	−2·6	−2·8
1963–8	−17·7	−6·4	−1·1	−5·3	−5·1	−8·1	−2·0	−3·5	−24·9	−7·2	−3·1	−3·9
1948–68	−13·2	−3·6	−2·3	−6·7	−2·8	−3·5	−0·4	−0·6	−16·0	−3·6	−2·7	−2·5
Total 1968	243·1		19·4		53·7		51·1		296·8		70·6	

*Including 11·4 thousand prisoners of war

Source: Agricultural Census

for leaving; the second has been to construct linear-regression models of labour outflow based upon time-series data from the agricultural census. Each approach has produced entirely compatible results. The survey data has attributed the drift from the land primarily to the low earnings of agricultural workers compared to those obtainable in other employment. Secondary factors have been longer hours, lack of prospects, the level of amenities in rural areas, rural isolation and living conditions.[18] The more econometric approach has demonstrated that migration from agriculture is related to the business cycle. Cowling and Metcalf, for example, have developed an increasingly sophisticated model involving predominantly economic variables derived from quantitative data on employment in agriculture, (regional) unemployment levels, wages, agricultural prices, age and education, and ignoring most of the more social factors such as housing, hours, etc., used in the survey-based approach.[19] The predictive power of their model, despite some criticisms which could be made, seems reasonably successful at the aggregate level (though the burden of prediction is now passed on to guessing future rates of unemployment). Cowling and Metcalf have shown the importance in accounting for the drift from the land of the ability of the agricultural worker to *choose* whether or not to leave agriculture. The effects of this can be quite startling – for example, they estimate that an increase of 1 per cent in industrial unemployment, evenly distributed across all regions, is likely to have the effect of reducing the drift from the land by up to 8 per cent.[20] Therefore, whatever the perceived deprivations of work on the land which may produce a *desire* to move on the part of the agricultural worker, these must be matched to the worker's opportunity to move without which occupational choice is a meaningless concept.

These points have been obscured by the desire of agricultural economists to conceptualize the topic of labour mobility in the sociologically irritating terms of 'push' and 'pull'.[21] The terms themselves are often used somewhat loosely as metaphors, but basically 'push' factors are those which are generated within agriculture reducing the demand for labour on farms, while 'pull' factors refer to the demand for labour in non-agricultural employment. Hence, during periods of low unemployment in non-agricultural industries 'pull' factors will predominate over 'push' factors, while the reverse is the case when unemployment increases outside agriculture. It is perhaps significant that the push–pull model has been developed by agricultural economists from a consideration of aggregate statistics on labour outflow. Here it may be useful to conceptualize labour as being pushed and pulled hither and thither by impersonal market forces, but it is important to recognize that this *is* only a metaphor applied to aggregate movements and need not represent the situation as perceived by individual agricultural workers (although this is not to deny that it *may* do). The push–pull distinction falls down at the individual level simply because, as the previous paragraph concluded, *both* factors are necessary before an agricultural worker will move. High wages in industry cannot 'pull' an agricultural worker off the land unless low wages in farming 'push' him off. Even at the most extreme example of 'push' – redundancy – workers will not be permanently pushed out of the labour force (they remain unemployed agricultural workers) if the 'pull' factors fail to operate. The *opportunity* to move into industry must present itself before the worker is capable of moving. The same arguments can be used, of course, concerning the decision to remain in agricultural employment – not only must the worker choose to remain on the land but there must be the opportunity for him to do so.[22] The push–pull conception must therefore be confined to what it is, a handy shorthand metaphor, but in no way must it be regarded as a viable model of individual worker behaviour. Unfortunately not all agricultural labour economists have been aware of its limitations.

It seems that a more sophisticated model of occupational mobility will need to incorporate on the one hand a theory of occupational choice with, on the other, a model of occupational opportunity. The latter will include the variables used in the econometric analysis of labour mobility, since it seems plausible to suppose that the most important factor concerns changes in the economic structure of the labour market. Occupational choice, however, can be understood only in terms of factors less often investigated by economists.[23] There is some evidence, for example, that the decision to enter agricultural employment is embedded in the structural context of the individual worker – the influences of immediate social networks, like the family, peer group and local community. (These are considered in more detail later in this chapter.) To reduce the complex process of occupational choice to a mechanical model akin to a pinball machine is too simplistic.

The extent to which occupational mobility in agriculture is caused by the disappearance of employment opportunities as opposed to a choice taken by workers to leave or remain in agriculture enables an assessment of job insecurity to be made. Econometric analysis has shown that behind the year-to-year fluctuations in labour outflow there is an 'underlying, strong, basic trend towards a reduction in the total labour force',[24] so that even in years of high unemployment in industry there is a decline in employment opportunities in agriculture owing to continuing mechanization and the adoption of other labour-saving techniques. These declining opportunities therefore act as a constraint on occupational choice and threaten the job security of the agricultural worker, a problem exacerbated by the fact that, almost by definition, the range of occupational choice in rural areas is small. It is mainly for these reasons that the rural labour market has traditionally been a buyer's market for labour.

As has already been pointed out, however, the rural labour market is not a uniform phenomenon and market conditions may vary quite sharply over different areas and according to the type of worker involved. There is, for example, an elite group of highly skilled and highly trained supervisory or autonomous workers – herd managers, stockmen, foremen, etc. – whose pay and conditions are superior to the majority of workers and whose labour market has national, rather than local, boundaries. These form around 15 per cent of the total work-force, and their degree of job security is considerable.[25] Indeed they are in quite a strong market situation, as a glance at the advertisement columns of the farming press will testify. For the mainstay of the arable labour force – the tractor driver/general farm worker – the situation can be somewhat different, however. Their skills are now of a kind that are relatively easily transferable to other industries, as they were not in the days of horses, and so it seems that their market situation is primarily affected by their proximity to industrial employment, although there is some evidence to suggest that migration from farms is not a simple function of distance from industrial labour markets at any given point in time. Gasson, for example, has argued that rural industrialization has a ripple effect on the surrounding labour market.[26] Losses of workers will be heaviest first in the immediate vicinity of towns, then in middle-distant areas and then in the most remote and inaccessible parts of the locality. The extent of the 'ripple' will be affected by the flow of information concerning industrial earnings and employment opportunities, the cost and availability of rural transport and the freedom of the worker's housing situation. It should be noted that some of these factors have worked against increasing freedom of access to alternative employment opportunities, so keeping certain sections of the labour force captive.

The most sensitive indicator of the agricultural worker's overall market situation, given its closer approximation to a perfectly competitive labour market, is probably income. This will be dealt with more fully in the following section, but it can be noted here that the trends since the war in the relative earnings position of agricultural workers *vis-à-vis* industrial workers hardly give rise to optimism. Indeed, if this is taken as an important indicator, then on average (admittedly a statistic which rarely means a great deal in agriculture) the agricultural worker's market situation has undergone a comparative deterioration. This is a burden to the agricultural worker and his family, since over the same period, as successive *Family Expenditure Surveys* have shown, it has become increasingly more expensive to maintain the same standard of living in the countryside as in the towns. Perhaps most ironically of all, it had by the late 1960s become more expensive to buy food in rural areas than it was in Britain's towns and cities. Farm workers' wives rely upon small village shops to purchase their family's food and cannot take advantage of the economies offered by supermarkets, unless they wish to add the price of transport to their shopping bills. It is cheaper to buy fresh meat and vegetables in the centre of London than it is in a Suffolk village.

One further indicator of the agricultural worker's market situation is the unemployment rate. Adult unemployment in agriculture is consistently higher than the national average for all economically active persons.[27] This is not surprising, since agriculture is a declining industry in terms of employment opportunities, continuing the well-established trend of shedding labour to the manufacturing and service sectors of the economy. Thus in rural areas, where agriculture has dominated the employment structure, unemployment tends to be above the national average. At this level the importance of the declining demand for labour as a causal factor in accounting for total labour outflow becomes more prevalent in relatively isolated rural areas than in areas near towns.[28] Rural unemployment is not a very visible phenomenon, for the absolute numbers are usually very small, so it has not received the attention that the much larger concentrations of urban unemployment occasionally receive. It conflicts oddly with the cosy image so prevalent in British society, yet like so many other aspects of rural life there is often a socially invisible but less reassuring underside to the bland exterior which is rarely explored.

National trends in the agricultural labour force cannot always be applied to local conditions, however. Circumstances vary considerably in different parts of the country and within small districts; even 'differences within almost individual parishes are very significant'.[29] A Ministry investigation[30] in Essex and Lancashire found considerable variations within these counties. In Essex, an outflow of 10 per cent per annum or more was found by Thames-side and around Chelmsford, compared with $3\frac{1}{2}$ per cent around Saffron Walden. In Lancashire outflows of 10 per cent were found around Manchester and Liverpool, compared with 7 per cent in the Fylde, 5 per cent in Furness and 1 per cent around Lancaster. Other local studies have produced similar results, endorsing the view that the areas which are meaningful as labour markets for most agricultural workers are extremely small. Differences at the local level may therefore cut across overall regional and national patterns, and it is perhaps not surprising that a number of local studies aimed at assessing the relative importance of 'push' and 'pull' factors produced conflicting results.[31] Similarly, just as it is impossible to extrapolate from local investigations to national estimates, so is the reverse process – given that most migration is over short distances and that labour markets are very localized, national and regional analysis of labour transfer may lead to misleading conclusions being drawn about individual workers.

In East Anglia gross unemployment rates consistently run at less than the UK average although they tend to rise above the average in rural areas.[32] However, during the 1960s weekly earnings have run on average 10 per cent less in East Anglia than in the country as a whole. Around 3 per cent of this shortfall is due to the greater predominance of agriculture in the region, for East Anglia has a greater proportion of employed labour resources engaged in agriculture than any region in Great Britain except the south-west. The remaining 7 per cent difference is accounted for by lower hourly wage rates rather than the economic structure. The general picture of the region is therefore one of a predominantly low-wage area, with agriculture occupying a more important role in the labour market than is typical of the country as a whole. In 1970, 10 per cent of the adult male population was engaged in agriculture, compared with 2·9 per cent nationally. Even 10 per cent may not seem a very high proportion, but this picture grossly understates the proportion of the employed population who depend upon agriculture for their livelihood – for example 20 per cent of the employees in manufacturing employment are in the food-processing industries.[33] Agriculture therefore dominates the region economically and in the less accessible areas continues to be in a virtual monopoly position over the purchase of labour. There are therefore large areas where a substantial proportion of the labour force would leave agriculture if given a realistic choice – Bessell, for example, found that the percentage of young male workers intending to leave agriculture but still on the land was the highest in the country: 26·4 per cent compared with an average of 17·0 per cent in England and Wales as a whole. For a number of rural school-leavers there is little choice but to find a job on the land and await the age at which a driving licence will enable them to extend their area of occupational choice.[34]

The extent of employee dependence upon agriculture at the local level and the consequent lack of occupational choice may be gauged by data collected from the survey of farmers and farm workers in Suffolk. Since the survey was not constructed with a view to in-vestigating labour mobility and the minuiae of the local labour market, it must be borne in mind that the survey results give only a partial view. Those agricultural workers who were interviewed form to some extent a residual population and to achieve a rounded picture of the extent of occupational choice and opportunities it would have been necessary to have interviewed a sample of workers who had left the land. Nevertheless, a number of insights can be gained.

The extremely localized nature of the labour market, to which much of the literature has drawn attention, was confirmed by the survey results in a number of ways. First, the workers in the sample were asked two hypothetical questions about their willingness to move and their willingness to travel each day to another job. As Table 12 shows, only 20·2 per cent of the workers were not willing to move house in order to obtain another job, a very low figure when compared with other groups of workers,[35] but one must bear in mind the proportion living in tied accommodation (62 per cent) for whom alternative employment would force them to move their home.

Altogether however, 58 per cent were not willing to move outside Suffolk. As one might expect, there was a significant tendency for younger, unmarried, workers to be willing to move 'anywhere', but there was a similar tendency among the more highly educated and highly qualified workers and those who were born outside Suffolk. There was also a much greater unwillingness on the part of those *not*

Table 12 Willingness of workers interviewed in Suffolk, 1972, to move home in order to obtain alternative employment

	No.	%
Would not move	47	20·2
Move within same parish	22	9·4
Move within ten-miles radius	27	11·6
Move within twenty-miles radius	18	7·7
Move within Suffolk	20	8·6
Move within East Anglia	13	5·6
Move anywhere	84	36·1
Don't know/No answer	2	0·9
	233	100·1

living in tied houses to move. Answers to a question on journeys to work, however, indicate that, for those unwilling to move far, their employment opportunities would be restricted indeed. In answer to the question 'How far would you be willing to travel each day to another job?', the median distance was 2·27 miles, with over a third of the sample unwilling to travel more than one mile (see Table 13) and more than half less than three miles. In many parts of rural Suffolk there are very few employers within a radius of 2·27 miles. These results must be treated with some caution, however, since the questions were somewhat hypothetical. One certainly had the impression that on occasions some respondents, particularly younger ones, would airily state their willingness to move anywhere with little thought, and indeed with some bravado. There is a tendency to give inflated replies to the first of these questions in particular, and so this information should be checked against the actual mobility of the respondents prior to being questioned. The picture that emerges is of a somewhat less mobile work-force than these replies imply – although again it must be borne in mind that the questions were put to a residual work-force in an era when agriculture has undergone a net loss of workers. Some extent of the geographical limits of the mobility of the farm workers in the survey can be assessed by comparing their

Table 13 Distance workers interviewed in Suffolk, 1972, were willing to travel to work

	No.	%
Less than one mile	78	33·5
1–3 miles	50	21·5
4–6 miles	33	14·2
7–9 miles	15	6·4
10–19 miles	35	15·0
20 or more miles	21	9·0
Don't know/No answer	1	0·4
	233	100·0

birthplace with their current workplace. Nearly one-third of the workers were born in the parish in which they were working when interviewed and over 85 per cent were born in Suffolk (see Table 14). Evidence on the location of their first job (which for 27·5 per cent is also their present job) indicates that, of the 15 per cent who had moved in from outside Suffolk, nearly a quarter moved because their parents had moved. Indeed, 43·3 per cent were currently working in the same parish as they had worked in after leaving school, with an additional 17·2 per cent in the neighbouring parish. Again, however, one must stress that this intense localism does not apply to the majority of those workers who possessed formal qualifications and had undergone some further education or vocational training (12·4 per cent of the sample). These were mostly foremen, stockmen and farm mechanics, many of whom were obviously participating in some national or lowland-area labour market and were consequently mobile over greater distances.

The predominantly local nature of the labour market for the majority of agricultural workers does not mean that they are completely sedentary, however. Indeed, 46·4 per cent of the sample had moved house immediately prior to embarking on their current employment, a high proportion which is no doubt accounted for by the tied housing situation, described later in this chapter. In all, the 233 workers who were interviewed had had 877 jobs (an average of 3·76

Table 14 Birthplace and location of first job in relation to workplace of workers interviewed in Suffolk, 1972

| | Birthplace | | Location of first job | |
	No.	%	No.	%
Same parish	70	30·0	101	43·3
Neighbouring parish	40	17·2	40	17·2
Parish in fieldwork area	36	15·5	26	11·2
Remainder of Suffolk	53	22·7	47	20·2
Remainder of East Anglia	18	7·7	9	3·9
Remainder of UK	13	5·6	6	2·6
Abroad	3	1·3	4	1·7
	233	100·0	233	100·1

per worker) and of these 362 (41·3 per cent) had involved moving residence. The overall pattern is therefore one of considerable geographical mobility but usually over very short distances indeed, certainly over a range within which the choice of occupation and of employer is extremely limited.

This localization of the labour market, taken with the sparse spatial distribution of employers in rural areas, would lead one to expect a highly particularistic market situation for most agricultural workers, where employers and employees know one another – and more importantly one another's reputation – on a personal basis even before the question of seeking and granting employment arises. The process, so well described by Littlejohn,[36] is still one in which the best workers and the best employers seek each other out, but the other side of this procedure is often less manifest, for it concerns what is defined as 'best' – in the past it has been difficult for workers who may be excellent at their jobs but have undesirable personal characteristics of one

kind or another to find employment without leaving the area. The
pressures for conformity over what constitutes a 'good' worker are
therefore often apparent in such a close, face-to-face situation, even
though the overt use of sanctions may be few and far between.
Agriculture is a job in which the *personal* relationship between employer and employee so predominates that farmers sometimes go to
what – by urban standards – seem extraordinary lengths to investigate
the 'character' (that is, the private life) of prospective employees who
are not familiar to them. This is not necessarily a surreptitious process
– although discreet telephone calls are often made – and where a
worker can afford to be choosy the process is sometimes reversed.
Nevertheless most farmers prefer workers they have known in-
timately from childhood and are deeply suspicious of formal qualifications and impersonal methods of hiring. (This point will be
elaborated in the final section of the chapter.)

This particularism emerges from the information given by farmers
about their hiring practice. The seventy-one employers of the workers
who were interviewed were asked how, the last time they had hired
a man, they had gone about it. They were asked this question
separately for 'specialized' workers – foremen, stockmen, etc. – and

Table 15 Method of hiring workers of farmers interviewed in Suffolk, 1972

	'Specialized' workers		'General' workers	
	No.	%	No.	%
Informal contact by farmer	9	22·5	20	35·7
Worker applied to farmer personally	14	35·0	21	37·5
Advertised locally (e.g. in shop window)	1	2·5	1	1·8
Advertised in local press	9	22·5	7	12·5
Advertised in national press	3	7·5	1	1·8
Employment exchange	1	2·5	1	1·8
Other	3	7·5	5	8·9
Total replies	40	100·0	56	100·0
Don't know/No such worker employed	31		15	

for general workers/tractor drivers. The replies are presented in Table 15. It can be seen how particularistic methods predominate: in both cases a majority of workers have obtained employment by approaching the farmer personally or vice versa. However, there is a significant difference between the two categories of worker – nearly three-quarters of 'general' workers were hired in this way, compared with just over a half of 'specialized' workers.

The proportion of workers who approached the farmer for a job suggests a high degree of dependence upon agriculture for employment. This aspect of the market situation can be explored further by

Table 16 Previous employment (each job counted once) of workers interviewed in Suffolk, 1972

	No.	%
Agricultural worker	662	75·5
Other agricultural employment:		
Farmer	3	
Agricultural contracting	35	5.6
Gardener/groundsman	9	
Forestry	3	
Armed forces (exc. National Service)	31	3·5
Building trade	23	2·6
Lorry driving	20	2·3
Engineering trades (inc. motor mechanic)	19	2·2
Food processing	13	1·5
Roundsmen	10	1·1
General labouring	8	0·9
Other	41	4·7
	877	100·1

considering the job histories of the workers who were interviewed. Altogether, 155 of these workers (66·5 per cent) had no experience of non-agricultural employment; and 27·5 per cent had only had the one job they were currently occupying. The breakdown of previous employment is shown in Table 16, which is a list of jobs, not respondents.

The results confirm the picture of alternative employment opportunities that has been conveyed by studies of workers who have left the land – a predominance of the armed forces, the building trade, transport, food processing and employment in service and distributive firms.[37] The dependence upon agriculture is considerable, particularly when one bears in mind that two-thirds of the sample had always been employed on the land. However, because this represents something of a residual population, further evidence is required before the extent of employee dependence upon agriculture can be fully assessed.

One proxy measure of dependence suggested by Mackay *et al.* in their comprehensive investigation of labour market conditions in the engineering industry is the voluntary quit rate.[38] Because voluntary leavers have *chosen* to leave, the voluntary quit rate enables an assessment of the constraints on choice to be made. The farmers in the sample were asked how many workers had quitted their job on their farm over the previous year and over the previous five years. Over the five year period the voluntary quit rate was 4·9 per cent; and over the previous year it was slightly higher at 5·8 per cent, suggesting a slight easing of the farm worker's market situation, although the five-year figure may be slightly depressed owing to the problems of recall. Both rates are, however, extremely low compared with the quit rates reported by Mackay *et al.* among engineering workers. These varied between 22 per cent in the 'tight' Birmingham labour market, 16·8 per cent in Glasgow, 7·6 per cent in north Lancashire and 5·6 per cent in Small Town – the last two being areas where the employment opportunities were much less favourable.[39] It may be noted that the voluntary quit rate among Suffolk farmworkers was on a par with the lowest of these.

The voluntary quit rate is not an entirely ambiguous measure, however. Although it may be low owing to competing industries it may also be low owing to the high job satisfaction involved in working on the land.[40] Additional evidence from both the survey and elsewhere, however, suggests that the latter factor is less important. The workers in the sample were asked whether, if they had their life over again, they would still choose a job in agriculture, and they were also asked later in the interview whether they would recommend their sons to choose employment on the land. Fifty-five per cent of the respondents replied that they would choose a different job if given the chance again and, of those with sons, nearly three-quarters (73·5 per cent) would recommend them not to work in agriculture but to try to find employment elsewhere. These figures can only be regarded as something of an indictment of conditions on the land and give some assessment of the extent to which the current labour force, even after the decades of drift from the land, continues to remain a captive one. This impression is reinforced by the fact that 38·2 per cent of the workers interviewed had thought of leaving the land, but had not yet done so. The main reasons for them wanting to do so were boredom with the job (31 per cent), poor pay (24 per cent) and bad personal relations with their employer (12·5 per cent). Nearly one half had not only thought of leaving but had taken positive steps to go. What kept them at their present job was primarily the absence of any alternative employment opportunities (45 per cent), age (28 per cent), the problem of finding a house because of the occupancy of a tied cottage (13 per cent) and family reasons (8·2 per cent).

The location of the barriers to occupational mobility which this disjunction between choice and opportunity indicates can be pinpointed by an appraisal of the workers' job histories. Their average length of service was 16·7 years (very long by industrial standards[41]) and their average age 39·7 years. Mean school-leaving age was 14·5 years and so the average length of employment experience was 25·2 years. Since the average number of jobs held by the respondents was 3·76, this means that *on average* a worker would change his job three or four times between the ages of fourteen and twenty-three, before 'settling down' into his current job. Now, although it is dangerous to argue from averages, especially in agriculture, this picture corresponds to a pattern of employment that has been observed by other investigators of the agricultural labour market.[42] It is a pattern of employment which affects movement not only within agriculture, but between agriculture and other industries. Wagstaff,[43] for example, has noted that a youth of fifteen will on average stay in agriculture for only seven years, although, if he is the exception and stays until he is thirty, the likelihood is that he will remain on the land for a further twenty-three years. Wagstaff linked this familiar pattern of agricultural employment with nationally derived data on inter-industry labour movements in order to analyse the pattern of recruitment and outflow of labour in agriculture. In the economy as a whole net inflows or outflows of labour disguise gross movements eight times as large, but agriculture is unusual in losing only two workers for every net decrease of one. As Wagstaff points out, 'A man is more likely to stay in agriculture than in several other industries, in spite of low wages.' Wagstaff's general conclusion is that this pattern can be attributed to 'skills which are not transferable to other industries, and the quite different characteristics of farm and non-farm life'.[44] This conclusion hardly squares, however, with his analysis of length-of-service expectations. These skills and characteristics were not a barrier until the workers reached their middle twenties (on average): what was the sudden transformation wrought afterwards? The reasons hardly seem to lie in the area of transferability of skills – there is no reason to suppose they suddenly become less transferable in the late twenties – or in a residual population who have chosen to remain in the face of opportunities to move – the Suffolk survey data does not suggest this. The barriers to movement must be elsewhere and one can only surmise that they lie not in the work at all but in the family life-cycle and, associated with this, the agricultural worker's housing situation, which in some way grossly restricts his opportunities for alternative employment. (This is investigated later in this chapter.) In any case it seems that the extremely low voluntary quit rate can be attributed in no small measure to a substantial proportion of workers who have lacked the opportunity to move rather than made a choice to stay.

There is an important distinction to be made between the lack of alternative job opportunities with which the Suffolk agricultural worker is faced and his job insecurity. It is quite possible that, although the farm worker's choice of occupation is highly restricted, he may nevertheless be immune to redundancy and dismissal in the job he has obtained. Overall, the decreasing demand for labour on farms due to mechanization and the higher unemployment rate in agriculture than the national average suggest a degree of underlying insecurity in the market situation of the agricultural worker. Nevertheless, this does not have a uniform impact over the whole agricultural labour force, as the results from the survey demonstrated. Only 12·4 per cent of the workers interviewed had ever experienced unemployment over a period of more than a few days between jobs, and of these the majority (nearly three-quarters) had only been unemployed once. This experience went back over many years, however, and a substantial number recalled unemployment in the 1930s. Only 6·4 per cent of the sample had suffered unemployment during the five years before the interview.

The workers' job histories also contained information relevant to their job security, and where employment was on a farm the reasons for leaving were extracted. They are presented in Table 17. These

Table 17 Reasons for leaving previous farm employment of workers interviewed in Suffolk, 1972

Reason	%
Dismissal	8·6
Redundancy	23·6
More money	19·3
Advancement	17·5
Dissatisfied	13·7
Family	4·2
War/National Service	9·5
Other	13·8
Farmer-initiated	32·2
Worker-initiated	40·5
Third-party-initiated	27·4

figures cannot be taken as an accurate guide to the present state of the labour market, since they cover a lengthy period of time and a number of geographical locations. However, they are not startlingly dissimilar from the results reported by Gasson of her survey of farms in certain parts of East Anglia. She found that worker-initiated quits ran at 47.4 per cent of all separations, farmer-initiated quits at 22·6 per cent and 'natural causes' (which included death and retirement, by definition excluded from this sample) were responsible for 40·1 per cent.[45] Nevertheless, a voluntary quit rate in the region of 40–50 per cent of all separations is markedly below that reported among engineering workers by Mackay *et al.* where the proportion of voluntary quits was between 69·1 per cent in the 'slack' labour market areas and 73·0 per cent in Birmingham. Employer-initiated separations accounted for between 16·4 per cent and 27·2 per cent.[46]

Farm workers therefore seem to have a generally much less secure market situation than most engineering workers, with movements initiated by factors beyond their control forming a much larger proportion of all moves. Nevertheless this aspect should, perhaps, not be exaggerated – work on the land today is nothing like so precarious as it has been in the past, particularly before the last war, and many of the old abuses of hiring and firing have now disappeared.

Table 18 Workers' and farmers' views on ease of replacement by type of worker, Suffolk, 1972

| | Specialized worker | | General worker | |
	Worker's view	Farmer's view	Worker's view	Farmer's view
With great difficulty	15·6	42·3	3·5	11·3
With some difficulty	42·9	33·8	42·0	26·8
Fairly easily	25·9	18·3	32·9	42·3
Very easily	15·6	5·6	21·7	19·7

In an attempt to explore the degree of insecurity felt by the workers themselves and the nature of their own perceptions of their position in the labour market, they were asked whether their employer could find it easy or difficult to replace them if they left. The same question was also put to their employers. The results are shown in Table 18. It can be seen that the supervisory and autonomous workers share their employers' view of the distinctly 'tighter' market for their skills. On the whole, however, the workers have a rather more optimistic view of their power in the labour market than the farmers and than is probably warranted by their position as sellers of labour under the conditions that predominate in most rural areas. Some clues to the reasons for this emerged when the workers were asked directly about the security of employment in agriculture. They were first asked whether they felt that *in general* farm workers had to worry about getting the sack and then how secure they thought their *own* job to be. Just under one-quarter (23·3 per cent) said that they felt farm workers in general did have to worry about losing their jobs; three-quarters believed that employment on the land was generally secure. Turning to their own job, however, only 6·1 per cent of the workers felt it was 'rather insecure', while the remainder felt it was 'fairly safe' (53·5 per cent) or 'dead safe' (40·4 per cent). There appear to be two major reasons for this discrepancy. First the question 'How secure do you think your own job is?' may not be a very good one for tapping the workers' feelings of job security. As in the traditional survey questions on job satisfaction, there may be a considerable element of rationalization involved in the replies, biasing the respondents towards answering in terms of security. It is not easy for anyone to admit to himself, let alone to a strange investigator, that his employment is not secure. Perhaps the distinction between 'dead safe' and 'fairly safe' is more significant here. A second reason suggests itself, however, by the reasons which the respondents gave for their replies (see Table 19). Not surprisingly the worker's view of his own job security is based not so much upon a consideration of the general market situation but upon his own experiences with his own particular employer. The meaning of the word 'security' therefore has to be considered in relationship to this experience, which of course varies from worker to worker. In both sets of replies the significance of the nature of the relationship with the farmer in promoting feelings of security is evident. This merely reinforces the impression gained from other data that the farm worker's market situation is a highly distinctive one in which the quality of the *personal* relationship between farmer and worker (reflected in the latter's length of service) is uppermost.

The overall typification of the agricultural worker's market situation which emerges from this analysis is one of considerable powerlessness in comparison with that of urban, industrial workers. The geographical boundaries of the labour market are, for the majority of workers, highly localized and consequently the opportunities for alternative employment are highly restricted. There is evidence to show that a substantial proportion of workers on the land are captive to the extent that they have accepted agricultural employment rather than chosen it. In this respect their market situation contains a number of paradoxes: although choice is restricted, employment on the land is reasonably secure (certainly, one suspects, very secure compared with conditions up until the Second World War); farm workers only partially correspond to the 'man and boy' caricature for there is considerable movement between employers, much of it involving moving home – but most of it in the early years and nearly all over very short

Table 19 Perceptions of job security and reasons for reply of workers interviewed in Suffolk, 1972

	Agricultural employment in general % (N = 177)	Own job % (N = 211)
Secure		
Good relationship with employer	36·7	37·5
Declining recruitment	50·8	17·1
Length of service	–	26·5
National employment situation	7·3	1·4
Possession of rare skills	2·8	9·9
Other	2·4	7·6
	100·0	100·0
	(N = 54)	(N = 15)
Insecure		
Tied house	57·4	23·3
Farm amalgamation/redundancy	18·7	53·3
Fatalism (e.g. 'you never know what's going to happen')	18·7	20·0
Other	5·2	3·4
	100·0	100·0

distances. In the last analysis, however, the majority of farm workers' powerlessness as sellers of labour must be reflected in the level of rewards they can command from their buyers. To this we can now turn.

Pay and Conditions

One word can be used to sum up the standard of living of the vast majority of agricultural workers, and that word is 'poor'. It is a word which most of them, with their own self-respect in mind, do not like to hear applied to themselves, but one which they would nevertheless accept. They are the rural poor and it is as well not to fudge this issue at the outset. Of course, this does not mean that the nature of the farm worker's poverty has not changed since Victorian times, or that starvation is a real threat in the Suffolk of the 1970s, as opposed to the 1870s. In absolute terms his standard of living has steadily improved along with everyone else's. Nevertheless by the standards of post-war, full-employment, welfare-state Britain the agricultural workers are among the poorest sections of society.

During the spring and summer of 1972, the time at which field-work was carried out, the statutory minimum wage for regular whole-time male workers over the age of twenty-one in agriculture was £16·20 for a 42-hour week. Average earnings in the year ending March 1972 were £21·42 for a working week of 47·3 hours, compared with average earnings in manufacturing industry of £34·50 for 44·3 hours. Earnings in agriculture are the lowest of any industry covered by the Department of Employment's six-monthly earnings surveys. Not only are average earnings in agriculture among the lowest in the country, however, but the spread of earnings is extremely narrow, resulting in an unusual concentration of low-paid workers within agriculture compared with other industries. Thus in 1972, earnings data from the Ministry of Agriculture's Wages and Employment Enquiry showed that those earnings falling between the quartiles (the central 50 per cent) were spread over a range of £6·70 per week, compared with £10·50 for all semi-skilled workers, who enjoyed, moreover, a shorter working week. This exemplified the conclusions of two Prices and Incomes Board investigations into agricultural wages in the late 1960s. In the words of the first report, 'The concentration of low-paid workers is higher than elsewhere ... Few industries, if any, provide for all payments above the minimum (other than overtime) within such a narrow span.'[47] In other words, agriculture does not contain simply a pocket of low-paid workers, but represents virtually *in toto* a low-paying sector.

In common with many other low-pay industries, the minimum standard of wages and conditions in agriculture are laid down by an industrial council, the Agricultural Wages Board (AWB). The AWB is therefore the cornerstone of wage bargaining in agriculture, an institution for which agricultural trade unions fought long and hard (its inception and organization are described in Chapter 4). The very existence of the AWB is, of course, a symbol of the very weak market situation of the agricultural worker. Its awards – in reality those of the neutral 'appointed' members, since employer and employee representatives invariably disagree – have on the whole been very conservative and as a result the proportion of workers paid the minimum wage in agriculture has declined dramatically from 33·7 per cent in 1950 to only 5 per cent in 1972, which suggests more than nine out of ten workers could achieve more in their own 'negotiations' face-to-face with their employer than their respective national representatives. It is mistaken, however, to view the AWB as an anachronism or as an irrelevancy: not only does it perform an important 'safety-net' function for the lowest-paid, and therefore often the most exploited, groups of workers who remain on the minimum wage – to be found mainly in the south-west, Wales and East Anglia – but the narrow dispersion of earnings makes AWB awards decisive in improving the standard of living of all workers. Because the basic pay so dominates total earnings in agriculture in comparison with other industries, negotiations over the statutory minimum wage remain vitally important despite the small proportion of workers actually receiving the basic amount.

The earnings of agricultural workers vary by occupation, as Table 20 shows. Extra payments to certain categories of workers can be accounted for by their longer working hours, and when this is allowed for the premium payments (basic pay above the statutory minimum) tend to even out over most categories except supervisory workers, who receive substantial premiums of more than one-quarter of their total earnings. In 1972 the somewhat haphazard and variable system of premium payments was institutionalized by the introduction of a statutory wages structure which provided for premiums of 10, 20 and 30 per cent for skilled and supervisory workers. This was of some significance to employer–employee relationships on the farm, for it introduced for the first time universal criteria of wage premiums into a situation which had hitherto been highly particular. Many farmers believed that they no longer had the freedom to pay their men what *they* thought they were worth, but must conform to standards laid down by the AWB. One farmer explained the problem like this: 'Now if I say he's not worth the grade A certificate and he says he is, we go to an arbiter. Now, if he says he is worth it, my chap is not going to think much of me for saying no. But if he fails, I can say, "I told you so," and we don't get a very good relationship that way either.'

The interviews with the workers in Suffolk were carried out immediately after the introduction of the wages structure in the spring of 1972. It was very noticeable how it had the effect of crystallizing the premium payments around the statutorily prescribed amounts.

Table 20 Average total weekly earnings by type of occupation on farms in England and Wales for year ending 1972

	£ per week	Percentage of workforce
Bailiffs, foremen	27·86	0·1
Dairy cowmen	28·84	1·5
Other stockmen	24·73	9·6
Tractor drivers	23·73	5·7
Horticultural workers	22·15	19·0
General farm workers	21·82	62·5
Other workers	25·58	1·6
All men	23·67	100·0

Thus, nearly half of the workers were being paid the current craftsman's rate of £17·82 for a basic week of 42 hours. Indeed this was becoming widely regarded as the 'minimum', rather than the lower basic rate of £16·20. The distribution of gross basic wage levels is in Table 21. The coalescence around the wages structure rates reflects the partial loss of many farmers' discretion over premium payments. It is perhaps significant that, of the three occasions when workers threatened official strike action while fieldwork was being carried out in the area, two were over the implementation of the wages structure, in each case the farmer wishing to grant the craftsman's rate only to certain members of his labour force and in each case the workers demanding that it should be given to everyone. On one farm matters reached such a pitch that a deputation of tractor drivers went to see the dairy manager to ask him to pull the bung out of the bottom of the milk tank. He refused; but eventually the farmer agreed to put all the workers on the craftsman's grade.

In addition to the basic wage and premiums, the remainder of the agricultural worker's earnings consist of overtime payments. The average of hours worked in agriculture is greater than that for manufacturing industry. Overtime varies considerably according to the type of worker – those dealing with stock perforce work longer hours

Table 21 Gross basic wage of workers interviewed in Suffolk, 1972

Amount	%
*Less than £16·20	4·8
£16·20	10·0
£16·21 to £17·81	6·1
£17·82	49·1
£17·83 to £19·99	14·3
£20·00 to £24·99	6·6
More than £25·00	9·1
	100·0

*At the time of the survey the statutory minimum adult rate was payable at the age of twenty-one. The minimum age for inclusion in the survey was eighteen. Altogether 12·9 per cent of the sample were on the minimum rate for their age.

– and the time of the year. The workers interviewed in the sample had an average working week of 51·6 hours; only 9·4 per cent worked no overtime, but 17·2 per cent said they worked 60 hours or more per week on average. There may have been some inflation in the replies, however, owing to the time of year during which the interviews took place. Certainly the average was above that of the Wages and Employment Enquiry (47·9 hours), even though the fieldwork was in an area with little livestock. Nevertheless it was substantially the same as the average in the NEDO study carried out at the same time.[48] Overtime payments pushed up the average gross weekly earnings of the workers interviewed to £23·79. The distribution of earnings is shown in Table 22.

Parity of earnings with workers in other industries is the long-cherished ambition of agricultural workers and particularly of their trade unions.[49] It is the comparison which all agricultural workers make when evaluating their own standard of living, and the size of the wages 'gap' is their principal point of reference in assessing their degree of satisfaction with their own income levels. Thus there was an almost complete correlation between satisfaction with present income and a perception of the wages gap gradually closing (101 respondents out of 102); conversely a perception of the gap having

Table 22 Gross weekly earnings of workers interviewed in Suffolk, March–August 1972

Amount	No.	%
Less than £15·00	8	3·5
£15·00–£19·99	47	20·5
£20·00–£24·99	82	35·8
£25·00–£29·99	64	27·9
£30·00–£34·99	21	9·2
More than £35·00	7	3·1
Total replied	229	100·0
Refused	4 or	1·7% of total sample

widened or remained the same led to workers being dissatisfied with their standard of living (129 out of 131).[50] Aggregate data on comparative earnings in agriculture and industry tend to be rather conflicting and frequently fail to take account of the longer hours worked by agricultural workers – weekly rather than hourly rates are compared.[51] There is some consensus, however, that the pre-war ratio of agricultural to industrial earnings was in the region of 50 per cent, but that agricultural labour shortages during the war considerably improved agriculture's relative position, enabling, with continued post-war governmental support, a new equilibrium to be achieved at around 70 per cent. Table 23 shows, however, how hourly earnings in agriculture have gradually fallen further behind those in industry and how the growth in the general level of earnings has increased the absolute size of the gap from just under £2 in 1949 to just under £12 in 1972. Apologists for the low level of earnings in agriculture often point to the extent of fringe benefits, especially payments in kind.

The Agricultural Wages Act overrides certain sections of the Truck Act and allows farmers to make certain payments in kind, but only according to a legally prescribed reckoning laid down by the AWB. They are primarily board and lodging, tied accommodation and milk, although some farmers also give other perquisites which lie outside the AWB orders, like potatoes, vegetables and fuel, and which

Table 23 Relative earnings of agricultural workers and manual workers in manufacturing industry, 1949–72

Year	Average weekly earnings (£ p.) Agri.	Ind.	Average hours Agri.	Ind.	Average hourly earnings (p.) Agri.	Ind.	Hourly earnings ratio*
1949	5·49	7·25	51·1	46·5	10·7	15·6	69·0
1954	7·34	10·26	51·2	48·2	14·3	21·3	69·3
1959	9·99	14·21	52·1	48·2	19·2	29·5	64·7
1964	12·68	18·68	51·2	46·9	24·8	39·8	59·7
1969	16·96	25·54	49·2	45·7	34·5	55·9	61·7
1970	18·30	28·05	49·1	45·7	37·3	57·1	61·5
1971	19·18	31·10	47·7	44·4	40·2	68·2	58·9
1972	21·45	34·50	47·3	44·3	45·3	75·8	59·8

*The ratio of the average hourly earnings of the industrial worker to those of the agricultural worker, multiplied by 100.

are not allowable against cash wages. As all of these perquisites are usually valued at far less than their market price, real earnings of agricultural workers may appear to be somewhat higher than their money earnings suggest, an accusation which agricultural workers have persistently had to suffer when they have complained of their poverty and which has occasionally taken the edge off any sympathy which might otherwise be due to them. It is therefore worthwhile examining the agricultural worker's fringe benefits in some detail.

Although many farm workers do receive occasional gifts of farm produce, their significance has often been grossly exaggerated. Total payments in kind as a percentage of the contract wage for all hired men has declined steadily since the war and by the early 1970s was standing at 2 per cent. Apart from accommodation, payments in kind have usually consisted of milk and potatoes, but their provision on many farms has been eliminated by the increased specialization of production. The typical East Anglian agricultural worker, for example, is hardly interested in taking home a sack of barley or sugar beet and there are fewer farms left with cows to provide free milk or with hens for free eggs. Even where edible produce might be available, new mechanized methods of collection (mechanized milking parlours, new methods of potato-harvesting, etc.) have made the distribution of free samples too troublesome. Hence there has been a decline in the provision of free produce. Most workers receive their milk in bottles on their doorsteps from the local roundsman like everyone else.

The provision of housing is, however, quite another matter. A very small percentage – less than 5 per cent – often receive subsidized board and/or lodging on the farm. They are mostly youths and the proportion is declining. The other form of accommodation is the tied cottage, or 'service accommodation' as it is sometimes euphemistically entitled. Here the proportion of workers has *increased* markedly from just over one-third to more than one-half since the war. The significance of the tied cottage extends far beyond its cash value, and this is considered in the next section of this chapter; nevertheless it composes an important, indeed predominant, part of all payment in kind.[52] The maximum rent which farmers were allowed to charge under AWB regulations in 1972 was 50p per week and this was the value which was adopted when official statistics on payments in kind were computed. Its value to the worker was, however, far more than 50p. The official estimates of rent and rates of local-authority property outside the Greater London area in 1972 was approximately £3·50 per week. This is probably a reasonably accurate assessment of the opportunity-cost of tied accommodation for most farm workers and compares with an allowance in the statistics of 16p. (indicating that over two-thirds of employers waived the rent). The house's value is also tax-free (although the farm worker earning average wages in 1972 would not be liable for income tax) and the cost of repairs and maintenance is borne by the employer. Thus, given that only half of the labour force is living in tied accommodation, the average additional value of housing was approximately £2·00 per week in 1972, or 9 per cent of average earnings.

Ostensibly this appears to narrow the wages gap considerably.

However, in order to compare like with like, it is necessary to examine the extent of payments in kind and other fringe benefits in industry. Most farms lack, for example, the kind of benefits that have become a matter of course in other industries, like superannuation and private pension funds, compulsory sick pay, medical facilities, low-cost canteens, etc. These add nearly 6 per cent on average to industrial wages and salaries – or approximately £2·40 per week in 1972. Moreover, it can be argued that agricultural employers receive benefits from the provision of tied housing which their industrial counterparts must pay for. These range from the partial de-rating of farm cottages to the lack of any 'stand-by' payments for the immediate on-the-spot availability of farm employees to deal with straying stock or rain-threatened harvests. By comparison, for example, water-authority workers received a weekly stand-by payment of £4·90 in 1972, county-council roadmen received two hours' payment on being requested to stand by, at overtime rates if necessary; and many industrial companies, from ICI to Allied Breweries, paid amounts ranging between 62½p. and £1·50 in addition to overtime. So, when the pros and cons of payments in kind in agriculture are worked out, it can be seen that the farm worker is only very marginally, if at all, better off than the average industrial worker in this respect. The size of the gap between real agricultural and real industrial earnings remains virtually unaffected by including payments in kind and the idea that employment on the land carried with it a cornucopia of concealed material benefits needs to be recognized for what it is – a myth.

There are many farmers, possibly a majority, who recognize the prevalence of low pay among agricultural workers, and leading representatives of the NFU can occasionally be heard expressing the belief that farm workers deserve improved wages. Why, then, do not farmers pay their employees higher wages? The farmers' own reasons have followed the interpretations offered by many agricultural economists, and relate to factors which were briefly considered at the beginning of this chapter. That is to say that many farmers acknowledge that the earnings of agricultural workers compare unfavourably with those of workers in industry but regard this as an associated aspect of the low-income problems of agriculture in general, which results in employers' earnings and returns on capital being below that of industrial employers. This view has been generally supported by many agricultural economists who have considered the problem of low returns to agricultural labour, and who have extended the model which explains the lower returns to farmers to explain why the earnings of agricultural workers have consistently failed to reach parity with those of industrial workers. Metcalf,[53] for example, derives the low income of agricultural workers in this manner, and Capstick has written about the phenomenon as follows: 'In the developed world total farm population is falling rapidly. In general the productivity of labour in agriculture is well below that in industry or the service trades, consequently earnings in agriculture are also low. But we may note the anomalous position of the British farm worker who is as productive as the average worker in the country (and therefore more productive than workers in some industries) but who is still at the bottom of the wages structure. This is partly a matter of tradition – the agricultural worker has always been ill-paid and an improvement in his earnings commensurate with his productivity would set off a round of wage claims from all other sectors of the economy. Partly also the low earnings of agricultural labour reflect the industry's structure; an increase in profit margins which would allow the 40 per cent of farmers who employ labour to pay wages comparable with those in industry would also increase profits for the 60 per cent of farmers who do not employ labour. The latter are the small farmers ... And thirdly, low returns to labour are part of the whole problem of less than average returns to total factors which is one of agriculture's perennial problems ...'[54]

The major point of weakness in this explanation is that an economic model which accounts for the low incomes of farmers, which are derived from the sale of farm products, cannot be applied indiscriminately to farm workers, whose income comes from the sale of their *labour*. Farmers may indeed be able to pass on their low returns in the form of low wages for their employees, but this is contingent upon the conditions of the, mainly local, labour market rather than the ability to raise overall returns to the agricultural sector. For this reason there is no very close correlation between farmers' incomes and the earnings of agricultural workers. In East Anglia, for example, where farmers are among the most prosperous in the country, the earnings of their workers are among the lowest; what renders the agricultural worker among the most poorly paid in the region is not the inability of farmers to pay higher wages, compared with farmers in the rest of the country, but the lack of competition for labour in what is a predominantly rural area, which in turn enables a sufficient quantity and quality of labour to be obtained at a lower price than elsewhere. Powerlessness in the market situation therefore seems a better predictor of low wage levels than an inability of farmers to 'afford' higher wages.[55]

In this respect farmers could justifiably argue that they are by no means unique in their entrepreneurial behaviour: they are in business to make a profit, not to act as charitable organizations for the relief of the working poor and the maintenance of profits requires a minimization of costs wherever possible, including labour costs. What is significant, however, is that this interpretation of low pay in agriculture in terms of labour-market factors is *not* what is offered. Overwhelmingly the interpretation which is presented to the farm worker is not one in which his low pay is determined by the impersonal exigencies of the market but by the personal, and often regrettable, inability of the farmer to pay more. This reinterprets a situation which otherwise could be regarded as mere cash nexus into one in which no conflict of interest between farmer and worker is admitted. Instead, even the most prosperous farmers argue that they cannot afford to raise wages and point to their own low returns on capital and inability to pass on their own increased costs to the public in support of this, emphasizing how low returns in agriculture affect farmers and workers alike. Only occasionally is this view challenged by individual farmers, who may, for example, point to the payment of higher wages in industrial areas and lower wages in remote rural areas as a phenomenon which hardly squares with this interpretation, and to the inherent weaknesses in the market situation of farm workers which may tempt some farmers to offer only as much as is necessary rather than as much as possible. Such a viewpoint in a letter to *Farmer's Weekly* in April 1972 opened up what the editor was to call 'the great wages debate' which filled up hundreds of column-inches as the letters flooded in over the next three months. The initial letter, headlined 'Farming's ludicrous minimum wage', came from the managing director of an *arriviste* farming company backed by a City finance house, who was later to prove himself a scourge of what he considered to be the outmoded nepotism and paternalism of British agriculture. The letter hinted that the NFU in its wages negotiations took advantage of 'the fact that (farm workers) could not strike, nor employ that delightful misnomer "work-to-rule", in order to depress the workers' wage levels'.[56] The ensuing correspondence, in the words of one letter, rang 'with praises for the virtuosity and loyalty of the farm worker and has set him up as a paragon of virtue to those in other industries'.[57] Apart from some discussion over the extent of low pay in agriculture (stimulating a parallel debate on tied housing) and some waspish comments on 'big business' buying into farmland, two themes emerged. One was summarized by a correspondent who called himself 'willing but poor': 'decent wages depend on decent prices for food . . . We would be only too ready to pay them, but meanwhile I suppose we shall just pay no attention to pious resolutions.'[58] The other was a series of suggestions that the NFU should bargain on behalf of their workers in the annual Price Review negotiations with the Ministry.

This correspondence represents only one example, but the arguments are repeated almost every year before and during the AWB round of wages bargaining. The real problem, farmers argue, is that the share of national resources allocated to agriculture is inadequate: that workers' *and* employers' earnings are intolerably low. The real conflict of interest lies not between farmer and worker but between the agricultural industry as a whole and the urban/industrial demand for cheap food. Again this kind of consensual interpretation is not unique to farmers and farming; however, it is more prevalent among agricultural workers than among many industrial workers (see below, Chapter 5) because the relationship between employer and employee has increasingly become a personal, diffuse one rather than impersonal and contractual. Most workers in any case have no idea of the extent of the profitability of the farm on which they are working and cannot judge the precise ability of the farmer to pay higher wages; on the other hand the arguments seem plausible – farmers *are* price-takers rather than price-makers and returns to capital in farming *are* lower than in industry on average. This is not to accuse farmers of being hypocritical: the vast majority are quite sincere in their arguments and even, in 1972, were angered when a workers' pay award was frozen by the government at the end of an exceptionally profitable farming year. (Many Suffolk farmers in fact made the payments illegally.) What is so significant is that farmers account for low pay in agriculture on other grounds than their own highly rational economic behaviour and that this is closely linked with a desire to stabilize and harmonize a *personal* relationship in which underlying conflicts of interest could otherwise emerge. Furthermore the institutionalization of wage bargaining at the national level in the AWB has removed from the arena of the farm what is customarily the most sensitive issue of all between employers and employees and the one which is most capable of highlighting any conflict of interest – as some farmers' experiences on introducing the wages structure demonstrate.[59] For these reasons pay is *not* a major obstacle to harmonious relationships between farmers and workers: among the workers interviewed, only 25 per cent blamed farmers (including only 8 per cent their own employer) for their unsatisfactory pay. However, what has remained is one institution which is potentially quite capable of crystallizing and symbolically expressing any conflict of interest between farming employers and employees, an issue which probably causes more polarization than any other – the tied cottage.

The Tied Cottage

There is probably no topic in agriculture which raises passions more than the tied cottage. Even the term itself can provoke anger, as it seems to stress the negative aspect of the system to the employee: many farmers prefer to use 'service accommodation', both because this is the legal term and because it describes the system as a service to the employee. The extreme sensitivity which surrounds the tied cottage is not without its sociological significance, but it has resulted in a welter of polemic, accusation, bitterness and exaggeration, although, at the time of writing, little hard evidence beyond three highly limited surveys and one case study. The *Farmer's Weekly* produced a 'great tied cottage debate' during 1973 and 1974 to match the wages debate of a year earlier, except that on this occasion there were more letters, it lasted much longer, was more acrimonious and was ultimately even more inconclusive. Readers of *Farmer's Weekly* could be excused a feeling of *déjà vu* during this period, for another lengthy correspondence on the subject between January and March 1965 covered the same ground and utilized the same arguments. To an outside observer, the question of why the tied cottage should generate so much controversy in agriculture (as opposed to other industries in which a similar system operates) is almost as interesting as the tied-cottage system itself – but then only an uninvolved outsider can afford the luxury of being so detached from its moral and material implications. For ultimately the arguments for and against the tied cottage are reducible to a particular moral stance, and this is probably why the arguments are in the last analysis irreconcilable on each other's terms.

Tied cottages are houses provided by a farmer as part of an agricultural worker's terms of employment – the worker may be required to live in tied accommodation as a condition of employment, or has made his own decision to do so. As we saw in the previous section, the farmer may make a deduction from wages of an amount regulated under the Agricultural Wages Act of 1948 (in 1972 50p. per week in most cases), but the worker does not pay any more of his wages in rent, otherwise he becomes a tenant in the normal sense. If, for any reason, the worker's employment ends, his security of tenure is lost, and he forfeits the right to the house one month from the date on which notice of the termination of employment is given. However Section 33 of the Rent Act, 1965, as modified by Section 99 of the Agricultural Act, 1970, provides that if the owner seeks a possession order for the house during the six months following termination of employment, the court must normally suspend this until the end of the six months' period. These provisions also apply to the widow or dependents of a deceased employee. It is no longer possible, therefore, for a farm worker to be thrown out of a tied house at a moment's notice on the whim of his employer: application must be made to a County Court judge for a possession order.

However, thanks to House of Lords' amendments to the 1970 Act, the court can choose not to suspend the order in the following circumstances:

1. if it considers it 'reasonable' not to;
2. if suitable alternative accommodation is, or will become, available during the period;
3. if greater hardship will be caused by suspension of the order than by its execution;
4. if damage is occurring to the property;
5. if the 'efficient management of any agricultural land or the efficient carrying on of any agricultural operations would be seriously prejudiced unless the premises are available for occupation by a person employed or to be employed by the owner'.

However the first condition on its own is insufficient grounds for failing to grant a suspension and it must co-exist with at least one of the other four conditions. The court can also extend or terminate the period of suspension and attach conditions to it, such as the payment of rent arrears or mesne profits.

This legal framework suggests that the agricultural worker has six months' security of tenure. However, in practice the agricultural efficiency clause is invoked in many cases and the courts do not make full use of their powers to vary the period of suspension. The farm workers' union maintains that the average period of suspension is one month, although the actual period of security could easily be longer than this because there is often a lag between termination of employment and application for an order. At the time of writing, however, no thorough study has been carried out into this question and one can only summarize the situation by stating that a proportion of workers – how large it is impossible to tell – are liable to eviction well within the six months following termination of employment.[60]

Nationally, the proportion of farm workers living in tied housing has increased from 34 per cent in 1948 to 52 per cent in 1972. The problems of insecurity which the system engenders are far from being purely notional: in 1964 the farm workers' union handled 210 cases of threatened eviction in the County Courts; by 1970 the number had increased to 417; and by 1973 to 561.[61] In the *Farmer's Weekly* survey of tied housing, reported by Thompson and Gasson in 1974,[62] 35 per cent of a self-selected sample of farmers almost certainly biased towards more enlightened employers admitted having used legal action on at least one occasion to remove a tied-cottage tenant. Undoubtedly some of these threatened 'evictions' are arranged between employer and employee in order to force the hand of rural local authorities, many of which refuse to admit farm workers to their council-house waiting lists while they are in possession of tied-cottage tenancies. The proportion of these colluded 'evictions' is not known, however, although it is a minority. Actual evictions are quite rare occurrences – probably no more than twenty per year – since the local authority is usually prevailed upon to act as a long stop in emergencies. Needless to say, evictions, when they do occur, are accompanied by a full panoply of publicity and their *symbolic* importance extends far beyond their numerical significance.[63]

Farmers are committed to the continuation of the tied-cottage system quite simply because they see it as an essential part of their ability to function properly and indeed to remain in business at all.[64] They argue that tied cottages, most of which are situated in the immediate vicinity of the farm buildings, are vital in an occupation like farming where unpredictable and fluctuating demands are constantly being made upon the whole labour force of the farm (including the farmers themselves). This particularly applies where the farm carries stock, since the stockman must be on hand to deal with emergencies at all hours of the day and night, especially during calving, lambing or farrowing. Farmers also see the tied cottage as essential in another sense, however. Without being able to offer accommodation, they argue, it would be impossible to attract labour at all, particularly those like skilled stockmen who are in short supply. Many farmers can recount the experience of advertising for labour without mentioning accommodation and receiving no replies, but being deluged with applications upon re-advertising with a promise of rent-free housing. This is interpreted as a demand for tied housing among farm workers and a vote of confidence in the continuation of the system as it is.

Most farmers will acknowledge that the tied-cottage system is occasionally abused by a handful of bad employers (for whom they have no sympathy whatsoever) and that this can lead to the odd case of indefensible exploitation or harassment. However, in the vast majority of cases they believe that the system works well, to the benefit of employers and employees alike. The handful of abuses by farmers are matched by those workers who obtain a job on the land merely to occupy a house rent-free and then promptly leave for a job in industry but refuse to vacate the house. The farmer is then faced with a situation in which he needs the house in order to accommodate a new employee. With a labour force of only one or two this may seriously threaten the running of the farm. It is cases of this type which, it is argued, form the vast majority of cases before County Courts; such is the shortage of skilled labour on farms today that any worker worth his salt has nothing to fear in any case – only the misfits cause trouble. In addition it is pointed out how the tied cottage represents a considerable tax-free addition to real earnings for the employee, but something of a sacrifice to the employer, who could often sell the house for a large sum to wealthy middle-class urbanites in search of country homes or let it on the open market at a sum often equalling the worker's total weekly wage. Farmers are therefore providing a service; indeed, given the state of local-authority housing in rural areas, without the tied cottage the provision of cheaply rented rural accommodation would collapse. For this reason, whatever the defects of the tied-cottage system, there has simply been no realistic alternative offered: if it were abolished tomorrow, thousands of workers would become homeless and the agricultural production of the country would suffer incalculable harm. Finally, farmers ask, what is all the fuss about? Many other industries use service accommodation for their employees without the same demands for its abolition. Why should not agriculture do the same? Policemen, coal miners, schoolteachers, vicars and even (inevitably in any argument this example is used) the Prime Minister in 10 Downing Street all live in tied houses and are happy to do so. In agriculture only those with vested interests (the trade-union leaders) or who are politically motivated ('agitators') desire the abolition of the tied cottage. The majority of workers wish to retain tied housing, recognizing that it enhances mobility within agriculture, enables experience of farming conditions in many districts to be gained and is essential for the success of good farming practice.

Agricultural trade unions have been implacably hostile to the tied cottage, viewing it as an intolerable restriction on the freedom of agricultural workers.[65] The tied cottage is identified with the exploitation of the farm worker by agricultural employers and as their principal device in maintaining a low-wage regime and consequent poverty on the land. The tied cottage is indeed regarded as the centrepiece of the system which has condemned the agricultural worker to poverty and dependence over the last 150 years or more. By restricting the mobility of workers between agriculture and other industries, the tied cottage literally ties the worker to the land. Thus terms like 'serfdom', 'captivity' and 'under the thumb' are part of the armoury of rhetoric brought to describe the dependent situation which ensues. Where an employer is also the landlord, the twin threat of dismissal *and* eviction is viewed as a concentration of power in the farmer's hands which removes the last vestige of independence and freedom from the already low-paid farm worker. This dependency is particularly extreme in remote rural areas where there is little alternative employment or housing. Here the subservience of workers and the payment of low wages is more easily enforced. In many cases, life 'under the boss' can lead to intolerable interference in the private lives of workers and petty restrictions on their leisure activities. The unions also recall that in the past the tied cottage has been used as a weapon against the spread of unionization or the threat of industrial action and that personal disagreements with employers over non-farming matters have resulted in genuine domestic hardships for the worker and his family. For these reasons the situation in 10 Downing Street has never seemed to be a proper analogy.

The tied cottage therefore symbolizes a master-and-servant relationship from which agricultural trade unions have sought to escape for more than a hundred years. It is believed to be responsible for an underlying sense of fear which is alleged to pervade farm workers and which prevents many of them speaking up for their rights. For this reason the cases of hardship that reach the courts are merely the tip of an iceberg; submerged beneath a placid exterior is a widespread feeling of resentment at the inferior pay and conditions of agriculture which many workers are afraid to voice. These feelings particularly pervade older workers who after years of loyal service are faced by the prospect of their household belongings stacked under a tarpaulin by the roadside watched over by a perplexed ex-employee and a wife frantic with worry. The actual proportion to whom this occurs should be discounted: the *threat* of eviction hangs over all workers, the argument runs, and is a deterrent which none but the most hard-hearted farm worker can afford to ignore when dealing with his employer. Moreover, the alarming rise in the number of court cases handled by the union shows that the problem is far from disappearing, especially when this is placed against the background of a decreasing number of workers on the land. Indeed, the fact that this decrease has been accompanied by a rising proportion of workers in tied accommodation shows what a tie the system is: disproportionately more workers leave agriculture who are *not* in tied housing. As a final barb it is often observed with some irony how the NFU protects its tenant-farming members against insecurity of tenure but then reverses its arguments when supporting the tied cottage.

As must be apparent, the two arguments are not easily reconcilable, for each side chooses different ground as a basis for its case. The case for retention is presented in largely pragmatic terms with reforms aimed at averting abuses of the system rather than the system itself; the case for abolition is quite the reverse, arguing that the way in which the tied cottage system is operated in practice by individual farmers is to a certain extent irrelevant – it is the system itself which must be abolished root and branch, since it is the system which produces the deleterious effects, however reasonable the actions of some individual farmers. For this reason there has been little room for compromise, although some half-hearted attempts have been made, such as the operation of an 'early warning system' for retiring farm workers in tied houses in counties like Hampshire and Essex whereby representations are made by both the NFU and the local trade-union branch to the local authority for rehousing; or legislation aimed at lengthening the period of security for tied-cottage tenants. Both are viewed by the union as mere palliatives, however.

Just as it is difficult to see how the arguments for and against the tied cottage can be reconciled on each other's terms, so it is not clear how they can be supported or refuted *empirically*.[66] Since they both start from different premises, the evidence which is marshalled in their support is viewed by the other side as being in the last analysis irrelevant. This has not prevented argument taking place. On the contrary, since neither side understands – or indeed wants to understand – the other's point of view, it has intensified the debate. But what it has done is make the arguments peculiarly inconclusive and repetitive.[67] To some extent this is inevitable, since, from their own point of view, both sets of arguments are substantially correct. From the farmer's point of view he *does* require service accommodation and while housing in rural areas remains in abominably short supply no alternative to the tied cottage *is* viable. Equally, from the worker's point of view, the system *does* tie him to the land, depress his wages and undermine his independence. There is a straightforward conflict of interest here which no amount of rhetoric can hide, a conflict of interest between capital and labour with each side pursuing its legitimate interest to the detriment of the other. The tied cottage symbolizes this conflict in a peculiarly vivid form and for this reason the issue has entered a wider political arena. A motion on its abolition has become the notorious 'hardy annual' of TUC and Labour Party conferences and a pledge to abolish the tied cottage has formed a part of every Labour Party general election manifesto since the war.

This party political involvement in the tied-cottage issue has in itself enabled the emotional temperature of the debate to remain high. The tradition of using the tied cottage as an oppressive weapon in agricultural labour relations also accounts for the debate having remained so alive for so long, while the trauma of eviction provides a spectacular reminder of injustice and hardship which provokes anger and bitterness all round. All these factors help to explain the continued emotive content of the tied-cottage issue. In themselves, however, they fail to explain why this hostility is so pronounced in agriculture compared with other industries. For it is mistaken to believe that many of the problems associated with service accommodation are entirely absent from other occupations.[68] Farm workers are, of course, in a very different position financially, for they cannot afford alternative forms of accommodation in most cases. This means that the agricultural worker is frequently faced by the dilemma that he cannot afford *not* to take on the tenancy of a tied cottage, even though, once in one, he cannot afford to seek alternative employment outside agriculture. The tied cottage is the carrot which may make a worker accept his low wage, but renders his ability to quit the land ever more remote as he becomes older. More than any other factor, however, the emotiveness of the tied-cottage issue is probably due to the close, personal nature of the relationship between employer and employee. If the provision of accommodation were merely a contractual matter, impersonal and legalistic as in many other industries, the severance of the contract would involve little personal acrimony. Living on a farm, however, strengthens the close relationship between employer and employee, relationships which often extend beyond work into the family life of both parties. While this can create its own peculiar problems, it nevertheless engenders a much greater *identity* between farmer and worker than is typical in large-scale industry. The problems associated with the tied cottage are likely to be more rancorous under such circumstances precisely because the relationship is a personal one: any threat to terminate the occupation of the house will flagrantly breach this identity between employer and employee built up by perhaps years of face-to-face relationships. Thus, like a family, such a social organization is likely to lead to greater harmony where mutual commitment pertains, but where it is flouted the resulting conflict, like a family quarrel, is likely to be all the more bitter and recriminating.

Sociologically, the tied cottage is therefore of great interest as a factor in the relationship between employer and employee. The customary divisive issue of wage negotiations has been banished beyond the farm gate in most cases, and only the tied cottage remains as a potentially irreconcilable conflict which threatens the generally close and harmonious relationship which employers wish to foster. By this argument the issue of the tied cottage represents a microcosm of the wider issue of class relationships in agriculture. The response of agricultural workers to the tied cottage may therefore follow a similar pattern to varying patterns of class consciousness in general, ranging from outright opposition, through varying degrees of ambiguity to outright endorsement of the existing system. Nor is this merely a matter of analogy: because the tied cottage involves rights over property, the purchase and disposability of labour and the level of monetary and non-monetary rewards, class relationships are, in the peculiar circumstances of agricultural employment, *reducible to* the tied cottage in most cases. In striking a particular attitude towards the tied-cottage system, the agricultural worker is therefore saying something, albeit in a modest, restricted and situationally defined way, about class ideology *tout court*.

It is this aspect of the tied cottage that can be explored empirically, although cross-sectional survey-generated data is only of limited use. This is because, for many workers, any conflict of interest with their employer over housing may only arise, so to speak, *post hoc*, that is, only when the worker is already on his way out of his job. The short-term hedonistic aspects of working-class culture apply to housing as elsewhere: there is a tendency among some workers to overlook the long-term threat of insecurity (for example, upon retirement) in favour of the short-term material gains. Evaluation of the tied cottage system will vary accordingly. Nevertheless attitudinal data can throw some light upon workers' perceptions of tied housing and suggest interesting lines of inquiry. At the time of writing investigation of the tied cottage in agriculture has, however, been extremely skimpy, although what evidence there is, including that from the Suffolk farm workers interviewed in this study, tends to point in the same direction.

Studies by Cowie and Giles, Fletcher and Gasson[69] have all demonstrated that as far as the standard of amenities is concerned tied cottages are, in the words of Fletcher, 'by no means the back-water of rural housing'.[70] The standards tend to be on average a little below that of local-authority housing but above that of private rented accommodation. There are, however, wide disparities: the best tied houses are far superior to even the best council houses, while the worst are rural slums. In his study in Devon, Fletcher found that the conditions tended to vary with the age of the occupant, older workers having to suffer lower standards. There is 'a clear indication', he writes, 'that improvements in housing conditions are undertaken by the employer-landlord, at least partly in order to attract and keep employees. Inevitably, it is the young who benefit from such a situation.'[71] Gasson has also indicated how the house was used as a bait for putative employees, particularly on the urban fringe. Larger employers were not only more inclined to offer housing, but where they did so it was generally of a better quality.[72]

Cowie and Giles explored the opinions of both tied cottage and non-tied cottage occupants of the advantages and disadvantages of their respective types of housing. For those workers living in tied cottages the main advantage was that of cost (33 out of 53 replies) with proximity of workplace (8 out of 53) a subsidiary reason. The two major disadvantages were being tied to agricultural employment (28 out of 62) and insecurity (20). Just over one-third of their respondents saw both advantages and disadvantages to the system, but more saw only disadvantages (29 out of 92) than saw only advantages to tied housing (20 out of 92). Those workers not living in tied accommodation tended to see the main advantage of their position as 'freedom' (18 out of 24); while the major disadvantage was financial (9 out of 13). Cowie and Giles' data, although based upon a small number of respondents, suggests therefore that the main reason why workers like the tied-cottage system is an instrumental one – it is cheap – while dissatisfaction is expressed in terms of restrictions on freedom of occupational choice and/or insecurity of tenure. They observe that 54 per cent of their sample in tied cottages were there because there was no suitable alternative accommodation available: 'The emphasis concerning suitable alternative accommodation was invariably placed on the cost of such alternatives and it was made clear that modern council houses did not constitute alternatives by this standard, being well beyond the pockets of most workers. In effect, then, it appears that certainly the bulk of tied cottage dwellers are involuntary victims of circumstances.'[73]

These conclusions can be linked to the comments made earlier in this chapter regarding the effects of the tied cottage upon perceptions of job security and occupational choice. Among the Suffolk farm workers the tied cottage was regarded as the largest single source of job insecurity and it was suggested that the constraints on occupational mobility lay in the area of the family life-cycle and housing situation. Cowie and Giles also noted how nearly one-third of those tied-cottage dwellers who would prefer to have other accommodation would leave agriculture if such an alternative offered itself.[74] Fletcher's data were even more startling: 40 per cent of the workers wanted to leave agriculture, and, although only one in ten said that the tied cottage was their reason for wanting to quit the industry, nine-tenths of those who wanted to leave said they had been prevented from doing so because of the lack of alternative housing. Fletcher therefore suggests that the housing situation is more important than family life-cycle in explaining the pattern of occupational mobility among agricultural workers. To some extent, Fletcher concludes, farmers have a 'captive labour force', but the workers do not normally express it in that way 'because relations with individual employers are for the most part good'.[75]

This suggests a source of acceptance, and even endorsement, of the tied cottage which can be investigated via the interviews carried out in Suffolk. The respondents' housing is shown in Table 24. The pro-

Table 24 Housing of workers interviewed in Suffolk, 1972

Type of housing	No.	%
Tied accommodation	144	61·8
Owner-occupier	19	8·2
Council housing	22	9·4
Private rented	5	2·1
*With parents	37	15·9
Other	6	2·6
	233	100·0

*Including fifteen respondents whose parents were living in tied housing.

portion living in tied accommodation is higher than the national average (52 per cent); and the proportion increases with the number of workers employed – from 26·7 per cent of workers on farms with only one employee to 71·1 per cent of those on the largest farms of more than twenty workers. Altogether 54·1 per cent of the workers lived on the farms, compared with 45·9 per cent living in the villages;[76] of the tied-cottage dwellers, however, 75 per cent were on the farms. All respondents were asked, 'Would you like to see any changes in the tied-cottage system?' The replies elicited as near a 50–50 split as an odd-numbered sample will allow, 116 advocating changes in the system and 117 not desiring any change. Not all of those who wished to see the system changed wanted outright abolition of the tied cottage, however – this view was limited to half of those who advocated changes, and nearly 30 per cent of the overall sample. These views are set out in Table 25.

Table 25 Attitudes towards the tied cottages of workers interviewed in Suffolk, 1972

	No.		%	
No change wanted	117		50·2	
Change wanted	116		49·8	
Abolition		69		29·6
Longer security of tenure		28		12·0
Better amenities		16		6·9
Other		3		1·3
	233	116	100·0	49·8

Those workers who wanted to see the tied-cottage system abolished invariably did so because of the restrictions it imposed upon their freedom to move off the land and because of the fear of insecurity in both house and job which the system engendered. In practice these aspects were so merged together that it made little sense to separate them for the purposes of categorizing the replies. The vehemence with which these views were spoken was also apparent – the feelings of those who wished to see abolition were deeply held and expressed with some force. The following examples illustrate these points:

'They should get rid of it. I'm in a (tied) house and I've got to do as I'm told. I'm at their beck and call. If I refused to work on Sundays, they wouldn't like it and I risk being thrown out.'

'You shouldn't be put out on the road. A lot won't say anything because they live under the boss and fear he may put them out on the road.'

'It's not so much leaving the job as leaving the house. In a private house you can say and do what you like, but I can't can I?'

'You do your job and that's that. You can't argue too much with the family in a tied house.'

'To go into a tied house is the worst thing anybody can do, but when you're married you need a home.'

'The biggest worry is tied cottages – that's the biggest headache. You worry, not so much of losing your job as being evicted from home.'

'Farmers always say they can't do without them, but that's a load of old codswallop. It's all very well saying they're worth an extra three quid a week, but who would have one for three pounds? The worst of it comes to old people – when you retire, what's going to happen then? If they say they want the cottage they can have you out. The Bench are all their friends. That's one thing we should fight for, to have the tied cottage cases in another area where the farmers haven't got any friends. Open-air life won't keep me when I'm old.'

Nevertheless two-thirds of the workers wished to retain the tied-cottage system in some form and a half did not want any change at all. The most important reason for allowing the system to remain unaltered was that no alternatives were believed to be viable (41·4 per cent), that it was essential for farmers (26·3 per cent) and that it was rent-free (22·2 per cent). Support for the tied cottage appears therefore to be of a somewhat negative kind – the lack of anything perceived to be better – rather than a positive support for their employers' justification, that it is an essential aspect of agriculture. There are, however, interesting variations in responses among the workers interviewed. Those workers who actually live in tied cottages, for example, were both more likely to want changes in the system and want outright abolition of the tied cottage than those workers who were not living in tied housing. In fact a majority of workers living in tied housing wanted changes (54·2 per cent) while only a minority (42·7 per cent) of those *not* in tied accommodation did so. While only a minority in all types of accommodation wished to see the system abolished the proportion was higher among tied-cottage tenants (32·6

per cent) than those living elsewhere (25·8 per cent). Actual experience of tied housing therefore appears to produce a greater antipathy
towards it.

Because fewer workers on the small farms live in tied cottages, and
because their contact with their employer at work is much closer, one
might expect greater support for the system among these workers
than among those on the larger, more impersonally organized farms.
However, as Table 26 shows, this is not the case. For the purposes of

Table 26 Attitude to tied cottage by mode of control of farms of workers
interviewed in Suffolk, 1972

	Mode of control			
	Patriarchal		Bureaucratic	
	No.	%	No.	%
No change	47	45·6	70	53·9
Change	56	54·4	60	46·1
Total	103	100·0	130	100·0
No abolition	68	66·1	96	73·8
Abolition	35	33·9	34	26·2
Total	103	100·0	130	100·0

this analysis the farms were divided, according to the nature of the
work situation described in Chapter 2, between those where there
was no intervening level of authority between farmer and worker –
'patriarchal' – and those where there were one and more levels of
authority between employer and employee – termed 'bureaucratic'.
(This is in fact a better predictor of frequency of contact between
workers and their employers than size of labour force *per se*.)[77] On
those farms where there was more extensive contact between farmer
and worker there was a slight but significantly greater likelihood of
the respondent wishing to change the tied-cottage system; on the
more impersonally organized farms, however, the distribution was
reversed: a majority of the workers on these farms wished to see no
changes in the system. Moreover, this pattern also emerged over the
question of abolition – a higher percentage on the 'patriarchal' farms

wished to abolish tied cottages altogether than those employed on the more 'bureaucratic' farms. This was an unexpected finding and, furthermore, the association stood when controls were made for age, length of service in agriculture and total size of labour force.

One plausible explanation of why workers on the 'patriarchal' farms should be more hostile to the tied cottage is that the living conditions of these tied-cottage tenants on these farms are inferior to those elsewhere. There is some evidence to suggest that larger farms provide better housing conditions for their workers[78] and, although the evidence is only impressionistic, this was confirmed during the period of fieldwork in Suffolk. Almost invariably those cottages with a poor standard of amenities were on the small farms, while the large farming companies provided accommodation at least equal, and often superior, to local-authority housing. Although there is some validity in this explanation, however, the fact that evidence from elsewhere in the survey shows that workers on smaller farms are less instrumental and less motivated by their level of material rewards suggests that instrumentalism alone is not sufficient. Instead it is necessary to turn to the reasons given by those workers who wished to retain the status quo in order to provide some enlightenment on this question. These are presented in Table 27, again broken down by organizational mode of control, with 'don't knows' excluded. The table shows that while

Table 27 Reasons for wanting no change in the tied-cottage system by mode of control of farms, of workers interviewed in Suffolk, 1972

| | Mode of control | | | | | |
| | Patriarchal | | Bureaucratic | | All farms | |
	No.	%	No.	%	No.	%
Rent free	4	10·0	18	30·5	22	22·2
Essential for farmers	16	40·0	10	16·9	26	26·3
Lack of alternative	17	42·5	24	40·7	41	41·4
Other	3	7·5	7	11·9	10	10·1
Total	40	100·0	59	100·0	99	100·0

the major reason for not wanting any change in the tied-cottage system – lack of alternatives – is virtually constant across all farms, there is an association between the organizational structure of the farm and the two other main reasons given. On the 'bureaucratic' farms the workers are more likely to justify the tied cottage on instrumental grounds, but on the 'patriarchal' farms the farmers' own point of view is much more likely to be echoed by the workers – indeed the association is even stronger when supervisory workers are excluded, since eight of the ten replies on the 'bureaucratic' farms which concerned the importance of the system for farmers came from foremen and managers, who might be expected to be closer to their employers' viewpoint.

Workers on farms where there is greater contact between employers and employees are therefore polarized in their attitudes towards the tied cottage. They are more likely than the sample as a whole to desire both changes in the system and complete abolition; but they are also more likely to identify with their employers' own justification of it. It does not seem implausible to conclude that these two attitudes are in fact linked together. Precisely because workers on the 'patriarchal' farms have been more thoroughly exposed to the vindication of the tied cottage in terms of its vitally essential role in agriculture, some of them have followed through the logic of the argument in the light of their own circumstances. That is to say that particularly on the smaller farms some of the workers are under no illusions about the importance of their own house to their employer, with the corollary that the farmer will require possession should the worker for any reason leave his employment, including retirement, ill-health or accident. It is also recognized that because these farms have a smaller housing stock there will be less room to manoeuvre. These workers therefore have both greater understanding of farmers' housing requirements *and*, in some cases perhaps because of this, a greater antipathy to their viewpoint.

It seems that over the tied cottage, almost uniquely in agricultural labour relations, the more pervasive contact between farmer and worker reinforces rather than obscures any conflict of interest between them. It is probably not coincidental that because it is a payment in kind it is a reward whose level cannot be assigned to an impersonal abstraction like the market, but which is the direct and irrevocable personal responsibility of the employer. There is no doubt that many farmers attempt to operate the system with as much humanity as possible, but even this must give way to economic necessity and it is the employee who consequently suffers. Individual farmers are not always aware of the suffering they, often inadvertently, cause. For example, during an interview on one farm in Suffolk, one of the workers suddenly collapsed and died of a heart attack. The solicitous employer informed the widow the following day that there was 'no hurry' to move out of the house. The farmer, who needed the house for another potential employee, obviously believed he was making a humane concession; the widow (and the other workers on the farm) believed he was callous to remind her of her insecurity at such a moment. The farmer's good intentions are not at issue here, merely that he had an ultimate interest to pursue which unconsciously determined his reaction to the situation. The majority of farm workers would not deny that interest, but equally they recognize their own interest in the provision of housing for themselves and their families. Because the tied cottage places this directly under the aegis of the farmer, rather than with a third party, as in the case of wages, the conflict of interest is particularly acute. Many farm workers are aware of this conflict, but simply leave it at that, and, unable to conceive of a way out of this dilemma, prefer to live with it and leave things as they are.

Traditionalism and the Labour Market

One of the conclusions which emerges from a review of the agricultural worker's market situation is the extent to which his life-chances are constrained by the traditional nature of the regulation of employer–employee relationships. The lack of occupational mobility, the intense localism – amounting in many cases to a literal parochialism – the particularistic nature of hiring practices, all contribute to the traditionalism of the disciplines and controls with which farm workers are faced in their market situation. This emphasis on traditionalism, however, is not an endorsement of the customary view of the countryside as involving an *unchanging* continuity of belief and custom. Although certain aspects of the agricultural worker's position are 'traditional' in this sense, being familiar to successive generations of workers on the land – poverty, the lack of alternative employment opportunities, the low level of pay and conditions compared with industrial workers – the concept of traditionalism is employed here to describe the way in which changes in the context of employer–employee relationships are interpreted to and by most farm workers, and the way in which that relationship is itself structured. Within the market situation ascription and particularism are particularly prevalent – indeed one could argue that it is only because overlapping work and non-work roles are so heavily ascribed that the hierarchical nature of rural society can become stabilized through traditional modes of control.[79]

These ascriptive qualities are, for example, reflected in a strong father-to-son tradition on the land – among those workers interviewed, more than two-thirds (67·4 per cent) were from agricultural backgrounds, and only 8·5 per cent were the sons of farmers.[80] Taken with the extremely limited extent (though not necessarily amount) of geographical mobility referred to earlier in this chapter and the high average length of service of farm workers, it is not surprising that employer–employee relationships are regulated as much by custom and habit as by instrumentalism. Because of these conditions traditionalism moulds the operation of the labour market in a variety of ways. This is not necessarily positively sought by farm workers, however, and indeed inter-generational continuity appears to be declining, for only 38 per cent of the *sons* of the workers interviewed who were in employment were working on the land.[81] The fact that this was still higher than the proportion who said they would recommend a job in agriculture to their sons (26·5 per cent) suggests that lack of alternatives rather than pre-adult socialization is responsible for this 'tradition' in many cases.

In general, family ties were strongly embedded in an agricultural milieu. The minority of workers whose fathers were not employed as agricultural workers tended to come from backgrounds connected with associated service industries, the most numerous being carpenters (3·6 per cent), general labourers (3·1 per cent), blacksmiths (2·7 per cent) and food-processing workers (1·8 per cent). Downward mobility was fairly common – 18·8 per cent were the sons of self-employed and/or non-manual workers, including farmers – although much of this reflected the disappearance of the independent rural craftsman, such as the blacksmith, wheelwright, etc. (On the other hand, three respondents could only be described as middle-class drop-outs, attracted into agriculture by the simple, idyllic life removed from the urban rat-race.) The strength of family ties with agriculture also extended to the occupations of brothers (46 per cent engaged in agriculture) and to the background of the respondents' wives (57·3 per cent were the daughters of farm workers). These findings merely repeat a pattern of relative self-containment found by other investigators. For example, Bessell, in a national survey of young workers, showed the importance of family background in occupational choice. Nearly 42 per cent of his respondents stated that familial factors had been influential in their decision to work on the land. Moreover, these factors were also significant in determining the young workers' intentions to remain in agriculture rather than leave after a few years' experience for a job elsewhere.[82] However, the family was a comparatively weak influence in East Anglia and this would support the impression that what is handed down from father to son is, in many cases, the conviction that the son would do better to look elsewhere if possible.[83] The constraints of the labour market nevertheless dictate what is possible and feasible and often the choice is between a job on the land – at least in the short term – and no job at all.

Until recently this situation has enabled agriculture to recruit far more than its share of school-leavers on to the land, and, although in the last ten years agriculture's share of school-leavers has declined, it is still nearly double the number that can expect to remain on the land until retirement. Heath and Whitby, in their analysis of the changing rate of recruitment in agriculture,[84] show that the recent decline can be attributed to the gradual deterioration in relative earnings of agricultural youths compared with industrial youths during the late 1960s. Nevertheless they show that agricultural youths' earnings were 89 per cent of industrial youths' earnings, whereas adult earnings in agriculture were less than 70 per cent. The relative position deteriorates as agricultural workers enter their twenties, at precisely the period when they take on commitments of a home and family of their own, and it is from this age-group that labour outflow is most pronounced. However, Heath and Whitby also indicate that much of this excess recruitment occurs because agriculture provides a stop-gap until other opportunities are opened up, notably, as Bessell points out, in motor transport.[85] Once again, therefore, the constraints on employment opportunities define the peculiar structure of the agricultural labour force. The gradual fall in recruitment since 1964, though still not sufficient to bring about an absolute decline without wastage, is nevertheless creating an ageing labour force. Nationally, one-third of farm workers are within twenty years of retirement, and in East Anglia – the region which, as was pointed out earlier in this chapter, contains the highest proportion of recruits planning to leave within five years – the proportion over the age of forty-five is nearly one-half.[86] In the sample interviewed in Suffolk, almost 40 per cent were from this age-group. A recent national survey showed that large, arable farms had workers with a higher average age than smaller, predominantly livestock farms,[87] so that a picture begins to emerge of the general farm worker who has been in agriculture since an age in which he was accustomed to hand labour and working with horses rather than with tractors and machinery. His chances of finding alternative employment in view of his age, lack of experience of non-farm jobs and his housing situation are extremely slim. Most of these workers will therefore stay on their present farm until they retire, hemmed in by these constraints. These workers are particularly significant in East Anglia, where they may form more than half of the total labour force.

There are often built-in disadvantages in rural areas which impede schoolchildren and students from obtaining the kind of qualifications which aid labour mobility. Rural schools have generally poorer facilities compared with many of those in towns, while access to further education, especially vocational training, is often restricted by the absence of near-by technical colleges or other centres of education.[88] In the sample interviewed in Suffolk the mean school-leaving age was 14·5 years, and only 12·4 per cent of the workers possessed any formal agricultural qualifications and/or had had formal agricultural training.[89] Attempts to introduce a formal training scheme in agriculture have until very recently been not only notoriously ineffective but regarded by most farmers with thinly veiled contempt. The initial proposals over the inception of the Agricultural Training Board, though at first agreed by the NFU hierarchy, produced a grass-roots revolt and a subsequent drastic modification of the scheme. Although many more young workers are now being trained than ever before, most farmers remain suspicious of 'paper' qualifications. As Giles and Cowie conclude after a perusal of advertisements in the farming press over a ten-year period, 'Even on the most optimistic interpretation of these figures no great comfort is provided

to those who would claim a substantial stirring of farmers' interest in
the formal further education of their workers.'[90] This pattern was
confirmed in the interviews with the Suffolk farmers. They were
asked whether they thought that the possession of formal qualifications made a man a better farm worker; 37·9 per cent believed that it
did; 60·7 per cent believed that it did not. The larger-scale farmers
and those with higher qualifications themselves were more likely to
value formal training, arguing that it made a man more interested in
his job and more competent to deal with complicated machinery.
However, those against formal training argued that farming was a
practical job which could not be learned 'from books'.

Training therefore tends to be particularistic and not conducive to
labour mobility. There seems little incentive to the agricultural
worker to undertake formal training, particularly as the large number
of small employers in agriculture allows no promotion ladder. Not
even the wages structure, although it will increase the relevance of
training, will alter this structural disincentive, although the increasing
specialization and complexity of the industry may make formal training more relevant. Like the wages structure, however, formal, universalistic training schemes strike at the very heart of the personal,
particularistic relationship between farmer and worker. They also
threaten to undermine the traditional authority of the employer,
since formalized training introduces new criteria of legitimate authority – knowledge and expertise – which may threaten the stability of
the relationship. As Black has remarked in a discussion of the farmers'
views of 'the ideal farm worker', 'farmers like to be ahead of their
men and feel that trained men will challenge or argue with them and
strain the relationship they consider proper'.[91] Most farmers, particularly those on the smaller farms where relationships with the
workers are extremely diffuse and personalized, therefore prefer to
restrict (albeit often unconsciously) their workers' access to knowledge which may jeopardize the latter's identification with their
authority on the farm. In this way the 'limited horizons', referred to
in Chapter I as being regarded as characteristic of many nineteenth-
century farm workers, are perpetuated through the work situation of
the smaller farms.

Earlier in this chapter, the particularistic nature of the labour market
in rural areas was outlined. The qualities which farmers seek in their
ideal farm worker tend not surprisingly, therefore, to revolve around

the personality of the worker rather than his skill at work. Of the Suffolk farmers interviewed, 66·2 per cent valued most of all the character of the worker and only 16·9 per cent his skill (11·3 per cent valued both equally). The characteristics most commonly mentioned as desirable were honesty, enthusiasm, conscientiousness, reliability and willingness to learn. It was apparent that the Suffolk farmers, like those interviewed by Giles and Cowie, 'decided on the type of person they are looking for and then proceed to find him'.[92] Furthermore, the market situation of the agricultural worker often enables them to do so. There are therefore strong pressures to conform in behaviour and demeanour to the stereotype of the 'ideal farm worker' as conceived by local employers. As Aronson pointed out many years ago, 'The number of farmers in a given district is comparatively small and they are personally known to one another. The whole life-history of the labourer is common knowledge and the ring of employers very nearly complete. The labourer knows that if he loses his job he will, in all probability, be forced to leave the district . . . This power might not be exercised . . . and in many cases it certainly would not be, but the very fact of its existence is sufficient to prevent any villager in employ from seeking to obtain rights or privileges which he might think would be repugnant to his employer.'[93] Because of the diffuse nature of relationships in rural localities, the farmer's authority in the labour market overlaps into other roles beyond that of employer, just as the subordinate position of the agricultural worker does not just relate to his market situation. It is quite clear that since Aronson's time the farmers' definitions of the ideal worker have altered to some extent and what was 'repugnant' to a farmer in 1914 would in many cases no longer be so today. Nevertheless the underlying structure of the market has remained remarkably resilient, despite vast changes in the work and community life of most rural areas: the number of farmers in the area meaningful as a labour market to farm workers remains very small and tightly knit, and the 'whole life-history' of local workers remains 'common knowledge'. No one would deny that the relationship has become more easy-going, but it seems that the source of this change is in the shifting attitude of the farmers rather than the workers. Few farm workers remain in doubt as to where the power to affect the situation resides.

In the official farming credo there is one method by which agricultural workers may, through thrift, hard work and some business acumen, haul themselves out of their subordinate market situation – the 'farming ladder'. There are frequent features in the farming press along the 'from rags to riches' theme involving, say, an ex-cowman who graduates through a smallholding and tenanted farm to become an owner-occupier on 5,000 acres. Closer inspection almost invariably reveals that self-help was not the only factor involved – for instance, our cowman turns out to be the grandson of a supermarket tycoon who conveniently died and bequeathed a substantial legacy at a strategic point in his heir's career; or that our cowman turns out to be a relative of a farmer; or that he has been taken under the wing of a wealthy patron and financial backer. It should be made clear that in East Anglia in particular the chances of a farm worker becoming a farm owner are on a par with winning the football pools – which indeed is the only way in which an East Anglian agricultural worker could amass sufficient capital to bid for an even modest tenancy. The 'farming ladder' remains a myth of rural revivalists. Certainly farm workers themselves have a realistic assessment of their chances of placing their feet on the first rung of the ladder and what they demand are improved pay and conditions, not 'three acres and a cow'.

Elsewhere, in upland England, where the price per acre of farmland is lower, the 'farming ladder' may have some basis in fact. However, even here one remains sceptical – the first rung of the ladder is likely to be well beyond the means of most hired workers with no kinship connections with farmers. Nalson, for example, found that in an upland area of North Staffordshire, where farms are small and comparatively cheap, only four farmers out of a total of 172 were the sons of farm workers. He concluded that 'such a ladder is not characteristic of this area. Indeed it is doubtful whether this notion of mobility within the farming industry has any basis in reality anywhere.'[94] The myth of the 'farming ladder' extending down to the farm worker has remained strong, however, and has at various times informed the decisions of Parliament, particularly around the turn of the century when rural revivalism was rampant. The result was a series of Smallholdings Acts, which empowered county councils, and later the Ministry of Agriculture through the Land Settlement Association, to purchase land and redistribute it in the form of smallholdings, giving preference to agricultural workers as tenants. The results have been disappointing: not only have the bulk of the tenants not been farm workers, but a recent Committee of Inquiry reported: 'On the whole statutory smallholdings have not provided the tenants with incomes high enough to enable them to build up sufficient capital to move to larger farms.'[95] Under the local authority scheme only fifty-five out of 15,000 tenants had succeeded in this.[96] Upward mobility into the employer class is therefore a pipe-dream in agriculture and because of the lack of large concentrations of workers within farming enterprises there are few opportunities to rise up a promotion ladder within the employed labour force either. This can only be achieved by spiralism,[97] and here again the 15 per cent or so of workers who are highly trained and have certain supervisory responsibilities provide an exception to these generalizations. Nevertheless such is the likelihood of upward mobility for the majority of agricultural workers that their life-chances are severely curtailed.

If this analysis is substantially correct, it is apparent that the traditionalistic character of the agricultural worker's market situation is not just a backward or residual aspect of his overall social situation – a sort of cultural lag. The economic organization of lowland arable agriculture is for the most part a highly rational exercise in entrepreneurial activity by farmers and landowners. The apparent paradox that certain aspects of their labour relations show the hallmarks of traditionalism is neither an oversight nor a coincidence, but derives from the social structure in which both workers and farmers are placed. From the worker's point of view he is surrounded by a circle of constraints upon his economic life-chances which contribute to his overwhelming dependence on agriculture, and even on an individual farmer, for employment. It is important to emphasize, however, that while the worker may recognize these limitations on his freedom he need not be embittered by them – he may regard them as legitimate or fatalistically accept them – and they may be mitigated by a close and harmonious relationship with his employer. This represents a source of ambiguity in the worker's perceptions of his social world that will be returned to later in this book.

Dependence may not in itself promote deference, for the 'causal sequence' between 'submission and sympathetic agreement' can vary either way.[98] But clearly farmers *do* have an interest in cultivating this conversion and in creating a stable and harmonious working relationship. Where conditions of dependency *and* personal, pervasive relationships predominate, as in many rural areas, it is likely that, other things being equal, these conditions will be more conducive to the stability of traditional authority than elsewhere. Even when farm workers do not identify with this traditional authority, their powerlessness is such that they will have little option other than to abide by it. Nor is there much evidence to suggest that these constraints are substantially weakening. On the contrary, the agricultural worker's level of earnings continues to fall further behind that of his industrial counterparts, and a greater proportion of workers are in tied housing. He remains the archetypal 'hired man'.

1. For details, see P. Self and H. Storing, *The State and the Farmer*, Allen and Unwin, 1962.
2. ibid.; J. G. S. and F. Donaldson, *Farming in Britain Today*, Penguin Books, 1972; *A Discussion of Current Politics and the Future Structure of Agriculture*, University of Newcastle, Agricultural Adjustment Unit, 1969; G. Mc-Crone, *The Economics and Subsidizing Agriculture*, Allen and Unwin, 1962.
3. D. G. Johnson, *World Agriculture in Disarray*, Fontana, 1973.
4. ibid.; J. R. Bellerby, *Agriculture and Industry: Relative Income*, Macmillan, 1956; D. Metcalf, *The Economics of Agriculture*, Penguin Books, 1969; M. Capstick, *The Economics of Agriculture*, Allen and Unwin, 1970.
5. Johnson, op. cit.; also K. Dexter, 'Some Economic Influences on Agricultural Policy', in University of Newcastle, Agricultural Adjustment Unit, op. cit.
6. Donaldson, op. cit.; Dexter, op. cit.
7. Self and Storing, op. cit. On the farming vote, see J. R. Pennock, 'The Political Power of British Agriculture', *Political Studies*, vol. 7, 1959, pp. 291–6; V. H. Benyon and J. E. Harrison, *The Political Significance of the British Agricultural Vote*, University of Exeter, Dept. of Agricultural Economics, 1962; R. W. Howarth, 'The Political Strength of British Agriculture', *Political Studies*, vol. 17, 1969, pp. 458–69.
8. Dexter, op. cit., pp. 16–17.
9. J. K. Galbraith, *The New Industrial State*, Hamish Hamilton, 1967, p. 190, cited by Dexter, op. cit., pp. 18–19.
10. See C. Bell and H. Newby, 'Capitalist Farmers in the British Class Structure', *Sociologia Ruralis*, vol. XIV, No. 1/2, 1974, pp. 86–107; Metcalf, op. cit.
11. See H. Newby, 'The Low Earnings of Agricultural Workers: A Sociological Approach', *Journal of Agricultural Economics*, vol. XXIII, no. 1, 1972, pp. 15–24.
12. See J. F. B. Goodman, 'The Definition and Analysis of Local Labour Markets: Some Empirical Problems', *British Journal of Industrial Relations*, vol. 8, 1970, pp. 179–96.
13. K. Cowling, D. Metcalf and A. J. Rayner, *Resource Structure of Agriculture: an Economic Analysis*, Pergamon, 1970, p. 85.
14. D. Robinson, 'Myths of the Local Labour Market', *Personnel*, December 1967.

15. C. Kerr, 'The Balkanization of Labour Markets', in E. W. Bakke (ed.), *Labour Mobility and Economic Opportunity*, Wiley, New York, 1954.

16. All agricultural statistics are from Ministry of Agriculture figures unless otherwise stated. The main sources are: *Agricultural Statistics*, HMSO, annually; the Ministry's *Wages and Employment Enquiry*, MAFF, annually; and *Farm Classification in England and Wales*, HMSO annually. This information has been consolidated in a number of publications, particularly *A Century of Agricultural Statistics, 1866–1966*, HMSO, 1968; *The Changing Structure of the Agricultural Labour Force in England and Wales, 1945–1965*, MAFF, 1967; *The Changing Structure of Agriculture*, HMSO, quinquenially; and *The Availability of Labour in Agriculture*, Memorandum to the Select Committee on Agriculture, 10 April 1968, MAFF.

17. *The Changing Structure of the Agricultural Labour Force . . .*, op. cit.

18. See W. F. G. Cowie and A. K. Giles, *An Inquiry into Reasons for 'The Drift from the Land'*, University of Bristol, Dept of Agricultural Economics, 1957; F. McIntosh, 'A Survey of Workers Leaving Scottish Farms', *Scottish Agricultural Economics*, vol. 22, 1972, pp. 147–52; R. Gasson, *Mobility of Farm Workers*, University of Cambridge, Dept of Land Economy, Occasional Paper No. 2, 1974.

19. K. Cowling and D. Metcalf, 'Labour Transfer from Agriculture: A Regional Analysis', *Manchester School*, vol. XXXVI, No. 1, 1968, pp. 27–48; K. Cowling, 'Agricultural Labour Supply and the Business Cycle: Some Regional Predictions', in the Economic Development Committee for Agriculture symposium, *Agricultural Manpower*, NEDO, 1969, pp. 10–17.

20. Cowling and Metcalf, op. cit., p. 45.

21. For example, Cowie and Giles, op. cit.; McIntosh, op. cit.

22. Thus Cowling (op. cit., p. 43) points out that 'even if a "push" factor is operating it need not necessarily push workers out of the agricultural labour force – they can become unemployed if the "pull" factors don't exist.' For a further critique of 'push' and 'pull' see R. C. Taylor, 'Migration and Motivation: A Study of Determinants and Types', in J. A. Jackson (ed.), *Migration*, CUP, 1969.

23. See the papers collected in W. M. Williams (ed.), *Occupational Choice*, Allen and Unwin, 1974.

24. House of Commons Select Committee on Agriculture, *Minutes of Evidence*, Session 1967–68, Q. 435, pp. 174–5.

25. See the evidence on pay in the National Board for Prices and Incomes, Report No. 25 (Cmnd 3199).

26. R. Gasson, op. cit., and 'Industry and Migration of Farm Workers', Oxford *Agrarian Studies*, vol. II, No. 2, 1973, pp. 1–20; also C. E. Bishop (ed.), *Geographic and Occupational Mobility of Rural Manpower*, OECD, Paris, 1965.

27. *Department of Employment Gazette; Annual Abstract of Statistics*, HMSO.

28. For Scottish evidence see F. McIntosh, op. cit.

29. Permanent Secretary in the Ministry of Agriculture, in evidence to the Select Committee on Agriculture, Session 1967–68, Q. 443, p. 176.

30. See *The Availability of Labour in Agriculture*, op. cit., p. 156.

31. cf. Cowie and Giles, op. cit.; McIntosh, op. cit.; M. Black, 'Agricultural

Labour in an Expanding Economy', *Journal of Agricultural Economics*, vol. 19, No. 1, 1968, pp. 59–76; Gasson (1974), op. cit.

32. In the Woodbridge Employment Exchange Area, for example, where the survey of workers was carried out, unemployment rates are consistently above the national average – see the *Structure Plan for the Ipswich Subregion. Report of the Survey: Employment*, Ipswich County Borough Council and East Suffolk County Council, 1972.

33. The above statistics in this paragraph are all from East Anglia Economic Planning Council, *East Anglia: A Study*, HMSO, 1968, and subsequent editions of their *Regional Planning Review*.

34. J. E. Bessell, *The Younger Worker in Agriculture: Projections to 1980*, NEDO, 1972, pp. 25–7; C. E. Heath and M. C. Whitby, *The Changing Agricultural Labour Force*, University of Newcastle, Agricultural Adjustment Unit, 1970, p. 51.

35. cf. the studies cited by J. H. Goldthorpe *et al.*, *The Affluent Worker: Industrial Attitudes and Behaviour*, CUP, 1968, pp. 150–51. However, this confirms Williams' findings in Ashworthy that farm workers were spatially the most mobile members of the community. See W. M. Williams, *A West Country Village: Ashworthy*, Routledge and Kegan Paul, 1964.

36. J. Littlejohn, *Westrigg*, Routledge and Kegan Paul, 1963, pp. 27–36.

37. cf. Gasson (1974), op. cit., Ch. 7, Bessell, op. cit., p. 27; McIntosh, op. cit.; Black, op. cit.

38. D. I. MacKay, D. Boddy, J. Brack, J. A. Diack and N. Jones, *Labour Markets under Different Employment Conditions*, Allen and Unwin, 1971, Ch. 7; see also R. van der Merwe and S. Miller, 'The Measurement of Labour Turnover: A Critical Appraisal and a Suggested New Approach', *Human Relations*, vol. 24, No. 3, 1971, pp. 233–53.

39. D. I. MacKay, *et al.*, op. cit., p. 169.

40. cf. R. Gasson, 'Turnover and Size of Labour Force on Farms', *Journal of Agricultural Economics*, vol. xxv, No. 2, 1974, pp. 115–27.

41. cf. MacKay *et al.*, op. cit., pp. 208–12.

42. e.g. Heath and Whitby, op. cit.; D. K. Britton, 'Agricultural Manpower: the Current Situation', in Economic Development Committee for Agriculture, op. cit., pp. 1–7; *Agricultural Manpower in England and Wales* NEDO, 1972.

43. H. R. Wagstaff, 'Recruitment and Losses of Farm Workers', *Scottish Agricultural Economics*, vol. xxi, 1971, pp. 7–16.

44. ibid., p. 13.

45. Gasson, 'Turnover and Size of Labour Force . . .', op. cit., p. 123.

46. MacKay *et al.*, op. cit., p. 206.

47. National Board for Prices and Incomes, *Report No. 25* Cmnd 3199, p. 19.

48. *Agricultural Manpower in England and Wales*, op. cit., p. 57.

49. See Self and Storing, op. cit., Ch. 7, and Ch. 4 below.

50. Moreover these questions were separated in the questionnaire – see appendix.

51. cf. Donaldson and Donaldson, op. cit., p. 29; J. R. Bellerby, 'Distribution of Farm Income in the United Kingdom, 1867–1938', in W. E. Minchin-

ton (ed.), *Essays in Agrarian History*, David and Charles, 1968, vol. II, p. 271; R. Gasson, 'Resources in Agriculture: Labour', in A. Edwards and A. Rogers, *Agricultural Resources*, Faber, 1974, p. 128.

52. Interestingly, Gasson has shown how the configuration of perquisites varies with distance from alternative employment opportunities, farmers near towns concentrating on housing, pensions and protective clothing, while those in more isolated rural areas followed more traditional types of benefit, like free vegetables and fruit. See Gasson, *The Mobility of Farm Workers*, op. cit., pp. 68–70.

53. Metcalf, op. cit., p. 118.

54. Capstick, op. cit., p. 40. See also Bellerby (1956), op. cit.

55. This argument is expanded in Newby, op. cit. See also A. Martin, 'A Comment on J. R. Bellerby's Explanation of the Level of Income in Agriculture', *Farm Economist*, vol. IX, No. 1, 1958, pp. 271–84.

56. *Farmer's Weekly*, 28 April 1972. See also A. Rosen, 'Increased Land Prices – Their Implications on the Future Structure of Agriculture', *Hampshire Harvest Review*, September 1973.

57. *Farmer's Weekly*, 9 June 1972.

58. *Farmer's Weekly*, 12 May 1972.

59. To this extent the fears of the NFU over the implementation of the wages structure, reported by Giles and Cowie in 1964, were fully justified. The NFU fought long and hard for the structure to be based on the grade of *man* rather than the job. This dispute is discussed more fully in the following chapter. See A. K. Giles and W. J. G. Cowie, *The Farm Worker: His Training, Pay and Status*, University of Bristol, Dept of Agricultural Economics, 1964, p. 25.

60. See B. Reed and C. Quine, *Freedom to Depend: A Report on a Pilot Study of Service Accommodation in Agriculture*, The Grubb Institute, 1974, pp. 3–5.

61. Figures from the National Union of Agricultural and Allied Workers' *Annual Reports*.

62. M. C. Thompson and R. Gasson, 'Do We Really Need the Tied Cottage?', *Farmer's Weekly*, 25 January 1974, pp. v–xxi.

63. Giles and Cowie have expressed this point very well: 'It is not a simple concept, this insecurity. Being in a tied cottage colours one's attitude to many of life's vicissitudes. Choice of employment becomes confined if it entails house removal as well. Illness is something to be feared more than normally because being laid off for any length of time involves the risk of being dismissed. Old age is viewed with great apprehension: retirement brings nearer the day when some alternative accommodation must be found; loss of physical strength may necessitate the abandonment of agricultural work some years before retirement, adding the task of finding other work to that of finding other accommodation. Redundancy also poses similar difficulties should it arise. The occasional news of some fellow-worker's plight under any of these vicissitudes, especially if his employer has been over-hurried in securing possession of his cottage, keeps such fears alive. Although there is little evidence that employers do use their powers of eviction either often or unfeelingly, the odd case in any district is sufficient to unsettle the workers for some time' (A. K. Giles and

W. J. G. Cowie, 'Some Social and Economic Aspects of Agricultural Workers' Accommodation', *Journal of Agricultural Economics,* vol. XIV, No. 2, 1960, p. 155). Also the same authors' *Accommodation of Agricultural Workers,* University of Bristol, Dept of Agricultural Economics, 1960, p. 26.

64. The arguments over the following two paragraphs are taken from the correspondence in *Farmer's Weekly* during 1973 and 1974.

65. The arguments over the following two paragraphs are taken from the *Land Worker,* the journal of the NUAAW, and from a number of the union's policy documents.

66. Thus even Giles and Cowie are eventually forced to abandon their data when it comes to assessing the competing arguments, since, they state, 'It is clear that both farmers and workers enjoy specific benefits from tied cottages.' It therefore becomes a matter of assessing whose benefit is the least, particularly if they are conflicting in some way. See Giles and Cowie, 'Some Social and Economic Aspects . . .', op. cit., pp. 156–7. And this in turn requires making value-judgements.

67. Compare the correspondence about the tied cottage in the *Farmer's Weekly* between 15 January and 26 March 1965 with that in the same journal during virtually the whole of 1973, particularly following the article 'House and Job' by Graham Harvey in the issue of 1 June, pp. 90–92. This article clearly sets out most of the pros and cons of the system.

68. See the report by Shelter, *Tied Accommodation,* Shelter, 1974.

69. Cowie and Giles (1960), op. cit.; P. Fletcher, 'The Agricultural Housing Problem', *Social and Economic Administration,* vol. 3, No. 3, 1969, pp. 155–66; Thompson and Gasson, op. cit.; Gasson, *Mobility of Farm Workers,* op. cit.

70. Fletcher, op. cit., p. 160.

71. ibid.

72. Thompson and Gasson, op. cit.; Gasson, *Mobility of Farm Workers,* op. cit., Ch. 8.

73. Cowie and Giles (1960), op. cit., p. 22. See their data on the advantages and disadvantages of tied cottages on pp. 19–20.

74. ibid., p. 23.

75. Fletcher, op. cit., p. 166.

76. 'On the farm' was the residual of these two categories, i.e. where the worker was living on the farm but the farm itself was situated in the centre of the village, he was coded as living 'in the village'.

77. See below, Chapter 5, for a full explanation.

78. See Thompson and Gasson, op. cit.

79. This is elaborated in the final chapter of this book and in H. Newby, 'The Deferential Dialectic', *Comparative Studies in Society and History,* vol. 17, No. 2, 1975, pp. 139–64.

80. This figure excludes those who were the sons of their present employer. All employers' relatives were excluded from the sample.

81. Even this figure is rather high compared with that reported by Gasson, *Mobility of Farm Workers,* op. cit., p. 79, in a more urbanized area.

82. Bessell, op. cit., p. 28.

83. cf. traditionalism among trawler-fishermen reported by J. Tunstall, *The Fishermen*, MacGibbon and Kee, 1962, pp. 106–7.

84. C. E. Heath and M. C. Whitby, op. cit., pp. 51–60; also Britton, op. cit.; and J. H. W. Wilder, 'The Manpower Problem', *Proceedings of the Twenty-First Oxford Farming Conference*, 1967, pp. 82–93.

85. Bessell, op. cit., p. 34.

86. R. Gasson, 'Who Will be Left on the Farm? An East Anglian Picture', unpublished paper, British Association for the Advancement of Science, 1971.

87. *Agricultural Manpower in England and Wales*, op. cit., p. 44.

88. See S. Hale, *The Idle Hill: A Prospect for Young Workers in a Rural Area*, Bedford Square Press (NCSS), 1971; Giles and Cowie, op. cit., p. 7.

89. This compares with the 9 per cent reported in the NEDO study, *Agricultural Manpower* ..., op. cit., pp. 52–3.

90. Giles and Cowie (1964), op. cit., p. 9; see also M. Black, op. cit.; cf. the particularistic training of clerks described by David Lockwood in *The Blackcoated Worker*, Allen and Unwin, 1958; and D. J. Lee, 'Very Small Firms and the Training of Engineering Craftsmen – Some Recent Findings', *British Journal of Industrial Relations*, vol. x, No. 2, 1973, pp. 240–55.

91. M. Black, op. cit., p. 69.

92. Giles and Cowie (1964), op. cit., p. 39. A *Farmer's Weekly* self-selected readers' survey at the time of the introduction of the wages structure indicated continued opposition to universalistic 'interference' in personalized wages bargaining. See 'Good Men Deserve Good Wages ...', *Farmer's Weekly*, 26 May 1972.

93. H. Aronson, *The Land and the Labourer*, Andrew Melrose, 1914, pp. 80, 161–2.

94. J. S. Nalson, *Mobility of Farm Families*, Manchester University Press, 1968, p. 120. For a similar verdict on the situation in the Fens, see H. G. Popplestone, 'Part-time Farming – The Use of Sociological Techniques', University of Cambridge, M.Sc. Thesis, 1965, p. 98.

95. Departmental Committee of Inquiry into Statutory Smallholdings, *First Report*, Cmnd 2936, para. 295.

96. *Final Report*, para. 243.

97. On spiralism see W. Watson, 'Social Mobility and Social Class in Industrial Communities', in M. Gluckman (ed.), *Closed Systems and Open Minds*, Oliver and Boyd, 1964.

98. M. Weber, *The Theory of Social and Economic Organization*, The Free Press, Gleneve, Ill., 1964, p. 327; Newby (1975), op. cit.

CHAPTER FOUR

Agricultural Trade-Unionism

The typical response of the agricultural worker to the constraints that have traditionally surrounded his market situation has been fatalistically to accept his lot and accommodate to it as best he can or to leave the land and seek employment elsewhere, often in the towns. Occasionally, however, to use a phrase employed by Arch, the worm would turn, and agricultural workers have attempted to create the conditions under which they would be able to determine their own life-chances.

As we saw in Chapter 1, such resistance was not always collectively organized nor of a self-evidently political nature. Nevertheless, along with Dunbabin, it is helpful to regard early nineteenth-century rural unrest as pre-political rather than apolitical and to interpret the contrasts between the Captain Swing riots and the 'Revolt of the Field' as a movement from 'primitive' to quasi-'modern' forms of working-class political action.[1] As Hobsbawm reminds us,[2] no country has a longer history of trade-union-like agitation among farm workers than England, but its consolidation into a sound and permanent form of modern trade-union organization is a relatively recent, twentieth-century phenomenon. Increasingly as the twentieth century has progressed the agricultural worker's protest against his conditions has become institutionalized through trade-unionism, and the pre-political activity of the rural underworld has slowly disappeared. Nevertheless joining a trade union remains a somewhat untypical activity for the farm worker; many more vote with their feet each year.

Two trade unions organize farm workers: the National Union of Agricultural and Allied Workers (NUAAW) which has a membership of around 90,000, about three-quarters of whom are farm workers; and the Transport and General Workers Union (TGWU) which has about 11,000 farm workers in its agricultural section concentrated mostly in certain areas like the north-west and Scotland. This chapter will concentrate mainly on the NUAAW, which can be considered the industrial union of agriculture, which consistently takes the lead in union activity for farm workers in England and Wales and whose stronghold has traditionally been situated in East Anglia. Like many aspects of the agricultural worker's life, rural trade-union activity is historically conditioned to a considerable extent. The history of agricultural trade-unionism during the twentieth century is believed by many union leaders to contain a number of lessons – particularly regarding the efficacy of militant action – which have been taken to heart with a vengeance, and consequently this history, or rather a particular interpretation of this history, has itself imposed constraints on contemporary agricultural trade-unionism. The Norfolk strike of 1923 (described below), for example, has dominated the thinking of the NUAAW leadership for more than fifty years on the topic of strike action in support of wage claims. At the beginning of the 1970s, as the old guard who had been active in the Norfolk strike began to fade away, so there were some signs of a more pragmatic approach towards the use of the strike weapon; yet in this as in many other areas of both NUAAW and TGWU policy it is impossible to understand present-day activity fully without reference to historical precedents.

Historical Background

As was pointed out at the end of Chapter 1, by the end of the nineteenth century the agricultural worker was left devoid of virtually any trade-union organization whatsoever. Joseph Arch was reduced to the status of a Liberal Party poodle, 'a loyal Liberal satellite', as the historians of British trade-unionism since 1889 have put it, '. . . drinking his bottle of whisky a day, but hardly opening his mouth for any other purpose'.[3] There was, therefore, no organization to protect the agricultural worker when, following the Liberal landslide victory in the General Election of 1906, many farmers took their revenge on their employees for having voted against the Tories in such large numbers. Victimization became rife as scores of men were dismissed and evicted from tied cottages on suspicion of radical views or having voted Liberal, many of them in Norfolk. A number of them turned for help to a local councillor and Liberal Party activist, George Edwards. Edwards had been active in trade-unionism in Norfolk in the 1870s and in the brief revival of 1889 had become secretary and a founder-member of the short-lived Norfolk and Norwich Amalgamated Labourers Union. After some hesitation Edwards, at the age of fifty-six, decided to establish a farm workers' union in Norfolk once more. He used his Liberal Party connections to appeal for money and help and on 20 July 1906 a conference was held in North Walsham from which emerged the Eastern Counties Agricultural Labourers' and Small Holders' Union. By the end of the year Edwards had set up fifty-seven branches, with a total membership of 1,600.[4]

There was a considerable overlap in both personnel and political style with the earlier movement of the 1870s. There was even a direct continuity between Edwards and many of the other union activists and the earlier local leadership under Banks and Arch. Edwards, like Arch, was a devout Primitive Methodist lay preacher and his autobiography is full of biblical references and metaphors. He would allow union meetings to be held on Sundays only 'on the condition that the meeting should be of a strictly religious character ... We always opened with prayer and lessons from the Scriptures were always read.'[5] The final words of his autobiography are the lines 'Labour, all labour, is noble and holy. Let thy great deeds be thy prayer to God.'[6] Consequently Edwards' political philosophy was one of moderation and conciliation. 'I can't explain it,' he wrote, 'but I always had, from the moment I took a leading part in the trade union movement, the greatest horror of a strike, and would go almost any length to prevent it.'[7]

In the early years the union was sponsored by the Liberal Party, for much the same reasons it had come to the aid of Arch. These were embodied in the founding resolution adopted at North Walsham: 'To take definite steps to form a union, the objects of which shall be to enable the labourers to secure proper representation on all local bodies and Imperial Parliament, protection from political persecution and better conditions of living.' This resolution would, as Madden observes, have served to found a radical political association rather than a trade union; a group of farm workers would have identified themselves more closely with the class which the union was designed to help and would have given more prominence to economic than political aims.[8] The creation of a trade union was a practical alternative method of organizing the rural Liberal vote, since few workers would pay subscriptions to local party associations from which they could see no tangible and immediate benefit. The first Executive Committee was therefore packed with prominent Liberals – the President and Treasurer were both Liberal M.P.s – who viewed with some alarm, along with Edwards, any sign of militancy among the rank-and-file members.

Within two years Edwards had built the membership up to 3,000, cycling over 6,000 miles a year around Norfolk in order to do so. Recruitment was relatively easily accomplished over this period, during which a fall in the real incomes of farm workers was combined with a gradual rise in farm prices. Many men wanted action to be taken over wages and conditions and a clash between political expediency and rank-and-file demands seemed inevitable. It came in 1910, when two general elections and a county-council election meant that most union officials spent more time electioneering for the Liberal Party than on trade-union business. In March there was a spontaneous strike in Trunch, a strong union village near North Walsham, and in May a more widespread strike in the village of St Faith's. The St Faith's dispute marked a significant step in the development of the union.[9] It was long and bitterly fought, with cartloads of strike-breakers being brought in under police escort, and achieved some national notoriety. With a further General Election announced for December, many Liberals on the Executive were anxious to divert the energies of the union organizers to canvassing for Liberal support and to end the strike which was becoming an embarrassment to the party's potential voters among employers and the middle class. On the very day after Asquith had dissolved Parliament the Executive decided to negotiate privately with the farmers for a return to work on the old terms and to ballot all the union's members for their consent 'in bringing the dispute to an honourable conclusion'. This loosely phrased mandate was granted, but, after an outraged St Faith's branch had demanded a second ballot making the alternatives clearer, the membership produced a small majority in favour of continuing the strike. Unabashed, the Executive, despite Edwards' protests, proceeded to settle on any terms. The strike was declared over on 6 January 1911, more than seven months after it had started. The men returned on the old terms and more than half were left out of work, victimized by their employers. They felt betrayed by the union leadership and even Edwards could not avoid some bitterness, referring to the settlement as the Valley of Humiliation.

The defeat at St Faith's is significant because it provoked the membership to cut its ties with the Liberal Party once and for all. At the following month's annual conference at Fakenham the Liberals on the Executive were swept out of office and what amounted to a Socialist take-over ensued, regarded with some apprehension by Edwards. The contrast with a somewhat similar situation after the lock-out of 1874 could not be more complete. On that occasion a set-piece conflict which had resulted in defeat was quickly followed by the disintegration of the union. In 1911, with many of the 'primitive', millennial overtones absent from the movement towards unionization, defeat produced an increased determination to succeed. Although sixteen Norfolk branches lapsed after the St Faith's defeat, the position was soon recovered and the union began to assimilate to itself all the accoutrements of political modernity. In 1912, its name was changed (somewhat pretentiously in view of the location of its membership) to the National Agricultural Labourers' and Rural Workers' Union (NALRWU). It registered as an Approved Society under the Health Insurance Act of 1911, the state not for the last time providing a stimulus to recruitment. Edwards retired through ill-health in 1913 and his successor, R. B. Walker, ushered in a more secular and radical style of leadership. Madden sums up the contrast well. '[Edward's] annual reports which always started with "Brethren" betrayed the author's close acquaintance with St Paul's epistles to the struggling early Christian churches. In these messages Edwards staked his faith in the triumph of the farm workers' cause through righteousness. His successor, who addressed his auditors as "Comrades", preferred the inevitable outcome of the class struggle.'[10] Certainly Walker's views were more 'advanced' than those of the majority of the membership, and probably of the Executive too, but this did not prevent him from quickly establishing his own authority over the direction in which union policy was moving.

In the meantime, the most successful area of union expansion was in Lancashire, where, by the beginning of 1913, 2,500 members had been enrolled. The centre of recruitment was the countryside around Ormskirk, which specialized in dairying, poultry and market gardening, a contrast with the arable/beef concentration in Norfolk, but, significantly, types of farming in which the cessation of work would have an immediate impact. The rate in south-west Lancashire, on the fringes of the industrial areas, was £1 per week, compared with 13s.

in Norfolk, but hours were longer and the local workers were becoming increasingly dissatisfied with their pay and conditions. Following a meeting of Lancashire branch officers in March to discuss strategy, they put their demands to the local employers in May 1913, asking for a Saturday half-holiday, a minimum wage of 24s. per week, 6d. per hour overtime and recognition of the union. The Executive, 'all Norfolk men meeting in Norfolk and out of sympathy with a demand which was for nearly double Norfolk wage rates', showed little enthusiasm for any conflict. 'In view of the changes which had taken place on the Executive at the beginning of 1911 and the issue which had caused them,' Madden writes, 'it is somewhat surprising to note that its temper had not become more militant. Despite its fervent Socialists the Executive was still relying on appeals to the employers and to the government for wage negotiations just as though the Liberals had not been removed.'[11] The Executive was, however, powerless to intervene; 60 per cent of the total membership were in Lancashire and not even strike pay could be denied since funds were being raised locally from sympathetic industrial unions.

The strike began in June and was a total success, thanks largely to the co-operation of the local branch of the National Union of Railwaymen, which refused to handle any produce from the strike area. Wages were raised to £1 10s. and all the other demands were met in full. It was on the conclusion of this strike that Edwards handed over to his former assistant, Walker. Walker's first important decision was over a request by the Lancashire members to maintain their own loosely knit branch federation in existence and to pay its own organizer with the £800 left over from the strike fund. When this was exhausted, they suggested, Lancashire subscriptions should be raised by an extra threepence per week in order to maintain a full-time officer in the area. To Walker the whole idea was an outrage, an affront to the centralized constitution of the union, in which he firmly believed and which he was prepared to go to almost any lengths to maintain. The prospect of a Lancashire Federation seemed to him to threaten the centralized control of the union from Norfolk, and yet, with a majority of the membership now residing in Lancashire, Walker had little option but to order a ballot on the proposal, which was duly accepted and came into operation at the beginning of 1914.

Walker soon took steps to regain the initiative. The Federation's nominee for the post of local organizer was given notice by the

Executive and was replaced by the officer responsible for Lincolnshire
and the Midlands. The Federation immediately objected and forced a
ballot on the issue of the Executive's and their own choice, upon
which the Executive humiliatingly caved in and withdrew their
proposal. But still Walker persisted and on his suggestion a new
method of representation to the 1914 Annual General Council was
introduced 'which seems to have been designed to preserve the
hegemony of Norfolk'.[12] Changes in branch representation at the
meeting were based upon the outdated 1912 records, which ignored
Lancashire's subsequent recruits, despite the fact that by the end of
1913 more than 70 per cent of the membership was in Lancashire. Of
the sixty-nine representatives, Norfolk sent forty-one, and as an
additional anomaly the new Executive was elected by this assembly.
Not surprisingly the Lancashire members were disgusted by what
they believed to be a cheap trick, and after some angry correspondence
the Federation organizer was dismissed and had by June 1914 carried
most of the Lancashire membership into a new organization, the
Farm and Dairy Workers' Union.

In many other years this move would have destroyed the
NALRWU but fortunately 1914 was a year which matched 1872 as
one in which a spontaneous 'explosion' of rural unrest erupted all
over the country. During 1914 strikes took place in Essex at Helions
Bumpstead, Steeple Bumpstead and other surrounding villages, and
in several areas of Norfolk, including Trunch again, Flitcham on the
Sandringham Estate (a notable success which led to demands elsewhere for 'the King's money and the King's conditions', and to the
publication of the union's first journal, *The Labourer*) and the Burston
School strike. Other strikes took place in Wiltshire, Cheshire, Lancashire, Kent, Northamptonshire, Oxfordshire, Bedfordshire, Herefordshire, Gloucestershire and Somerset.[13] Nearly all of them were
successful, farmers generally being willing to concede demands on
the basis of growing prosperity in agriculture and a slowly tightening
labour market.

By 1914 the NALRWU was not the only union organizing farm
workers, however. Following a short-lived experiment in 1899,[14] in
1912 the Workers' Union, an urban-based general industrial union,
began seriously to recruit agricultural workers, concentrating in an
area around Herefordshire and Shropshire, which was organized by
Sidney Box, a former Liberal Party agent. Later in the year a small

Midlands agricultural union, formed by Robert Hornagold, merged with the Workers' Union, which then proceeded to extend its recruitment to Yorkshire, East Anglia and the Home Counties. Within a year the Workers' Union had established 150 branches in fourteen counties and the union began to consider seriously a confrontation with the farmers on the question of wages and conditions. The demands were moderately formulated and presented, but the leaders believed that the standard of living of their members could not be adequately raised without ignoring the widely varying conditions of different districts, and the conflicting priorities of the workers' own intentions. 'The solution,' writes Hyman, 'was to adopt a policy of decentralization: the labourers in each area were left to formulate their own demands, with the assistance of union organizers, in the light of local conditions and local needs.'[15] This policy was the complete reverse of that of the NALRWU.

During 1914 significant gains were made in both wages and membership and Green estimates that in this year the Workers' Union contained 5,000 agricultural members.[16] This early success was no doubt due to the fact that employers had 'shown a more conciliatory spirit than in times past ... There are indications that the Farmers' Union may be prepared to discuss a schedule of rates of wages and code of rules for the labourers'.[17] But as the year wore on, the employers became more resolute and by August 'the general pattern was that members in some counties were already on strike ... while others were preparing for a future confrontation'.[18] Both sides seemed to be girding themselves for the kind of winner-takes-all combat which had occurred in 1874. Then, on 4 August, came the outbreak of war.

In common with all other union leaders, those in agriculture were faced with a choice between class and country. Edwards, whose health was restored and was again doing organizing work, decided 'to put ... the nation's interest before any other consideration' and in a letter to the *Eastern Daily Press* he appealed to 'the working women of Norfolk, the wives and mothers and sisters of our brave boys'[19] to take up land work as part of the war effort. To Walker, this smacked of an open invitation to farmers to undermine the union's negotiating position by importing non-union labour to alleviate the labour shortage on farms. Walker and Edwards quarrelled and Edwards resigned his organizing duties. The Workers' Union, as part of the general industrial truce, allowed its wage claims to drop and existing disputes were quickly settled. With a virtual moratorium on industrial conflict, farm workers found other means of escape from their intolerable conditions. Within a year, an astonishing 243,000 farm workers had joined the Services and by the end of the war this figure had risen to 400,000, of which 250,000 were volunteers.[20] Inevitably these included many union members and activists, and in East Anglia 'practically in every village the great bulk of the young men have joined the Army. In this way we have for the time being lost nearly all our active and energetic members'.[21] According to Madden's estimates the NALRWU lost nearly one-quarter of its members between 1914 and 1916, and in the Workers' Union the extent of the collapse was even more striking.[22] From 250 agricultural branches in 1914, there were less than 40 by 1916. Both unions were thus too weak to press for any general increase in wages, despite the rapid advance in the cost of living. Labour shortages helped to propel wage rates upwards, but, at a time when farmers were making abnormal profits, the conditions for farm workers were deteriorating rapidly. The Parliamentary Secretary to the Board of Agriculture estimated in 1916 that since the outbreak of war agricultural wages had risen on average at only half the rate of the cost of living.

The fortunes of agricultural trade-unionism were revived by purely external factors. In a few months German submarines provided a bigger boost to trade-unionism on the land than more than eighty years of indigenous agitation since the Tolpuddle Martyrs. The effects of their blockade in 1916 led the government to act decisively upon its wartime preoccupation with increasing domestic food production. In February 1917 Lloyd George announced a new policy designed to induce farmers to bring more land under the plough by guaranteeing cereal prices for six years. As a *quid pro quo* to the unions, he also promised to establish a statutory minimum wage in the industry, to be negotiated through Central and District Wages Boards. Under the shadow of the submarine menace, the government therefore implemented a policy first mooted under similar circumstances in 1796. Following the collapse of trade-unionism in 1896 it had frequently been demanded by liberal sympathizers, and in 1909 both agricultural trade-unionists and the TUC had demanded that agriculture be included in the Trades Board Act which regulated pay and conditions in the 'sweated' industries. On that occasion the government had turned the idea down on the grounds that it entailed a change of precedent due to the extension of the Act into an industry of predominantly male employment. Private members' Bills also failed in 1913 and 1916, despite receiving support from both some Liberal and Conservative M.P.s. The NALRWU leadership, and Edwards in particular, had campaigned unceasingly for the establishment of an Agricultural Wages Board, having soon realized that without some institutionalized form of collective bargaining the chances of improving the conditions of an isolated and scattered labour force by unionization alone were extremely slender. Despite disappointment at the initial minimum wage of 25s.,[23] Edwards could therefore justifiably rejoice at the achievement of something which he had been striving to obtain for over forty years.[24]

The Corn Production Act became law in August 1917. It set up a Central Wages Board, consisting of sixteen representatives of the workers, sixteen employers and seven neutral 'appointed' members, who were to arbitrate if no agreement could otherwise be achieved. As well as the appointed members, half the employer and employee representatives were nominated by the government and approved by the Minister of Agriculture. The Board set up District Wage Committees for England and Wales, and left each side to select their own representatives on them. Separate machinery was set up to cover Scotland, where a separate union, the Scottish Farm Servants' Union, existed, led by Joe Duncan. Conditions in Scotland were frequently very different from those in England and Wales and neither the NALRWU nor the Workers' Union recruited members there.

Of the eight elected union representatives on the Central Wage Board, six were from the NALRWU and two – John Beard and George Dallas – from the Workers' Union, reflecting their relative strengths in the country. There were bitter arguments between Walker and Dallas over the composition of the District Wages Committees, with many disputes requiring the intervention of the appointed members, and equally vehement disputes over policy within the NALRWU, especially between Walker and Edwards. Edwards was not an elected union representative, but appointed by the Minister following his exclusion from the NALRWU six. Walker, in keeping with his policy of centralization, disliked the whole idea of district committees and sought wherever possible to direct uniform agreements from the central board; Edwards preferred local agreements, locally negotiated, with the function of the Central Wages Board to be merely that of ratification. A dispute soon arose along these lines concerning overtime rates. For three months the workers' side fought for a simplified system against the resistance of the farmers, who were supported by Edwards. 'In taking up this attitude,' Madden observes,[25] 'Edwards was being consistent with earlier views expressed at General Council meetings but he was acting contrary to the decision arrived at by the workers' representatives, whose meetings he ignored. Part of his attitude would appear to be his distaste for the notion that a meeting in London could override agreed decisions of Norfolk men concerning Norfolk matters, but in addition, he found it easier to oppose Walker than to support him.'[26] The two men were indeed diametrically opposed in temperament and outlook and their relationship had not been improved by an early skirmish on the Board over the implementation of an agreed Saturday half-day, over which Walker had accused Edwards of 'joining hands with the farmers to defraud the men'.[27]

The establishment of a state-sponsored negotiating machinery suddenly made unionization relevant to the individual farm worker. As the price of wheat rose, so did the farm worker's wage, and so did the membership of the unions.[28] The Corn Production Act transformed what was, despite its title, a small regional organization into a genuinely national union. Even as late as 1913, the existence of the N A L R W U was unknown to as eminent an observer of the agricultural scene as Sir Daniel Hall, who was moreover by no means unsympathetic to the existence of trade unions on the land.[29] But in the four years between 1916 and 1920 membership grew from less than 4,000 to 93,000 and Hyman estimates that in addition the Workers' Union had by then achieved an agricultural membership of 120,000,[30] reinforced in 1918 by the amalgamation of the Farm and Dairy Workers' Union, the former Lancashire Federation which had broken with the N A L R W U in 1914. These were heady days for the union leaders. The end of the war did little to remove labour shortages and significant advances were made in wages, together with a reduction of hours. Although the earlier awards were merely catching up lost ground, by 1920 wage rises had overtaken increases in the cost of living since 1914 and had also risen faster than average rates in industry. All this was achieved with little resort to the threat of strike action, since farmers were prospering, too. Furthermore the Agriculture Act of 1920 continued the provisions of the Corn Production Act, including the guaranteed prices, wages boards and the minimum wage. As if to set the seal on its success, in 1920 the NALRWU changed its name to the National Union of Agricultural Workers (NUAW).

In keeping with their new nationally recognized status, leaders of both unions found themselves being increasingly drawn into wider issues of agricultural politics than merely minimum-wage legislation. Wartime conditions had revived agriculture as a major topic of political controversy and both unions necessarily became involved, both on their own account and through the Labour Party, in the formulation of policy over such matters as smallholdings and allotments, the abolition of the tied cottage, the implementation of a rural public-housing programme, free trade and the level and extent of state support for agriculture under postwar conditions. In July 1919 the government announced a Royal Commission 'to inquire into the economic prospects of the agricultural industry in Great Britain', which was to include union representatives – Walker and W. R. Smith, the NALRWU's President, Dallas from the Workers' Union, Duncan from the SFSU and the Radical author F. E. Green, who was also active in the Workers' Union. The government demanded an interim report on the question of guaranteed prices by the end of September, but the Commission was hopelessly divided on the question: of the twenty-three Commissioners, twelve signed a majority report recommending their continuation, and the remaining eleven in a minority report favoured an abandonment of guarantees.[31] No final report was ever produced, the government dissolving the Commission when it began to consider the politically sensitive issue of land tenure at the beginning of 1920. The minority report, with its proposal for the abolition of price guarantees, was vehemently supported by all the union representatives, who were equally vigorous in their attacks on the government for accepting the majority report and pressing ahead with the passing of the 1920 Agriculture Act. The Workers' Union journal referred to the Commission as the government's 'tame creature', and the NUAW's President, Smith, opposed the Agriculture Bill in Parliament.[32]

Within six months the government took the farm workers' representatives – and, it should be added, the National Farmers' Union – at

their word, and in June 1921 announced its intention of repealing the
Agriculture Act, abolishing both price guarantees and minimum-
wage control. Thus passed into farming folklore what both farmers
and farm workers have regarded as the 'great betrayal' of British
agriculture by conniving urban politicians. But as Madden wryly
points out, 'The government, which six months earlier had legislated
the main recommendations of the majority report, was now extending the same courtesy to the minority report by abolishing both
ceilings and guarantees, cultivation powers and husbandry standards.'[33] It was not altruism which provoked the reversal of policy,
however, so much as the fact that, with the armistice having freed
shipping and allowed increased cereal production once more in North
America, the price guarantees were for the first time going to cost
money. Within a few days of the government's announcement, and
well before the Corn Production Acts Repeal Bill was presented to
Parliament, the employers' side of the Wages Board served notice on
what the probable effects of the new situation were likely to be by
moving an immediate reduction of minimum rates (from 46s. to
40s.) in all counties. Despite union resistance, an appointed members'
amendment was carried to give a general reduction of 6s., subject to
a minimum of 42s. The new rates came into effect in September 1921,
just before the Wages Board ceased to exist.

As a sop to Labour Party protests, the government agreed to try to
set up voluntary Conciliation Committees, area bodies composed of
farmers' and workers' representatives under a neutral chairman. The
committees could agree on minimum rates for their areas and submit
their recommendations to the Minister of Agriculture for confirmation, upon which the rate would become implied terms in the
workers' contracts of employment in the district. A worker could
then enforce the proper rate through the civil courts. But as Groves
rightly states, 'The Conciliation Committees were useless . . . Being
voluntary, no one was obliged to set them up; if set up, the committees were under no obligation to reach an agreement; and if they
reached one, under no obligation to submit it to the Minister for
confirmation. In the first year's working of this scheme only seven
committees submitted agreements . . . out of sixty-three committees
set up . . . and by the end of [1923] the number had fallen to four.'[34]
The committees were unworkable and did little to stand between the
farm worker and an increasingly depressed labour market. Through-

out 1921 and 1922 agricultural prices fell heavily and rapidly – the price of wheat was halved in six months – and farmers began to contract their area of cultivation and shed labour in thousands. The unions were powerless to prevent cuts in wages and at the end of 1922 they were down to 30s., lower in real terms than the depressed level of 1914 and the rate obtained by Arch in the 1870s. Rural unionization was once again threatened: the NUAW lost three-quarters of its membership in three years and the impact on the Workers' Union was worse still. 'As a result,' writes Mejer, 'and under the depressed economic conditions generally, employers had the whip hand over the workers' interests and there was a general drift back from collective to individual bargaining.'[35] Despite the movement of its headquarters from Fakenham to London in 1918, the NUAW became once more virtually a local union based on Norfolk, so that by the end of 1921 conditions had again been created whereby Norfolk had become the test county for the whole country.

Walker soon came to regret his removal to London, since negotiations in Norfolk were in the hands of a conciliatory district organizer, Sam Peel. In the latter half of 1921 and at the beginning of 1922, Peel was defying his Executive and signing agreements with local farmers which were not only unacceptable to the Executive but which it was powerless to prevent becoming the national norm. Peel, however, had the agreement of the Norfolk County Committee and was mindful of 40 per cent of his local members being unemployed. In January 1922, the Norfolk farmers suggested a wage of 28s. and Walker characteristically attempted to regain centralized control and outflank Peel by ordering a ballot of the Norfolk membership. The Norfolk members rejected the offer by a seven-to-one majority and Walker prepared to serve strike notices on the Norfolk employers. With this in mind, he made an effort to obtain the co-operation of the Norfolk County Committee, only to discover that Peel, on their behalf, had been continuing negotiations and was on the point of signing an agreement on the basis of 30s. for 50½ hours. There was little Walker could do, since Peel was a lay member who could not be directed or dismissed, as could organizers elsewhere. Walker reported another defeat to his Executive, who proceeded to pass a motion condemning the union representatives on the Norfolk Conciliation Committee and calling for their resignations. This motion was circulated to all Norfolk members before the next meeting of the Norfolk County

Committee, whereupon the Conciliation Committee representatives resigned as requested.

The manoeuvre of sending out the circular requesting the resignations to all branches before informing the County Committee was bitterly resented by the Norfolk union leaders and was raised at the Biennial Conference in June. Peel, who was there as a Norfolk delegate, giving some indication of where rank-and-file support lay, accused Walker of trying to discredit the conciliation machinery. He was supported by a fellow Norfolk delegate, a farming journalist named Edwin Gooch, who 'thought the Union should continue along the lines of conciliation, because they would get better terms than by uttering threats against the farmers'. Walker replied that 'if the Union decided at any time that the Committees were a force or a failure, it would have no greater supporter than [myself]'. Madden believes that Peel was probably correct in trying to avoid a strike, since, according to his estimates, the membership in Norfolk had fallen by over 6,000 (out of 17,000) between the harvest of 1921 and February 1922. 'This was hardly the situation in which to call a strike.'[36] But underlying the dispute between Walker and Peel, there was the familiar issue of centralization versus regionalism and the pique of Norfolk members over the move to London. Walker's eagerness to cause the breakdown of the conciliators' machinery was certainly motivated by his long-standing concern to retain centralized control and a fear that it would delay any possible return to a Wages Board. This, for Walker, was 'the only solution' to the plight of the farm worker and if his subversion of conciliation allowed the writ of the NFU to run untramelled by contrary argument, this was a risk he was prepared to take.

In July 1922, Peel resigned as Norfolk organizer, having accepted the presidency of a newly formed National Union of Landworkers, a breakaway union under the aegis of the New Agricultural Party, which had been launched by farmers and landowners with the object of returning M.P.s pledged to the protection of British agriculture. For a time the NUAW Executive was clearly worried by the prospect of a Norfolk secession, and a vote of thanks to Peel at the next meeting of the County Committee was only narrowly defeated, 10–7, despite Peel having founded a rival organization, and despite the attendance of Smith and Walker. Shortly before, George Edwards, now seventy-two years old, but retaining an immense prestige in Norfolk, had issued an impassioned appeal to 'Stick to the Union that has stood by you'.[37] It seems that Edwards had managed to sway what was clearly a crucial meeting; and the unity of the NUAW was maintained.

In October the Norfolk farmers offered 25s. for 50 hours to operate over the winter months. The NUAW representatives, now under Edwards, walked out of negotiations, but this did not prevent 25s. becoming generally operative throughout Norfolk at the end of 1922. In February 1923, the employers requested a new meeting and proposed to cut wages further, with various configurations of pay and hours, the final one being 24s. 9d. for a 54-hour week. This was expressed as 5½d. per hour, with the implication that farmers would renege on a guaranteed weekly wage and deduct 'wet time', bringing wages down to 18s. per week or less. This pushed the union beyond endurance and a strike was called. It was recognized by both sides as a test battle and Groves argues convincingly that the farmers' move was deliberately designed to create a situation which might bring government action to help agriculture. Indeed the first response was a joint farmers' and workers' deputation to 10 Downing Street, but to no avail. The Executive then moved quickly to control affairs in Norfolk. A strike committee of national and local leaders was set up, and Jim Lunnon, the national organizing secretary, was despatched to Norwich to take charge. There was a brief period of 'phoney war' during which attempts were made to reach an agreement, but they were a failure, and on Saturday, 24 March 1923, the strike began in earnest.

The NUAW Executive wisely decided to concentrate its effort in one area only, north and west Norfolk, where it possessed its greatest strength. Those members in south and east Norfolk, and in Shropshire and Lincolnshire where sympathy strikes were threatened, were told to stay at work in order not to dissipate the strength of the union. The significance of the strike was in any case recognized by both sides and went far beyond its narrow geographical confines. Groves, in his inimitable style, summarizes the position well: 'It was the farm workers' biggest battle since the great lock-out of 1873. To farmers and farm workers throughout the country it was a trial of strength: what happened in Norfolk could help decide what would happen elsewhere. The downward fall of wages would be checked or intensified by the outcome of the dispute. And more – its effects on outside opinion, and on the Government were important to both sides. The farmers wanted help for agriculture: the farm workers wanted State regulation of hours and wages. Much – very much – depended upon this fight in Norfolk.'[38]

Lunnon, 'sitting at a trestle table beneath a large engraving of John Wesley preaching in the open air',[39] organized a system of mobile pickets, who were sufficiently effective to bring in a large number of police from surrounding counties, up to 600 on one occasion. This led to lurid newspaper stories about 'war' in the Norfolk countryside, most of which were greatly exaggerated, but there seems no doubt that the dispute was in places very bitterly fought indeed. At the 'Battle of Holly Heath Farm', for example, pickets were fired upon by an irate employer. Luckily no one was injured and Groves reports, 'The men went away singing the "Red Flag" and "Onward Christian Soldiers".'[40] This mixture of bitter class conflict and Christian sense of overwhelming social injustice characterized the actions of the strike committee. Gooch, who was its treasurer, asserted 'That a country which calls itself Christian should tolerate such a state of affairs passes my comprehension ... Will the labourer win? He must and he will. The mantle of Kett and Arch has descended upon him. His sun is rising and best of all, God is on his side.'[41]

Many employers were clearly taken aback by the strength of the workers' resistance and quite soon the strike spread to Workers' Union members in Cambridgeshire and West Suffolk. However, behind their brave statements the union leaders must have been anxious about the progress of the strike. At the beginning of March, 20,000 strike notices had been sent out, but by the end of the month the largest number of pre-strike members who had actually withdrawn their labour was less than 5,000 – and this in the union's strongest area in the whole country. Moreover, the union was paying out nearly £4,000 per week in strike benefits and, despite some financial assistance from other unions, was heading fast for bankruptcy. As April progressed the financial situation was becoming perilous and there was a slow but discernible drift back to work – more than 1,000 in the second week of April alone.[42] On 9 April NFU and NUAW leaders met in Norwich, but could reach no agreement. Walker was convinced, as he later wrote, that 'the whole action of the farmers could only be explained as an attempt to force the government to give more and more concessions to the farm employers'.[43] On 9 April, however, the government fell and, with a General Election in the offing, the Labour Party leader, Ramsay MacDonald, was anxious to reassure electoral opinion by acting as peacemaker and establish that his party did not merely consist of strike leaders and agitators. Mac-Donald invited both sides to meet him at the House of Commons to discuss possible conditions for a settlement. On 18 April agreement was finally reached: there was to be a guaranteed week of 50 hours for 25s; further hours up to 54 were to be paid at a rate of 6d. per hour; above 54 hours special overtime rates applied. After some delay a further clause was added: 'There shall be no victimization.' This was interpreted by the union to mean that all strikers could have their jobs back; but the farmers' interpretation was that none of the men's jobs would be given to outsiders. The result was that hundreds of ex-strikers remained unemployed – by June 1,200 men were still out of work. This took away a great deal of the satisfaction felt by the leadership on the conclusion of the dispute. A full page of the *Land Worker*, the NUAW's journal, in July 1923, was given over to an account by Walker of how 'the farmers of this country are not to be trusted to keep agreements', but his rage was limited only to issuing vague threats about what the Labour Party would do if it won the coming election. Financially the NUAW was in no position to call the men out again, even if the enthusiasm was there to do so, and certainly the union could not afford to be seen overthrowing an agreement sanctified by no less a figure than Ramsay MacDonald (whose subsequent behaviour was not very edifying) when the NUAW would need the vigorous moral and financial support of the whole Labour movement.

For the NUAW the Norfolk dispute and its settlement were undoubtedly the most important in its whole history. It was represented as a glorious victory, and symbolically it certainly was. The line had been held at 25s. for a 50-hour week and the guaranteed week had been retained. There was to be no return to the pre-1917 horrors of casualization. It therefore marked a definite turning-point in the modern history of the farm worker's fight for better pay and conditions. But in a more immediate sense the outcome could not give rise to much optimism. In the NUAW's strongest area, only 25 per cent at a *maximum* had obeyed the union's strike call, and the union was reduced to penury. In five weeks, almost two years' worth of the total membership's subscriptions had been paid out in strike pay. The terms of the settlement provided, in all conscience, little reason for satisfaction – in real terms the union had made no progress in forty years. Added to this the leadership could do nothing other than impotently watch many strikers victimized, left homeless as well as jobless, with no option but to take this treatment lying down. And all this in a dispute which was fought half-heartedly by many Norfolk farmers, who had an eye only for government intervention. In time, the lesson drawn by those involved in the Norfolk strike – including two future presidents, Gooch and Bert Hazell – was a simple one: the future of the union lay in the establishment of a wages board and working within its statutory framework; except in the most exceptional circumstances strike action could lead only to the demoralization of the membership and the speedy self-destruction of the union.

The early history of the NUAAW has been dwelt upon in some detail, not because it represents an interesting curiosity, but because the policy issues raised in these early years have remained up until the present day. It is no exaggeration to state that the events of the years between 1906 and 1923 have dominated the philosophy of the union's leadership for the subsequent fifty years. For example, at the 1972 Biennial Conference the union's President recalled in his address the 'years in the history of our Union when membership ebbed to a very small figure, when members were having to accept wage cut after wage cut, when hours were increased not decreased ... Those who guided the destiny of this Union in those days ... "kept the faith". I am certain we have no intention of departing from the course they took.' Despite much progress since those years, the problems facing the NUAAW today bear a striking resemblance to those which faced the early pioneers.

Uppermost among these is the sheer scale of the problem involved in recruiting, organizing, servicing and, above all, retaining membership in the face of a declining labour force whose structure is hardly conducive to unionization. Agriculture had, and continues to have, more employers than any other industry in Britain, the vast majority employing only a handful of workers. This scattered and often isolated labour force presents enormous problems of organization to any union – representation in every village would mean tens of thousands of branches. A less obvious but more insidious problem, however, is the propensity of the workers not to join a trade union even when availed of the opportunity to do so. Here outright oppression and exploitation were often less of a problem to Edwards and other early pioneers than the benevolent paternalism of a personally known and trusted employer. Hence the enthusiasm of the workers for union could be raised at village meetings, only for it to be dissipated in the following days when the isolated worker was alone with his thoughts and alone to face the persuasive arguments of his employer. The face-to-face relationship of farmer and worker, as was outlined in Chapter I, provided an enduring basis to paternalism which union organizers found difficult to overcome. Even though the average labour force was much larger at the beginning of the century, most farmers were far from being remote and impersonal figures. Beard, an early Workers' Union organizer, despaired that 'whilst a successful meeting would cause many men to enrol, a few weeks later the spirit of revolt would be killed by the suggestion of the farmers, made individually to the men in the fields, that they were only paying money to create big salaries for agitators'.[44] A high turnover of membership was therefore endemic to early agricultural trade-unionism (it remains also today) and the apparently indefatigable efforts of the early organizers in putting over the message were always likely to be brought to nothing by any adverse change of circumstances. Fluctuations in membership therefore hid gross inflows and outflows often several times larger, and all this meant that large amounts of time, effort and money were required to minimize losses wherever possible. Nevertheless hard-won increases in membership were easily wiped out, as Table 28 shows. It was no coincidence that the centre of union support during the long years of retrenchment was in the eastern counties, where the larger farms and nucleated agricultural village provided a basis for the occupational and communal solidarities which could foster unionization.

It was over these organizational difficulties that an early policy had to be evolved on how best to fashion a structure for the unions which recruited an agricultural membership. The NALRWU and the Workers' Union sought differing solutions to this problem. Once Edwards' union began to have national aspirations, symbolized by the change of title in 1912, it began to adopt an increasingly centralized form of administration. Madden makes it clear that the breakaway of the Lancashire Federation in 1914 was the result of a premeditated choice on the part of the Executive, in which Walker, though instrumental, was by no means pre-eminent. It was apparent that by maintaining a high degree of centralized control, the Executive was

Table 28 Estimated[45] membership of the NUAAW, 1906–70

1906	349	1939	37,225
1907	1,580	1940	39,268
1908	3,052	1941	42,183
1909	3,133	1942	59,913
1910	3,189	1943	71,279
1911	2,753	1944	88,064
1912	2,008	1945	98,586
1913	3,546	1946	113,695
1914	4,734	1947	124,134
1915	4,145	1948	136,839
1916	3,649	1949	134,372
1917	7,678	1950	127,863
1918	40,542	1951	129,582
1919	72,696	1952	124,459
1920	93,448	1953	125,550
1921	79,067	1954	125,297
1922	35,663	1955	125,316
1923	28,804	1956	128,457
1924	22,085	1957	129,173
1925	24,190	1958	125,881
1926	24,546	1959	126,881
1927	24,021	1960	123,330
1928	24,482	1961	113,646
1929	23,246	1962	116,201
1930	23,831	1963	118,467
1931	24,301	1964	126,654
1932	22,868	1965	115,472
1933	22,524	1966	115,892
1934	23,455	1967	113,243
1935	25,291	1968	108,744
1936	26,892	1969	103,426
1937	30,962	1970	94,497
1938	35,098		

deliberately seeking to abolish regional wage differences instead of perpetuating them, and to pave the way for the national collective bargaining in which it was poised to participate. By 1914 Walker and his Executive had gained control of the initiative on wage movements. Whereas previously they had given often grudging and belated approval to grass-root wage demands, throughout the war years they made the running, spurred by an Executive Committee resolution of 1914 which, in the aftermath of the Lancashire defection, made the establishment of a nationally uniform wage the union's policy for the first time. Henceforth Walker skilfully exploited every opportunity to complete a centralized uniformity of union administration and policy, and from 1914 up to the introduction of the Wages Board the order of county wage movements indicates that the union was consolidating from the centre. Thereafter the institution of the Central Wages Board only reinforced this tendency and in the light of this Walker's hostility to the Conciliation Committee formed in 1921 is understandable.

The Workers' Union, however, adopted a completely contrary policy of decentralization. This was in part the natural outcome of its objective to become a general union, for which a federal structure was the most appropriate form in which to organize workers in diverse industries in many parts of the country; but it was also a recognition that farming conditions varied enormously between different areas, each of which would need to formulate its own demands according to what was necessary and feasible in the locality. The difference in policy also doubtless reflected a difference in motivation behind the unionization of agricultural workers in the first place. The Workers' Union remained a solidly urban-based union, whose purpose in organizing the rural labour force lay as much in the desire to prevent the dilution of industrial wage rates by the importation of cheap rural labour as it was by the plight of the farm workers themselves. The rural branches therefore tended to be regarded as peripheral outposts which were expensive in time and energy to maintain, and which could easily be lopped off when circumstances demanded a concentration of effort on the centre of union activities among its industrial membership. For this reason the decline in agricultural members between 1914 and 1918 and again in the 1920s was far more catastrophic in the Workers' Union than in the N U A W. It was in these years that the latter's policy of centralization was vindicated, for retrenchment could be controlled and limited in a way which was impossible without some centralized co-ordination. If the worst came to the worst, the NUAW could always retreat into its Norfolk heartland and retain the rump of its membership, which provided it with a firm basis for expansion again when the opportunity arose. Otherwise its membership would have been decimated and, like the Workers' Union in 1929, the NUAW would probably have been forced to seek the shelter of the Transport and General Workers' Union, leaving agricultural workers without an organization tailored to meet their own peculiar problems.

The centralization of the NUAW's administration was not without its consequential problems, however. The logic of its policy, and indeed its clearly stated aim, was to drive it willingly into the arms of a centrally organized, state-sponsored bargaining institution. This relationship could be, and was, both a loving embrace and an immovable fetter. The NUAW leadership believed that, without firmly established collective bargaining procedures, the union would lose its *raison d'être* and the trends in recruitment between 1906 and 1923 seemed to support this. This led the NUAW to give implacable support to the union leadership at times when the Board's verdicts were not to its, and its members, liking, a not infrequent occurrence, since it soon became apparent that the appointed members were paying precious little attention to the strength of each side's arguments and were basing their awards on the profitability of the industry, or, in more mundane terms, the price of a sack of wheat, a commodity whose price did not always move faster than the Index of Retail Prices.[46] The NUAW could not be seen to support the concept of a Wages Board on the one hand and then take direct action against it on the other when it received an unfavourable award. A brief allusion from the NFU as to the likely consequences to the future of the Board of abandoning agreed procedures would be sufficient to bring about the grudging acceptance of the situation.

The Workers' Union, however, had no such compunction. Its leadership, especially Dallas, had never been as enthusiastic about minimum-wage legislation as Edwards and the NUAW. Hyman writes that 'there is no evidence that the question received any serious attention within the union' and, although a supporter of the Wages Board, Dallas was not unaware of its drawbacks, stating as early as 1917 that if this machinery fell into the wrong hands the agricultural worker would be 'worse off than ever'.[47] With a lesser commitment than the NUAW, the Workers' Union was therefore not averse to by-passing the Wages Board and using direct action. Its view was explicit: the sole purpose of the statutory machinery was to set a legal minimum to protect the weakest sections of farm workers, but it was perfectly legitimate to seek higher wages by negotiation, and to use strike action in support of its demands. In some areas its semi-autonomous district organizers used these tactics successfully, for example in Lancashire, Cheshire and Northumberland in 1919. Indeed, in the north-west, local Conciliation Committees were set up which by-passed the Wages Board procedure entirely. The NUAW clearly viewed these developments with some alarm, for, when the Workers' Union planned a strike in Essex in June 1920, the local NUAW organizer, on the day before it started, issued a statement to the press urging his members not to cease work, and to abide by the Central Wages Board's decisions. Such was the commitment of the NUAW to the Wages Board that, it seems, it was prepared to commit one of the most heinous crimes in the trade-unionist's book and sabotage a fellow union's dispute. Not surprisingly conflict between the two unions was never far below the surface thereafter.

The NUAW's reluctance to engage in direct action did not just stem from its loyalty to the Wages Board, however. Its propensity to militancy was governed by a complex set of relationships between three variables – how far the objective conditions of the agricultural labour market and work situation made strike action feasible; how these conditions were *perceived* by the union leadership and their ideologies which largely governed their perceptions; and whether the rank and file was prepared to move. Events between 1906 and 1923 showed that successful strike action to raise the standard of living of farm workers was possible, but it also clearly demonstrated some of the limitations of militancy.

The nature of the production cycle and the economic structure of agriculture have always made a withdrawal of labour a somewhat less than draconian constraint on farming employers. The farm hardly suffers from an immediate cessation of work as do many manufacturing and service industries. There are long periods during the year when an arable farmer can watch his land unattended without much concern, saving money on wages and calculating, usually correctly, that he can survive for longer than his men can exist on little or no strike pay. Only at seed-time and harvest is a strike likely to embarrass him, and then it is always possible, as Arch discovered, to concede demands only to counter-attack with a lock-out once the seed was in the ground and the harvest safely gathered in. The livestock farmer, whose production cycle is far shorter, could usually manage by using family labour. Even the most militant union leaders recognized therefore that the strike weapon could be used only very selectively, principally, as their experience up to 1914 shows, to accelerate wage awards which rising agricultural prices and a tightening labour market would probably have brought about in any case. Strikes were therefore most successful against conciliatory employers not spoiling for a confrontation and usually involved such issues as the restoration of traditional regional differentials (as in Lancashire and Northumberland in 1919) or the enforcement of wage increases granted in one locality to the remainder of the district. However, both the St Faith's strike in 1911 and the Norfolk strike in 1923 showed that against determined and well-organized employers' opposition even the highest pitch of organization of which the union was capable could not guarantee a stoppage of production in the area of dispute. At the time of these disputes the total withdrawal of hired labour engaged in British agriculture would still have left a labour force equal to about one-third of the male adults, that is the farmers themselves (this proportion is now up to 45 per cent), plus a substantial number of family members and other kin who would be prepared to help out. More than half the farms (those employing the equivalent of one or less full-time worker) would be unaffected. And even in East Anglia, where there were above-average concentrations of hired workers, it was found impossible to prevent non-unionist blacklegs from being imported. Farmers quickly organized themselves to meet any strike threat, using fully the panoply of economic and, through their domination of the local Bench, coercive power that was at their disposal. Activities were co-ordinated by local Farmers' Federations and eventually the NFU, founded in Lincolnshire in 1908 as a direct response to the spread of workers' unionization in that county.[48]

The organization of farm workers therefore provoked the employers to organize themselves too, and, given the resources available to them, the NFU and local employers' organizations were consistently in a far stronger position than the corresponding workers' unions. In situations of outright confrontation, agricultural trade unions have thus been unable to combat a determined employers' resistance on their own, and have been forced to appeal for both public and trade-union support, particularly for finance. There was an ominous significance to the success of the Lancashire strike in 1913, which had been achieved only by the co-operation of the local railwaymen and, to a lesser extent, dockers. It was apparent that even in an area where agriculture had only a short production cycle an immediate impact could be achieved only by involving the support of transport unions to prevent the forward movement of produce. If strike action against hostile employers was successful only under such circumstances then the logic of the situation was for farm workers to be organized by the likes of the TGWU. But in turning down a proposed merger in 1929, the NUAW leaders doubtless had in mind the farm workers' experiences under the former Workers' Union, which had shown itself to view its rural membership as expendable during periods of difficulty. There were also important areas of potential conflict between rural and urban workers – a cheap food policy being the most obvious – which made the NUAW leadership justifiably wary of losing their identity inside such a huge urban, industrial-dominated union. Several subsequent attempts to woo the NUAAW have been fended off for much the same reasons. Nevertheless the obvious dilemma remains even today.

The circumstances under which strike action was feasible were, then, highly limited, but these constraints do not in themselves account for the complete absence of strikes in agriculture since 1923. The willingness of the union leadership to contemplate strike action also played an important part, particularly after 1914. Hyman even argues that had the NUAW been prepared to strike in 1921, as it was compelled to do in 1923, the national collapse in wage rates might have been checked. This seems highly questionable given the conditions in Norfolk and elsewhere at that time, but certainly a much stronger case can be put forward that during periods of comparative agricultural prosperity the reluctance of the leadership on occasions to sanction strikes and only be driven into open conflict by a more militant rank and file hampered the rapid improvement of wages and conditions. These comments would seem to apply to the period between 1911 and 1914 and again after the Second World War. Throughout its history it has been possible to observe within the NUAAW leadership two differing philosophies which have had implications for the readiness to engage in militant action. The first, personified in the early years by Edwards, is the tradition of non-conformist Radicalism which has long characterized the rural areas of Norfolk; the second, of which Walker was representative, was a crypto-Marxist Socialism which owed more to urban syndicalism than the radical traditions of the countryside. The former faction was generally more moderate and more conciliatory, desiring social justice and an *equitable* wage for the farm worker. The latter, although Walker was certainly no revolutionary, was more prepared to strike and far more concerned with the class struggle and the rapid achievement of a Socialist agriculture through the instrument of nationalization. The centralization of the NUAW's structure allowed the whole style of the union's activities to be governed according to which of these two ideologies its principal officers were devotees. This is not to accuse the union of being undemocratic, far from it: the Executive was not averse to giving its principal officers the occasional rap over the knuckles and neither was the Biennial Conference to the Executive, even over quite major policy decisions. However, such was the centralized control over the day-to-day running of affairs that a dominant figure – the General Secretary or the President – could usually steer both the Executive and the membership in the requisite direction. The ideological differences between the two factions could lead to quite bitter internal disputes – Edwards, for example, conspicuously omits Walker from the list of union notables thanked at the end of his autobiography – but it is to the credit of the union's democratic commitment that their sincerely held differences have never allowed one faction entirely to expunge the other.[49] In general, the moderate wing has been in the ascendancy, continuously so since 1928 when Walker resigned and the *de facto* leadership was wrested back to the Norfolk, nonconformist, radical tradition, in the person of Edwin Gooch.

These differences were discernible not only in the leadership's attitudes towards direct action, but over the question of smallholdings, which occupied a considerable amount of the early union's attention. The word 'smallholder's' was not without reason incorporated into the union's first title, and Edwards was personally very keen indeed on promoting smallholdings, calling the Smallholdings and Allotments Act 'the workmen's charter'. Walker, however, was less enthusiastic; he 'could hardly have looked with equanimity on the Union's efforts to turn the rural proletariat into individualistic petty proprietors'.[50] Smallholders were, though, prominent on the Executive, being one of the few groups with the time and, more importantly, independence to engage in union activities; and so the union retained its attachment to the smallholdings movement even though this created some confusion because of the simultaneous espousal of a more efficient (and therefore larger-scale) industry which would provide better wages and conditions. Gooch, however, was an advocate of smallholdings and so ensured that this somewhat contradictory stance remained for many years.[51] Even today the NUAAW is by no means hostile to smallholdings.

The ideological differences within the union's leadership have also often (though not always) tended to overlap with whether the personalities involved came from a rural or non-rural background. Such was the threat of victimization during these years that local branch officials were often recruited from outside agriculture – railwaymen and schoolteachers were particularly prominent. The lack of agricultural representation on the early Executives was even more pronounced, for few farmers would allow their workers the time off to attend meetings. Walker and Smith were both from urban backgrounds, with little knowledge of the intricacies of agricultural production. Up until the First World War, a policy of 'more wages and less hours' sufficed, but the union's very success in achieving a nationally recognized status as a participant in the debate over agricultural affairs propelled it to the conference table at a time when it lacked a clearly thought-out agricultural policy of its own. This seems to account for the débâcle of the 1919 Royal Commission Minority Report – 'the biggest single error of judgement on policy to be made by the leadership throughout the Union's history'.[52] All the unions' leaders were merely following the urban-based Labour Party orthodoxy of free trade, even going so far as to advocate a switch from cereals to grass, and from agricultural to non-agricultural employment on the grounds of 'relative advantage'. The conflict between a cheap food policy and its members' interests took a long time to be perceived by the NUAW, such was its leaders' attachment to Labour Party policy. They opposed a sugar-beet subsidy in 1924; they rejected a demand from Norfolk for a duty on imports of malting barley in 1926; and in 1928 the Executive attacked agricultural de-rating. This was all due to the lack of some long-overdue policy thinking inside the union beyond the immediate issue of pay and conditions, which left it 'without even a theory – much less a policy – of wage and membership movements'.[53] It was Gooch's great contribution to the NUAW's development that he provided this policy and during the 1930s convinced his Executive that the farm worker's interests were not necessarily identical with those of the industrial worker. He was also brave enough to lead his union into the political wilderness which the break with Labour policy implied. Thereafter Gooch sought common cause with the NFU on agricultural policy matters.

As far as one can judge, most rank-and-file union members shared their leaders' lack of interest in policy and preferred to consider the more immediate issues of pay and conditions. But it must be remembered that union members were only a minority of farm workers and those prepared to engage in strike action only a minority of union members. Isolated and scattered, working singly or alongside their employer, it was impossible to apply moral pressure or the threat of ostracism to many workers in other than the most sporadic or attenuated form. The trauma of the 1923 strike was an important corrective to any tendency to overestimate the militancy of agricultural workers: a 25 per cent turn-out in the union's strongest area, although denying the caricature of the supine clodhopper, nevertheless hardly reinforced confidence in the efficacy of strike action. In the light of subsequent experience this certainly seems to be how the events of those five weeks were interpreted by Gooch and his successors. For under other conditions strike action had proved effective and a salutary experience to the employers. This, however, was overlooked admist the renewed devotion to the statutory control of wages.

Modern Unionism

For most of the inter-war years the NUAW was fully stretched in retaining the rump of its earlier membership and dealing with the routine cases of injustice and exploitation which the Depression encouraged farmers to perpetrate. This is the period which is recalled with such great bitterness by farm workers today – 'hate all round'. The union did what it could to alleviate the most flagrant examples, including some notorious tied-cottage evictions, mostly by appealing to public sympathy. That the NUAW remained in existence at all is a tribute to the determination of its officials that it should not go the same way as had Arch's union under similar circumstances at the end of the nineteenth century. They were undoubtedly helped by the re-introduction of statutory wage control during the Labour Party's short tenure of office in 1924, a prize which the Norfolk strike had belatedly won for the farm worker. However, this success was tempered by the passing of a Liberal amendment which took away from the Central Wages Board its power of amending wage rates and hours suggested by the County Committees. As a result there was a great variation in hours and wages from county to county, although overall for those workers *in employment* there was a slight improvement in wage rates between 1924 and 1939 and a slight improvement of the farm worker's comparative position *vis-à-vis* industrial workers.[54] In 1936, a notable success was achieved when a special scheme for unemployment insurance for agricultural workers was introduced. For the first time since 1834 the shadow of the workhouse was lifted from the farm worker.

In a remarkable repetition of events between 1914 and 1918, it was the Second World War which again transformed agricultural trade-unionism. Labour shortages on the land enabled the NUAW to press successfully for large wage increases and this in turn stimulated membership (see Table 28). In 1940 the Central Wages Board was given the power to derive a national statutory minimum wage and hence-forth County Committees could only vary their awards upwards not downwards. This wartime measure was consolidated in 1947 by the passing of the Agricultural Wages (Regulation) Act which provided for the present Agricultural Wages Board for England and Wales (and a separate Board for Scotland). The machinery was streamlined, with a smaller Board consisting of eight trade-union and eight NFU representatives, together with five appointed members. On the workers' side the TGWU was given, somewhat generously, the right to nominate three members, and the NUAW five. The estab-lishment of the AWB represented the culmination of over forty years of trade-union agitation. The NUAW's sense of achievement was only dampened by the failure of the Labour government to honour its associated pledge and abolish the tied cottage. There began a renewed campaign for abolition as a result of the government's re-fusal to include such a measure in the Agricultural Wages (Regulation)

Bill and throughout 1947 and 1948 the *Land Worker* continued
to carry a barrage of propaganda against the tied-cottage system.
Nevertheless, despite this disappointment the *Land Worker* could hail
the end of 'the Union's greatest year' in December 1946. 'The story
of the Union is at once a record of enormous gains for the workers
and a romance,' the leader writer stated. 'A new country life has been
born. Minimum wages are now fixed by law. The earnings of farm
workers are now comparable with those of many other workers . . .
It is mainly due to the efforts of the Union that the land worker is
now treated not as a serf, but as a citizen.'[55]

The chief architect of what was virtually a new union was Edwin
Gooch. It was he who had shepherded the NUAW through the lean
years of the 1930s and had ensured that the organization remained
intact and ready to take advantage of the opportunities which the war
had presented. Gooch was also primarily responsible for the re-
framing of union policy during these years, a re-appraisal which took
account of the dependence of union growth on the changes in farm
workers' money wages, and of wages on the movement of farm
prices. Gooch had therefore began to champion agricultural protection, a policy which was bound to take the NUAW closer to the
NFU. An editorial in the *Land Worker* of July 1931 entitled 'A
Common Meeting Ground?' marked the first attempt to convert the
membership to the new policy. By 1935 sufficient accord had been
reached between Gooch and farmers' representatives over agricultural
policy that he was unanimously elected President of the Norfolk
Chamber of Agriculture. This moved the *Eastern Daily Press* to
comment: 'If it had been predicted but a very few years ago that we
should live to see the President of the Agricultural Labourers' trade
union unanimously and cordially elected to the presidency of the
Chamber of Agriculture nobody would have believed it possible . . .
It betokens a new sense of common purpose and common interests
between master and man in the agricultural industry, a realization
that . . . neither of them can serve that interest effectively except upon
a basis of the prosperity of their common industry.'[56] These sentiments were echoed by Gooch himself in his acceptance speech.
Clearly Gooch's growing acceptability was not only influenced by
his commitment to agricultural protection but by a growing reorientation of the NUAW under his leadership away from an outright advocacy of Socialism in agriculture and the destruction of

capitalism to an acceptance of the existing order (whatever the rhetoric). Better wages and conditions were becoming an end rather than a means, with the ultimate aim being the right of the farm worker to equal social status with the urban worker and a recognized, if junior, role in a capitalist agriculture – 'a place in the sun' as Gooch was to call it.[57]

The proliferation of wartime committees that were set up as part of the state control of agriculture brought the NUAW and NFU leaders even closer together and made them work for a common purpose. Gooch, in an address to the National Farmers Club in December 1941, suggested that if agriculture were again threatened after the war a Defence Council should be set up representing all interests, and in 1944, with the end of the war in sight, private consultations began with the NFU. The opening of the 1944 Biennial Conference was preceded by an Executive Committee meeting attended by Sir James Turner and J. K. Knowles, the NFU's President and Secretary. At this meeting it was resolved to seek Conference approval for future joint consultations. The long Conference debate, extensively reported in the *Land Worker* beneath a photograph of Gooch and Knowles shaking hands, was 'remarkable for the number of references to leopards and spots',[58] but the Executive's recommendation was given grudging approval by the narrow margin of 55 votes to 43. The District Organizers, meeting at Oxford shortly afterwards, were perplexed by Gooch's initiative. To them the NFU 'did not mean the diplomatic Turner and Knowles but the backwoodsman who did his stint for the NFU on the District Wage Committee, the evicting farmer and the underpaying farmer'.[59] As it turned out the Joint Consultative Committee achieved little and it finally foundered upon the election of the Labour Party in 1945, whereupon the possibility of legislating NUAW policy through Labour's agricultural proposals seemed more realistic than it had ten years earlier. The NUAW sponsorship of seven Labour candidates in the election compared with none in 1935 demonstrated the extent to which the difference of opinion over agricultural policy had been resolved.

In retrospect these conciliatory moves can be seen to have had unfortunate consequences for the maintenance of farm workers' living standards in the decade following the end of the war. As Table 23 (p. 172) showed, the euphoria generated by the immediate post-war

wage levels was premature: in comparison with industrial workers
the position soon began to deteriorate. It became apparent that the
farm workers' faith in the new AWB was somewhat misplaced, for
throughout the 1950s the AWB's awards were extremely conservative. If the NUAW was prepared to contemplate the strike weapon
under the unfavourable conditions of 1923, this surely was an
opportune time to adopt a more militant approach in order to preserve the hard-won ground of the late 1940s. The idea of strike action
was raised at the Biennial Conference in 1946 for the first time in
twenty years, but was firmly rejected by Gooch and the resolution
was lost.[60] It seems unlikely that Gooch, in the aftermath of his conciliatory approaches to the NFU, had any enthusiasm for direct
action, but overlying this was the old problem of the threat which
such action represented to the continuation of the statutory wage
system. Gooch and his Executive did not feel they could subvert the
decisions of the AWB which they had fought for so long to establish.
Yet while the AWB continued to give its miserly awards farm
workers were losing ground against their industrial counterparts. This
dilemma was illustrated in 1952, when a particularly niggardly award
provoked a flood of branch resolutions demanding its rejection and
the recall of the Biennial Conference with a view to further action.
The Berkshire County Committee suggested a token one-day strike,
but this was repudiated by the Executive, who gave a sharp reminder
that only they were empowered by the union rule book to call a
strike. It then decided that 600 branch protests were a poor response
and decided to accept the AWB's offer. While acceptance of the
Wages Board machinery was the cornerstone of the NUAW's
policy, there was little option but to accede to its decisions, however
much they were to be deplored.

The 1950s and 1960s saw the relative position of agricultural
workers' earnings drift slowly downwards and the wages gap grow
correspondingly wider. In fact, between 1949 and 1955, *real* wages
actually declined.[61] The proportion of hired workers receiving the
minimum wage also declined substantially from nearly 34 per cent in
1950 to 5 per cent in 1970, suggesting that a growing number of
workers were doing better in their own 'negotiations' with their
employers than their representatives on the AWB. It also suggests
that increasingly over this period the AWB was achieving little for
the agricultural worker beyond ratifying changes in their labour

market situation which had been attained by other means – principally the drift from the land and the general level of unemployment in the economy[62] – and providing a 'safety net' for an ever-diminishing number of badly exploited workers, principally in Wales, the south-west and East Anglia. The NUAW leadership was therefore caught between a disenchantment with the results of negotiation through the AWB and a lack of any policy other than a firm commitment to it. Moreover this dilemma was exacerbated by the realization that the feasibility of strike action was becoming more questionable as time went on. The changes wrought by technological innovations and the altered composition of many rural villages were destroying the old occupational and communal solidarities upon which militant action had been based in the past. As the number of workers per farm declined so those that remained were being drawn into a more diffuse, personal relationship with their employers, hardly conducive to a desire for strike action. Furthermore the invasion of rural villages by a largely alien, urban, immigrant middle class tended to lead farmers and workers to close ranks against what was frequently a common antagonist. Even where closer relationships did not prevail – for example because of farm amalgamations – the growing percentage of workers in tied housing was a factor which was likely to make many workers wary of militancy. Even as late as 1969, therefore, the union leadership was unable to share the general disaffection with wages councils voiced by the TUC. During the post-Donovan discussions on the topic the NUAAW's General Secretary stated: 'The predominant pattern in agriculture is one or two [workers per unit], and half of them are living in the tied cottages of their employers. We would not take the view, in relation to our industry, that the abolition of statutory wage enforcement in broadly its present form is a practicable proposition, in the interests of the workpeople in that industry, for a considerable time to come.'[63]

The method by which the NUAW leadership eventually sought to overcome its dilemma over wage bargaining was through an advocacy of a statutory system of plus rates in agriculture. Such a wages structure had first been suggested by the appointed members of the AWB in 1945 and had been enthusiastically taken up by the TGWU, which had considerable experience of negotiating differential rates in industry. The NUAW was, however, more cautious. A mildly hostile article appeared in the *Land Worker* in April 1945, but readers' opinions were also invited. The main fear was that a graded system would depress the minimum wage, and so the Executive turned the idea down, doubtless influenced by the NFU's enthusiasm for such a scheme, which was indeed motivated by such a prospect. In 1950, the issue was raised again at a meeting of district organizers, who felt that some form of wages structure was required if an increasingly mechanized industry was to retain its skilled workers. At that year's Biennial, however, a motion allowing the Executive 'to explore a wages structure in the industry in the light of changed conditions' was thrown out by a ten-to-one majority.[64] Nevertheless, as the 1950s progressed and the shortcomings of the existing AWB machinery became clearer, so the Executive's conviction – led by successive General Secretaries, Alfred Dann and Harold Collison – grew that future wages policy lay in the formulation of a wages structure. On the other hand, the membership remained sceptical.

A wages structure sub-committee was eventually set up with the TGWU in 1955. It was decided to grade the job and not the man and to make the scheme compulsory. The report was endorsed by the Executive and presented to the Biennial Conference for approval. To the Executive's chagrin, and at the union's Jubilee Conference of all places, the platform was defeated and the proposal was lost by 80 votes to 69. For the following two years a vigorous campaign was conducted by the Executive in favour of the wages structure, and its benefits were extolled in the columns of the *Land Worker*. In 1958, they duly had their way and the conference gave the go ahead for negotiations. Unfortunately it was over this same period that the NFU was having second thoughts about the wisdom of the scheme, viewing it as a disguised method of raising wages across the board (exactly the aspect which was commending itself to the NUAW). Characteristically the NFU demanded that the man should be graded and not the job he was performing and it became adept at finding 'practical' difficulties which provided an excuse for proceeding only slowly, or not proceeding at all. Negotiations, indeed, dragged on, with the NUAW now convinced of the desirability of a wages structure, right through the 1960s until a scheme was finally initiated in 1972, twenty-seven years after it was first mooted by the AWB.

The significance of the wages structure, and the debate on the issue within the union, lay far beyond the matter of wages, rendering it the most important policy matter in the post-war period. Undeniably the conversion to the proposed wages structure was encouraged by the belief that if the qualifications could be formulated widely enough a wages structure would provide a method of surreptitiously raising the earnings of the majority of agricultural workers. Reading between the lines of the union's policy statements over the years, there also seems to have been a realization that the replacement of the somewhat haphazard and privately negotiated premium payments by a statutory scheme would also render the AWB more relevant to the individual farm worker, allowing, by virtue of this, the efforts of the NUAW on the Wages Board to have more impact at the grass-roots level. The wage packets of a much higher proportion of farm workers would therefore be determined solely by the fiat of the AWB and the activities of union negotiators. In this manner the NUAW hoped to extract itself from the dilemma which threatened its continued attachment to the AWB. Concern with material benefits was not the only incentive, however, for underlying these considerations there was another which was given equal prominence: the status of the farm worker *vis-à-vis* workers in industry. Since their inception both agricultural trade unions had aimed not only at placing the farm worker on an equal financial footing with the industrial worker, but at achieving a comparable status in the eyes of society at large. A long campaign had been fought against the customary image of the agricultural worker as an unskilled, uncouth yokel, symbolized by a growing sensitivity to the use of the word 'labourer'. Although in the early years the NUAW had been quite happy to apply this term to its own members, a growing familiarity with its less prestigious connotations caused an increasingly strong reaction to its use. Farm workers, and especially their union leaders, resented (with some justice) the implication that they are unskilled and regarded the use of 'labourer' when applied to them as 'an insolent and offensive relegation of farm workers to a lower social status'.[65] The establishment of a craftsman's grade was therefore regarded as an acknowledgement of the farm worker's skilled status, particularly if it was attached to an apprenticeship scheme. It would remove for good the stigma of being considered a mere 'labourer'. So through a wages structure the agricultural worker could in another, but equally important, sense achieve his 'place in the sun'.

Opposition to the wages structure was led by the left-wing faction within the NUAW, who found common cause with many of the adherents to the union's nonconformist radical traditions. Both groups were moved by a desire to see the union's first priority as the raising of the minimum wage so that all 'comrades' or 'brethren' (according to whether they were disciples of Marxism or Methodism) could move forward together. The former group were naturally fearful of status differentials weakening the class consciousness of the farm worker – 'to adopt such a principle makes Socialism impossible. Let us be clear in our minds and repeat that a wages structure means reward for ability. It is the foundation of, and results in, the "haves" and the "have nots" '.[66] The latter were equally concerned that the union would be side-tracked from its fundamental aim of raising the living standards of the downtrodden farm worker, no matter what his abilities, but they were more easily mollified by the Executive's declared policy of grading the job and not the man. It was therefore this group which swung the vote in favour of a wages structure in 1958, leaving only the left wing to continue a campaign against it throughout the 1960s. When agreement with the NFU was finally reached in 1971 the result was something of a compromise. By attaching the new grades to the simultaneously introduced New Entrant (Apprenticeship) Training Scheme or, for existing workers, an employer's declaration of competence (capable of being challenged by taking a proficiency test) it was clear that the man rather than the job was being graded. On the other hand the unions had succeeded in broadening the scope of the craftsman's grade sufficiently to include the majority of workers, thus obtaining a concealed rise in the statutory minimum, and had reasserted some control over the previous haphazard system of payments. The crystallization of premium rates around the new grades (see Chapter 3) has shifted the focus of plus-rate-bargaining back from the farm to the AWB, reinvigorating the unions' negotiations there.

The very longevity of negotiations on the wages structure, together with its symbolic and intrinsic importance, have meant that this issue has dominated the post-war history of the NUAAW, so that other policies than those connected with wages and conditions have assumed something of a secondary role. The predominance of the wages issue has led the NUAAW to see its future more and more in promoting the worker's advancement *as a worker*, rather than in encouraging him to become a smallholder or farmer. Such a philosophy has also enabled the union to appear more attractive to workers in ancillary industries – food-processing, etc. – in which great efforts have been made to recruit new members to compensate for the decreasing pool of agricultural workers from whom recruitment is possible. This policy was symbolized by the incorporation of the word 'Allied' into the NUAW's title in 1968. But seeing the future in terms of better pay and conditions has meant a consequent support for farm nationalization and larger farms, which has conflicted with the traditional support for smallholdings. Indeed this problem has been exacerbated because the NUAAW has simultaneously pursued a policy of land nationalization. Thus its most recent policy document, *Farming for the Future*, published in 1965, commends statutory smallholdings schemes while also advocating larger productive enterprises as being in the best interests of its members,[67] but this has to be seen as an attempt to embrace a difference of opinion within the union stemming from its differing traditions.

The very birth of the NUAAW in 1906 had been viewed by the Liberal Party as part of its whole strategy over the 'land question' and an early proposal was made that the then Eastern Counties Agricultural Labourers' and Smallholders' Union should be modelled on the Irish Land League. Although this was ruled out as being of no use to the farm worker, it was decided that the union's rules be so framed that it was able to assist members to obtain land, including its own purchases of land, which could subsequently be let to members. Attachment to the Labour Party and the influence of Walker, however, also introduced the objective of land nationalization, which appears as one of the five major aims of the union in the *Land Worker* of 1919, with no mention of smallholdings. As was pointed out earlier in this chapter, the two policies remained uneasy bedfellows in the union's overall policy. The contradiction became more open shortly after the Second World War when land nationalization was omitted from the Labour Party's immediate plans. At the 1950 Biennial Conference the Executive opposed a motion demanding immediate and complete land nationalization and in a subsequent speech Gooch argued that 'nationalization would have a disastrous effect on British farming. The Union was against it and the Labour Party had no intention of introducing it.'[68] The 1952 Conference voted against land nationalization, and then the 1954 Conference voted in favour.[69] Not surprisingly an Executive meeting involved in drafting the policy document that was to become *Health and Wealth Under Our Feet* resolved that 'nationalization of land was controversial and references

to it in the final draft should be guarded',[70] but at the 1956 Conference
a motion that a much stronger policy statement be included was
passed. Land nationalization henceforward became union policy, but
it would be fair to say that it was adopted only reluctantly by the
leadership, who were determined to relegate to the background such
a contentious issue which seemed to them to be only marginally
related to their fundamental aim – improved wages and conditions.

Groves, writing in 1948, summarized this position quite well. He
pointed out that 'it would be wrong to leave the impression that the
NUAW as a whole has yet expressed its final opinion on the future
of Britain's agriculture. So far, it strives against capitalist agriculture
only to get better conditions for its members, it seeks adjustment
rather than drastic change. This, however, puts the NUAW in a
halting place, a half-way house, untenable in modern conditions.'[71]
Although land nationalization was included in the policy statement
Farming in the Future in 1965, it was regarded very much as an *ultimate*
goal, impracticable for the immediate future. There was not, in any
case, any large groundswell of opinion among the membership that a
great deal of attention be paid to this problem: wages remained pre-
eminent. Consequently the union's policy in this area was never
clearly worked out and although nominally in favour of land
nationalization the NUAW loyally supported Gaitskell over Clause
Four and remained very much in the 'moderate' wing of the Labour
Party. By 1962, Self and Storing were concurring with Groves'
assessment: 'there is still too much uncertainty and division of opinion
for the union to speak with conviction on the crucial question of how
agriculture should be organized . . . The difficulty is that nationalization has to be discussed in terms of some notion of what the government should do with the land when it gets it, and there has been little
discussion of this point in the Union. The principle continues to be
supported, with decreasing enthusiasm, by the leaders because it is
part of Union lore and because its abstract quality masks, at least for
the time being, harder questions.'[72]

By the early 1970s the NUAAW had moved a little way towards
developing a more coherent strategy on long-term agricultural policy,
including land nationalization, so that Self and Storing's conclusions
are no longer entirely valid. The death of Gooch in 1964, followed by
several further changes in the leadership by 1970, brought about the
critical period of re-appraisal that Self and Storing had foreseen in

1962.[73] Their suggestion that the NUAAW's voice in agricultural politics was weak because it could not decide whether its future lay alongside the Labour Party or the NFU is no longer tenable – if, indeed, it ever was. The reasons for its weaknesses lie elsewhere – in its organizational problems, its lack of resources and the inability to escape from the toils of everyday issues like wages and the tied cottage to devote time and energy to longer-term policies. There is now no question of the NUAAW not committing itself to a large-scale and nationalized agricultural structure, seeking its 'place in the sun' through the Labour movement as a whole, alongside fellow industrial workers. Even land nationalization has, thanks to the price inflation of 1972–3, become less of a contentious issue. Nevertheless, while it is true that the NUAAW has a much clearer perception of its future than Self and Storing suggest, it continues to devote little attention to a detailed formulation of long-term agricultural policy and how it could be implemented. In this area the NUAAW seems content with its subaltern role to the NFU, and rarely challenges the employers' prerogatives over these matters in public by developing a coherent Socialist critique. But then, one suspects that the majority of the membership are more interested in the size of the wage packets than the complexities of agricultural policy planning.

The NUAAW in the 1970s

Of the three types of trade-union government outlined by Turner, the NUAAW follows in almost every important respect that which he calls 'popular bossdom'. This somewhat unflattering description is applied to those unions 'marked by a generally low level of membership participation, and by the greatest difference between the members and the professional officials on which they depend. In their case, the full-time officers' expertise necessarily embraces a range of affairs which is quite beyond the ordinary member's experience ... And thus, in them, the relations which actually exist between the membership and the key officials will depend very much on the latters' style of leadership ... And since such leaders largely choose (or at least mould) the assistants who will inherit their place, a particular "leadership style" may be transmitted down the line of succession.'[74] An

isolated and scattered membership, combined with a highly centralized administrative structure in which little decision-making autonomy is available at the local level, has made this style of government
inevitable in the NUAAW, but it would be mistaken to regard its
structure as an unconscious outcome of factors beyond its leaders'
control. On the contrary it is the result of a conscious policy, fiercely
defended when the need arises.

Basically the NUAAW consists of a four-tier hierarchy of
decision-making.[75] Every member must belong to a branch, which is
the basic unit of the NUAAW's structure. For certain purposes the
branches are grouped together into District Committees, which are
composed of one delegate from each branch in the district. From
within each District Committee delegates are elected to County
Committees which form the next layer of the union hierarchy. The
fourth, and most powerful, committee is the Executive Committee,
which consists of twelve members, each elected by the membership of
one of the divisions into which the country is divided for this purpose.
Each division has a roughly similar number of members, so their geographical extent may vary according to the density of unionization
within their boundaries. Although this four-tier structure forms the
mainstream of everyday union decision-making (at least in theory),
there are three important centres of power which lie outside it. First,
there is the Biennial Conference, the union's supreme decision-
making body which lays down the policies to be implemented by the
Executive Committee. It consists of delegates elected by the branches
on a county-by-county basis, the number of delegates being determined by the size of the membership. Secondly there is the administrative headquarters of the union, 'Head Office' as it is known, presided over by an employee of the union, the General Secretary, who
is elected by the whole membership. Finally there are the District
Organizers, again employees of the union appointed by the Executive
Committee, whose duties are to organize (that is, recruit) and service
the members within their areas. The *formal* structure is represented in
the diagram opposite.[76] The informal structure of decision-making
is, however, as in most organizations, rather different.

As the earlier parts of this chapter have sought to demonstrate, the
consistent policy of the NUAAW's leadership since its very early
days has been to consolidate and maintain a centralized control over
almost all important items of union policy and action. As a result the

NUAAW has often appeared to consist of two groupings only: the national leadership based in London, consisting of the Head Office, exemplified by the General Secretary, and the Executive Committee; and on the other hand the local branches and committees under the wing of the District Organizers. The centralization of the union's authority has left the membership with little or no autonomy at the

Structure of the NUAAW

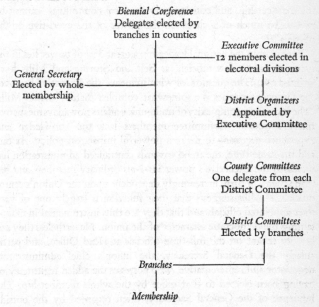

Biennial Conference
Delegates elected by
branches in counties

Executive Committee
12 members elected in
electoral divisions

General Secretary
Elected by whole
membership

District Organizers
Appointed by
Executive Committee

County Committees
One delegate from each
District Committee

District Committees
Elected by branches

Branches

Membership

local level, so that branch activity is often moribund and, perhaps because of this, the rank and file largely passive. The Biennial Conference therefore rarely represents a threat to the chosen policies of the national leadership; occasionally the delegates will flex their political muscles, but more often the power vacuum which the denial of localized decision-making has created is easily filled by the national leadership. Indeed, the relationship is reflected in the conduct of the conference itself. Delegates present their motions, there is a discussion, the 'platform' (the national leadership) gives its views on the matter, and usually their guidance is accepted by the 'floor'. For the rank and file to reject the declared views of the platform on important matters of policy – such as in the wages structure debate in 1956 – is a rare occurrence, and – as again in the case of the wages structure – usually short-lived. The platform is thus adept at controlling the Biennial Conference, whatever its subordinate constitutional position. Thus, despite a nominally diffuse decision-making structure 'popular boss-dom' may survive as long as it is reasonably sensitive to the feelings of the membership, and consequently the local committees 'cannot be said to be much of a check on the power of the executive or the officials'.[77]

Even within the national leadership a great deal of power lies in the hands of only a few officials, as Self and Storing and Mills have pointed out. 'The question of what influence the Executive has over the Union's activities is a somewhat complex matter,' writes Mills. 'The increasing complexity of trade-union affairs nowadays means that many Executive Committee members lack the knowledge and experience necessary to make a powerful impact on policy. At one and the same time, the trend towards centralized administration has increased the Executive's power *vis-à-vis* ordinary members and has made them, in turn, increasingly dependent upon the Union's senior officials.'[78] Mills suggests that their function is largely one of veto over appointed officials and that they are thus instrumental in main-taining the democratic character of the union. Nevertheless they are heavily reliant on the full-time officials at Head Office, and parti-cularly the General Secretary, the union's chief administrator, negotiator and representative, who possesses the added legitimacy of having been elected to that office by the whole membership. The influence of the General Secretary, often regarded by the outside world as not so much an employee of the union as its leader, can be considerable, for he is a full-time expert advising a part-time lay com-mittee, most of whom (because of the time involved and the inability to obtain leave of absence from most employers) are not usually farm workers. His only peer is the President, who chairs the Executive Committee and is elected by the Biennial Conference. He is virtually a full-time official and is the constitutional leader of the union. How-ever, the extent of his personal power *vis-à-vis* the General Secretary may vary according to the personalities involved. As the recognized leader of the union Walker was General Secretary and Gooch was

President. On other occasions responsibility has been shared, but together these two posts carry considerably more *de facto* authority than is suggested by the NUAAW's constitutional structure.

By the standards of British trade-unionism the NUAAW is a thoroughly democratic institution and this can be exemplified by the continuation of lively debate and factional conflict within the union, argued and fought according to the rules of union democracy.[79] Conflict between the Executive and the senior officials is rarely endemic and the former's power of veto is, as far as can be judged, used sparingly. Internal conflict tends, rather, to take place elsewhere. Two important divisions can be observed. The first is the continuing schism between the moderate grouping within the NUAAW and a more militantly inclined, neo-Marxist left wing. This has created a degree of factionalism within the NUAAW from top to bottom. Generally the moderates have held the ascendancy and often the left wing has taken on the role of a kind of loyal Opposition, or ginger-group within the union, thus allowing the political conflict to become institutionalized and almost ritualized. On other occasions, however, the factionalism has become more bitter and more damaging, particularly during a rather unhappy period in the union's history between 1968 and 1972.

The second dimension of internal conflict has been between the national leaders and the local leaders, especially the thirty-one District Organizers. As Self and Storing point out, 'Although assigned and paid by headquarters, the organizer *is* the National Union of Agricultural Workers on the local scene, and is so regarded by himself and others.'[80] Not unnaturally the organizers tend to equate centralization with remoteness and their relationship with the leadership has not always been a harmonious one. The organizers' duties bring them into constant contact with individual members, not only recruiting them but servicing their needs in a bewildering variety of ways. They are the 'front line', dealing on the spot with tied-cottage evictions, accident inquiries, industrial tribunals and, judging by the union's *Annual Reports*, a not insignificant proportion of personal welfare problems – for example, 'DO obtained cost of new dentures shattered on biscuits', 'DO obtained refund for unjustified service charge for TV', 'DO recovered money in connection with repairs to member's car', etc., etc.[81] Their close contact with the membership makes them powerful centres of influence which the leadership have persistently attempted to constrain. Consolidated action by local organizers has been discouraged and, as a counter-measure, an extra-constitutional device has been introduced, the annual County Conference. This is attended by branch officers and is used by the leadership to maintain contact with the grass-roots. A senior official from headquarters attends these meetings and, as if to emphasize his subordinate role, the organizer must make a report to the conference on his activities. The number of organizers who may attend the Biennial Conference is also heavily circumscribed and neither are they allowed to become members of the Executive. The NUAAW also has an unenviable reputation for sacking: Clegg and his colleagues found that dismissal was the single most frequent cause for the departure of NUAAW organizers. Consequently, the District Organizers have their own registered trade union – unique in Britain – which negotiates with the NUAAW over pay and conditions.[82]

Frequently the two areas of conflict overlap, for there are many organizers who are more militant than headquarters. In 1963 there was something of a *cause célèbre* when a Marxist District Organizer was sacked after disagreements over policy with the Executive. This made the District Organizers more circumspect in their actions, but the lack of harmony can remain. In an interview one left-wing organizer complained that on most matters of policy the objective was 'defeat us, not the good of the union'. But a more moderate District Organizer expressed the reverse argument: 'We've got a few left-wingers on the Executive, unfortunately – or fortunately you might think, I don't know. But I know that if I were a militant I would lose half the membership straightaway.' From an opposite political viewpoint each was prepared to express the lack of trust which often prevails between the Executive and the local organizers. A very senior official at headquarters concurred: 'Of course this union is far, far, far out to the Right politically ... The main conflicts here are not between the union and the farmers, but between the union and its own employees.' He then elaborated his own explanation of this: 'It's a very bureaucratic union because of the scattered and, if I may say so, not very sophisticated membership. There are certain formalities – elections and so on – to go through, but there's not much participation and once in power it's very easy for the bureaucracy to be manipulated.' There is an echo here of Self and Storing's verdict: 'The structural rigidity at the top is an attempt to compensate for the lack of solid foundations, and it is this lack, not the "communist threat" or "the undue influence of the organizers", that is the Union's real organizational problem.'[83] Whatever internal difficulties the NUAAW may have, therefore, stem less from personal animosity than structural weaknesses, which lead to any criticism being perceived, more often than not, as a threat. In a very real sense the NUAAW is only as strong as the recruitment and organization of its members allows it to be.

It is at the grass-roots, at the basic level of union government, the branch, that the major difficulties lie. The vast majority of the NUAAW's three thousand branches are based upon the village rather than the place of work. On only a tiny number of the very largest farms, and in a larger proportion of ancillary enterprises, is there a workplace branch where some degree of plant bargaining, handled usually by the District Organizer, may occur. For the most part, however, branches are community-based, and consequently branch activity has tended to suffer along with the decline of many rural villages as occupational communities. Branch secretaries no longer accrue to themselves the status that they once did. Many branches never meet and some have no secretary, their existence only prolonged by the District Organizer assuming this role. Most branches which hold meetings only do so infrequently. Mills, in his survey of the union's activities, was quite shocked by this display of apparent apathy,[84] but, quite apart from the social changes which lie behind their moribund appearance, the union's constitution allows the branches precious little to hold meetings for, apart from stirring up enthusiasm for the annual wage negotiations, forwarding resolutions to the Biennial Conference every two years, or showing the occasional film on such matters as farm safety. Whereas once the branch meeting was an excuse for a local social event, the decline in the agricultural population and increased access to alternative sources of entertainment have taken their toll: 'The village is no longer an isolated, self-contained social unit, dependent upon its own people for the provision of its entertainment. The young lads seek, and get, motor-cycles which will take them into town any evening they wish to go, with the girls on the pillion. Those who are not so young, and who are tired after a full day's work and overtime, get all the entertainment they want from the television by their own fireside. The Union branch meeting, once a monthly social event, can no longer compete with TV quiz shows and regular radio features. Contributions, once collected with comparative ease at well-attended meetings, now have to be called for, thus increasing considerably the work of the branch secretary.'[85]

The decline in the number of agricultural workers has meant that the number of potential recruits within the village has decreased markedly since the war. Organizationally, therefore, the NUAAW has been squeezed between a falling average branch size and the increasing cost of administering such an enormous number of branches. As Mills points out, merely keeping in touch with over 3,000 branches presents the union with problems of a kind and scale not usually found elsewhere in British trade-unionism, and this in itself partly accounts for the NUAAW's rather top-heavy administration. Only the TGWU has more branches than the NUAAW and no union has a smaller average branch membership than the NUAAW's thirty or so. Simply collecting subscriptions, the branch's main function, can be an extremely complex business, as the NUAAW's ill-starred flirtation with a computer accounting system in 1970–1 vividly brought home. In order to cope with these problems a number of innovations have been tried, such as the introduction of a number of area branches, run by secretaries provided with a moped by the union to collect subscriptions, and the appointment of national recruiting officers to ease the load of the District Organizers and to organize recruiting drives in particular areas (they have now been discontinued on the grounds of cost). More successful has been the attempt to move into new areas of recruitment altogether to boost the union's flagging agricultural membership, especially into the ancillary industries where workers do not 'come out the gate in ones and twos' and who are consequently easier to recruit and organize.

Because of the presence within the NUAAW of many of these 'allied' workers, it is not easy to state exactly the proportion of agricultural workers who are unionized. Mills estimates that between 30 and 35 per cent of the membership are not agricultural workers, but it is likely that this proportion has increased since the early 1960s, when Mills carried out his investigations, owing to substantial success in organizing workers in the food-processing industry, particularly poultry-packers. Assuming the non-agricultural section of the membership amounts to 40 per cent of the total, the NUAAW contains approximately 40 per cent of the total regular full-time hired workers in England and Wales. Their geographical distribution is far from random, however. Three counties – Lincolnshire, Norfolk and Yorkshire – account for nearly two-fifths of the membership and, generally speaking, the NUAAW is strongest in the arable areas where the concentration of workers is highest. Thus, Norfolk is 72 per cent unionized, Lincolnshire 63 per cent and Huntingdonshire 52 per cent; at the other extreme the whole of Wales only accounts for 2 per cent of the membership and most of the north and west are sparsely unionized (Dorset is an exception with 55 per cent membership).[86] Overall the 60 per cent or so of farm workers who are not in the NUAAW are a constant drag on its resources, depriving it of not only the cash but often the authority to fight for the interests of farm workers wherever and whenever the need arises.

In the eyes of the NUAAW leadership this need arises frequently. Part of the philosophy of granting the agricultural worker his 'place in the sun' has been for the union to demand representation on every body that might affect the agriculture industry or rural life in general. Since agriculture is encumbered with a larger apparatus of statutory control than most British industries, the representation of the workers' interests on a multitude of official and quasi-official bodies is in itself a considerable business, involving 'every aspect of country life from the village dog show to the county hall'.[87] The central activity of the NUAAW is, of course, wage negotiation, but its inherent weakness in this aspect of its work has led it to emphasize the subsidiary aspects of its activities as an attraction to potential members. Its friendly society benefits receive wide publicity in the *Land Worker* and the union's Legal Department is constantly dealing with National Insurance and industrial injury cases, workmen's compensation, road accidents (members can obtain cheap motor-car insurance) and various miscellaneous claims. The union also handles wage arrears and redundancy payments for its members and, most importantly, tied-cottage cases when possession orders are applied for. In general it is engaged in the myriad activities of any modern trade union – public relations, education, political representation within the TUC and the Labour Party, international relations through the International Federation of Plantation, Agricultural and Allied Workers, and as a watchdog on farm safety and health.[88] All this is obtained for one of the lowest subscription rates in British trade-unionism, and as a result there has been a chronic financial shortage since the mid-1960s.

Because of the absence of strike action the NUAAW often appears to the outsider more like a friendly society than an orthodox trade union. The problems of recruitment and organization have inhibited the use of the strike weapon, yet without it the NUAAW renders itself unable to raise the standard of living of its members beyond the level determined by a free labour market. This in turn threatens to make unionization irrelevant for the individual agricultural worker, who has less incentive to join. In many cases the union can hardly be said to give him a better deal than a friendly chat with the boss. Hence the NUAAW has become trapped within a vicious circle – its lack of power is based ultimately upon a low level of organization which in turn stems partly from its weakness in wage bargaining. However, in order to investigate this question, it is necessary to look at how the individual agricultural worker regards trade-unionism more closely, through data gathered in the survey.

Agricultural Trade-Unionism in Suffolk

Being an adjacent county to Norfolk, Suffolk was penetrated by trade-union activity at quite an early stage. The first branches were established around Halesworth in the parishes of Holton, Walpole and Wenhaston in 1917. The county shared in the national upsurge of activity after the First World War and by 1919 a further eighteen branches had been established, mostly in the Halesworth area, but also around Stowmarket. By 1926, a further eleven branches were in existence. Halesworth was the centre of early agitation and help was obtained from the local branch of the National Union of Railwaymen. In 1919 a harvest strike occurred in the area which was supported by munitions workers in Norfolk who collected donations for the strike fund. 'Hardly "Silly Suffolk" now!' enthused an early report in the *Land Worker*.[89] Much of the stimulus came from the Norwich ILP, and generally the movement marked a southward extension of the geographical boundaries of the union's Norfolk stronghold.

Unfortunately, in common with the nationwide setback in the growth of unionization, the position could not be held. Although the appointment of a full-time organizer enabled a further spate of branches to be opened in the early 1920s, the declining overall numbers, it was reported in 1922, 'display a frame of mind that makes work difficult'. In common with organizers elsewhere (one from Nottinghamshire began, 'My report is scarcely a report but an appeal') the Suffolk representative was obviously finding the going tough: 'The ruthlessness of employers, the drought, the extension of unemployment, have produced a very disquieting feeling among the workers. Men are asking if this is what they fought for.'[90] By 1926, the union appeared on the verge of extinction in the county. 'Suffolk County Committee met on 7 April,' reads a report in the *Land Worker*. 'It was agreed to approach the EC to see if a grant could be made to help Suffolk to organize, seeing that the men there were largely unorganized, and it is difficult for the county committee to do much with very small funds.'[91] In 1931 attempts were made by Suffolk farmers to cut the wage in the county from 30s. to 28s. – the kind of reduction which had provoked the Norfolk strike in 1923. Despite union protests and a successful appeal to the Labour Minister of Agriculture, Addison, to order the Suffolk Wages Committee to reconsider, the recommendation was confirmed. The membership was balloted on a strike proposal but was split 324–345 against strike action. However, on the same day a joint meeting of the NUAW and NFU led to an agreement to maintain the wages *status quo* in return for joint action to obtain import quotas on wheat.[92] Nevertheless the episode seems to have somewhat revived the fortunes of the union in Suffolk, and the existing branches scraped by with only a few cases of extinction until the Second World War brought about a considerable revival.

In 1972 there were 122 branches of the NUAAW in East Suffolk and thirty-six in West Suffolk, where many farm workers are organized by the TGWU. Until 1972, East Suffolk had its own NUAAW organizer operating from Ipswich, but henceforth West Suffolk has been added as part of the union's reorganization scheme which reduced the number of District Organizers on their payroll. Many of the East Suffolk branches can date their foundation from the period immediately after the Second World War: forty-four branches were established between 1945 and 1949 alone. The strongest area remains in the north of the county. There is hardly a parish between Eye and Halesworth without a branch of the NUAAW and some of them, for example Laxfield, are very large. Branch organization is thinner, however, in the very north-east in the area known locally as 'the Saints', where farms are small and hired workers thinner on the ground, and in the immediate hinterland of Ipswich (although some of this region is covered by an area branch at Pettistree). The concentration of branches in the Halesworth–Eye area is not associated with any concentration of larger farms – indeed large employers of labour are disproportionately represented in the south-east of the county where unionization is much weaker. However these comments are all based upon figures taken branch by branch and parish by parish. Branch and parish do not always coincide by any means, nor do aggregate parish statistics allow for variations in farm size within each parish, so in order to understand the nature of agricultural trade-unionism in East Suffolk it is necessary to begin at the individual level.

Investigating the precise composition of the NUAAW membership is not, as researchers in other counties have discovered,[93] an easy business. Probably the only person who can give an accurate guide is the branch secretary – the District Organizer, let alone Head Office, has only the vaguest notion of either the size or the composition of the membership. In 1963–4, Head Office inquired into the member's occupations by sending out questionnaires to all branch secretaries. In East Suffolk only sixty-eight out of 119 branches replied, and an examination of the original questionnaires shows the data to be not totally accurate. Nevertheless, in so far as it confirms a pattern found in other counties, it arguably gives a reasonably representative picture of the situation at that time. Where the member's occupation was specified, 72·1 per cent were agricultural workers, the next most numerous being retired workers (5·7 per cent), building workers (3·2 per cent), agricultural contractors (2·0 per cent), council roadmen (1·9 per cent), gardeners (1·8 per cent) and lorry drivers (1·5 per cent). Since 1964, there has been a growth in the non-agricultural membership, due mainly to the unionization of food-processing plants, so that the proportion of agricultural workers in the membership has probably dropped below 70 per cent. Nevertheless, taking this latter figure as an estimate of the proportion of members who are agricultural workers, and using the method of estimating the membership from subscriptions devised by Madden,[94] the proportion of regular full-time farm workers in East Suffolk who were members of the NUAAW in 1972 was calculated as being 48·6 per cent. In the survey carried out in the forty-four parishes, 46·8 per cent of the respondents were members of the NUAAW and 1·7 per cent were in the TGWU, making an overall percentage unionized of 48·5.

The survey provided some information on the characteristics of those agricultural workers who were trade-union members. As might be expected farm foremen were under-represented, only 42·9 per cent being unionized, although one foreman also stated that he had applied to join the Association of Scientific, Technical and Managerial Staff (ASTMS) but had been refused membership. Stockmen were also under-represented, with 40·4 per cent. However, the main determinants of union membership seemed to be unrelated to the type of worker involved. One important factor was the agricultural worker's work situation – that is, there was a clear relationship between union membership and the bureaucratization of the farm. Thus, 60·2 per cent of the workers on the 'patriarchal' farms were not members of a trade union, compared with 44·6 per cent on the 'bureaucratic' farms. However, when the degree of bureaucratization was taken into account the relationship became curvilinear, as Table 29 shows. This

Table 29 Trade-union membership against number of levels of hierarchy in farm structure, workers interviewed in Suffolk, 1972

| | Levels of hierarchy | | | | |
	1	2	3	4	All workers
Unionized					
No	41	30	17	25	113
%	39·8	66·7	51·5	48·1	48·5
Non-unionized					
No.	62	15	16	27	120
%	60·2	33·3	48·5	51·9	51·5

demonstrates that there is by no means a straightforward relationship between unionization and the bureaucratic nature of farming enterprises (and *a fortiori* size) that has sometimes been assumed. Increased social distance between farmer and worker, together with contact with fellow workers, certainly promotes trade-union membership, but as farms become larger and more bureaucratic there are also economies of scale from which workers may benefit in the form of better pay and conditions. There is, in fact, a very clear relationship between the size and organization of the farm and the workers' gross weekly earnings (see Chapter 5), and so workers on the larger farms may feel that they obtain an equitable standard of living from their employer without the necessity of joining a trade union. The workers most likely to be union members are therefore those working on the medium-sized farms which have been bureaucratized, thus removing the pervasive contact between farmer and worker, but which are not paying superior wages (usually through failing to provide unlimited overtime) and/or providing inferior housing, compared with the very large farms. Apart from being associated with this combination of bureaucratic rule *and* low earnings, trade-union membership was also found to be associated independently with tied-cottage occupancy, the unionization of the respondent's father and, rather weakly, with residency in a village defined as an occupational community (see Chapter 6).

The union members in the sample were asked why they had joined. Their replies are shown in Table 30. The most prevalent reason was so that they could obtain the NUAAW's friendly society's benefits

Table 30 Reasons for joining trade union of workers interviewed in Suffolk, 1972

	No.	%
Friendly society benefits	39	34·5
Pressure from workmates	22	19·5
To fight for higher wages, better conditions, etc.	19	16·8
Generalized collectivism ('you need someone behind you', etc.)	15	13·3
Pressure from kin	7	6·2
In tied house	5	4·4
Other	6	5·3
	120	100·0

(accident benefit, cheap car insurance, etc.), which no doubt vindicates the prominence the union gives to them in its recruiting literature. Overall the replies show a situation not dissimilar to that discovered by Mills in Berkshire and Oxfordshire. Using a different question, which asked respondents which of the union's activities they most valued, 'negotiations of improved wages and hours' was given first priority (28 per cent), then friendly society benefits (27 per cent) and 'general availability of union help when needed' (24 per cent). In addition to the wages issue it is apparent that the general feeling of security which unionization gave was a highly significant factor. There was a clear concern with what Mills calls, 'some aspect or other of the "peace of mind" derived from knowing that in case of "trouble" they could always rely on the backing of the Union'.[95]

A further factor, however, is the pressure to join from workmates. This can be seen as being related to the location of union activists. There was a strong tendency for branch secretaries to be employed on the very large farms, whose workforce then formed the nucleus of the local branch. By no means all branch secretaries within the forty-four parishes were practising agricultural workers – indeed one of the largest branches in the county was run by a retired carpenter and part-time caretaker who was not even a NUAAW member! Nevertheless of the branch secretaries whose occupations were known (thirteen out of seventeen), eight were agricultural workers and the average size of the workforce on the farms on which they were employed was 17·4. Larger farms are an obvious and prominent source of union members and the eye of the District Organizer is likely to alight on them when it comes to cajoling a member to undertake the chore – for this is usually how it is regarded – of becoming branch secretary. Certainly the assumption of the post hardly seems to be associated with a militant stance on union issues; although the sample was admittedly based upon very small numbers, the branch secretaries interviewed were *less* willing to engage in strike action if called upon to do so by the union than the rank-and-file members.

Beyond collecting and forwarding subscriptions most of the branch secretaries in the area seemed to regard their role in the NUAAW as a passive and minimal one. For them, as for most members, the union was essentially a benefit society which in a very last resort could aid members and protect them from the excesses of a few eccentric employers. At least one branch secretary confessed to being somewhat embarrassed by an ideologically committed member who brought him a stream of new recruits, thereby adding considerably to his clerical burden. Meetings were rare events and often poorly attended. This was sometimes attributed to the decline of the village pub as a

social centre, but in Suffolk the union ran a successful darts tourna-
ment in an attempt to maintain interest. Nevertheless 68·1 per cent of
the members interviewed had never attended a branch meeting in the
year before the interview. Moreover, 23·5 per cent of the members
could not even state accurately which branch they belonged to. The
main reasons given for not attending branch meetings were: 'not
interested' (34·2 per cent), no meetings held (20·5 per cent), 'no time'
(15·1 per cent) and 'not informed' (9·6 per cent). This display of
apathy at the branch level is, of course, by no means unusual in the
trade-union movement as a whole, nor, given the members' predominant orientation to the union, is it particularly surprising. Since
most members rely on the existence of the NUAAW as a safety net
which is simply 'there' in times of need, like an insurance policy,
there is little incentive to engage in active participation in union
affairs.

The majority (51·5 per cent) of the respondents who were not in
any trade union were asked a number of questions concerning their
attitudes towards trade-unionism in general and the NUAAW in
particular. Just under one-third of them had been trade-union members at some time in their lives, mostly in the NUAAW (27 out of
37). The main reason for their lapse of membership related simply to
organizational problems – either they had moved and had lost contact
with the union or the collector had ceased to call for subscriptions.
Together they accounted for 40·5 per cent of lapses, followed by disagreements with union policy (18·9 per cent), the failure of the union
to help over a particular problem in the past (16·2 per cent) and apathy
– 'just left' – which accounted for 13·5 per cent of lapses. Among all
the non-union workers only a small fraction (14·2 per cent of the
non-union workers and 7·3 per cent of the total sample) expressed
what might be termed 'ideological' objections to joining a trade
union, such as 'I don't agree with strikes', 'They're all Communists',
etc. Apathy and the failure of the union organization to penetrate to
their situation represented by far the main reasons for non-unioniza-
tion. The hard-core opposition to trade-unionism is very small in
view of the supposedly deferential character of farm labour.

A detailed examination of the agricultural worker's class attitudes is
presented in Chapter 7. However, at this stage some brief reference to
their attitudes towards trade-unionism and militant action may be
made. All respondents were given a battery of attitude questions

(discussed more fully in Chapter 7) from which those most relevant to trade-union activity are presented in Table 31. Overall their attitudes towards trade-unionism seem ambivalent and even contradictory: a strong belief that trade unions in general are too powerful in this country combines with a view that farm workers need a

Table 31 Responses to selected attitude questions of workers interviewed in Suffolk, 1972

	Agree %	Disagree %	No opinion %
The trade unions have too much power in this country	84·1	12·0	3·9
Farm workers need a stronger trade union to fight for their interests	70·8	20·2	9·0
Farm workers do not get their fair share of farm income in wages	64·8	24·0	11·2
Farmers are getting more than their fair share of farm income	37·8	40·3	21·9
Workers should follow the lead of farmers rather than trade-unionists in national affairs	31·8	38·6	29·6*

*Includes respondents who replied 'neither'

stronger trade union to fight for their interests, for example. However, compared with the cross-section of urban workers studied in Peterborough by Blackburn and Mann[96] the agricultural workers' responses were more moderate. Some of these apparent contradictions can be reconciled by allowing for the agricultural worker's strong sense of distinctiveness *vis-à-vis* urban, industrial workers. Trade unions are for the most part viewed as urban, industrial phenomena, part of the urban conspiracy in favour of cheap food which depresses the returns to both farmer *and* farm worker. Hence the relationship between wages and profits need not be regarded as zero-sum. Although 56·2 per cent of the respondents expressed themselves as 'dissatisfied' with their present level of wages, when they were asked whom they blamed for this state of affairs (and the emotive term 'blame' was introduced deliberately), only one-quarter blamed their employer or farmers in general (see Table 32). Agencies beyond the farm gate were held to be most accountable, reinforcing the point made in Chapter 3 that centralized collective bargaining has enabled a more harmonious relationship between employer and employee to be maintained on the farm itself.

Table 32 Blame attributed for earnings dissatisfaction of workers interviewed in Suffolk, 1972

	No.	%
AWB independent members	30	25·0
Government/cheap-food policy	27	22·5
NUAAW	20	16·7
Farmers in general	20	16·7
Own employer	10	8·3
Industrial workers	8	6·7
Other	5	4·2
	113	100·0

This raises the question of the agricultural worker's willingness to strike for higher wages. All respondents, both unionized and non-unionized, were asked whether if the union called a strike (for higher wages) they would come out. A majority – 55·4 per cent – said that they would refuse to strike, but 42·9 per cent stated that they would withdraw their labour (1·7 per cent did not know). Although there was a degree of bravado in some replies which provoked doubts as to the ability of some respondents to put their words into action, the proportion willing to engage in strike action seems surprisingly high in view of the numbers in tied housing, the absence of a tradition of militancy in the Suffolk countryside and, not least, the professed harmony of relationships with their employers (see Chapter 5). The proportion of union members willing to engage in strike action was even higher: 60 per cent compared with only 28·8 per cent of the non-union members. Indeed union membership was the main determinant of willingness to engage in strike action, so that those factors associated with this attitude were those which were also associated with unionization, including the curvilinear relationship with farm size. The conventional wisdom that workers on the very large farms are the most conducive to strike action was not confirmed by the interviews.

The workers who were interviewed were asked for the reasons for their reply. These are shown in Table 33, with 'don't knows' elimin-

Table 33 Reasons for attitude to strike action of workers interviewed in Suffolk, 1972

Reason willing to strike	No.	%
Would have to because of pressure from fellow members, workmates, etc.	44	44·0
Only way to obtain higher wages	25	25·0
Must support the union	21	21·0
Must stand up for rights	8	8·0
Other	2	2·0
	100	100·0

Reason unwilling to strike	No.	%
Could not let livestock suffer	36	28·1
Ideological – 'Do not agree with strikes', etc.	30	23·4
Not union member	17	13·3
Fear of dismissal	15	11·7
Could not let employer down	10	7·8
Cannot afford to	6	4·7
In tied house	6	4·7
Other	8	6·3
	128	100·0

ated. These replies offer a caution to an unduly high expectation that agricultural workers favour militancy, since the main reason for indulging in strike action was a negative one – the fear of sanction from fellow workers. Those workers who expressed a positive belief in the justice or efficacy of strike action numbered only one-quarter of the entire sample. Among those workers who stated that they would not strike, loyalty to their employer seemed less prevalent than a general aversion, even revulsion (fieldwork took place in the wake of the miners' strike at the beginning of 1972), to strikes in general. In addition, nearly all the workers who handled stock were adamant that they could not allow the animals in their charge to suffer and that they were not prepared to go on strike and see this happen. This question was then followed by another which allowed the issue to be probed further: 'But farm workers do not usually go on strike, do they? Why do you think this is?' This enabled the workers interviewed to express their own perceptions of the apparent docility of the agricultural worker. Their replies are shown in Table 34. Perhaps significantly most of the replies are couched in terms of the impracticalities of militancy rather than the personal qualities of agricultural workers, which were referred to by only just over 20 per cent

Table 34 Reasons why farm workers in general do not take strike action given by workers interviewed in Suffolk, 1972

	No.	%
Insufficiently unionized	77	33·0
Too scattered/isolated	52	22·3
Too conscientious	26	11·2
Too friendly with employers	22	9·4
Will not allow livestock to suffer	16	6·9
Cannot afford to	9	3·9
Too apathetic	7	3·0
In tied house	7	3·0
Other	5	2·2
Don't know/No answer	12	5·2
	233	100·0

of those interviewed. However, the distinction should not be drawn too rigidly – perhaps the most prevalent reply involved a recognition that militant action was impracticable because of the nature of the work situation, but also that the work situation was such that grievances rarely reached the stage where militancy could even be contemplated. Some comments from the respondents themselves may exemplify this:

'There are too many bosses. There are only four men to one boss on nine out of ten farms. In industry it's three thousand to one boss. A lot of farmers and workers are friendly – you talk to them as you do to your workmates.'

'Working together. We don't think of ourselves as master and man, we work together. He'll talk to me like I'm talking to you. He tells you the prices, everything. We're too loyal to him sometimes – I've pushed my dinner away to help him.'

'Too scattered – agitators can't do anything like in industry.'

'Fifty per cent of farm workers don't belong to the union, so most farms would carry on with non-union labour. Our wages go before the Wages Board and every year you get a little rise. Farm workers are peaceful people and that keeps them satisfied. They're too scattered. Farmers are more like friends and workmates than bosses.'

'We're more isolated in little units. Relations are better between farmers and workers than in big concerns – you can talk it over if anything goes wrong.'

'Not enough in the union. Take this farm – I'm the only one in it! What would happen when I came back? There'd be victimization. When they (workmates) talk to the boss they turn the other cheek and smile.'

'We're the most loyal workers in the country. We work alongside the employer and feel a lot happier about it. Any grievances you can soon air them and finish with them on the spot. Farmers won't ask you to do a job they wouldn't do themselves.'

These comments highlight the complex problems which underlie the supposedly deferential characteristics of the agricultural worker. Most agricultural workers recognize that there is little that they are capable of achieving by engaging in some form of industrial conflict, even if they wished to do so. On the other hand some of the factors which produce this incapacity – notably, from the above examples, the nature of the work situation – also promote definitions of the situation which allow conflict to be dissipated or never to arise. Nevertheless, a not insignificant number of the workers interviewed declared themselves willing to engage in strike action, so that, as was envisaged in Chapter 2, it becomes necessary to try to relate these variations to certain typifications of the agricultural worker's overall social position. This matter is taken up again in Chapter 7.

In the spring and summer of 1972, the question of strike action was, it should be emphasized, far from academic. At the NUAAW's Biennial Conference in May, the following motion (No. 125) was put to the delegates:

'That this conference demands a minimum wage of £20 for a five-day, 40-hour, Monday to Friday working week for workers in agriculture and horticulture. Furthermore to call upon the Executive Committee to formulate a plan, whereby workers can take positive and direct action in support of this claim if it is not met in full by February of 1973. Also to call upon all workers to unite and support in full any action they may be called upon to take in support of this claim.'

Although the motion itself did not mention strikes, it was interpreted as such by all concerned (its proposer later confided that what he had had in mind was not total strike action but sporadic one-day strikes in different areas). A lively debate ensued which not only reflected the factional differences within the NUAAW (the Executive had, according to the proposer, spent a good deal of effort trying to persuade him to withdraw it, but he felt unable to do so since it had been passed by both his District Committee and County Conference) but also acted as a microcosm of the divisions of opinion among farm workers in general. Those delegates pressing the motion came mainly from north Norfolk, North Yorkshire and Essex. In these areas the members were reported as being 'ready for action'. The Essex County Conference, for example, had voted unanimously for strike action with the support of local milk-tanker drivers who were members of the TGWU. Essex has a very energetic County Committee and is generally on the left of the union. The market situation of farm workers in the county is stronger than most because of ample alternative employment opportunities. However, even here appearances can be deceptive: one Essex delegate admitted privately, 'Well, I can't strike because of the cattle, but I told my boss I might take a bit longer over the lunch break.' Later, in correspondence, another commented that 'the boredom generated by the raking over of the illusory ashes from imaginary fires inspires nothing more than a county yawn that stretches from Southend to Waltham Abbey to Saffron Walden to Harwich back to Southend'.

Opposition to the motion was led by the platform. The General Secretary denied that the Executive had been laggardly in pressing wage claims and that in any case they could move only with the support of all members. Yet when, after the previous award, 3,200 branches had been circularized for advice on what action should be taken only sixty-one had replied. Only eight members had turned out to lobby the AWB (five from Lincolnshire, two from Middlesex and one from Wiltshire). A number of speakers made the point that, until the labour force was 100 per cent unionized, strike action was the equivalent of industrial suicide and would drive the NUAAW into amalgamation with another union. Eventually Motion No. 125 was carried against the advice of the platform by 47 votes to 46. One delegate thereupon shouted, 'I'm a farm worker – I work on a *farm*. Not like most of you bloody lot around the room.' The Suffolk delegation, which had voted solidly against the motion, concurred with this view. As one put it, 'Among all those hollerin' for strike action there were none of them farm workers. There were roadmen, cabinet makers, council workers and anything else. There was only one farm worker and he has a branch with 270 members. Most of them don't know what they're talking about.' Certainly one detected a distinct change in atmosphere moving from Suffolk to the conference hall in Weymouth and back again, but in the light of the data from the interview the Suffolk delegation was possibly as unduly pessimistic of the chances of effective local direct action as those in favour of the motion had been optimistic.

As it turned out, events could hardly have taken a more ironic twist. At its meeting in October the AWB considered the NUAAW's new claim for £25 for a 40-hour week as demanded by the Biennial Conference. It awarded an extra £3·30 on the minimum rate, a rise of 20 per cent to £19·50. However, before it could be implemented the award was frozen as part of the Conservative government's wages standstill under the Counter-Inflation Act. The 'positive and direct action' which the Executive decided to take was to instruct County Committees to consider the proposals and send their comments. At the same time several suggestions for selected stoppages were put to the committees, as, for example, in respect of sugar-beet and potato-lifting, fruit-picking and pea-vining, and work in connection with milk production. In the meantime the farm workers' frozen pay award was receiving much national publicity and sympathy. Farmers, particularly in the Eastern Counties, had had an embarrassingly profitable year. In Suffolk the local NFU decided at a meeting to press strongly for the farm workers' pay award to be implemented in full. If anything, the local farmers seemed more out-raged than their employees, their feelings partly kindled by guilt over their own unhampered profit-making as contrasted with the depriva-tion imposed on their workers, but also by a universal recognition of their responsibilities. 'Don't worry,' one NFU official told a NUAAW branch secretary. 'We're going to help you out.' Several farmers decided to pay the award before it was officially ratified by the AWB in order to avoid the freeze. Others simply broke the law and told their men to put an extra couple of hours' overtime on their time-sheets. This, as the District Organizer pointed out, was the first time in nearly thirty years in Suffolk that he had heard of farmers being prepared to break the law so that they could pay their men *more* money. He had always spent a considerable amount of time pursuing through the courts employers who were underpaying their men.

Meanwhile the Suffolk County Committee of the NUAAW decided to take no action. They were not alone. The returns to Head Office could not have been very promising because by the time of the February 1973 edition of the *Land Worker* the General Secretary was doing his best to make a virtue out of necessity: 'Yet, if we are realistic, we should recognize that the position as it affects farm workers could be worse – a good deal worse. They have been cruelly penalized while their employers have made big profits – yes; and we have made this clear to both the government and the public. There is, however, one important favourable factor. The award will be paid IN FULL.'[97] The leader of the unofficial Action Committee, which had been established by a number of left-wing members to co-ordinate any resulting campaign, resigned in disgust. At the Sax-mundham District annual dinner the Suffolk District Organizer reassured his audience that they should not 'worry [*sic*] about getting a strike notice tomorrow'. In the end the union's 'positive and direct action' was reduced to a routine lobbying exercise.

Had a militant rank-and-file been betrayed by a hesitant and prevaricating union leadership, as some left-wingers suggested? Or were the gloomier prognostications of the opponents of Motion No. 125 at Weymouth vindicated by a reassertion of grass-roots opinion? The answer, in the light of the interviews, is probably neither. The Executive had shown itself capable of a more pragmatic approach to direct action than hitherto, admittedly pushed from behind by a narrow Biennial Conference vote. On the other hand its lead had met with no enthusiastic response, except in two or three counties. Had a more flexible approach been adopted these counties could perhaps have been given their head, and allowed some headline-seeking disruptive activity at a local level. However, the old principle of centralized control reasserted itself and an 'all-or-nothing' policy seems to have been adopted. The interviews demonstrated that a national strike was out of the question for the foreseeable future, so that localized, sporadic activity seems the only alternative to no direct action at all. The interviews showed *some* basis for such activity, provided it is carefully organized and co-ordinated, yet official union policy continues to stifle this approach. Morale, or consciousness depending upon one's terms of reference, seems unlikely to be raised until this policy is changed.

The NUAAW and the Future

It is apparent, then, that trade-unionism in agriculture has never been sufficiently strong to raise wages beyond that which the labour market has determined.[98] Many areas, such as Norfolk, which are highly unionized continue to contain some of the lowest-paid agricultural workers in the country. On the whole an improvement in life-chances through collective trade-union action has not proved possible. Of course, the agricultural worker has improved his standard of living over the years along with everyone else, yet he still has to find his 'place in the sun' and has lost ground since the war against industrial workers. Such a situation is both a cause and a consequence of the weaknesses of agricultural trade-unionism and was bound eventually to create serious problems for the NUAAW. By the end of the 1960s, beset by a declining membership and a diminishing pool of potential recruits, there were signs that it was beginning to experience chronic financial difficulties.

These difficulties have been accentuated by the parsimonious attitude of successive Biennial Conferences over the level of subscriptions, which, despite the inevitably high cost of organizing such a widely scattered membership, remains one of the lowest in British trade-unionism. With agricultural workers being themselves so lowly paid the resistance to any increase in subscriptions has been forceful, but it has weakened the union organization and contributed towards maintaining low wages. The data on trade-union finance unearthed by Latta reveal the precariousness of the situation. By 1970 the NUAAW had become one of the ten unions which relied most upon members' subscriptions for their income and with the highest proportion of their expenditure going on working expenses (92·5 per cent and 82·9 per cent respectively). In 1960 it had been among neither of these groups. Most other unions in this situation were the fast-expanding white-collar unions which had not yet built up large investments. 'The major exception,' writes Latta, 'to the equation of rich *equals* contracting or "stable" and "poor *equals* expanding", were the NUAAW, poor but contracting, which has never been able to get a high subscription rate.'[99] The state of the NUAAW's finances would be of less concern were it expanding its membership; however, given the contrary circumstances the situation was becoming dangerous.

Aware of these problems the NUAAW embarked upon a major reorganization scheme between 1970 and 1972. The number of District Organizers was reduced from forty-two to thirty-one and further economies were made elsewhere. Although these were essential measures to save the union from bankruptcy, they clearly weakened its long-term effectiveness. In spite of dire warnings from Head Office, however, subscriptions still failed to keep pace with inflation (or, indeed, the wage increases of agricultural workers), so that the financial health of the union has shown little sign of a sustained recovery. Between 1964 and 1973 contributions failed to cover gross expenditure by an average of £42,963 per year, reduced by investment income to an average deficit of £17,055 per year. Over the same period the value of investments was virtually halved – from £433,000 to £222,159 – as they were eaten into in order to reduce working losses. Only a large and rapid increase in subscriptions could rectify this situation, yet the danger is always that such a sudden movement would drive away a substantial proportion of members.

This financial malaise was paralleled during the late 1960s by an unfortunately acrimonious interlude in the internal politics of the NUAAW, during which the power vacuum left by the death of Gooch in 1964 was being competed for. There was an unusually fast turnover in the personnel occupying some of the leading positions in the union and, in the ensuing jostling for power, rivalries emerged and personal relationships became somewhat embittered, resulting even in litigation. The election of a new General Secretary in 1968 to succeed Lord Collison was described by the successful candidate, Reg Bottini, as a 'symbolic blood-letting' and he went on to call for a return to unity within the union.[100] The NUAAW was certainly in danger of losing its way and becoming stymied by internal squabbles. However, while internally the different factions may still 'hammer hell out of each other in private debate', they have succeeded in achieving a 'synthesis of effort'[101] against the common enemy, wherever it may be found. This has partly been a result of a more pragmatic approach to what has customarily been the main bone of contention – militant action. Since the election of Bottini the NUAAW leadership has, it seems, been more willing at least to consider the possibility of direct action, rather than to rule it out completely from the beginning, though as yet it has preferred to follow rather than lead rank-and-file opinion on this question.

The difficulties of the NUAAW have not escaped the notice of its traditional rival in the unionization of agricultural workers, the TGWU. In 1971 it renewed attempts to negotiate a merger with the NUAAW, but was given short shrift by the latter's leadership. Given the history of the NUAAW its wariness of the dangers of becoming just one section of a larger and apparently stronger union are not difficult to comprehend. The strong sense of possessing a peculiar identity which the individual agricultural worker feels easily transmits itself to the very top of the NUAAW. There is an instinctive objection to losing this identity in an organization run predominantly by and for urban, industrial workers. At the Biennial Conference in 1972 the NUAAW President, Bert Hazell, strongly supported these sentiments and set his face against any prospect of a merger. In many respects the TGWU's track record over peculiarly rural problems, like the tied cottage, does not inspire a great deal of confidence and there are fears that in supporting urban demands for cheap food the TGWU might not serve the best interests of the farm worker. Many NUAAW members have, on this basis, felt that once part of the TGWU they would be regarded as peripheral encumbrances, difficult and expensive to organize and easily lopped off in times of stringency. At least a union designed specifically for farm workers presents no such danger. On the other hand, a number of union activists have recognized that quick, effective industrial action is often possible only with the help of the TGWU – for example, the aid of bulk-tanker drivers in cutting off milk supplies. With the industrial might of the TGWU behind the farm worker, it is argued, the narrowing of the gap between industrial and agricultural wages could easily be brought about.

In the long term a merger with the TGWU may prove to be a logical step, even if financial difficulties do not drive the NUAAW to seek shelter there in the meantime. The falling numbers of agricultural workers, the urbanization of large tracts of once 'truly rural' countryside and the changing nature of the farm worker's skills may all conspire to undermine the belief that agricultural workers 'do different'. Furthermore, if the fall in the number of workers continues to outpace the rate of farm amalgamation, so that the average size of the labour force continues to shrink, then the more personalized quality of employer–employee relationships may well, other things being equal, render unionization and particularly industrial action more difficult to contemplate. A merger with the TGWU, however, might enable the farm worker's life-chances to be improved, while only a minority of them would need to engage in industrial action against their own employers.

1. J. P. D. Dunbabin, *Rural Discontent in Nineteenth Century Britain*, Faber, 1974, Ch. XIV.
2. E. J. Hobsbawm, 'Social Banditry', in H. A. Landsberger (ed.), *Rural Protest: Peasant Movements and Social Change*, Macmillan, 1974, p. 152.
3. H. Clegg, A. Fox and A. F. Thompson, *A History of British Trade Unions Since 1889, Volume I, 1889–1910*, OUP, 1964, p. 248.
4. G. Edwards, *From Crow-Scaring to Westminster*, NUAW, 1957, Chs. 9–10.
5. ibid., pp. 116, 117.
6. ibid., p. 237.
7. ibid., p. 140.

8. M. Madden, *The National Union of Agricultural Workers, 1906–1956*, Oxford University, B.Lit. thesis, 1957, p. 2. Madden, a former NUAW member and Ruskin scholar, provides the most comprehensive and analytical history of the first fifty years of the union. It is, alas, unpublished.

9. It is described in detail in Madden, op. cit., pp. 16–22, in R. Groves, *Sharpen the Sickle!*, Porcupine Press, 1949, pp. 117–22, and in Edwards, op. cit., Ch. 12.

10. Madden, op. cit., p. 26.

11. ibid., pp. 26, 27.

12. ibid., p. 30.

13. Groves, op. cit., pp. 143–9; F. E. Green, *A History of the English Agricultural Labourer*, P. S. King and Son, 1927, pp. 214–32.

14. Described in R. Hyman, *The Workers' Union*, Clarendon Press, Oxford, 1971, pp. 27–8.

15. R. Hyman, *The Workers' Union*, Oxford University, D.Phil. thesis, 1969, p. 265.

16. Green, op. cit., p. 322.

17. *Record* (journal of the Workers' Union), 1914, cited by Hyman (1969), op. cit., p. 266.

18. Hyman (1969), op. cit., p. 267.

19. Edwards, op. cit., pp. 190, 191.

20. Groves, op. cit., p. 149. See also R. Blythe, *Akenfield*, Allen Lane, 1969, Ch. 1.

21. Workers' Union, *Annual Report*, 1914, cited by Hyman (1969), op. cit., p. 268.

22. Madden, op. cit., p. 299; Hyman, op. cit., pp. 268–71.

23. Madden, op. cit., p. 40. Madden suggests that the award of 25s. was due to the fact that it represented a 66 per cent increase on the level of wages in 1914, just as the guaranteed wheat price did. Retail prices, however, had risen by 88 per cent.

24. Edwards, op. cit., p. 196.

25. Madden, op. cit., p. 58.

26. ibid., pp. 58–9.

27. Edwards, op. cit., p. 199.

28. Madden, op. cit., p. 279.

29. See A. D. Hall, *A Pilgrimage of British Farming*, John Murray, 1913, p. 443. Also A. H. Baverstock, *The English Agricultural Labourer*, Vineyard Press, 1912, p. 45.

30. Hyman (1969), op. cit., p. 274. Because of the extremely rudimentary records that were kept by both unions, these figures are only rough estimates.

31. Royal Commission on Agriculture, *Interim Report*, 1919, Cmd 479.

32. See Hyman (1969), op. cit., p. 294.

33. Madden, op. cit., pp. 93–4.

34. Groves, op. cit., p. 172.

35. E. Mejer, *Agricultural Labour in England and Wales*, Part II, 1920–50, University of Nottingham, Dept of Agricultural Economics, 1951, p. 29.

36. Madden, op. cit., p. 75.

37. *Land Worker*, August 1922, p. 4.

38. Groves, op. cit., p. 184.

39. ibid., p. 185.

40. ibid., p. 188.

41. *Land Worker*, April 1923, p. 8.

42. Details in Madden, op. cit., p. 81.

43. *Land Worker*, May 1923, p. 9.

44. Cited by Hyman (1969), op. cit., p. 261.

45. Since the NUAAW itself has no information on the precise number of its members, the membership has to be calculated on the basis of inferences drawn from the union's subscription income. The total number of regular workers in England and Wales in a random year is multiplied by the appropriate rates for males, females and juveniles. This produces the membership equivalent of each £1 of subscriptions. This method probably produces a slight understating of the membership at any one point in time since it derives a figure which would apply to the number of members of one year's standing. The method is described in detail in Madden, op. cit., Appendix D, pp. 301–3, and in F. D. Mills, *The National Union of Agricultural Workers* (University of Reading, Ph.D. thesis, 1965, Appendix 3, pp. 355–8. The base year used here is the same as that of Mills, i.e. 1954.

46. See Madden, op. cit., p. 262 ff.

47. Hyman (1969), op. cit., p. 273.

48. Many of the reasons for the weak unionization and low level of militancy among agricultural workers are summarized by J. A. Venn, *The Foundations of Agricultural Economics*, CUP, 1933, pp. 227–8.

49. One exception to this was the decision to expel a District Organizer in 1963. As Self and Storing (op. cit., p. 164) point out, there were suspicions of Communist infiltration in Dorset, where an Organizer of seventeen years' standing was sacked because 'he had failed in his capacity as a full-time officer of the Union to conform to Union policy' (*Land Worker*, April 1963, p. 5). This was carried through despite an appeal from the representatives of the other Organizers and a deputation from the Dorset County Committee.

50. Madden, op. cit., p. 47.

51. See Self and Storing, *The State and the Farmer*, Allen and Unwin, 1962, pp. 169–72.

52. Madden, op. cit., p. 92.

53. ibid., p. 131.

54. A. L. Chapman, *Wages and Salaries in the United Kingdom, 1920–1938*, CUP, 1953, Ch. IV.

55. *Land Worker*, December 1946, p. 3.

56. Reported in the ibid., September 1935, p. 7.

57. ibid., January 1944, p. 6.

58. Madden, op. cit., p. 163.

59. ibid., p. 165.

60. *Land Worker*, June 1946, p. 13.

61. K. Cowling, D. Metcalf and A. J. Rayner, *Resource Structure of Agriculture: An Economic Analysis*, Pergammon, 1970, p. 65.

62. D. Metcalf, 'The Determinants of the Earnings Gap in Agriculture, England and Wales, 1948–1963', *Farm Economist*, vol. XI, No. 2, 1966, pp. 67–82.

63. TUC, *Collective Bargaining and Trade Union Development in Wages Councils Sector*, TUC, 1969, p. 44.

64. Madden, op. cit., pp. 220–21.

65. *Land Worker*, January 1950, p. 7. Ironically the union's first journal was entitled *The Labourer*. These matters are considered more fully in Chapter 6.

66. *Land Worker*, May 1958, p. 15.

67. ibid., July 1965, p. 11.

68. ibid., November 1950, p. 8.

69. The intervening period was one of lively controversy over this issue – see ibid., July 1953, p. 5; September 1953, pp. 6–7.

70. Madden, op. cit., p. 252.

71. Groves, op. cit , p. 235.

72. Self and Storing, op. cit., p. 172.

73. ibid., p. 176.

74. H. A. Turner, *Trade Union Growth, Structure and Policy*, Allen and Unwin, 1962, p. 291.

75. The decision-making structure of the NUAAW is described in great detail in Mills, op. cit.

76. cf. B. C. Roberts, *Trade Union Government and Administration in Great Britain*, Bell, 1956, p. 504.

77. F. D. Mills, 'The National Union of Agricultural Workers', *Journal of Agricultural Economics*, vol. XVI, No. 2, 1964–5, p. 234. See also Self and Storing, op. cit., pp. 159–65.

78. Mills (1964–5), op. cit., p. 236.

79. The survival of faction is the criterion of union democracy suggested by R. Martin, 'Union Democracy: An Explanatory Framework', *Sociology*, vol. 2, 1968, pp. 205–20.

80. Self and Storing, op. cit., pp. 161–2.

81. These examples are taken from the NUAAW's *Annual Report* for 1970.

82. See H. A. Clegg, A. J. Killick and R. Adams, *Trade Union Officers*, Blackwell, Oxford, 1961, pp. 62, 77–82.

83. Self and Storing, op. cit., p. 164.

84. Mills (1964–5), op. cit., p. 231. The voting figures published in the *Land Worker* after union elections give the impression of very high turn-outs. This, however, is misleading, since the votes actually cast are multiplied up to give a proportional vote of the entire branch membership.

85. *Land Worker*, September 1960, p. 10.

86. Mills (1964–5), op. cit., p. 250. The previously published estimates of the density of union membership among agricultural workers have varied quite widely, though none have been as high as the NUAAW's own (50 per cent). Cowling and Metcalf (in 'An Analysis of the Determinants of Wage inflation in Agriculture', *Manchester School*, vol. 33, 1965, p. 184 n.)

estimate it at 17.63 per cent; Madden (op. cit.) gives 37 per cent; Mills
takes 33 per cent; and Hindell ('Trade Union Membership', *Planning*,
vol. 28, 1962, p. 156) judges it to be 26 per cent.

87. Cited by Self and Storing, op. cit., p. 165.
88. See Mills (1965), op. cit., for details.
89. *Land Worker*, No. 8, 18 December 1919, p. 5.
90. ibid., March 1922, p. 7.
91. ibid., May 1926, p. iv.
92. Madden, op. cit., p. 117.
93. cf. Mills (1965), op. cit., p. 22 f.
94. See n. 45 above.
95. Mills (1965), op. cit., p. 34.
96. See R. M. Blackburn and M. Mann, 'The Ideologies of Unskilled
    Workers', in M. I. A. Bulmer (ed.), *Working Class Images of Society*,
    Routledge and Kegan Paul, 1975.
97. *Land Worker*, February 1973, p. 4.
98. See Cowling and Metcalf, op. cit., p. 192.
99. G. Latta, 'Trade Union Finance', *British Journal of Industrial Relations*,
    vol. 10, No. 3, 1972, p. 406.
100. *Land Worker*, January 1970, p. 4.
101. ibid.

CHAPTER FIVE
The Work Situation

Work on the land has customarily been regarded as a qualitatively different experience from work in any other industry. Even today, despite wholesale mechanization, agriculture remains surrounded by a set of symbolic boundaries which separate it off from other types of employment and create an air of uniqueness with which farmers and farm workers alike identify. The move from agricultural to non-agricultural employment is still regarded as involving a much more severe dislocation than any other kind of occupational mobility. The agricultural worker tends to think of himself as being part of a distinctive breed, divorced by temperament and environment from the urban, industrial majority. The actual work itself is therefore an exceedingly important attribute of the farm worker's personal and social identity – more than many other jobs it defines for the farm worker what he *is*.

This partly explains the importance of the work situation as a structural component of the agricultural worker's overall social situation. However, as was pointed out in Chapter 2, the nature of the work situation has a number of other important implications owing to the frequent overlap of work and non-work roles. When the rural village was an occupational community such an overlap was virtually complete; and even today the large proportion of workers living 'on the job' (54·1 per cent in the Suffolk sample) ensure that the division between home and work is nothing like as great as in many other industries. It is the purpose of this chapter to describe the nature of the agricultural worker's work and to analyse his workplace relationships, both with the employer and fellow employees. Particular attention will be paid to one of the theoretical problems raised in Chapter 2: the mode of control operated by the employer, particularly the extent of bureaucratization, and its implications for the kind of worker commitment and loyalty which ensues. These are the kind of issues usually associated with the so-called 'size-effect' – the effect of plant size on worker identification.[1] In agriculture, because workplace relationships so often spill over into the surrounding community, the way in which employer–employee relationships are handled and legitimated will clearly have implications in the wider social setting, just as the latter will help to define the worker's expectations of his work situation. However, broader questions concerning the relationship between the work situation and the agricultural worker's overall 'image of society' are left to Chapter 7.

By the standards of most other sociological studies of occupational groups it is apparent that the agricultural worker's work situation is a somewhat peculiar one. In 1970 there were over 300,000 agricultural holdings in the United Kingdom, 171,000 of which were full-time with an average size of 154 acres. At the same time there were an average of 1·7 regular whole-time workers for every full-time holding. Therefore one is inevitably dealing with small-scale em-

Table 35 Distribution of holdings by labour size groups, 1972

	Suffolk %	Eastern Region %	England and Wales %
Size groups, regular whole-time workers:			
1	36·4	37·0	49·1
2	20·3	19·9	23·6
3	12·4	12·1	10·6
4	9·0	7·8	5·3
5–9	15·3	15·3	8·2
10–14	3·0	4·1	1·7
15–19	1·5	1·7	0·7
20+	2·0	2·1	0·8
Holdings with regular whole-time workers	47·5	39·8	35·6
No. of regular whole-time workers per holding	1·82	1·58	0·93
No. of regular whole-time workers per full-time holding	2·86	2·73	1·7

Source: MAFF Statistics

ployers of labour, and, although the trend is towards larger units in terms of production and acreage, so far the rate of diminution of the labour force is sufficiently outpacing the rate of farm amalgamation to reduce the average size of the labour force – in 1965 it was 2·1. In 1970 nearly three-quarters of all agricultural holdings employed no full-time workers at all and a further 13·9 per cent employed only one. So the distribution of the labour force is highly skewed towards the lower size groups: 21·4 per cent of the labour force are employed on their own and 62 per cent are employed on units of four or less men; only 7·8 per cent of the workers are on farms employing twenty or more employees. Comparative data on the distribution of holdings by the number of workers per holding is shown in Table 35.

Work and Work Orientation

Agricultural work, despite all the technological changes of recent years, remains distinctive in one important respect: the length of the production cycle and the rhythm of working on the land remain largely governed by the seasons of the year. The very length of the production cycle on an arable farm often results in a telescoping of time perception: ten years ago is only ten 'products' ago – almost yesterday to the Suffolk agricultural worker. Technological change, while it has drastically altered the work situation in other respects, has not removed this, for while the pace of work has been affected this rhythm remains. The basis of this apparent paradox is not hard to find. Operations in arable agriculture, unlike those in most areas of manufacturing industry, *must* take place sequentially rather than concurrently. Thus in replacing hand or horse power by machines the practice of carrying out production in sequential steps is not disturbed, as it is in the changeover from handicraft to mechanized manufacture in industry. As a result the consequences of technological innovation in agriculture have merely been a spectacular change in the implements of production, whereas in industry changes in the organization of production have been much more thoroughgoing.[2]

This is not to say, of course, that technological change in agriculture has not transformed the nature of the workplace social structure. In particular there has been a dramatic reduction in the division of labour as mechanization has allowed the production sequences to be carried out more quickly and with less labour than hitherto. On most farms the division of labour among the workers is minimal, with only one major division remaining – between those workers who work primarily with livestock and those involved in crop production which most involves driving machinery. On the smaller farm even this division is bridged. One consequence of mechanization, then, has been an increased variety in the work of the individual farm worker. Agricultural workers have always had to be extremely versatile, but whereas the nineteenth-century Suffolk horseman's life revolved entirely around his horses, his modern counterpart must not only be a tractor driver and mechanic, but often a stockman and general labourer too. In addition to this increased job rotation, mechanization has also removed much of the routine drudgery and certainly the physical effort from working on the land. The major drawback has, however, been the isolation of the modern farm worker, increasingly a rather lonely figure in a noisy tractor cab with sometimes only an attenuated and desultory contact with his workmates, of whom there are fewer and fewer around.

To try to reconstruct the work experience of the 'typical' farm worker is a somewhat fruitless exercise, since no farm worker could be regarded as typical in this sense. However, such is the social (and literal) invisibility of much farm work that it seems important to convey some idea of the nature of the farm worker's work experience, particularly as it is exactly this aspect of rural life which is usually absent from the conventional English cultural perspective. Most of the farms in the Suffolk sample were arable/pig enterprises, that is to say they were mainly concerned with growing crops, mostly cereals, and incorporated a pig unit which utilized home-produced feed. The end-product of these farms was therefore pigs, although many of the crops, including some cereals, were sold on the open market. Because of its predominance in the sample this type of farm can be taken as an example of the nature of the Suffolk agricultural worker's work, but it must be realized that such a description is intended to be illustrative rather than exhaustive. Certainly there are many Suffolk farming enterprises where the experiences of the workers do not conform with those given below.

A 600-acre Suffolk farm of this type, situated on clay land and away from the river valleys, would in 1972 have employed perhaps five general farm workers/tractor drivers and one pigman, perhaps more, perhaps less depending upon the involvement of the farmer and his family. With the enticing prospect of entry into the EEC and buoyant cereal prices, perhaps two-thirds or more of the farm would be under cereals, barley and wheat, the remainder being taken up with sugar beet, peas for freezing, beans and perhaps a few acres of other vegetables such as potatoes, swedes, cabbages, dwarf beans, brussels sprouts, etc. Small plots of land might be given over to growing bat willows or conifers, which not only have a commercial value but are useful for taxation purposes, while they, together with any residual woodland, provide some cover for that other important source of entertainment and revenue, the pheasant. Although there may be some specialization over pig production, many farms still see their charges through from farrowing to fattening, using some sort of rota whereby batches of fattened pigs leave the farm perhaps every three weeks or so, destined more often than not for one of the large food-processing firms which often contract out pig production to individual farmers or farmers' co-operatives.

On such a farm the pigman's job is perhaps the most routine, involving a daily round of preparing the feed and distributing it to the pigs, as well as generally keeping an eye on them for any sign of malady. He may also be involved in mucking out at regular intervals, although this will involve help from some of the other workers, since the muck will be transported by trailer around the farm to make muck heaps, later to be spread on the land prior to ploughing. The pigs will also need to be weighed (which will also involve some help) once a month and appropriate records will be kept. Less predictably the pigman will also look after farrowing, which in many cases will involve the constant supervision and awkward hours to which most stockmen have become inured. The cycle of farrowing, weaning and fattening is quicker than the production cycle on the arable side (it takes between twenty-two and thirty-one weeks from birth to despatch), but the process may also be carried out concurrently so that all the stages are taking place simultaneously. On very intensive livestock units, especially poultry, such tendencies have been followed still further to produce 'factory' farming methods (the term itself is, of course, significant), allowing for an extreme division of labour, associated with routine and repetitive work for those involved. Few Suffolk arable/pig farms could in any way be compared with this, however.

The work of the arable workers tends to be more constrained by seasonal factors, although it is not without its daily or weekly routines. January and February, generally a very slack time devoted to maintaining machinery, tidying up around the yard, oiling and painting, according to the weather, represent the nadir of the farming year. The major outdoors activity is hedging and ditching, a job which most farm workers dislike intensely because of the cold, wet and often filthy working conditions, and because the job is essentially destructive rather than constructive. With more and more fields having been amalgamated and hedges removed, more ditching than hedging is nowadays involved. Increasingly both tasks are mechanized – one sees very few traditionally 'laid' hedges in East Anglia these days – and on some farms the work is carried out by contractors, who possess the necessary equipment, rather than by the farm's own labour force. For the farmer on heavy land hedges and ditches are an irksome nuisance, occupying expensive land which could otherwise be rendered productive, costly to maintain and perpetuating an inefficient field pattern that has been inherited from a pre-mechanized age. Since the job is not a popular one among the workers either, and since there have been cash incentives for field amalgamation, hedges have been removed, and ditches replaced by drains all over south and eastern England. The result has been a change in the appearance of the countryside – with by now notorious repercussions among those who wish to preserve the 'traditional' rural English landscape – but for the farm worker a reduction in time spent on a job which he continues to regard with some distaste.

The end of this slack period depends very much upon weather conditions and how quickly the land will have sufficiently dried out to allow men and machinery to venture upon it, but most farmers hope that around the second or third week in March it will be possible to start preparing for one of the most frenetic periods of the year – seed-time. At this time new potatoes are sown and there is some early seed-drilling if the weather allows, beginning with spring beans. By April the preparation of seed beds, drilling and rolling are in full swing, beginning with barley and then wheat, peas and sugar beet. Timing is of the essence and if weather conditions have been adverse during March and early April it is not unusual to see drilling taking place at night by the light of the tractor's headlights. 'Winter' cereals – cereals sown during the previous autumn which have overwintered – are rolled and harrowed and late potatoes are sown. In addition the winter cereals are top-dressed with artificial fertilizer. All these activities ensure that the farm labour-force is fully stretched over this period. Overtime is usually plentiful and welcomed by most farm workers after the lean winter months and with summer holidays to look forward to. The necessities of the situation are also fully understood, so that there is little need for the employer to justify the imposition of long hours and weekend work upon his workers. Indeed most workers are as anxious to complete a successful sowing as their employers.

During May there is a further lull, punctuated by some crop-spraying. In the last week of May the hand-hoeing of sugar beet begins. Until very recently sugar beet has been sown in a continuous row and a great deal of hand labour is required for chopping out and singling the seedling to allow single plants to grow to maturity. The crop also needs to be kept free of weeds so that later in the year further sessions of tractor hoeing between the rows may take place. Hand-hoeing is an important event for a number of reasons. It is almost invariably paid for by piece-rate, the minimum rate for which is decided upon each year by County Wages Committees consisting of NFU and NUAAW representatives. Individual farms can, and sometimes do, vary the rate upwards, so some 'plant-bargaining' is by no means uncommon. Because of the operation of piece-rates, overtime is virtually unlimited and there is a further opportunity to obtain extra money for summer holidays. But perhaps the most important aspect from the sociological point of view is the fact that the operation is so labour-intensive that casual labour is often taken on, usually in the form of retired workers and workers' wives. Sugar-beet hoeing is therefore something of a social occasion, indeed under modern agricultural conditions it is virtually the last remaining farming activity in which the whole farm labour force (and often their wives) is gathered together with the possibility of easy and continuous communication between them. There is often a quasi-festive air about the proceedings – picnic lunches, etc. – tempered only by the competitive element introduced by piece-rates. Throughout June the usually depopulated fields of East Anglia take on a faintly – and temporarily – bucolic appearance for the one and only time in the agricultural year. However, even this is fast disappearing, since weeds are increasingly being controlled by chemicals and the singling operation has been superseded in many cases by precision drilling and monogerm seeds.

June is also the month for haysel or hay harvest. The increased specialization of most East Anglian farms, and the consequent disappearance of cattle from many of them, means that this is no longer the job it once was. Once haysel began in June and continued until mid-August, when it linked up with harvest; now it is of no concern to most Suffolk farmers and even for those who keep cows it has diminished in importance. A few runs round with a tractor and it is all over in a few weeks. For the arable/pig farm June is a month of watching and waiting once sugar-beet hoeing is completed. It is a time to take holidays or visit agricultural shows. It is also a time for lifting early potatoes, usually with the help of casual female labour, and for irrigating the main crop. Otherwise the tending of crops is limited to spraying – sugar beet for yellow virus, wheat for yellow rust, peas for weevil, etc.

In July the pace of work quickens once more. The early part of the month may be spent on routine maintenance work, the lull before the harvest storm, particularly going over the combine harvester before it is brought into use for its period of brief but intense activity. However, increasingly in Suffolk the main event of this month is pea harvest. Some peas are grown for seed and some for canning, but most of the crop, particularly on farms within easy reach of the factory at Lowestoft, is for freezing. Pea harvest is a fascinating spectacle, as far removed from the traditional smock-and-scythe image of agricultural work as it is possible to go. The keynote of the whole operation, which is carried out with an almost military style of planning and execution, is speed and precision of timing. The production of the crop is closely controlled by the food-processing firms – in Suffolk, mainly Birds Eye – in order to ensure both quality and a continuity of supply. The companies dictate to the individual farmers when to sow, when to spray and when to harvest. The farmers in turn combine into growers' groups in order to bargain with the companies, but also to pool machinery, labour and other resources at harvest time. In the case of one growers' group in the Suffolk fieldwork area this involved in 1972 the purchase of nine 'viners' – the machines which harvest the peas and which look like gigantic combine harvesters – worth £100,000, a water carrier, several tractors and the hire of a fleet of thirty lorries, plus the labour to operate them on a twenty-four-hour basis. This caravan of machinery and men moves around from farm to farm at the instigation of the factory in Lowestoft. The whole operation is radio-controlled from the factory and the peas have to be from field to freezer in ninety minutes, otherwise they are dumped. The harvest is carried out around the clock with a lorry leaving for the factory every twenty minutes (even if it has only a few peas in it).

For the workers, life 'on the peas' represents a qualitatively different experience from life during the other ten months of the year when they are on their own farms. They work shifts, something completely novel in agriculture, but generally receive higher wages. They also have the excitement, and status, of operating bigger, more expensive and more complex machinery than they have been accustomed to. More importantly the work is more disciplined and the mode of control more impersonal and formal than on most farms. However, the greatest significance probably lies in the opportunity which the pea harvest represents for workers from a large number of farms to come together, compare their circumstances and assess conditions on the farms they visit. This allows a degree of comparison over such matters as wages and conditions, not to mention husbandry techniques, which would otherwise not be available to many workers. Some of their verdicts are carried back to their colleagues who have remained on their regular farms and these help to establish and perpetuate evaluations of various farming employers, including their own, in the surrounding area.

Once the pea viners have departed, the opportunity is usually quickly seized to prepare the land for the next crop before corn harvest begins. This involves first muck-spreading and then plough-ing in preparation for, later in the year, the drilling of winter wheat or winter barley. By the middle of August pea harvest will have ended, although some of the team is kept together to harvest dwarf beans. By the end of the first week in August, however, most farmers on heavy land will have hoped to have the cereal harvest under way (earlier on light land), beginning with winter barley and finishing around the second week in September with spring wheat. This is traditionally the year's great climacteric, but while it remains a very busy period its importance both as a period of hectic work and as a social ritual has diminished considerably in recent years, though some of the mythology may remain. What was once simply 'harvest' is now often referred to as 'corn harvest' in order to distinguish it from other equally busy, and in some cases busier, periods. As long as it is not too extreme, modern grain driers have even reduced the importance of the weather (although driers can be expensive to operate). As if to perpetuate a version of harvest that is now fading away, farmers who otherwise hardly touch a tractor from one year's end to the next can be seen on board a combine harvester at this time of the year, while they also keep an anxious eye on the sky. The workers also keep a weather eye open, but for rather different motives – for them a difficult harvest means more overtime and higher wages.

Before the 1950s, grain harvesting involved a complex series of interconnected tasks involving the mobilization of a large labour force. The crop was first cut and bound into sheaves by a binder and the sheaves were 'stooked' in order to ripen and dry before being carted and stacked. The stacks were thatched to protect them from the weather, and later, over the winter months, it would be threshed to separate the grain from the straw.[3] Today some farmers earn a great deal of money by harvesting the odd field in such a manner and charging the public admission to come and watch them do it. Moreover by growing older strains of wheat without a pith in the straw they can often sell the straw for thatching commuters' cottages for a higher price than the grain. Needless to say, harvest for the most part is no longer carried out in this way. Now all the work is performed by combine harvesters which empty the grain from their tanks directly into trailers or lorries to be taken away in bulk to be cleaned and dressed elsewhere. A combine harvester can complete in a day what would have taken weeks using the old technology. In many fields harvest will take just one day, with possibly one more to bale and cart the straw. Alternatively the straw and stubble may be burned, so that by the end of August it can seem that the whole of the countryside is aflame, much to the consternation of surrounding residents, especially urbanized newcomers.

After harvest there is a brief interlude of muck-carting, ploughing and rolling in preparation for autumn drilling before the busiest time of the year for most East Anglian farms begins around the last week in September. October marks the confluence of a number of farming activities: the beginning of autumn ploughing and muck-spreading, the main drilling of winter barley, wheat and beans and the harvesting of spring beans, sugar beet and main crop potatoes.

This month has now replaced August as the really hectic month of the year, when overtime is often unlimited and when work continues over weekends and sometimes even into the night. Although this period has none of the aura of corn harvest, in terms of sheer work-load it forms the climax of the farming year before the slack winter months arrive. Ploughing and sugar-beet harvesting continue, weather permitting, into November and December and even beyond. The harvesting of sugar beet is now mechanized, thus removing one of the most laborious and detested jobs of the farming year, for pulling sugar beet in often freezing conditions was not only uncomfortable and arduous but a cause of sinovitis of the wrist which could result in permanent disability. Ploughing still results in a public statement of the farm worker's skill, but it has become less and less a status-enhancing quality in most rural villages. Some farm workers admit to being bored driving up and down the large East Anglian fields day in and day out for two or three months on end.

Most of the farm workers in the Suffolk sample experienced this kind of work pattern, although clearly it varied from farm to farm according to variations in the husbandry of the holdings and the division of labour among the workforce. Among the factors which emerge as being of importance is the tremendous variety involved in the work tasks, a variety enhanced by changes in the weather, soil and other contextual factors, so that farm workers will readily admit, with only minor exaggeration, that the work is never the same two days running. Most farm workers are also concerned with the production of living and growing things which they see through from beginning to end, so that they feel the sense of achievement familiar to most suburban gardeners when their crops or animals are finally brought to maturity. Compared with most other manual work, agriculture offers far greater non-economic rewards in terms of job interest, judgement, discretion, challenge, responsibility and control, so that intrinsic job satisfaction remains extraordinarily high. This is not to say that agriculture does not contain its boring, repetitive aspects nor its routine drudgery, but few farm workers leave the land because they dislike the work itself; on the contrary many would gladly return were it not for the low wages and poor prospects predominating throughout agriculture.[4]

These comments are supported by the findings of the survey. The vast majority (93·1 per cent) found their job interesting all the time or mostly interesting, and, although it is well known that a high proportion of all workers consistently affirm their job satisfaction in such a manner, the percentage is nevertheless very high in comparison with the various groups of workers to whom Blauner[5] put the same question (see Table 36). The workers were also asked for the reasons

Table 36 Job satisfaction of agricultural workers interviewed in Suffolk, 1972, and industrial workers interviewed by Blauner, 1964

	Agricultural workers %	Blauner's sample			
		Auto-mobiles %	Textiles %	Chemicals %	Printing %
Interesting all the time	31·3	33·0	45·0	52·0	58·0
Mostly interesting	61·8	33·0	37·0	38·0	37·0
Mostly dull and monotonous	6·0	16·0	10·0	8·0	4·0
Very dull and monotonous	0·9	18·0	8·0	3·0	–
	100·0	100·0	100·0	100·0	100·0

for their feelings of satisfaction or dissatisfaction. The small proportion who were dissatisfied overall cited boring, repetitive work, poor pay and poor working conditions as the main reasons. The variety of the job was overwhelmingly the major cause of satisfaction, together with the intrinsic pleasure derived from watching crops grow or stock mature. In general, as Table 37 shows, what some industrial sociologists have called intrinsic job factors predominated to the virtual exclusion of extrinsic factors.[6] Money was mentioned by only one respondent.

This question was probed further by asking the respondents first what they liked most and then what they liked least about their jobs. As Table 38 shows, most of the factors valued by the workers interviewed were of a somewhat nebulous kind (although none the less real for that) such as intrinsic interest, variety, autonomy, open-air, etc.[7] One particular task was mentioned with some frequency, however, and that was work with machinery. Operating modern farm

Table 37 Reasons for job satisfaction of workers interviewed in Suffolk, 1972

Reason	No.	%
Variety	116	53·5
Satisfaction from seeing crops and animals grow	52	23·9
Work with machinery	13	6·0
Outdoors	11	5·1
Autonomy	6	2·8
Friendly workmates	3	1·4
Friendly boss	3	1·4
Other	9	4·1
Don't know/No answer	4	1·8
	217	100·0

Table 38 Most valued aspect of job of workers interviewed in Suffolk, 1972

	No.	%
Working with machinery	48	20·6
Satisfaction from seeing crops and animals grow	41	17·6
Outdoors	34	14·6
Variety	23	9·9
Autonomy	18	7·7
Money	11	4·7
Friendly workmates	9	3·9
Friendly boss	6	2·4
Other	3	1·2
No difference	30	12·9
Don't know/No answer	10	4·3
	233	100·0

equipment undoubtedly represents a challenge to the skill and judgement of the agricultural worker which is capable of retaining his interest in the job. However, more than this is involved. Many farm workers assume an unyieldingly proprietorial air about the machinery they drive, resenting anyone else handling it whether he be a new

Table 39 Most disliked aspect of job of workers interviewed in Suffolk, 1972

	No.	%
Cold weather	28	12·0
Weekend work	22	9·4
Mucking-out	21	9·0
Working with animals	19	8·2
Poor pay	15	6·4
Dusty/dirty conditions	13	5·6
Hoeing sugar beet	11	4·7
Hedging and ditching	9	3·9
Spraying	6	2·6
Other	22	9·4
Nothing/No difference	56	24·0
Don't know/No answer	11	4·7
	233	100·0

apprentice or the employer himself. To drive a newer and bigger combine harvester or four-wheel drive tractor than anyone else on the farm or in the district is a matter of pride and status enhancement. Farms are judged by the machinery they purchase and farm workers share fully their employers' fascination with new mechanical innovations at agricultural shows and machinery demonstrations, treating them almost as a child views a new toy. While for the farmer there are overtones of conspicuous consumption, for the worker to handle such machinery is a badge of his modernity. It is one of the few ways in which the agricultural worker believes he can convey an impression of his skill to an otherwise largely uncomprehending non-agricultural population in terms which he believes they will understand.

The answers to the question on the most disliked aspects of the job tended to be more specific. A substantial proportion (28·4 per cent) mentioned particular tasks such as mucking-out, working with animals (something of a synonym for the former), hoeing sugar beet, hedging and ditching, and spraying. Most of these are either repetitive tasks or involve particularly unpleasant working conditions. Most of the other replies referred to cold weather, awkward hours, particularly weekend work, and poor pay. Nearly a quarter of the sample, however, could think of nothing that they particularly disliked about their job, an indication, perhaps, of their high degree of overall intrinsic job satisfaction.

Ostensibly the replies to these questions appear to indicate that the agricultural worker's orientation to work is an expressive rather than an instrumental one.[8] Pay does not figure particularly highly as a source of either satisfaction or dissatisfaction and what are generally considered to be expressive factors rate quite highly as a source of evaluation. This is not a surprising finding: the conventional wisdom is that nowhere is the contrast between low pay and high job satisfaction more starkly expressed than in agriculture and that the instrumentally oriented workers are filtered out by the customary outflow between the ages of twenty-one and thirty-five; those that remain are, almost by definition, the expressively oriented members of the labour force. This interpretation runs into difficulties, however, when the extent of instrumentalism among the farm workers in the survey is examined more closely. This instrumentalism was tapped using a question employed by Ingham in his study of Bradford engineering workers.[9] All respondents were asked 'Supposing you were offered a job outside farming in this district, but at 50p. a week more. Would you accept it?' If the answer was 'no', the 'offer' was increased to £1, then £3, £5 and £10. Those who would only move for £1 or more, and those who would not move even for an increase of £10 per week, were then asked the reasons for their answer. Although inflation makes direct comparison with Ingham's sample rather meaningless, the Suffolk farm workers interviewed appear roughly comparable with the expressively oriented workers in the small firms in Bradford: only 16·7 per cent would move for an increase of £1 or less, while 30·9 per cent would not leave at all. The reasons for their answers require a rather different interpretation, however.

As Table 40 shows, when respondents were asked why they were prepared to remain in their present job and lose the requisite amount of money, only a minority, 23·4 per cent, answered in expressive terms. The remaining answers took into account non-cash payments, particularly a free or virtually free house, or barriers to mobility such as age, family circumstances (for example dependent relatives living near by) and inability to undertake any non-agricultural employment. In the majority of cases, therefore, the low responsiveness to more money indicated not so much a lack of instrumentalism but a realistic assessment of either payments in kind or the weakness of the respondent's own market situation. On the whole it would appear that farm workers are much more instrumental in their orientation to work than has been supposed, but that this instrumentalism is often masked – and may, indeed be rationalized – by constraining factors which reduce the range of realistic alternatives to be considered.

How is the instrumentalism revealed by the answers to this question to be reconciled with the expressive orientation to work suggested by the previous replies? Clearly the two sets of questions were tapping different sets of needs or expectations and these results seem to confirm the utility of a distinction drawn by Daniel – between satisfaction *in* a job and satisfaction *with* a job. As Daniel points out: 'All surveys show that nearly all workers are satisfied with their jobs. They have made the best bargain in terms of their opportunities as they see them and they accept it. So it is not surprising that these workers are satisfied with their jobs ... This satisfaction is largely associated with sources of attachment to the job, which is a very different thing from the relative opportunities that different jobs provide for positive satisfaction at work through intrinsic interest, the exercise of abilities and the opportunities for growth, and the relative deprivations they furnish in terms of boredom and physical and emotional stress. In this case satisfaction with the bargain one has made does not make the cost painless.[10] Daniel is writing in the context of a debate with Goldthorpe over the value of an orientation-to-work perspective in the understanding of the industrial behaviour of Luton car workers.[11] In the case of Suffolk agricultural workers, the data suggests that the distinction equally holds, though the nature of the relationships is reversed: while nearly all agricultural workers are satisfied in their job, only a minority are

Table 40 Reasons for remaining in agriculture while foregoing more pay against amount of pay willing to forego, given by workers interviewed in Suffolk, 1972

	Amount of pay willing to forego					N	%
	50p.	£1	£3	£5	£10		
Unable to work elsewhere/possess skills uniquely suited to agriculture	20·0%	17·8%	–	7·4%	12·5%	22	10·5
Personal (e.g. age, family life-cycle, etc.)	–	13·3%	12·0%	7·4%	48·6%	49	23·4
Not worthwhile moving for less	66·7%	13·3%	6·0%	–	–	19	9·1
Value of tied house	–	24·4%	62·0%	44·4%	9·7%	61	29·2
Other instrumental reasons (e.g. availability of overtime, perquisites, etc.)	6·7%	4·4%	4·0%	3·7%	4·2%	9	4·3
Intrinsic job satisfaction	6·7%	13·3%	16·0%	37·0%	25·0%	49	23·4
	100%	100%	100%	100%	100%		
N	15	45	50	27	72	209	100
% of sample	7·2	21·5	23·9	12·9	34·4	100	

satisfied with it. Thus, while only 7 per cent of the sample expressed job dissatisfaction (that is, dissatisfaction *in* the job), a majority (56·4 per cent) were dissatisfied with their pay, 55 per cent would not take up farm employment if they had their life over again and 73·5 per cent would not recommend a job on the land to their sons.[12] This hardly suggests an overall satisfaction with the 'bargain' struck with their employers and also accounts for the 'frustrated instrumentalism' revealed in Table 40.

If agricultural workers possess both instrumental *and* expressive expectations of their work in such a manner, this hardly bolsters the utility of orientation to work as an independent variable to explain their workplace behaviour. Indeed, in the case of agricultural workers at least, it may be discounted, and for two major reasons. First on empirical grounds, it seems that the nature of the worker's market situation, especially the constraints on occupational choice, as mediated through the work situation, retain greater explanatory power than the kind of work-orientation approach favoured by Goldthorpe, *et al*. While the latter may or may not be suitable in the case of a more mobile and less dependent labour force like the Luton car-assembly workers, it is simply too voluntaristic to be appropriate here. As Chapter 3 showed, the constraints upon the agricultural worker's market situation are such that genuine choice between realistic occupational alternatives is not a predominant feature: farm workers are not, by and large, offered the luxury of carefully weighing the intrinsic and extrinsic aspects of a number of jobs open to them – they must take what they can, and often be grateful for it. Secondly, there is a certain circularity involved in an orientation-to-work approach which is particularly apparent in the case of farm workers. The expectations and needs which the farm worker is alleged to bring with him through the farm gate and apply to his work situation must be derived from some social milieu (unless one wishes to adhere to a rather naïve notion of universal human needs – an approach which the very voluntarism of the orientation-to-work perspective denies). The most obvious sources of this orientation are the family and the social system of the immediate locality – the village community. Yet not only are the great majority of workers themselves from agricultural families, but the communities in which most of them have been born and brought up have been shaped by the occupation upon which so much of rural society is by definition based – agriculture. Thus, even if an orientation-to-work approach were to be admitted on other grounds, the fact that the workers' orientations would largely be determined by the nature of the work situation in agriculture would lead to a somewhat arid circularity in the argument.[13] In an occupationally more heterogeneous area than rural Suffolk it might suffice, but such is the overlap between work and non-work roles and such is the overwhelming predominance of agriculture in the locality that the orientation-to-work approach, even allowing for its other weaknesses, is somewhat vacuous.

Relationships between Workmates

Changes in agricultural technology and the accompanying diminution of the labour force have wrought fundamental changes in the nature of workplace relationships among most agricultural workers. Much of the thriving rural working-class sub-culture described in Chapter 1 was based upon the twin supports of village and workplace conviviality. Nowadays both have become attenuated. At the workplace an occupational sub-culture with its own set of draconian norms and values was once reinforced by the comparatively large number of employees, often working in gangs with a horse-and-hand technology which allowed for easy and persistent communication between workmates. Today the number of employees on each farm has been drastically reduced, work in gangs has virtually disappeared as far as the regular farm labour-force is concerned and the new machine technology not only physically isolates one worker from another but renders communication difficult owing to the increased pace and noise associated with it. Working on the land is now a rather lonely occupation.

Nationally more than one-fifth of the agricultural labour-force are employed on their own and so have no regular full-time workmates at all; in the Suffolk sample this proportion was 8·6 per cent. For many of these workers, of course, their workmate is their employer, for many of the employers on farms of this size will also perform manual labour alongside their employees. As farm size increases, not only does the pervasiveness of this relationship decline but there are often greater opportunities for more sustained contact with fellow workmates. Thus among the workers interviewed in Suffolk, while overall the proportion who stated that they worked on their own 'a great deal' was 60·1 per cent, the figure varied between 66·7 per cent on the farms employing between two and four regular workers and 55·3 per cent on those employing twenty or more. Perhaps equally significant, however, is the absolute percentage – it is doubtful whether between a half and two-thirds of the workers would have given this reply twenty or thirty years ago. As it was, only 14·6 per cent worked alone 'hardly at all', which indicates that the great majority of agricultural workers spend a substantial proportion of their time separated from their workmates.

The extent of this isolation varies not only according to the size of the work force and the nature of the farm worker's job but according to the particular work task being performed. This in turn obviously varies according to the season of the year. The extreme variety in the work, illustrated earlier in this chapter, involves changes in the nature and extent of the contact between workers at work. For example, they may still work together in groups on such jobs as mucking-out, sugar-beet hoeing and the odd jobs performed around the farm during the slack winter months. On the other hand there are lengthy periods when they work predominantly on their own, especially during ploughing, drilling, spraying and even, because of the noise, dust and location of the driver's position on a combine harvester, at harvest. During work close to the farm buildings, tea breaks may be taken together, but otherwise they are taken alone out in the field. Mechanization has also allowed many workers to drive home for lunch on their tractors rather than eat communally against a hedge as was customary in the past. Contact between workers has therefore become more desultory and less regular. Workers interact with each other at work less often and less extensively than in the past and so there are fewer opportunities to maintain the workplace sub-culture which so often characterized the arable farm before mechanization.

One suspects, therefore, that the friendship network of the agricultural worker consists less of fellow agricultural workers than has been the case in the past. The workers who were interviewed were asked to give the occupations of their four closest friends, and although agricultural workers predominated (53·3 per cent of all friendships recorded) the proportion who were, or had been, workmates was 32·2 per cent.[14] This seems quite low, although there is no historical data with which to compare it. Older workers were more inclined to have friends who were workmates, as were those living on the farm rather than in a village. In both cases this can be understood in terms of availability (younger workers have a smaller proportion of peers employed on the land), although in the case of older workers it seems likely that it also signifies the greater importance of the work situation in the formation of friendships in the previous generation. In addition, the respondents were asked how many of their workmates were 'close friends'. What was understood as a 'close friend' obviously varied considerably (one respondent mused, 'A close friend ... That's someone I'd die for, isn't it?'), but for what it is worth 47·7 per cent stated that all their workmates were close friends while 20·4 per cent stated that none were. In addition, 55·8 per cent said they saw their workmates 'regularly' off the farm, 33·1 per cent occasionally and 11 per cent rarely or never. The most favoured meeting places were in the pub (40·4 per cent) and at home (33·3 per cent).

Although changes in the work situation are not the only factor involved, it is apparent that they have played an important part in undermining the kind of occupationally based sub-culture which used to be typical of the East Anglian village. Many aspects of this culture have declined, whether they be ploughing matches or poaching, while others, like the 'horseman's word',[15] have disappeared entirely. The oppositionist elements in this sub-culture were always sustained by close-knit workplace relationships and the associated fear of ostracism which they engendered. Workplace solidarity often consisted of this mixture of identification with an alternative set of norms and values to those imposed by the employers and a fear of 'doing different' from one's mates. Although this still applies in places today it is far less prevalent, and ostracism is hardly a sanction which can be applied as effectively as it once was. On the larger farms in the remoter, more agricultural areas one can still observe the persistence of this traditional proletarian culture in something like its old form, but elsewhere it has become extremely attenuated.

One example may be used to illustrate this point empirically – the willingness of the farm workers interviewed to engage in strike action. As was shown in Chapter 4, the single most important reason given for being willing to go on strike was the expectation of pressure from workmates to do so – 44 per cent of those who would go on strike mentioned this. However, the proportion increases with the size of labour force – from 35·9 per cent on farms employing less than four workers to 63·6 per cent on farms with more than twenty. Moreover unwillingness to engage in strike action is also associated with the tendency to work alone, as Table 41 shows. It seems clear

Table 41 Extent of working alone against willingness to engage in strike action of workers interviewed in Suffolk, 1972

	Extent of working alone		
Willingness to strike	'A great deal' (N = 137) %	'Now and then/ hardly ever' (N = 92) %	All workers (N = 229) %
Yes	37·2	53·3	43·7
No	62·8	46·7	56·3
	100·0	100·0	100·0

that, while the disadvantageous position of the agricultural worker remains, in comparative terms, much as it was before the onset of wholesale mechanization, changes in the work situation have resulted in fewer opportunities to sustain the animosities of class conflict which often flourished, albeit covertly, in the past. The work situation was not the only source of this sustenance, of course; the village community was, and occasionally still is, the other important basis of rural working-class culture. This, however, will be examined more closely in the following chapter. Here it is sufficient merely to note, firstly, that this culture, which once enabled the farm worker to maintain an alternative interpretation of his situation to that pre-scribed by farmers and landowners, is no longer supported to the extent that it once was by frequent and pervasive workplace inter-action; and, secondly, that this sub-culture was not a *source* of the conflict but merely ensured that a conflictual interpretation of employer–employee relationships was constantly available to the individual agricultural worker. In order to understand the course of the conflict, and how changes in the work situation have affected *this*, it is obviously necessary to investigate the relationship between employer and employee.

Workplace Modes of Control

Changes in technology and the associated decline in the average size of the farm labour force have also had a profound effect upon the relationship between farmer and farm worker. As was pointed out in Chapter 1, during the nineteenth and early part of the twentieth century the existence of a coherent, hegemonic and easily identifiable rural ruling class of landowners and farmers ensured that class divisions were strictly defined and maintained. Attempts to stabilize class relationships generally involved the exercise of paternalism, but this tended to occur outside working hours through the fulfilment of obligations in the village community. The work situation served mainly to reinforce class divisions rather than remove them, not only because of the existence of an oppositionist sub-culture among the workers, but because the employer was often a remote and authoritarian figure, whose contact with his workers at work was often only minimal. Orders were usually given to workers through a succession of intermediaries – bailiffs on the largest farms, foremen and charge hands elsewhere – and personal contact at work was often limited to the payment of wages, a literal case of cash nexus. The comparatively large amounts of labour employed necessitated this rigid, formal and somewhat impersonal mode of control, so that the work situation often reflected the class relationships characteristic of the wider rural society.

Most farms today present a vivid contrast. The gap in wealth, income and general life-style between farmer and worker is probably as wide today as ever it was, yet the changed nature of the work situation blurs class divisions rather than reinforces them. Perhaps no single factor has more influenced the agricultural worker's perception of his own objective situation than this change. The decline in the labour force, the removal of most gang labour and the tendency for a growing proportion of workers to live on the farm have all resulted in the growth of closer, more personal and informal relationships between farmer and farm worker, extending to consultation about day-to-day farm management and even outside working hours into the domestic sphere. Increasingly relationships have become established on a face-to-face, 'gaffer-to-man' basis, with farmer and worker often seeing each other several times a day, sharing break-times (often in the farmhouse kitchen) and even working alongside each other on the jobs that demand it. Thus the decreasing size of the labour force has enabled the traditional authority typical of agricultural employers to become more securely rooted. A number of studies of small industrial firms have shown how the more widespread level of interaction in small-scale organizations may produce a network with a high degree of 'connectedness' which creates a patriarchal normative system governing instrumental activities and fosters a high level of identification on the part of employees.[16] With the tendency for the average size of the agricultural labour force to fall there has been a trend towards this diffuse, particularistic mode of control being adopted by farming employers, other things being equal.

There has therefore been a tendency for a kind of size-effect-in-reverse to be operating in agriculture, with the prevailing trends reinforcing rather than breaking down traditional forms of authority. In terms of sheer numbers of workers employed, however, size *per se* is not a very satisfactory variable for understanding the work situation in agriculture. This is particularly apparent if one compares farms with the average kind of industrial enterprise – what in agriculture is a very large firm of, say, twenty employees would be considered tiny in most other industries. Clearly there are certain spatial constraints on the size of unit in agriculture owing to the importance of land as a factor of production, but associated with this is the capital-intensive nature of modern arable farming which has provided technological constraints on the organizational control structure not often found elsewhere. Hence farms bureaucratize, in the sense of introducing intermediate levels of authority between employer and employee, at a much smaller size than is customary among most industrial enterprises. This can be illustrated from the Suffolk sample, where no farm employing more than eight workers was without some level of authority, foreman and/or manager, interposed between employer and employees. Below this threshold farmers clearly have a degree of choice over how to organize their labour force – indeed some farmers with a very small number of employees may appoint managers because they either have no knowledge of, nor interest in, farming as an occupation (as opposed to a life-style). For this reason size of labour force and levels of organizational hierarchy are by no means completely correlated, nor are size of labour force and frequency of interaction between employer and employee. Indeed the number of levels of hierarchy in the organizational structure of the farm is a better predictor of the frequency of farmer–worker interaction than the absolute number of workers employed.

The proliferation of more than one level in the organizational hierarchy is often significant for the nature of employer–employee relationships in that inevitably the efficacy of traditional authority decreases when a patriarchal mode of control cannot be operated. This has occurred where farm amalgamation has reversed the trend towards a smaller labour force and personal authority. Here there are often associated tendencies towards the rationalization of authority: relationships become more universalistic and instrumentally specific and the mode of control is more by reference to impersonal mechanisms operated through a set of formalized procedural rules. There may be little or no contact between the owner of the farm and the workers, and day-to-day supervision is once again in the hands of managers and foremen, who may institute contact with workers through weekly 'assemblies' or by the use of personal two-way radios fitted to tractor cabs. This bureaucratic mode of control is often pursued on those farms run by large farming companies, particularly those with industrial or commercial connections which have recently been active in farm purchase in East Anglia. These new 'farmers' make no pretensions to traditional forms of authority[17] and are treated with suspicion by their neighbours as a result. In the Suffolk sample, however, all the farms, whatever their precise legal status, were to all intents and purposes family proprietorships. With one exception (described below) all the farmers operating a bureaucratic mode of control were nevertheless attempting to exercise traditional (rather than rational-legal) authority. A bureaucratic structure was therefore in existence either because of farm amalgamations stimulated by a desire for the more profitable use of capital resources or because the size of the labour force, despite reductions over the years, was still sufficiently large to support intermediate levels in the farm hierarchy, for example on surviving farm estates run by traditional landowning families.

The continuing exercise of traditional forms of authority by agricultural employers may seem paradoxical in the light of their economic rationality in other respects, and especially so given the decline of traditionalism as a criterion of legitimate authority in British society as a whole. However, the situation becomes more understandable when set in the context of rural society in general. Not only were all the farms which were investigated family proprietorships, but two-thirds of the present farmers had inherited the farm from their fathers. Many of them had been born and brought up in the same village as their workers and had 'served their time' working alongside their employees before assuming responsibility for running the business. Moreover, some farmers had an acute feeling for the stability which traditional authority conferred upon farmer–worker relationships. One farm, for example, was in the process of becoming more bureaucratically organized during the period of fieldwork. Two other farms were taken over and a new farming company was formed with arable and stock managers hired to run the respective parts of the new enterprise. The farmer was removed from daily contact with his workers but he maintained a visiting rota whereby he periodically saw the workers in their homes during the evening. He ensured that his secretary informed him of his duties at the required time. This, it was felt, improved the 'morale' of his employees, and 'ironed out any difficulties' resulting from the new structure (in the early weeks the workers complained of 'too many bosses').

Only one of the farmers in the sample had exercised the choice that was open to all of them and had consciously abandoned any notion of traditional authority at all. Perhaps significantly, he was the youngest farmer in the sample, having inherited the farm in his late twenties on the sudden death of his father. He had completely re-organized the structure of the farm into virtually autonomous units, and, following the recent industrial relations fashion for job enrichment and job enlargement, individual workers were given charge of one unit each and paid according to their output on what was virtually a profit-sharing basis. Two managerial overseers dealt with most of the day-to-day problems of running the enterprise and the workers rarely, if ever, saw their employer. He devoted most of his time to buying and selling through an associated marketing company, ensconced in the inner sanctum of a converted farm bungalow in a remote and lonely part of Suffolk which served as an office. To enter this building was a somewhat surrealistic experience, for inside were all the trappings of industrial bureaucracy: secretaries, typists, air conditioning, telex machines, telephones and modern Scandinavian decor. One other farmer in the fieldwork area also refused to abide by the conventions of traditional authority, but he unfortunately refused to be interviewed. He ran the largest farm in the area, employing nearly fifty workers, and his relationship with his employees was purely and explicitly that of cash nexus.

What was particularly interesting was the reaction to these two exceptions of the other farmers in the area. They were constantly being brought up as a point of reference in a disparaging way in order to condemn the economically instrumental nature of their relationships with their employees. Exaggerated accounts were given about the gross use of overtime on both farms and about the alleged injustices in the way the workers were treated (for example, the ploughing-up of their cottage gardens). Apocryphal stories were told with the intention of debunking their achievements, such as hints at dubious sources of finance or the non-payment of debts. This culminated in a slanderous account of the ancestry of the two farmers concerned, told with great relish and obvious sincerity about one or the other, by several of the more traditionalist farmers in the area. This myth seemed to serve a necessary social function, and it was hardly coincidental that it was applied only to the two most economically instrumental employers. As one farmer summed it up, 'People like x and y, they farm by the accounts book – they don't really know what farming is. They haven't been brought up to it [literally this was not true]. They're only interested in a return on capital, just a figure. It's not a way of life to them, just a business. They don't do anything for their men or for the farming community.'

Those farmers who are 'not brought up to it' quickly assimilate themselves into the prevailing pattern of employer–employee relationships. The newcomers with little or no farming background or experience are, indeed, those who, if anything, most overplay the traditionalist employer role. This is because they have been attracted into agriculture by the life-style and other non-pecuniary factors and enter fully-prepared, indeed eager, to assume a diligent paternalism both inside and outside work. This can occasionally lead to a somewhat over-zealous, and therefore resented, assumption of traditional authoritarian roles, particularly in the local community, before their credentials have been fully established. However, for many – and especially the substantial proportion of retired armed services' officers for whom such duties are a natural extension of their former obligations – the exercise of traditional authority in one of the remaining sections of British society where traditionalism continues to prevail is one of the main attractions which underlies their choice of farming in the first place.

The second group of newcomers are those who have a farming background and whose movement into the area can be understood in terms of either spiralism or the kind of familial circumstances which forces younger sons to move in order to remain in farming.[18] The most recognizable group are the significant number of Scottish farmers who moved into East Anglia during the Depression, buying derelict farms at knock-down prices. Much less traditionalistic, both in social and economic terms, than the local Suffolk farmers, many of them have become rich and successful farming businessmen. Their initial tendency was to treat their men in a similarly instrumental manner, paying them higher wages and disavowing the more traditional aspects of the employer's role in rural society. 'This was a very feudal sort of place,' said one Scottish immigrant. 'I was an outcast here because I paid a pound or two above the minimum'. Yet now the Scotsmen are indistinguishable from their local neighbours, paying the (craftsman's) minimum rate in the same way as virtually everyone else. Another former Scot had assumed many of the squirearchical roles in his village, having become president of numerous local associations and societies and the provider of the appropriate amounts of men, money, machinery and land to support its activities, from the village fete to the best-kept village competition. His workers, while all on the craftsman's minimum wage, were in receipt of a variety of gifts and perquisites.

The mechanisms by which such assimilation takes place are not too difficult to discern. Most farmers are integrated into a dense and close-knit social network with other farmers, both informally on the farm or in the pub and in an institutionalized way through regular meetings of the NFU, farmers' clubs, livestock associations, show committees, the Conservative Association and various charity organizations. 'It doesn't matter which social function I go to,' said one farmer, 'but it still looks like an NFU meeting.' In many cases these relationships stretch back over many generations and they are renewed regularly in innumerable ways. Whatever the situation among agricultural workers, gossip and ostracism remain potent regulators of behaviour among farmers (aided by one further technological innovation, the telephone), particularly in a situation where few alternative sources of local friendship are available. The norms of specifying the 'correct' way to 'look after' employees on the farm can therefore be strictly enforced. 'Looking after' workers most definitely does *not* mean paying higher wages, as the experience of the Scotsman quoted above shows. Indeed a few of the larger and more efficient farmers stated that they were willing to raise the wage rates of their workers, but that they were under strong pressure from other farmers in the area not to do so. Instead, 'looking after' the workers implies a genuine concern for their personal welfare, including help with personal and domestic problems, the provision of decent housing facilities, the provision, in so far as it is possible in agriculture, of safe and pleasant working conditions, and frequent individual acts of generosity like small gifts on family birthdays and at Christmas, periodic gifts of farm produce where possible and the provision of 'treats' like harvest suppers, days out at shows, etc. In other words the good employer is one who extends his relationship with his workers beyond the wage bargain – an employer who *cares*. In effect these attributes bear a remarkable similarity to, and are the modern equivalents of, the accoutrements of nineteenth-century paternalism. They represent the personal touch which takes the edge off what for most agricultural workers are the harsh realities of their market situation.

The decreasing average size of the labour force has allowed this personal, particularistic form of interaction to take place more readily. In the Suffolk sample, 65·5 per cent of the workers saw their employer at least once a day and 89·2 per cent at least once a week. However, the frequency of contact decreased on the bureaucratically organized farms. This tendency becomes particularly marked in relation to the extent to which the workers actually work alongside their employer: 14 per cent of the workers on the bureaucratic farms never worked with their employer and all those who did so regularly were on the patriarchal farms. These results are shown in Table 42. The organization of the work situation and the associated modes of control therefore act as a constraint upon the opportunities open to the employer to legitimate his authority and to convey his interpretation of the work situation, and of his workers' place within it, to his employees. The personal, diffuse nature of the relationship on those farms operating a patriarchal mode of control helps to ensure not only in a positive sense that the workers' identification with the

Table 42 Frequency of contact with employer and frequency of working alongside employer against mode of control of farms of workers interviewed in Suffolk, 1972 (supervisory workers excluded)

| | | Mode of control | |
	Patriarchal ($N = 103$) %	Bureaucratic ($N = 115$) %	All workers ($N = 219$) %
Frequency of contact with employer			
Every day	84·5	44·3	63·3
Less than daily, but at least weekly	14·6	34·8	25·2
Less often	0·9	20·9	11·5
	100·0	100·0	100·0
Frequency of working alongside employer			
Regularly	21·4	–	10·0
Occasionally	37·9	3·4	19·6
Rarely	16·5	2·6	9·1
Never	24·3	94·0	61·3
	100·0	100·0	100·0

farmer and farm are reinforced, but negatively in the sense that any conflict which arises is not put down by the workers to an abstract and inevitable consequence of any conflict of interest between employer and employee, but to a clash of personalities of the two parties involved. On the more bureaucratic farms, employer and employee tend to confront each other more as abstract categories and less as individuals, resulting in less affinity between the form in which the employer expresses his authority and the intermittent nature of the relationship reinforcing it. This in turn leads to the question of how far bureaucratization leads to a disjunction between the paternalism of the farmer and the kind of worker commitment to his employer that ensues.

Relationships with the Employer

Before examining this question some general comments can be made about the prevailing nature of employer–employee relationships. At the personal level this relationship is overwhelmingly viewed by the agricultural worker as being a good one: altogether 56·7 per cent of the respondents in the survey stated that they got on with their employer 'very well' and a further 42·5 per cent 'quite well'. Only two respondents – less than 1 per cent of the sample – were prepared to admit that they got on 'badly' with their employer. Both farmers and farm workers recognize that in what is overwhelmingly a close personal and particularistic relationship there are inevitable fluctuations from day to day which may affect this generally harmonious state of affairs. Most of the assessments were prefaced by something like, 'We have our ups and downs, but . . .', and there were a number of analogies drawn with marriage. However, there was a general recognition, as in their perceptions of marriage, that the relationship was not a conflictual one.

This conclusion is reinforced by other data gained by the survey. Of those workers who had worked on more than one farm, 64·4 per cent thought that their present farm was the best of those that they had worked on. In addition the respondents were asked the question traditionally employed by industrial sociologists to assess the workers' perceptions of their relationship with the employer in terms of harmony and conflict – whether a farm is 'like a football team' or whether farmers and workers are 'really on opposite sides'.[19] Again the relationship was overwhelmingly seen as harmonious, with 75·1 per cent characterizing the relationship as one of teamwork and 22·3 per cent as one of opposition (2·6 per cent did not know). This sense of teamwork is undoubtedly engendered by the farmer's willingness on many farms to work alongside his men as the need arises, particularly at harvest. Where this does not pertain, a sense of camaraderie may be generated by other means. For example, as one respondent pointed out in reply to this question, 'Every year we're in the competition for the best-kept farm. This year we were in and we won it again. If we were against him we would say, "Bugger it," and wouldn't bother. We don't think of ourselves as master and men, we work together.' One farm, however, could do even better than this: they actually played together as a cricket team – employer, manager and employees – so that not only did the analogy have a peculiarly apposite meaning for them, but, perhaps uniquely in British sociology, one was able to observe this alleged teamwork in action!

Although the expression of employer–employee relationships in terms of the 'team *versus* opposite sides' metaphor may be appropriate for the study of industrial relations in a factory it had certain limitations in tapping the nature of this relationship on the farm. Many workers preferred, quite spontaneously, to use an analogy with the family. By this, it should be emphasized, they meant that the relationship with the farmer was more harmonious and emotionally deeper than is implied by the word 'team', with its rather contractual overtones. Family metaphors cropped up constantly and could with profit have been employed in the question – in other words the 'team' analogy did not in many cases go far enough in discriminating the nature of the farm worker's attachment to his employer. Moreover the use of the family anology is full of sociological implications; in one sense on the smaller farms the analogy is a realistic assessment of the patriarchal nature of the farmer's authority, but on the other hand it raises interesting Freudian questions about how the farm worker can bring himself to revolt against the father.

The use of this family analogy to describe relationships at work suggests that, while they are generally harmonious, the extent of the involvement and attachment on which this harmony is based may vary. This can be examined by looking at the reasons the workers interviewed gave for their evaluations of their employer and by relating these reasons to the extent of farm bureaucratization. In other words, it should be possible to assess how far the use of more impersonal procedural rules on the more bureaucratized farms affects the nature of the farm worker's identification with his farm, by inhibiting the personal transmission of the farmer's values and beliefs about the work situation. In particular it is possible to gauge how far the harmony between employer and employee rests not so much on the latter's moral involvement with the farmer but on a more calculative basis which runs contrary to the tenets of traditional authority.

Table 43 shows the reasons the respondents gave for considering their farm the best farm, according to the mode of control operated by their employer. Worker attachment on the bureaucratically

Table 43 Reason for considering present farm the best farm to work on against mode of control of farms, given by workers interviewed in Suffolk, 1972[20]

| | | Mode of control | |
	Patriarchal (N = 58) %	Bureaucratic (N = 81) %	All farms (N = 139) %
Reason for considering present farm best farm to work on			
High pay	12·1	32·1	23·7
Efficiency	20·7	36·9	30·2
Good boss	39·6	8·6	21·6
Variety of work	6·9	1·2	3·6
Everything good	20·7	14·8	17·3
Other	–	6·2	3·6
	100·0	100·0	100·0

organized farms is notably more calculative, with 68 per cent giving the reason for their high evaluation of the farm in terms of high pay or the high efficiency of the farm (from which higher wages are assumed to spring). Only 8·6 per cent on these farms gave as their reason their respect and appreciation of the personal qualities of the farmer, compared with 39·6 per cent on the patriarchally run farms. A similar distinction also held, though more weakly, for the reasons the respondents gave for their good relationship with their employer. Although on both types of farm the major single reason concerned the personal qualities of the employer as a reasonable, even-tempered individual, the autonomy of the worker – his *lack* of frequent contact with (and by implication interference from) the employer – was a much more important factor on the bureaucratically organized farms. These results are shown in Table 44.

The nature of the relationships between farmer and farm worker can be summarized, then, by stating that, while most farm workers perceive it to be a generally happy and harmonious one, they do so for often very different, and even opposing, reasons according to the organization of work. Whichever mode of control is operated, the

Table 44 Reason for good relationship with farmer against mode of control of farms of workers interviewed in Suffolk, 1972 [21]

	Mode of control		
	Patriarchal (N = 103) %	Bureaucratic (N = 102) %	All farms (N = 205) %
Reason for good relationship with farmer			
Length of acquaintance	24·3	17·6	21·0
Personal qualities of boss	45·6	37·3	41·5
Appreciation of work	6·8	5·9	6·3
Autonomy	21·6	30·4	21·4
Other	10·7	8·8	9·8
	100·0	100·0	100·0

workers seem not only to comply with it but to evaluate their own kind of work situation highly. Clearly the involvement of the workers on the more bureaucratically organized farms is more 'calculative' than 'moral', to use Etzioni's terms [22] – that is to say, identification is more a matter of impersonal, economic nexus than of personal duty and obligation towards the employer. In the case of the farm workers interviewed, however, this did not imply any reduced *commitment* to the farm or the job – merely that the nature of this commitment was different. In order to measure the extent of the workers' commitment to the farm, a similar procedure was used to that adopted by Ingham. [23] The respondents were asked to choose between two different normative orientations towards absence from work:

A 'A man should not stay away from work in any event, except when it is really necessary as in the case of genuine sickness.'

B 'It's a free society and a man has the right to take a day off work once in a while if he wants to.'

The results, shown in Table 45, indicate that overall the farm workers interviewed have a high degree of attachment to their employment and that this hardly varies according to the organization of the farm.

Table 45 Attitudes to absence against mode of control of farms of workers interviewed in Suffolk, 1972[24]

		Mode of control	
	Patriarchal (N = 100) %	Bureaucratic (N = 111) %	All farms (N = 211) %
Attitudes to absence			
A man should not stay away from work except in the case of genuine sickness	63·0	64·9	63·9
It's a free society and a man has the right to take a day off if he wants to	37·0	35·1	36·1
	100·0	*100·0*	*100·0*

Moreover, unlike that found among the engineering workers studied by Ingham, this homogeneity remains when the reasons for their replies are taken into account.[25] For example, of those who agreed with alternative A, the proportion citing their duty or responsibility to the farm varied only between 44·4 per cent on the patriarchal farms to 40·3 per cent on the bureaucratic farms.

This hardly suggests, therefore, that the variations in evaluative criteria employed by the farm workers in the sample when assessing their farm and their employer can be accounted for in terms of different orientations to work, with the instrumental employees gravitating to the more bureaucratically organized farms and the more expressively oriented workers moving to the patriarchally run farms. As was argued earlier in this chapter, farm workers seem to possess *both* sets of expectations, and while it is reasonable, on the evidence presented above, to suppose that the more bureaucratic farms do indeed employ workers with a more calculative attachment to their jobs, it cannot be maintained that this rests upon their *prior* orientation to work. Although the evidence is more negative than positive, such differences seem to depend not on differences in work orientation but on a combination of self-selection and socialization on the farm.

This can be supported by considering for a moment the alternative case. A plausible view of the mobility pattern of farm labour would be to suppose that the movement between jobs during the first few years of employment represents instrumental employees seeking out instrumental employers and expressively oriented workers gravitating towards similarly inclined farmers. Then, once this matching process has been completed by the early twenties, the worker's mobility ends, and this would account for both the overall high evaluation of their employer given by the respondents in the survey and their differing criteria of evaluation. There may be some validity for such a model in the case of the more mobile, more highly trained and more specialized workers who form the highly paid elite group among farm workers, but for the majority this explanation is, as was pointed out earlier in this chapter, simply too voluntaristic. As the data presented in Chapter 3 showed, only a minority of moves are worker-initiated and even the 'settling-down' period during the early twenties is attributable less to factors associated with employment than with the housing market and the stage reached in the family cycle. Moreover there is little evidence to support the idea that farmers, even on the bureaucratically organized farms, use monetary rewards to attract workers, except again in the case of specialized workers – and even here other factors such as responsibility and autonomy probably count equally highly. The informal, particularistic and traditional ways in which the labour market operates, with strong sanctions against offering higher wage rates than those prevailing in the area (see Chapter 3) militate against this. Indeed, such economistic notions conflict with the traditionalism that prevails among agricultural employers. And, given the constraints of the labour market, the normative prescriptions which count are in general those of the employer rather than the prospective employee.

Hence the allocative process consists of good workers being sought out by farmers, rather than, except in the case of a fortunate few, the converse. On the smaller farms, as Table 43 suggests, the most important factor is the personal qualities of the employer and the consequent ability to 'get on' amicably. Labour mobility on these farms is much more likely to be due to the inability of the personalities concerned to mix together harmoniously. On the larger farms, however, the 'good' farmer is the efficient farmer, one who is innovatory, especially concerning new machinery, and a highly regarded exponent of crop and animal husbandry. Such farms offer not so much higher *rates* of pay as greater oppportunities for overtime (see Table 46). This is an important distinction, for overtime is typically

Table 46 Gross basic wage and gross weekly earnings against mode of control of farms of workers interviewed in Suffolk, 1972 (supervisory workers excluded)

	General workers		Specialized workers	
	Mode of control		Mode of control	
	Patriarchal (N = 81) %	Bureaucratic (N = 72) %	Patriarchal (N = 21) %	Bureaucratic (N = 44) %
Gross basic wage				
Less than £16·20	6·2	4·2	9·5	2·3
£16·20	12·3	13·8	14·3	–
£16·21–£17·81	5·0	9·7	9·5	2·3
£17·82	58·0	56·9	19·0	40·9
£17·83–£19·99	16·0	12·5	9·5	13·6
More than £20·00	2·5	–	38·1	40·9
	100·0	100·0	100·0	100·0
Gross weekly earnings				
Less than £15·00	7·4	–	–	2·3
£15·00–£19·99	29·6	16·7	33·3	9·1
£20·00–£24·99	38·3	45·8	23·8	20·5
£25·00–£29·99	18·5	27·8	33·3	40·9
£30·00–£34·99	5·0	5·6	4·8	20·5
More than £35·00	1·2	4·2	4·8	6·7
	100·0	100·0	100·0	100·0

regarded as the *gift* of the good employer, along with various payments in kind, like the standard of housing, food and fuel perquisites, etc., and *not* as an intrinsic part of the formal wage bargain (except for stockmen). Thus the granting of opportunities for overtime can be seen as part of the process of 'looking after' workers on the large farms, an extension of traditionalism, which in its *consequences* can threaten to be counter-traditionalistic. It panders to the more instrumental needs of the workers on the large farms and may indeed act as a substitute, as far as they are concerned, for the lack of more expressive satisfaction caused by the greater division of labour and the less pervasive personal contact with the employer.

Thus the differing evaluative criteria employed by the workers on the 'patriarchal' and 'bureaucratic' farms would appear to be due to the normative structure prescribed by the employer rather than the worker's prior orientation to work. To a certain extent this is perpetuated by the typically particularistic method of engagement, 'based first and foremost on employing the right type of man for the job in question'.[26] Those who do not 'fit in' are quickly eased out by one means or another, and this would account for a good deal of the movement between jobs in the early years rather than the movement of instrumentally oriented workers to the more bureaucratic farmers and expressive workers to the smaller, patriarchally run units. Thus, of the workers interviewed those on the bureaucratically run farms were not notably more responsive to money – 35·9 per cent of workers on the patriarchal farms were willing to move for £3 or less compared with 36·2 per cent on the bureaucratic farms. Nor did the workers on the larger farms exhibit the characteristics usually associated with an instrumental orientation to work:[27] they were *not* disproportionately younger, nor did they have more dependent children, nor were they more mobile, geographically or occupationally, nor did they have any greater experience of non-agricultural employment. Thus one is driven back to an explanation based upon socialization on the farm, which seems to offer a more likely source of variation in expectations of the work situation than prior orientation to work.

The stability of employment after the twenties (aided, of course, by the constraints on mobility discussed in Chapter 3), the geographical and social isolation of many farm workers from other groups of manual workers, the growing isolation of the farm worker from his colleagues at work and the increased contact between employer and employee on those farms which have not amalgamated – all these factors have made the work situation more conducive to the transmission of the employer's definition of the situation and the socialization of the agricultural worker into it. The more calculative nature of the workers' attachment on the more bureaucratic farms is due to the greater constraints upon maintaining the norms of traditional authority which the organization of these farms dictate – a higher division of labour, less variety in the work, more attenuated personal contact between employer and employee, the possibilities of maintaining a workplace oppositional sub-culture among the increased number of workmates and a greater reliance upon formal, impersonal rules and regulations. However, in general the changes in the nature of the work situation which have been wrought mainly by changes in agricultural technology have evinced a greater degree of contact between farmer and farm worker and a decline in the strength of the oppositional sub-culture of the workers themselves. Thus while on objective criteria like pay and conditions, the market situation of agricultural workers continues to deteriorate in comparison with other manual workers, the trends in the work situation, in so far as they affect the farm worker's perceptions and evaluations of his position, have not been ones which would lead one to expect them to express their dissatisfaction. Indeed, as far as these trends are concerned, the farm worker is more likely, in general, to endorse the dominant definition of his situation as it is conveyed to him from above, rather than question the legitimacy of the rewards that accrue to him.

The 'Size-Effect' – Some Preliminary Conclusions

Although the investigation of the relationship between the nature of the work situation and the agricultural worker's overall ideology is not to be taken up until Chapter 7, a few preliminary conclusions about the operation of the 'size-effect' may be made here. To establish a structural explanation of 'size-effect' we begin here by considering the work situation primarily in terms of the mode of control operated by the farmer. Thus the issue of size has been essentially couched in terms of the problem of order: how far there is an affinity between the traditional authority exercised by the farmer and the mode of control that he employs to organize his labour force. Thus, following Ingham's work on the size of industrial organization and worker behaviour, the 'size-effect' has been understood in terms of 'the effectiveness of *inter*personal as opposed to *im*personal controls in determining the level of organizational identification'.[28] The data from the survey of Suffolk farm workers suggests that, while the mode of control operated on the farm does determine the *kind* of identification which ensues, it does not seem to affect the *level* of organizational identification and commitment as measured by normative orientations towards absence from work. Nevertheless the more calculative involvement of the workers on the bureaucratic farms is not the kind of commitment which the employers on these farms, with one exception, would hope for, since this commitment does not conform to the established pattern of loyalty which they are trying to put across.

To a certain extent this is due to the very impersonality of the organizational structure on the bureaucratic farms, which conflicts with the personal loyalty to the employer that is embodied in the notion of traditional authority and which the farmer hopes to foster. The propensity of increasing size to bring about functional specialization and bureaucratization necessitates the use of a more impersonal, formal administration of the farm and renders the employer a more remote, authoritarian figure. It also restricts the opportunities open to the employer to socialize his employees into the norms and values of the enterprise and to obtain their personal commitment. In addition, however, the greater number of workers on these farms promotes the creation and sustenance of workplace sub-cultures by allowing greater interaction among fellow workers, while removing the opportunities for interaction between employer and employee. In this way, the workers on these farms are more likely to be insulated from exposure to dominant values and therefore less likely to accept their situation as a natural and legitimate one.[29] One would expect therefore, other things being equal, to find workers with more oppositional values – 'traditional proletarians' in Lockwood's terms[30] – on the bureaucratic farms, while those on the patriarchally run farms would be more deferential.

In some important respects, however, other things are not always equal. Undoubtedly, given the very high job satisfaction and the extent to which the agricultural worker takes his self-definition from his employment, the work situation is of great significance in defining the farm worker's *Weltanschauung*. However, the work situation cannot be considered completely in isolation from the other sets of relationships he enters into. The agricultural worker's perceptions and evaluations to some extent depend on his exposure to other sets of values off the farm and in the local community. There is no reason to suppose, for example, that frequency of interaction between employer and employee in itself produces a more harmonious relationship. Such a view 'mistakes the prevalence of face-to-face contacts ... for a prevalence of warm and satisfying relationships. It forgets that intimate personal contacts can be every bit as unbearable as the impersonality of the market place.'[31] As was noted in Chapter 1, what characterized the stability of nineteenth-century agrarian class relationships was the hegemony of landowners and farmers both in the work situation *and* in the local social system. Some degree of totality was therefore inherent in the situation, so that any access to alternative evaluations of the legitimacy of this rural ruling class was prevented. Stacey made much the same point in her first study of Banbury: 'In the traditional sector economic, social, religious and political values and attitudes are closely linked and traditional industry closely related to the social system.'[32] Thus the identification with traditional authority at work was inextricably linked with the stable and accepted criteria of legitimacy in the local system of stratification. This suggests that the stability of traditional authority is most guaranteed where the social structure is both small-scale *and* total, and it is perhaps in these terms that the so-called 'size-effect' is best understood.

This chapter has concentrated on associated aspects of scale in the work situation, particularly the mode of control and its implications for the kind of workplace interaction which ensues. In order to assess the degree of totality involved in the agricultural worker's exposure to traditional forms of authority, however, it is necessary to go beyond the work situation and examine his position in the local social structure of the village community.

1. See G. K. Ingham, *Size of Industrial Organization and Worker Behaviour*, CUP, 1970.

2. See J. M. Brewster, 'The Machine Process in Agriculture and Industry', in K. A. Fox and G. D. Johnson, *Readings in the Economics of Agriculture*, Allen and Unwin, 1970, pp. 3–13.

3. There are a number of detailed descriptions of this process available in the literature – see, in particular, G. E. Evans, *Ask the Fellows Who Cut the Hay*, Faber, 1956, Chs. 11–13; *The Pattern under the Plough*, Faber, 1966, Ch. 13; *The Farm and the Village*, Faber, 1969, Ch. 6–8.

4. See J. E. Bessell, *The Younger Worker in Agriculture: Projections to 1980*, NEDO, 1972, Ch. 4. The most comprehensive study of this issue, though now dated, is B. M. Osborne, *Recruitment to Agriculture*, Central Office of Information for the Social Survey, 1949.

5. R. Blauner, *Alienation and Freedom*, University of Chicago Press, 1964; for a detailed discussion of comparative rates of job satisfaction, see Blauner's paper, 'Work Satisfaction and Industrial Trends in Modern Society', in W. Galenson and S. M. Lipset (eds.), *Labor and Trade Unionism: An Interdisciplinary Reader*, Wiley, New York, 1960, pp. 339–60.

6. See the authors cited by Alan Fox, *A Sociology of Work in Industry*, Macmillan, 1971, Ch. 1.

7. In the samples reported on by Bessell (op. cit., p. 19) and Osborne (op. cit., p. 22) working outdoors was the most commonly cited reason, followed by intrinsic interest and working with machinery (Bessell) or mechanization and 'freedom, variety, interest' (Osborne). Both 'working with machinery' and 'outdoors' may, in some cases, be a disguised way of expressing a desire for autonomy.

8. On this distinction, see J. H. Goldthorpe, 'Attitudes and Behaviour of Car Assembly Workers: A Deviant Case and a Theoretical Critique', *British Journal of Sociology*, vol. 17, 1966, pp. 227–44, and J. H. Goldthorpe, *et al.*, *The Affluent Worker: Industrial Attitudes and Behaviour*, CUP, 1968.

9. G. K. Ingham, op. cit., pp. 91–2.

10. W. W. Daniel, 'Industrial Behaviour and Orientation to Work – A Critique', *Journal of Management Studies*, vol. 6, No. 3, 1969, pp. 366–75.

11. For further contributions to this debate see J. H. Goldthorpe, 'The Social Action Approach to Industrial Sociology: A Reply to Daniel', *Journal of Management Studies*, vol. 7, No. 2, 1970, pp. 199–208; W. W. Daniel, 'Productivity Bargaining and Orientation to Work – a Rejoinder to Goldthorpe', ibid., vol. 8, No. 3, 1971, pp. 329–35; and J. H. Goldthorpe 'Daniel on Orientation to Work – A Final Comment', ibid., vol. 9, No. 3, 1972, pp. 266–73.

12. Mostly for instrumental reasons like poor pay (41·0 per cent) and poor prospects (30·3 per cent).

13. See G. Mackenzie, 'The Affluent Worker Study: An Evaluation and Critique', in F. Parkin (ed.), *The Social Analysis of the Class Structure*, Tavistock, 1974.

14. The figure relates to the whole sample. It is depressed slightly by the

inclusion of workers with no workmates (including the much smaller proportion who have never had any).

15. See G. E. Evans, *The Horse in the Furrow*, Faber, 1960.

16. See Ingham, op. cit.; S. Cunnison, *Wages and Work Allocation*, Tavistock, 1966; S. Cleland, *The Influence of Plant Size on Industrial Relations*, Industrial Relations Section, Department of Economics and Sociology, Princeton University, 1955; E. V. Batstone, *Aspects of Stratification in a Community Context*, University College, Swansea, Ph.D. thesis, 1969; P. Hollowell, *The Lorry Driver*, Routledge and Kegan Paul, 1968.

17. See, for example, the remarks by Anthony Rosen of Fountain Farms Ltd, in the Rank-Hovis-MacDougall *Hampshire Farming Review*, 1973, in a paper entitled 'Increased Land Prices – Their Implications on the Future Structure of Agriculture' that 'there is no "divine right to farm" and that the best qualification to be a good farmer is not necessarily to be a farmer's son' (p. 11).

18. cf. W. M. Williams, *A West Country Village: Ashworthy*, Routledge and Kegan Paul, 1964.

19. cf. Goldthorpe *et al.*, op. cit.; Ingham, op. cit.

20. Workers employed on the farm where the farmer made no pretence at traditional authority are excluded, along with supervisory workers and 'don't knows'.

21. See note 20.

22. Etzioni, A., *A Comparative Analysis of Complex Organizations*, New York, Free Press, 1961.

23. Ingham, op. cit., pp. 119–21.

24. See n. 20.

25. Ingham, op. cit., p. 119.

26. A. K. Giles and W. J. G. Cowie, *The Farm Worker: His Training, Pay and Status*, University of Bristol, 1961, p. 41. See also M. Black, 'Agricultural Labour in an Expanding Economy', *Journal of Agricultural Economics*, vol. XIX, No. 1, 1968, pp. 59–76.

27. See Ingham, op. cit., Ch. 10; Goldthorpe *et al.*, op. cit., Ch. 7.

28. Ingham, op. cit., p. 28.

29. cf. the argument of Frank Parkin in 'Working Class Conservatives: A Theory of Political Deviance', *British Journal of Sociology*, vol. 18, 1967, pp. 278–90.

30. D. Lockwood, 'The Sources of Variation in Working Class Images of Society', *Sociological Review*, vol. 19, 1966, pp. 249–67.

31. R. Bendix, *Work and Authority in Industry*, University of California Press, 1956, p. 37. Also C. Bell and H. Newby, 'The Sources of Variation in Agricultural Workers' Images of Society', *Sociological Review*, vol. 21, No. 2, 1973, pp. 229–53.

32. M. Stacey, *Tradition and Change*, OUP, 1960, p. 37; Lockwood, op. cit.; also Ingham, op. cit., p. 54.

CHAPTER SIX
Changes in the Rural Village

Juxtaposed with the agricultural worker's world of work there lies the world of the local community.[1] In the past the village often represented the boundaries of his social world, an arena for the acting out of his biography and a source, along with his work, of his own identity. This may apply less rigidly today, but the rural village still remains an important source of values, beliefs and meanings upon which the agricultural worker can draw when evaluating the world around him and his own place within it. Moreover the structure and control of relationships in the local community are important in maintaining certain kinds of social imagery and political outlook. For example, by the degree to which the village community subjects the agricultural worker to the social control of his fellow workers during leisure hours, or exposes him and his family to other standards of conduct than those which prevail at work, or by the degree to which it provides opportunities for interaction across class lines, the structure of village life plays a crucial part in either reinforcing or weakening the evaluations of the prevailing social hierarchy which the agricultural worker acquires in his role as a worker.[2]

For many agricultural workers, however, the social composition of the rural village and its associated set of activities have changed within their lifetime in such a swift and bewildering fashion as to match the upheavals in the technology of agricultural work itself. The 'drift from the land' has denuded many villages of a substantial proportion of their former working population and this exodus has in many areas of lowland England been compensated for only by the arrival of a car-owning, overwhelmingly middle-class group of immigrant urbanites whose impact upon the local community has been prodigious. It is an impact, however, which has been very complex in its effect upon the nature of the relationship between the agricultural worker and his local community, and certainly more complex than simple *gemeinschaftlich* views of the rural community imply. As was suggested in Chapter 2, the changes which have taken place in recent years in many former agricultural villages cannot be subsumed under the rubric of *Gemeinschaft–Gesellschaft* or rural–urban dichotomies, but relate more to the impact of national changes on the local social situation, mediated through particular class and status groups in the local social structure. The purpose of this chapter is to describe these changes in so far as they have impinged upon the agricultural worker, with particular emphasis on how they have affected his status in local village society. The status accorded to the individual agricultural worker in his own village and the criteria which he adopts for allocating status to others clearly constitute an important element in his endorsement or rejection of the legitimacy of social inequality in contemporary rural life. Therefore the consequences of the changing social composition of many villages for the status hierarchy within them are particularly important to investigate.

'Attributional' and 'Interactional' Status

The concept of status has been a notoriously difficult one in sociology, so that before entering into an analysis of the status situation of the agricultural worker in local village society, it is necessary to make a few preliminary comments on the approach to be adopted here. This is not simply an abstract, conceptual exercise, however, since the distinctions drawn in this section can be applied in a very real sense to the recent changes in the social structure of rural communities.

Much of the confusion over the concept of status results, as Parkin has pointed out, from an insufficient distinction having been made between status as a reputational attribute of *persons* and status as a formal attribute of positions.[3] In many cases the two may empirically coincide, but in the case of the agricultural worker it is of fundamental importance to maintain this distinction and to be absolutely clear about which type of status is being referred to. Status as a reputational attribute is what Littlejohn refers to as 'esteem' and Plowman, Minchinton and Stacey as 'interactional status'.[4] It arises out of the face-to-face interaction of individuals, who, as a consequence of pervasive personal interaction, do not allocate status uni-dimensionally on the basis of some readily observable trait, but around a complex set of criteria arrived at through close personal acquaintance. Parkin characterizes such interactional status as 'a social increment which individuals build up and sustain through regular amounts ...; as such it has little or no transferability outside the restricted setting in which it emerges'.[5]

This may be contrasted with the alternative use of status as an attribute of positions in society, which Plowman, Minchinton and Stacey refer to as 'attributional status'. Attributional status is essentially an emergent property of the class structure. It is, then, embedded *within* the existing power structure, the source of which must be elsewhere and not within the development of social honour itself. 'The development of status', wrote Weber, 'is essentially a question of stratification resting upon usurpation ... But the road from this purely conventional situation to legal privilege, positive or negative, is easily travelled as soon as a certain stratification of the social order has in fact been "lived in" and has achieved stability by virtue of a stable distribution of economic power'.[6] Such attributional status, then, emerges from the imposition of the social evaluations and moral judgements of those who occupy dominant positions in society. In view of this it is not surprising that the attributional status hierarchy tends to follow closely the class hierarchy in British society as a whole, for it legitimates economically based domination and converts it into authority. Thus the easily discernible criteria of prestige allocation are basically material – occupation, income, wealth and conspicuous consumption – and thus all attached to the economic order. This renders attributional status a universal system of prestige allocation which can be, and is, transferred from one local *milieu* to another.

Interactional status and attributional status rankings can be regarded as quite separate phenomena, since the latter constitutes a national prestige structure and cannot be regarded as merely the aggregate of the reputational qualities of individuals earned in interactional status situations. Indeed attributional status is quite independent of the extent of the actual social interaction which may occur between the groups concerned. Thus in a local social situation like the rural village, individuals are more or less automatically assigned an attributional status position on the basis of being representatives of nationally recognized status groups, irrespective of *personal* evaluations. This is important when one comes to appraise the status of newcomers to the village. On the other hand interactional status forms a basis for social acceptance or rejection in the context of face-to-face relationships. Because these judgements *are* particularistic it is difficult to generalize concerning the criteria which form the basis for such evaluations, but among those which appear in the literature on local interactional status systems in community studies are: the distinction between 'rough' and 'respectable' families in working-class areas (in itself an interesting example of how dominant values penetrate even into this situation); the willingness to engage in reciprocal acts of help and kindness, particularly in times of domestic crisis; and, particularly important as far as agricultural workers are concerned, the possession of highly prized job skills. In many cases, however, such interactional status-enhancing characteristics amount to little more than personality differences.[7]

It is quite feasible for the two systems of status to co-exist within the same local community, particularly where class boundaries are clearly defined so that interactional status occurs among class peers rather than enveloping all social classes. (Indeed different social classes may even operate with differing criteria of *interactional* status under conditions in which their relative social separation ensures that these inconsistencies rarely become manifest.) For the most part evidence suggests that where conflict exists between attributional and interactional status rankings, the former takes precedence. An agricultural worker may be highly esteemed, but he remains an agricultural worker, and therefore lower in status than the land-owner, whatever the latter's personal qualities. Not all members of the village may accept this ranking by any means, but, as Parkin points out, most working-class individuals at least recognize this state of affairs and act according to the norms of the attributional status order, particularly in their social encounters with those higher up the social scale.[8] After all, in the last instance they may be constrained to do so, given the system of power and privileges on which such an order rests. In most instances, however, such a dilemma need not arise, for, in the case of the rural village, it is quite often possible for the agricultural worker to see his relationship with a landowner as being different in *kind* (because it is a relationship with *authority*) from his relationship with a fellow worker and for different criteria of status to apply in each case. Moreover these criteria need not be consistent with each other, for, unless circumstances demand that the individual confront these inconsistencies, he may continue to draw upon the normative prescriptions appropriate to each situation without considering the contradictions between them. (These matters are explored further in Chapter 7.)

Thus, in considering the status situation of the agricultural worker, it soon becomes apparent that it is not so monolithic nor so uni-dimensional as its encapsulation in the phrase *the* status situation implies. One must not only examine carefully the extent of the consensus which implicitly underlies all concepts of status, but ask, given a particular structure of relationships, *which* status system is it that is the most meaningful to the agricultural worker. It is quite apparent, for example, that while on attributional status criteria the ranking of the agricultural worker is very low indeed, his subjective interpretation of his status situation, which may be based upon his interactional status in the local community, may be at complete variance with this – or it may not. In either case, the interpretation of his situation will be based upon which status hierarchy seems most relevant to the social milieu in which he finds himself and, since this milieu has in turn changed rapidly in recent years with the changes in the social composition of the majority of rural villages, it is quite likely that his interpretation will have changed accordingly.

Change in the Rural Village – A Typology

Recent social change in the rural village has been a patchy and uneven affair, occurring at a different pace at different times and in different geographical areas. Nevertheless the underlying pattern of these changes has, whatever the variations experienced in particular villages at particular points in time, been similar – the changeover from a situation where the bulk of the village population both lived and worked locally to one in which many, if not most, work else-where in urban-based employment. These changes were first ex-perienced on the fringes of major urban centres and have proceeded generally outwards from them, first along the main lines of com-munication. Today, as Pahl has pointed out, the commuter frontier has enveloped virtually the whole of lowland England, so that the waves from London have met those from Bristol to the west and those from the Midlands to the north.[9] In East Anglia, however, there are areas which still have to feel the full brunt of these developments, thanks mainly to the poor system of road and rail communications. Here it is still possible to observe the impact of the kind of changes which Sturt was writing about in Surrey before the First World War,[10] but which in large areas of Suffolk and Norfolk are still a recent phenomenon.

As a starting point it is possible to take the rural village as it was outlined in Chapter 1, that is the village as an *occupational community*. Its main feature was that one industry – agriculture – dominated the employment of its inhabitants, and moreover, since at least in East Anglia the majority of the employers lived not in the nucleated core of the village but on the farms around its periphery, the agricultural village contained a virtually homogeneous class structure. It consisted almost entirely of agricultural workers, together with those workers employed in servicing the agricultural population. To reiterate some of the main points made in Chapter 1, this composition gave the village many of the characteristics that have been noted of working-class occupational communities elsewhere: a strong sense of shared occupational experience, a distinctive occupational culture, an overlap between work and non-work roles and loyalties, a prevalence of closely knit cliques of friends, workmates, neighbours and relatives and generally a strong sense of group identity which marked off the village from the others that surrounded it. This strong sense of attachment to primary groups was partly a function of geographical isolation and a common occupation, but it was also forged out of the economic necessities of living close to poverty which promoted the values of mutual aid and neighbourliness.

These characteristics meant that the East Anglian agricultural village on the whole conformed more to the pattern of urban working-class occupational communities[11] than to the more loosely stratified rural communities of upland Britain which form most of the literature on rural community studies. Thus, on the basis of the limited historical evidence available, it seems reasonable to conclude that the distance in wealth, income, life-style and, most importantly, authority decisively marked off the occupational community of the agricultural worker from the more geographically widespread network of the local farmers and landowners, creating the kind of 'us and them' social imagery characteristic of urban working-class communities and allowing nascent conflict never to be very far from the surface of day-to-day relationships. Many of the radical movements described in Chapter 1, particularly Primitive Methodism and trade-unionism, both fed upon and nurtured these underlying antagonisms, while simultaneously moulding them in their own image. At the same time it can be acknowledged that the reverse side of rural autocracy was often rural benevolence, but in either case the agricultural worker had no doubt where the power in the local community lay, and whether he preferred to defer to the authority of his 'betters' or fight against it or merely accept it as a fact of life and accommodate himself to it, he recognized that there was a qualitative difference between this relationship and that with his fellow workers.

In the rural village, therefore, the status situation of the agricultural worker consisted of a duality. In terms of attributional status he was at the bottom of the status hierarchy, part of the lowest of the three 'natural orders' of rural life, but even within the working class itself his low-paid and apparently unskilled job assigned him to a low place in the status order, with only the casual, itinerent workers, like tinkers, sweeps, gipsies and tramps, below them. As Evans points out, 'Strange as it must seem now, the skill of the old horse ploughman was not recognized outside his own immediate circle. All farm workers were *labourers* with that term's implication of unskilled and unintelligent toil; and that label stuck to them until recent years. And it must be admitted that the low level of wages the farm-worker received appeared to the uninformed justification enough for not changing their image of him.'[12] The farm worker was often quite aware that outside the boundaries of the occupational community these judgements were generally accepted, especially in the towns. Flora Thompson notes how fond were the agricultural workers in her village of 'explaining to an outsider that field work was not the fool's job that some townsmen considered it'.[13] He was, as far as society at large was concerned, the 'bottom dog',[14] existing in the backward state akin to serfdom which was all part of the 'idiocy of rural life'.

Within the occupational community, however, the status of the individual agricultural worker could be very different. As was suggested in Chapter 1, what counted in the closely knit network of workers which formed the occupational community were not the attributes of income and conspicuous consumption but the esteem gained from skill at work. Although this was not the *only* criterion of interactional status, it does seem to have been the most important one as far as the individual agricultural worker (though not necessarily his wife and family) was concerned. It allowed the agricultural worker to possess a degree of status in his own immediate set of relationships which could be at complete variance with that attributed to him by the rest of society. And all the evidence, from East Anglia at least, suggests that it was his interactional status in the local community which was more socially significant to him. In addition to being an economic necessity, his work was a serious business of status enhancement, institutionalized in formal ploughing and drawing matches. In addition the worker was often subjected to the more informal, but equally exacting, judgements of his peers each day in the field or on Sundays in the pub.[15] Thus, when the village was an occupational community, the individual agricultural worker could accrue to himself a great deal of the esteem and self-respect which was often denied to him in the rest of society

It is this interactional status system which the recent changes in the social structure of most lowland English villages have threatened to undermine. Indeed the occupational community is in danger of becoming a historical anachronism and in East Anglia it survives only in a few areas, such as those isolated by bad roads from urban centres. It has been destroyed by the twin assault of the decline of employment opportunities in agriculture and the creeping urbanization of the rural village. As the job opportunities in rural areas have decreased so the rural working population has moved out, to be replaced in many areas by commuters, retired couples and weekend-cottagers who have been attracted by a combination of cheap housing (until the late 1960s) and the idealized view of rural life which Pahl has called 'the village in the mind'.[16] The new immigrants possess a life-style in which the village is not the focus of their social activities, for not only do they not work locally, but their pattern of leisure activities – shopping, visiting friends and relatives, entertainment – often takes them outside the immediate locality as well.[17] This influx of strangers, therefore, can quite rapidly affect the nature of village society: suddenly everybody does *not* know everybody else. The newcomer, moreover, does not enter the village as a lone individual who has to win social recognition locally in order to make life tolerable. Instead the newcomer is one of a large group of recently arrived immigrants, whose values, behaviour and life-style, being similarly based upon an urban, middle-class pattern, are very similar, while being notably different from those of the natives. It is therefore no longer so essential that the newcomer should adapt himself to the mores of the village; if necessary, social contacts can be established among fellow-newcomers or even outside the village altogether. Quite quickly, then, a new social division may arise – between on the one hand the close-knit 'locals', who form the rump of the old occupational community, and, on the other, the newcomers. The former occupational community then tends to retreat in upon itself and become what might be called an *encapsulated community*,[18] since the locals now form a community within a community – a separate and dense network encapsulated within the total local social system.

In many villages the agricultural worker becomes part of what can almost be a residual category imprisoned by spatial and occupational constraints. Pahl, for example, refers to the growing polarization in the village population between 'the poor whose work keeps them there and the rich who have chosen to be there (perhaps only at weekends and holidays)'.[19] This is likely to continue as long as the deteriorioration in public transport facilities in rural areas, exacerbated by the influx of car-owning immigrants, continues to increase spatial constraints to the extent that the poor locals become more firmly imprisoned, while only the rich can afford the personal means of mobility which will enable them to overcome them. This gulf between the resident poor and immigrant rich in the encapsulated community means that there is often little contact between the two sides. Also, new dimensions of social conflict tend to be created, to replace the rural class antagonisms of the occupational community.

Conflict is likely to be generated over two main issues (although they are closely connected). The first is local housing. Housing is the crucial resource over which competition is fiercest in the encapsulated community. The newcomers, on the whole, are not competing with the local agricultural workers for jobs, since both they and their children are more mobile and more highly educated and are competing in an entirely separate – usually professional and managerial – labour market which is national in scope. Housing is an entirely different matter. In Chapter 1, reference was made to the strategic importance of control of rural housing in the control of the rural labour market – and, indeed, of rural society as a whole – in the nineteenth century. In many ways the chronic shortage of housing in rural areas is a legacy of this historical state of affairs, but it is also a function of the domination of rural local government in the twentieth century by property-owning ratepayers with an interest in keeping rates as low as possible and hence the expenditure on local-authority housing to a minimum. For the vast majority of agricultural workers, of course, the purchase of privately owned housing has been, and remains, completely out of the question, given the extremely low level of their incomes. The meaningful housing market for the agricultural worker was in the past, therefore, either privately rented property, local-authority housing or the tied cottage. The arrival of middle-class newcomers has not only finally put paid to any hopes of owner-occupation by the few aspiring farm workers but it has also priced most of them out of the privately rented market, too. Owners of ex-farm worker's cottages can obtain far higher rents from commuters, retired urbanites, holiday makers or weekend-cottagers than from local workers. These owners – principally local farmers and landowners, but also occasionally local shop keepers and other tradesmen – can also make large capital gains by selling their property to newcomers at what by local standards are vastly inflated prices. The supply of privately rented accommodation at a rent suitable for the agricultural worker has thus declined alarmingly (aided in East Anglia by another class of immigrants who offer a more lucrative return – American airforcemen). As a result the agricultural worker has been forced to fall back on the two remaining alternatives: tied cottages and local-authority housing.

The provision of local-authority housing links up with the second basis of the conflict between locals and newcomers. The newcomers have a set of stereotyped expectations of village life. What has attracted them to life in the countryside in the first place is the romantic vision of the English village, to which attention was drawn at the beginning of this book. They come to escape and to retreat; to escape from the turmoil and strife of urban life and to retreat into the peace and quiet of a tranquil and harmonious rural community. Their expectations therefore contain both an aesthetic and a social dimension: not only do they hold ideas on how the village should *look*, but on how the villagers should *act*. Their 'village in the mind' leads them to be aggressively protective against any changes in the village that threaten their image. Hence, typically, it is the new-comers who form village amenity societies, complain about uprooted hedges or diverted footpaths, and who, most significantly, protest against any plans to build more houses in the village, especially council housing, which is considered in both its aesthetic *and* its social connotations as being, in that well-used phrase, 'detrimental to the character of the village'. Needless to say, such attitudes hardly commend themselves to the agricultural worker, for whom the increased provision of council housing has become a dire necessity because he has been priced out of the privately rented market by precisely that group which now obstructs, as he sees it, any new housing development suitable for him. Such protests strain the already wary relationship between the locals and the newcomers.

This conflict, which merely adds to those created by the differences in background, class and life-style, is also overlaid by the new-comers' expectations of the locals' behaviour. The newcomers like to see farm workers around the village since it reminds them that they do indeed live in a 'real' rural community, as opposed to a kind of rustic suburbia. However, the agricultural worker is expected to conform to the demeanour expected of him in the idealized village – a 'character', a bit of a wit perhaps, a source of homespun rural philosophy, but above all he must be deferential. After all, conflict, strikes and the whole range of activities which result from workers not knowing their 'place' is part of the urban maelstrom from which many of the newcomers are trying to escape, and such behaviour hardly befits the situation they expect to find in an idyllic rural setting. The farm workers which the newcomers expect to find are therefore pet farm workers, 'props on the rustic stage' as Pahl has called them[20] who help to define the village, along with the church bells, the green and the thatched cottages, but whose behaviour must not intrude into this peaceful vision. To the farm worker, however, the newcomers' brand of paternalism simply seems insufferably patronizing and he frequently withholds the expected deferential response on the grounds that not only have they taken over 'his' village but that they lack any of the accoutrements of traditional authority.

This attitude towards the agricultural worker on the part of the newcomers is a consequence of the largely attributional status system that they bring with them into the village. They tend to share the predominantly urban view of the agricultural worker as a somewhat slow, unskilled and servile individual whose proper place is at the bottom of the village status structure. They therefore personify the penetration of the interactional status system of the occupational community by the more universalistic system of attributional status, based largely upon occupational prestige ranking, income and conspicuous consumption. The prospect of being judged by such criteria in his own village clearly threatens many agricultural workers with a loss of their former esteem based upon skill at work. The newcomers, of course, are almost entirely unappreciative of these skills – as they drive around the countryside they cannot distinguish between a well-ploughed field and a badly ploughed one or between a faultlessly drilled seed-bed and one that has gone haywire. They can only judge by criteria with which they are more familiar, and this for the most part means life-styles that are principally determined by income. The agricultural worker, on low wages, cannot compete in this league. Instead, threatened with being deprived of his former status in the community, he changes the rules of the competition. He responds to the new situation by excluding the newcomers from his social group, since non-acceptance on the basis of length of residence is one of the few ways in which the local workers can retain any of their old status in the community.[21]

Hence the process of encapsulation brings about a separation of the locals from the newcomers and a change in the local status system. By altering the criteria by which status is conferred to include length of residence, local prestige is withheld from the affluent newcomers. The locals become encapsulated in their own local social system, which, depending upon the morphology of the local housing, may also be physically located in one part of the village. The locals, for example, tend to congregate in the council-house estate, where they may retain their closely knit patterns of neighbourly association and preserve their own leisure activities, particularly their own pub, or one of the bars within a pub. Corralled in this way into one part of the village, interaction across the local/immigrant schism may be limited only to certain symbolic occasions like the parish meeting or the village fete, but even here social interaction may be highly ritualized and rudimentary. Village fetes in particular often reflect the divisions in the village rather well, with the locals, usually dressed in their Sunday best, keeping themselves very much to

themselves in the beer tent or at the vegetable show while the
affluent newcomers, easily distinguished by their proletarian denims
and corduroys, concentrate on the flower arrangements and the
wine-making, while congratulating themselves on the conviviality
of village life. Fetes and other social occasions are therefore more of a
symbolic coming together than a real one. Otherwise the only
regular contact between the two sides lies in the actions of a few
'go-betweens', such as small tradesmen and shopkeepers and those
employed part-time by the newcomers, such as domestic cleaners –
the 'little woman' who comes in two or three times a week to 'do'
and who is probably the wife of an agricultural worker grateful for
the extra money – and gardeners, who are likely to be retired farm
workers. These individuals will be very influential in defining the
locals' image among the newcomers, while at the same time they
define the newcomers' image among the locals by reporting back
and spreading their gossip around closely knit networks of friends
and relations.

This situation easily lends itself to mutual stereotyping. If the locals
consider the newcomers 'snobbish' or 'jumped up', the newcomers
are equally vehement in their complaints about having to have 'three
generations in the churchyard before you're accepted around here'.
They confess somewhat ruefully: 'They say the first fifty years are
the worst.' One village immigrant, for example, has expressed his
exasperation at the lack of friendliness among the local pub regulars
as follows: 'Admission to a Masonic Lodge is easy compared with an
entry into this coterie of diehards. The qualifications of a candidate
appear to be: *one* he must have attained the age of seventy years;
two his family must have resided in the parish for 200 years; *three*
he, and his father before him, must have been against the Parish
Council on the water question; and *four* he must have taken an active
part in the age-long dispute with the local estate concerning the right
of way across Shepherd's Close. These old men have a simple
expedient for dealing with any untoward situation that arises or any
intrusion on their sacred precincts at the inn. They just "drink up"
and walk out in a body, muttering under their breath.'[22] This
description is, of course, exaggerated, but it contains a number of
elements of truth which many newcomers to villages would recognize.

In the encapsulated community, therefore, the agricultural worker is no longer integrated into village society as a whole, but only into his own encapsulated section of it, and he tends to treat the newcomers, even though they are resident in the village, with the same mixture of suspicion and disparagement that 'furriners' from surrounding villages were subjected to when the village was an occupational community. Thus the old us/them antagonisms become redefined: 'us' are now the locals; 'them' are the newcomers. This affects the nature of the relationship between farmer and farm worker, since the farmers are also locals and therefore 'one of us'. Reinforced by the changes in the work situation described in the previous chapter the changes in the local community bring farmers and farm workers closer together than was customary under the old regime. The farmers themselves have not been immune to the impact of the newcomers on the tenor of local social relationships. They, too, suffer the consequences of 'the village in the mind'. The newcomers' tendency to treat the countryside as a vast municipal park, across which they can walk their dogs and their children gallop their ponies, often leads them into conflict with farmers and farm workers alike. Farmers and newcomers are also frequently antagonists over the question of the effects of modern farming practices upon the traditional features of the English landscape. The newcomers expect, for example, to see hedges rather than tower silos or asbestos barns. They complain vociferously about the removal of hedgerows, the use of modern insecticides and herbicides, the re-routing or obliteration of footpaths, the burning of straw and stubble and a number of other activities which the farmer looks upon as essential for the maintenance of an efficient and profitable farming enterprise.[23]

Farmers and farm workers in the encapsulated community therefore exhibit a tendency to close ranks against a common adversary. This is aided by the reduction in the number of authority roles held by farmers in the local social system as enthusiastic newcomers take over the running of local associations, become local councillors and assume positions of local responsibility. Thus farmers and landowners are no longer the figures of local omnipotence they once were, though they remain powerful as local employers. Nevertheless, farmer and farm worker share a common understanding of agriculture, so that, unlike the newcomers, the farmers at least continue to appreciate the nature of the farm worker's skills. As a result most farm workers obtain much higher esteem from their employers than from the attributional status ranking of the newcomers. Consequently local farmers are exempted by their workers from the antagonisms which might otherwise have arisen in the wake of the middle-class urbanites' arrival in the immediate vicinity. While farm workers may have become more aware of existing national class divisions and inequalities, their encapsulation in a local, agricultural social system – helped, it must be repeated, by changes in the work situation – has tended to insulate them from any generalized growth of class consciousness. Indeed, in so far as the encapsulated community marks a partial breakdown in the solidarity of the occupational community, it seems likely that class conflict has been reduced and with it there has been brought about a diminution in class consciousness. The rural underworld, for example, has largely disappeared. Those indulging in poaching activities today are more likely to be motorized petty criminals from the nearest town and the agricultural worker is as likely as not to be found standing shoulder to shoulder with his employer defending the farm and its game. The parameters of local social conflict have been altered and so absorbed the old class enemy.

Probably much more subversive of social order than the arrival of the newcomers have been the changes that have sometimes occurred within the locals' interactional status system in the encapsulated community. In those villages closest to the urban centres – closest, that is, in terms of journey-to-work time rather than sheer physical distance – it is not only the middle-class newcomers who live in the village and work in the town.[24] A diminishing proportion of even the local working class may forsake employment on the land nearby for the prospects of higher pay and better conditions in urban-based employment. Such a change creates, from the agricultural worker's point of view, a much more damaging modification to the local status system. Since a growing number of even the locals may not work locally in agriculture, status can no longer be allocated among them on the basis of quality of work. The work of those commuting to nearby industrial centres can no longer be judged publicly, while these workers, like the newcomers, may well lack the ability to evaluate the more openly displayed work of their neighbours who have remained on the land. In this situation, therefore, the local interactional status system becomes contaminated with the values of attributional status. It is when their friends, neighbours and kin, rather than the newcomers, are capable of supporting a more grandiose life-style that the agricultural workers in the village are made fully aware of their lowly situation. In turn, as the working-class locals who are employed in industry begin to adhere to the prevailing standards of attributional status, so they begin to apply these standards in the village. They begin to demonstrate their status by conspicuously consuming consumer durables (cars, colour television sets, etc.); and by joking with the farm workers about the latter's poor pay. In a myriad of subtle ways they remind the farm worker of his inferiority.

In certain areas, then, even within the local traditional element of the village, status is becoming increasingly based on life-styles that are determined by occupation and income. Such a change has helped to broaden considerably the 'limited horizons' of many agricultural workers and to raise their material expectations beyond those which were formerly specified by the values of the interactional status system of the occupational community. This would seem to account for certain changes in the policy of the NUAAW, for example, which, as a national organization, has always been the prime mover in any efforts to increase the attributional status of the farm worker. Although in the past it was often stymied by the 'limited horizons' of many of its potential members, the increasing impact of urbanization on the rural village has wrought a number of changes in union policy. As was pointed out in Chapter 4, the NUAAW has determinedly sought the farm worker's 'place in the sun' primarily in terms of parity of status with the urban worker. At its inception, however, it was quite happy to call its membership 'labourers', and its first journal was even given the title *The Labourer* since 'there cannot be any disgrace in being called a "labourer"'.[25] Later, however, it was to inform a miscreant journalist that 'farm workers resent being called "labourers" because in other industries the word "labourer" usually implies an unskilled man who does odd jobs. The farm worker is a skilled craftsman. The Ministry of Agriculture and the Agricultural Wages Board do not use the word "labourer" in their official notices. The farming papers dropped it long ago. Farm "workers" is the modern and accurate designation of the men who feed us.'[26] Today any reference to the term 'farm labourer' is seized upon with equal vigour as 'crude and insolent'.[27] The growing recognition which this embodies of the low attributional status of the farm worker has also been the stimulus behind the adoption of the wages structure in agriculture (see Chapter 4) and remains part, but only a part, of the denigration of the tied cottage, an obvious symbol of the continuing dependence of the agricultural worker.

The status situation of the agricultural worker in the encapsulated community is therefore a rather variable one. Much will depend upon the precise morphology of the local housing market and the opportunities for locals to commute to urban-based employment. Proximity to an urban area may increase the number of locals in the agricultural worker's social network who have been attracted to higher-paid industrial employment, but elsewhere, and where the village contains a suitable council housing estate, the social network may continue to consist predominantly of other agricultural workers. Here the interactional status system based upon workplace skills may be retained and the individual agricultural worker's esteem among his peers may continue to be at considerable variance with that assigned to him by the outside world. The situation is, however, a fluid one and may vary considerably from one local situation to another. It is in this context in particular that suitable community studies are lacking. Pahl's work concentrates on the adventitious rather than the agricultural population, as does Ambrose's study of Ringmer.[28] Apart from Blythe's portrait of 'Akenfield', which is full of literary insights into these trends but hardly a systematic examination, only Harris's study of the Norfolk village of 'Hennage' has set about investigating this area.[29]

In some villages this process of encapsulation has been taken still further, however. Where there is no suitable housing for agricultural workers, especially where there is no council estate, the village may have been taken over entirely by urban newcomers. This particularly applies in some of the better-preserved showpiece villages, which not only conform more exactly in their appearance to 'the village in the mind' (and therefore attract more newcomers) but on account of their beauty are subject to draconian planning policies which forbid the intrusion of local-authority housing. Unable to buy and with no council houses available many agricultural workers are forced to seek accommodation in the only alternative open to them – tied cottages. Here they will join workers already in tied housing for other reasons – for example, because they prefer the economic advantages of a virtually rent-free house, or because on a low wage they find even local-authority rents an onerous financial burden. Tied cottages are predominantly sited not in the village, but on the farm, and so the 'community' for these workers tends to become the farm itself. Indeed such a situation may be called the *farm-centred community*.

On the farm the worker is both physically and socially isolated from the village. Not only the increased distance but the virtually complete takeover of the village by strangers will render his contact with it perfunctory and largely instrumental, often limited to occasional visits for shopping and the use of other amenities. Otherwise the farm worker and his family will lead a somewhat privatized life mitigated by the pervasive contact with neighbours/workmates in the other tied houses. Since his employer is also a neighbour, the degree of interaction between farmer and farm worker is increased, and may be considerably greater than in the other two local social situations already described. This situation, indeed, bears much more resemblance to the patterns of interaction described by Rees, Williams, Jenkins and others in the upland farming areas of Wales and England.[30] Patterns of interactional status remain fairly established given the extent of propinquity and the overlap between work and non-work roles. In fact for workers in this situation the division between 'home' and 'work' virtually ceases, especially for those workers who handle stock. They are constantly 'popping in and out' between home and workplace and the actual hours worked may bear little relation to contract hours, or even to those for which the worker is paid. On the other hand, the employer will frequently appreciate this and be prepared to be flexible about working hours and work practices. These 'indulgency patterns'[31] operate across the whole range of the employees' work and leisure activities, for the farmer is now not only an employer and a neighbour, but often a friend. Workers frequently borrow farm equipment for their personal use or the farm Land Rover for personal transport. Similarly the farmer will not hesitate to call upon them at any hour of the day or night if urgent help is required, again particularly where stock is involved. Moreover this situation has become an increasingly common one as the proportion of workers living in tied cottages (not all of which will be on the farm, of course) has increased.

In such an isolated and self-contained situation, patterns of interactional status continue to assert themselves, and since all members of the farm-centred community share a common form of employment and even a common workplace, their skill at work remains an important evaluative criterion. However, such is the complete overlap between home and work that home-centred criteria can assume a greater importance even among the men – for example, the extent of neighbourly co-operation, cleanliness and so on. The status system of the farm-centred community may appear to be, therefore, a kind of occupational community in microcosm, but there is one crucial difference: the farm-centred community includes the farmer and hence does not embrace the homogeneous class culture of the agricultural village. For this reason it is unlikely to support the oppositional social imagery characteristic of the occupational community. The employer, like the workers, is able to earn high esteem by conforming to the necessary prestige requirements. The greater his conformity to the appropriate image of the good farmer, the more effectively he may be able to inspire sufficient *personal* loyalty on the part of his employees to inhibit across-the-board judgements of farmers as an undifferentiated group. Under these circumstances, then, it is far easier for the farmer to obtain the identification of his employees than in the occupational community. There are fewer opportunities to sustain the animosities of class conflict generated under the old conditions. The gap in wealth, income and general life-style between farmer and worker remains as wide as ever, but the small-scale solidarities of the farm-centred community help to ensure that the relationship is rarely stripped down to the cash nexus and that any conflict which may arise is put down to a clash of personalities rather than a product of the system. When the farm represents the 'community', therefore, the agricultural worker's interpretation of his situation is often commensurate with the farmer's own views, for he can often directly experience the social influences and judgements of his employer.

Change in the Rural Village – The Farm Worker's View

The threefold typology of occupational, encapsulated and farm-centred community situations presented above is based upon a reading of the rather meagre literature on rural change in lowland England and upon fieldwork experience gained in the forty-four

Suffolk parishes which formed the area in which the sample of farm workers was interviewed. Survey-generated data is only of limited use in exemplifying the changes inherent in this typology, however, because inevitably a survey produces only a cross-sectional 'snapshot' of what is a rapidly changing situation and is less successful at providing an understanding of the social processes at work. Nevertheless the interviews with the Suffolk farm workers provided a good deal of information that was relevant to the question of how changes in the population of many villages has affected the status of the farm worker within them and the extent of his integration into the local social system. In order to try to compensate for the weakness of the survey methodology the fieldwork area was deliberately chosen so as to represent a variety of community situations under the differential impact of urbanization.

In 1972, six of the forty-four parishes remained occupational communities,[32] albeit somewhat tenuously in one or two cases, for even in the north of the area, which was the most remote from Ipswich, the villages were beginning to undergo an influx of exurbanites. In some cases their agricultural identity had been preserved by the tenacity of a dominant landowner who, in one case, by owning the village's entire housing stock, had managed to keep out newcomers altogether. These villages contained 12 per cent of the workers interviewed. Seven other parishes[33] contained no nucleated village settlement at all, but consisted of a scattered set of farms and cottages. In these parishes, therefore, the farm-centred community predominated, but all the parishes contained situations of this kind, usually consisting of isolated groups of tied houses, often sited around the other farm buildings, so that in all 54·1 per cent of the workers interviewed lived in this kind of situation. The remainder of the villages were encapsulated communities, containing 33·9 per cent of those interviewed. The proportion of newcomers could vary considerably, however. Some villages had been almost entirely overrun, while in others it was the newcomers who were in the minority, contained within a newly appended housing estate, while the locals retained quite a firm hold on the remainder of the village and its institutions. Very much depended upon the local housing mix, especially the balance between local-authority and tied housing on the one hand and privately owned property on the other.

The disintegration of the rural village as a traditional occupational community in Suffolk is often represented locally as having involved a loss of 'community spirit' or 'sense of community'. The 'eclipse' of community in the Suffolk village is a live issue in the county, frequently discussed in the local press and often referred to in public statements by those in positions of local responsibility. This concern has even prompted the Suffolk Rural Community Council to commission a report on social trends in Suffolk, with an eye to the possible lack of integration of newcomers into the rural way of life. The report,[34] based on a survey of a sample of the population in four Suffolk Rural Districts, confirmed the conclusions of previous surveys in Hampshire, Norfolk, Hertfordshire, Kent and elsewhere, namely that the newcomers were overwhelmingly of a higher social status, more affluent and more highly educated than the locals. Although both the urban immigrant and native rural population found their own village a friendly place to live in,[35] they tended to diverge on their attitudes towards the changes taking place in Suffolk, urban migrants being on the whole more critical of change.[36] Obviously the 'village in the mind' remains a potent symbol. The report concluded that the immigrants were reasonably well integrated into their communities, but this was based upon the somewhat banal index of voluntary association membership and, as Green has observed,[37] to measure the vitality of rural social life in this way gives only a narrow and incomplete view. Unfortunately the data were not broken down by occupation, so the views of farm workers are not discernible.

The agricultural workers in the forty-four parishes were asked a number of questions aimed at assessing their relationship with the local village community and at discovering their perceptions of their status within it. Most of the workers interviewed were aware of the changes that had taken place in their local village, although occasionally they would assert that 'everyone in this village works on the land' when a new housing development proclaimed the contrary. The impact of the newcomers could remain invisible to the farm worker for quite long periods until a particular event would bring it home to him. Often, it was either the closure of the local pub, or a 'facelift' which converted it into an environment more congenial to the up-market clientele, which many farm workers refer to disparagingly as the 'gin-and-Jag' trade. Given the importance of the pub in the agricultural worker's pattern of leisure-time sociability, however, these changes do have real as well as symbolic consequences. The pub is not only the most important – in many villages, the only – meeting place outside work where agricultural workers and their friends can come together to meet and exchange gossip, it is also an arena in which the conventional wisdom of local and national affairs is established and transmitted.[38] The demise of the local pub therefore often alienates the agricultural worker from his own village much more than many of the other consequences of the arrival of newcomers, and its closure is regarded as being synonymous with the decay of the local community.

There is, then, often a lag between the wholesale influx of newcomers into the village and the perception by the farm worker of concomitant changes. In so far as this affects his attachment to the village this needs to be taken into account when interpreting the replies to the questions which were put on this matter. An abridged series of indicators of local attachment is shown in Table 47.[39] As might be expected, the most mobile workers were those in the farm-centred community situation. Since most of the houses in this situation were tied houses (94·4 per cent) they contained a more than proportional number of spiralist supervisory workers (71·4 per cent) and stockmen (72·4 per cent). A substantial proportion of these were born and brought up outside the area altogether and some had expectations of moving again in furtherance of their career, so not surprisingly they were less inclined to be sorry if they had to move away. However, the general workers in this situation were also less attached to their place of residence and showed less interest in village affairs than the other workers. They were also more socially isolated than the other workers who were interviewed – clearly a function of their greater geographical isolation from the village, although often the cluster of houses on the farm did provide opportunities for a great deal of social contact between workmates and neighbours outside working hours. Thus while quite a high proportion of friends would be seen almost every day to speak to, these would also be workmates in many cases, and workers in this situation socialized with friends or went out to the pub less often than average.

Their situation can be contrasted with those workers at the other extreme, living in the villages classified as occupational communities. Although the relatively small number of respondents of this sort must make generalizations rather tentative, the consistency across most

Table 47 Various indications of attachment to locality by type of community situation of workers interviewed in Suffolk, 1972

	Type of community situation			
	Occupational ($N = 28$) %	Encapsulated ($N = 79$) %	Farm-centred ($N = 126$) %	All workers ($N = 233$) %
Residence less than 10 years	19·5	22·3	29·4	26·1
Born in the parish	44·1	39·3	27·0	34·3
'Very sorry' if had to move away	42·7	35·6	34·4	35·8
'Very interested' to know what goes on in the village	29·4	23·3	22·2	24·0
'Not at all interested' to know what goes on in the village	14·4	24·9	31·7	26·6
'Very many' of the villagers known personally	70·4	49·1	40·8	45·7
'Most' or 'all' of friends live in the parish	58·9	29·0	27·2	31·9
Friends in the parish seen 'almost every day' to speak to	67·9	29·0	42·1	36·8
Go out visiting relatives or receive visits from relatives 'more than once a week'	19·1	11·8	15·1	13·7
Go out visiting friends or receive visits from friends 'more than once a week'	33·6	28·7	20·6	25·8
Go out to the pub for a drink 'more than once a week'	71·4	40·8	35·7	41·2

of the indicators suggests that these workers are indeed the most integrated into their locality and the most attached to it emotionally and socially. They are the least mobile and they would also be the most sorry to leave if they had to. They also show the greatest interest in village affairs and their friendship networks appear by far the most locally based – 70·4 per cent knew 'very many' of the villagers personally, 58·9 per cent had most or all of their friends living in the parish and 67·9 per cent saw their friends to speak to almost every day. The replies also exhibited the importance of the local pub as a centre of social activity, with 71·4 per cent of the respondents in the occupational community paying a visit more than once a week compared with only 35·7 per cent of the farm-centred workers. Although the precise percentages may not be too significant in absolute terms the pattern that is established is a relatively clear one: the agricultural workers who are the most integrated into their locality are those living in occupational communities and those least integrated are those living on the farms. The workers living in the villages classified as encapsulated communities generally are in between, although, from fieldwork experience, the variation within the encapsulated community is probably as great as the differences between it, as represented by the mean statistics represented in Table 47, and the other two situations.

Table 48 Perception of the status of the farm worker in British society as a whole and in immediate locality of workers interviewed in Suffolk, 1972

| | Status ranking of farm worker | |
	Nationally (N = 207) %	Locally (N = 203) %
Very high	–	12·8
Quite high	26·5	41·9
Same as everyone else	1·9	29·6
Quite low	12·1	5·9
Very low	53·6	7·9
Other (e.g. 'don't know about us')	5·8	2·0
	100·0	100·0

In order to assess how far these changes had affected the farm
workers' perceptions of their own status, those interviewed in the
survey were asked four questions directly related to prestige ranking.
First, they were asked, 'What sort of view do you think people in
general have of farm workers?', and then, after having asked for the
reasons for their reply to this question, they were also asked, 'What
about here in (place of residence)? What sort of view do you think
other people in (place of residence) have of farm workers?' Their
replies were then grouped into the categories shown in Table 48.
What emerges is a considerable inconsistency across the sample as a
whole between the farm worker's perception of his own status in
the village and that in the outside world. Whereas their local social
status was adjudged to be very high or quite high by 54·7 per cent of
the respondents and very low by only 7·9 per cent, the corresponding
figure for the general social status of farm workers was 26·5 and 53·6
per cent respectively. Many of the replies to the question on general
social status revealed the extent of their bitterness at the stereotyped
image of them which they believe most people not working on the
land possess. For example:

'If you're a farm worker, you're nothing.'

'People laugh at us. They think, "Working on the land – they
can't do anything else."'

'A lot think we're soft, daft – just bloody yobos.'

'I hide it I'm a farm worker if I go out – I won't tell anybody.'

'Any young girls who know you're a farm worker take the micky
out of you, call you a clodhopper. They won't go out with you.'

'If you see anything on TV they've always got old clothes on and
chewing a bit of straw. They think we're the local village idiots.'

' "He's just an old sod," they think, as they see us mucking out.'

'Goes back to the days of serfs – that's how we're still regarded.'

The image of the agricultural worker presented by the mass media
all too often gives the farm worker good cause to feel embittered.
In 1972, the *Guardian* twice in quick succession published articles on
farming illustrated by a man hand-ploughing with horses, one under
the headline 'The Rural Scene Too Many Take for Granted'.[40]
As one anguished correspondent observed, 'If that is the degree of
observation the countryside can expect from the average city-

dweller then the arrival of the final bulldozers and asphalt spreader is nearer than sometimes it seems. Why don't you rattle up here in a carriage and see for yourself?' In the same year Macmillan's published a well-intentioned series of booklets for remedial school-leavers called 'The Way to Work'. Along with other occupations presumably believed to be suitable for remedial children (like 'fetching and carrying') there was a booklet entitled *The Farm Labourer* (*sic*).[41] Such examples, and they are frequent occurrences, merely help to confirm the farm worker's view of the ignorance of the urban-dweller. It even taints what would otherwise be his appreciation of sympathetic media treatment of his plight. Thus newspaper articles and television programmes which aim to show the poverty of the agricultural worker and thereby to evoke action on his behalf, often, by presenting a downtrodden image of him, alienate the farm worker still further so that he entirely fails to appreciate any of the intended sympathy.

Under these circumstances it is not surprising that the individual agricultural worker may regard the network of village locals as a cosy enclave against an ignorant and denigrating world. Nor is it surprising that his status in the local social system is more meaningful to him, for not only is it reinforced by personal, face-to-face contact, but high status can be acquired locally, whereas nationally the farm worker's powerlessness over financial rewards makes high status almost unattainable. This distinction can be demonstrated by referring to the reasons the respondents gave for the appropriate status situation of farm worker, both nationally and locally. As Table 49 shows, the general social status of the agricultural worker was believed to rest mainly upon attributional criteria – pay, skill and so on. The urbanization of many rural villages has resulted in the importation of this attributional status system into the local community, and, if the data shown in Table 50 is anything to go by, this has occurred to a considerable degree. The most frequently cited criterion of local social status was money and/or conspicuous consumption and other attributional criteria figured prominently – for example, social class, occupation and landholding. The social-class category refers to the explicit use of this term and it ranks surprisingly high; however, the frequency of these replies may have been biased upwards owing to the fact that the questions on status occurred in the questionnaire shortly after a detailed and prolonged probing of the respondents'

Table 49 Criteria of general social status of farm workers, as perceived by workers interviewed in Suffolk, 1972

Criterion	No.	%
Low-status reasons:		
Poor pay	43	22·4
Tradition of being regarded as unskilled	43	22·4
Ignorance	30	15·6
Dirty job	20	10·4
Other	6	3·2
High-status reasons:		
Essential job	16	8·3
Hard working	11	5·7
Mechanization	8	4·2
Improved pay	5	2·6
Other	10	5·2
	192	100·0

Table 50 Criteria of local social status, as perceived by workers interviewed in Suffolk, 1972

Criterion	No.	%
Money/conspicuous consumption	45	23·5
No difference – all farm workers	30	15·6
Social class	25	13·0
Occupation	22	11·5
Personality	22	11·5
'People who help out', etc.	21	10·9
Landholding	14	7·3
Length of residence	7	3·7
Politics	2	1·0
Religion	2	1·0
Education	2	1·0
	192	100·0

class imagery and therefore the term was fresh in their minds. The use of length of residence to evaluate local social status seems low, but many of the other criteria were used as an idiom in which this distinction could be expressed. Money, social class and occupation often served to identify newcomers to the village – they were more affluent, middle-class and in urban-based employment. The criteria which could be recognized as signifying the continuing importance of interactional status were mentioned by only 38 per cent of respondents. These included the denial of differences in social standing on the grounds that everyone in the village was a farm worker (15·6 per cent), personality differences (11·5 per cent) and the willingness to help out in times of crisis, play a leading part in performing village chores (cutting the grass in the churchyard, for example) and generally play a full role in village social activities (10·9 per cent). In general, therefore, the opportunity for farm workers to compensate locally for their otherwise low attributional status seems to be somewhat attenuated, as one would expect under modern village conditions. Nevertheless the distribution of status-enhancing characteristics was far from uniform across the range of community situations in which the respondents were located, so that this needs to be taken into account before making any general conclusions.

Although the data are by no means clear-cut, the replies to questions on local social status confirm the effects upon the status situation of changes in the rural village as outlined in the typology earlier in this chapter. In terms of the assessment of their overall status ranking in the locality it was those workers in the encapsulated community who tended disproportionally to regard it as low – 17·4 per cent did so, as opposed to 11·1 per cent of those in the farm-centred community and only 5·1 per cent of those in occupational communities. The greater predominance of interactional status in the occupational community is also illustrated by the criteria of local social status which were expressed by the respondents. Interactional criteria predominated in the occupational community to the extent that 63·6 per cent of these respondents replied in those terms, compared with 26·3 per cent in an encapsulated community and 38·3 per cent of those on the farms. These results are shown in Table 51. The disruption of local interactional status systems is therefore confirmed as being greatest within the encapsulated community, where the farm worker is most exposed to the impact of newcomers; these changes are also apparent in the farm-centred community, but here the retreat into a more isolated and self-contained social world makes such disruption more unlikely.

Such changes, in so far as they are tending to align the farm worker's status situation more closely to his market situation, are

Table 51 Criteria of local social status by type of community situation, as perceived by workers interviewed in Suffolk, 1972

| | Type of community situation | | |
| | Occupational (N = 28) % | Encapsulated (N = 57) % | Farm-centred (N = 107) % |
Criterion			
No difference – all farm workers	29·9	10·7	16·8
Personality	20·7	7·8	8·4
'People who help out', etc	13·0	9·3	13·1
Money/conspicuous consumption	10·5	30·1	22·5
Social class	10·2	13·6	13·2
Occupation	5·0	14·5	12·1
Landholding	6·4	7·8	10·3
Length of residence	2·5	4·6	3·8
Other	1·8	1·6	2·8
	100·0	100·0	100·0

clearly of considerable importance in determining his own interpretation of his situation. In the encapsulated community, for example, many farm workers have for the first time seen at first hand a superior standard of living which previously they had only heard of or believed to be solely the preserve of local farmers and landowners. They observe the newcomers' life-styles and can begin to realize just how far down the social scale they really are, a feature which was previously obscured from them in the more self-contained occupational community, and may remain somewhat obscured in the farm-centred situation. One possibility is that this heightened awareness of material inequalities could produce a raising of class consciousness among agricultural workers. However, this would be to ignore the fact that these changes have also undermined the coherence of the former rural ruling class of farmers and landowners and have co-incided with changes at work which have seriously weakened the formation of workplace class antagonisms. Because of this the dis-satisfaction of the agricultural worker tends to be directed at the immediate cause of his declining social status, the newcomers, and not at the employers, either individually or collectively, in spite of the fact that it is they who are more responsible for the low pay upon which his low social status has become increasingly dependent. Thus the declining social status of the farm worker may not lead him to express his dissatisfaction in class terms at all. Indeed it may prompt a feeling that farm workers have more in common with farmers than ever before, so that class consciousness diminishes rather than in-creases.

Contact with Non-Agricultural Workers

Earlier in this chapter it was suggested that a more potent force for raising the expectations of the agricultural worker than the arrival of middle-class newcomers in the locality would be contact with locals who grew up with the farm worker in his own surroundings, but who had sought higher-paid employment in industry, usually in near-by towns. To the agricultural worker this group represents one of the few sources of exposure to the values and beliefs of workers who have no connection with farming. The geographical isolation of the agri-cultural worker, together with his strong identification with a job regarded as being qualitatively different from all others, have tradi-tionally prevented many farm workers from recognizing any shared interests with other, particularly non-rural, groups of workers. This lateral identity of interest has also been inhibited by the more ready recognition of another interest which cuts across that of class – the agricultural interest. Here the enemy is seen to be the urban, in-dustrial population which demands cheap food, producing depressed returns to the agricultural industry as a whole. The agricultural in-terest consequently tends to regard itself as an embattled minority in an alternatively hostile and indifferent world, subjected to the whims

of urban politicians. In such a situation all those involved in agriculture tend to close ranks, for, as Self and Storing put it, 'The
shadow of an immense urban majority falls across the interests of
agricultural workers as well as those of farmers and landowners'.[42]

This great urban conspiracy against agriculture is embodied (or, at
least, was until British entry into the EEC) in the cheap-food policy
which has dominated the state control of agriculture in this country.
Many farm workers view the policy as being responsible for their low
wages, an interpretation which is encouraged by farming employers
who plausibly point out that while urban manufacturers can, and do,
raise the price of their products in order to finance wage increases for
their employees, this is not an option which is open to farmers, for
their prices are controlled by the government. Whatever the plausibility of this explanation (and it is dubious on several counts) it has
not only been accepted by many farm workers, but it has conveniently shifted the blame for his poverty on to a section of the
population with whom he has had little direct contact. Dissatisfaction
with low pay has therefore often been expressed as anti-urbanism as
much as in terms of class conflict. Moreover it is significant that not
only are the newcomers to the village overwhelmingly middle-class
but they are also *urban* and are therefore often seen as the local representatives of this urban conspiracy against agriculture. Locals who go
to work in near-by towns are, however, exempted from such stric-
tures. As locals they are known personally as individuals and some of
them may have worked on the land themselves. Their common background will often ensure that the agriculture worker will take more
notice of their opinions and beliefs, and it is through interaction with
them that the agricultural worker's anti-urban and anti-industrial
prejudices are more likely to be overcome than through the rather
more formal contact with middle-class newcomers. This group
therefore forms a link, however tenuous, with the values and beliefs
of the British working class as a whole, but its emergence in the
village is a relatively recent occurrence, so that this kind of contact
may be the prerogative of only a minority of agricultural workers.

In order to make some assessment of the extent of this exposure to
broader working-class values, it is helpful to look at the survey data on
the occupational composition of some of the workers' immediate
associates, both friends and kin. This is shown in Table 52 (p. 356).
The data on kinship confirm the situation briefly referred to in

Chapter 3, namely the extent to which the agricultural worker's relatives themselves work on the land. More than two-thirds of the workers interviewed were themselves the sons of farm workers; only a very small proportion (5·6 per cent) were the sons of employees in manufacturing industry, and many of these had been employed in small engineering workshops in rural areas, particularly those firms engaged in the manufacture of agricultural machinery and implements. The proportion of agricultural workers from genuinely urban, industrial backgrounds was minute, so few that they stood out as individuals – for example, one or two of the spiralist supervisory workers, a couple of urban middle-class drop-outs, a farm mechanic who had moved for the sake of his wife's health, one ex-war evacuee who never returned. Since agriculture has been shedding labour rather than attracting a net inflow, this pattern was hardly surprising, and the 'drift from the land' also accounts for the decreasing representation of agriculture as one moves down through the generations, with 67·2 per cent of fathers and 57·3 per cent of fathers-in-law having worked on the land, but 46 per cent of brothers and only 38 per cent of children.[43] Most of the immediate kin not employed in agriculture were engaged in various service industries, especially transport, and in the building industry; there were many brothers and sons who were lorry drivers or builder's labourers. It is significant that both the road haulage and the construction industry are characterized by work situations very similar to that of agriculture: a numerical predominance of small family firms, a relatively high degree of workplace autonomy and independence and in both cases the deployment of skills not very dissimilar from those acquired working on the land.[44]

Over 70 per cent of the workers who were interviewed were married, but only 20·6 per cent of the wives were in regular employment. Notwithstanding their occasional employment as casual labour on farms for fruit-picking, potato-lifting, etc., most wives were therefore economically dependent upon their husbands. Within the field-work area there were few opportunities for female employment on any scale and, of the minority of wives who had regular employment, the highest proportion (41·2 per cent) were engaged in domestic service. The most common forms of employment after this were work in the food-processing industry, like chicken-packing or mushroom production (14·7 per cent) and assisting in shops (14·7 per cent), followed by agricultural work (11·8 per cent). In general, however, the geographical isolation of many workers' houses, the presence of young children and the difficulties of rural transport all conspired to tie most farm workers' wives to the home. In the home, if the children are at school or have married and moved away, the farm worker's wife can be isolated in the extreme, especially in a lonely farm cottage which may be some distance from a road or a bus route, let alone other houses and shops. A substantial proportion of wives are completely alone between 8.30 a.m. and 4.00 p.m. most Mondays to Fridays, a loneliness punctuated only by the call of roundsmen or the visit of a neighbour or friend. Those living in villages are more fortunate in this respect, but as more and more workers move into tied housing, which is usually situated on the farm, this is becoming more of a problem.

For the farm worker's wife the difficulties of a lonely domestic existence often accentuate those which derive from the low wages of her husband. The monotony of work in the home is often increased because she cannot afford to go out for entertainment during the week or at weekends as often as she would like. Not all wives find their domestic duties boring by any means, but certainly there are fewer compensations for them than for their husbands by way of job satis-faction to make up for low wages. This, together with the fact that most wives do not have the same degree of contact with their hus-band's employer, makes them more militant, on the whole, about pay and conditions in agriculture than the farm workers themselves. They are also much more conversant with the real value of the wage, since they carry out most of the shopping, usually in expensively priced village stores rather than cheaper supermarkets in the towns. It is the wife who is more fully aware of the extent of rising prices and of the sacrifices that must be made in order to retain the solvency of the family budget. And it is often she who first applies pressure for higher agricultural wages. As one NUAAW organizer has put it, 'It is the pressure from the wives that is making our members realize that in-dustrial calm is too high a price to pay for the low wages they receive.'[45]

Whether pressure from the wife leads directly to increased mili-tancy on the part of farm workers is, however, rather dubious, for it ignores the prevailing pattern of authority within the family. An equally likely outcome is a phenomenon familiar to many farm workers and the butt of many pub jokes – the nagging wife. The majority of farm worker's families are extremely patriarchal institutions, almost entirely untouched by the kind of egalitarian tendencies alleged to have affected the relationship between spouses elsewhere in society. Those workers living on patriarchally run farms therefore tend to move back and forth between one patriarchal institution and another, the difference being that in one he is exercising traditional authority, while in the other he is subjected to it. It does not seem too fanciful to suppose that under certain circumstances his domestic authority may help to compensate for his powerlessness in the world of work – his home is *his* castle. The wife's position *vis-à-vis* her husband is therefore somewhat analogous to that of the farm worker *vis-à-vis* his employer – and likewise economic dependence, powerlessness and unremitting socialization are likely to produce identification, compliance and accommodation but rarely an outright questioning of the system. Nagging is simply a form of domestic rick-burning.

For the exercise of her traditional authority the wife may turn, together with her husband, to her children, whose position when they are young allows for a complete socialization into parental authority and who can be physically controlled when the need arises. In this way can the traditional patriarchal authority structure of the family be maintained. Problems arise, however, when the children leave school and seek employment of their own. As Table 52 shows, a majority of those farm workers' children in employment were not working on the land. A substantial proportion of farm workers' sons find employment instead in relatively high-paid jobs in the building industry, as garage mechanics and later as lorry drivers, excavator drivers or even as engineering workers in local factories, having saved enough for a deposit on a motorbike to allow a greater degree of mobility. In this kind of employment many sons are soon earning as much, if not more, than their fathers, and not surprisingly they often demand the independence from parental authority that their economic independence allows them. The opportunities for domestic conflict are obvious. Unfortunately even if the agricultural worker is made more aware of his lowly position in society in this way and even if he is exposed more to alternative norms and values as a result, it usually occurs at a stage in his life-cycle when his position in the labour market has become seriously weakened because of his age. Realizing that it would be difficult to find another job, he is unlikely

Table 52 Occupations of various kin and friends of workers interviewed in Suffolk, 1972

	Father (N = 224) %	Brothers (N = 381) %	Father-in-law (N = 157) %	Children (N = 111) %	Friends (N = 871) %
Agriculture	67·2	46·0	57·3	38·0	62·5
Agriculture-related services	5·6	2·9	4·4	10·0	3·3
Other services	12·2	27·3	15·9	23·2	17·9
Other extractive industries	–	–	0·6	–	0·3
Manufacturing industries	5·6	6·5	11·1	11·7	4·1
Construction industries	9·0	13·9	8·2	17·1	11·0
Armed forces	0·4	3·4	2·5	–	0·9
	100·0	100·0	100·0	100·0	100·0
Small firm	85·3	66·7	76·4	n.a.	84·1
Large firm	9·4	21·8	12·1	n.a.	10·4
Local and national govt	4·5	7·6	8·3	n.a.	3·8
Armed forces	0·9	3·9	3·2	n.a.	1·7
	100·0	100·0	100·0		100·0
Workmate	22·0	8·7	4·5	n.a.	32·6
Not workmate	78·0	91·3	95·5	n.a.	67·4
Manual	87·3	90·3	90·0	82·0	87·5
Non-manual	12·7	9·7	10·0	18·0	12·5

to engage in any activities that might jeopardize his present one. Thus, there is little reason to suppose that the consequences of this – or, for that matter, the presence within the immediate kinship network of other non-agricultural workers – extend to a general questioning of the legitimacy of established patterns of authority. Unless a radical working-class sub-culture is on hand to interpret contemporary changes in the farm worker's situation in a way conducive to increased militancy (which in general it is not) the more likely outcome is a reassertion of the old-established patterns of authority rather than their overthrow. Most middle-aged and older farm workers have seen in their lifetime rapid changes at their work, a middle-class, urban invasion of their local village and their own consequent loss of status within it and finally their own sons and daughters beginning to question their authority, an authority which they had previously taken for granted. One common response has been one of sheer bafflement – 'I don't know what the world is coming to nowadays'. The other is nostalgia for the old days when each person knew his place, and was secure within it, when the old were respected and when the world was slower-moving and more predictable.

As Table 52 shows, the occupational composition of the agricultural worker's friendship networks was not altogether dissimilar to those of his kin. Each respondent in the survey was asked for the occupation of the four men with whom he was most friendly. Although there was some slight 'inflation' in the replies by some respondents trying to impress with the high status of some of their acquaintances, and although the meaning of 'friend' could differ between respondents, the data probably gives a reasonably true reflection of the situation. Once again the predominance of fellow agricultural workers is apparent (including nearly one-third who were workmates), with the majority of the remainder being employed in either service trades or in the building industry. The overall impression is of a notably self-contained network into which the values of those working-class groups who are likely to hold dissimilar beliefs to those prevailing in agriculture hardly enter. The proportion of friends employed in manufacturing, for example, was lower than among any of the kinship groups, at 4·1 per cent. This degree of separation is obviously partly a cause and partly a consequence of the anti-urbanism which prevails among most agricultural workers. It certainly helps to preserve the agricultural worker's sense of possessing a unique and separate identity from other workers and helps to massage his anti-urban prejudices and stereotypes. For most farm workers the urban, industrial working-class is a group with whom they feel they have little in common.

The self-containment of the agricultural workers' network of friends is increased by the fact that their leisure activities do not tend to take them away from their immediate locality or to bring them into contact with others who live outside it. Most farm workers' leisure activities are based upon a triumvirate of the garden, the pub and the television set. The exceptions to this are the young, unmarried workers whose friendships tend to be based on age rather than any other criterion and whose leisure activities are centred around the pub, the motor-bike and members of the opposite sex. In all three regards they tend to venture further afield. The majority of the married farm workers who were interviewed appeared to be very home-centred, however, making occasional visits to the local pub. A great deal of time was spent in the garden, partly out of intrinsic interest but also for sound economic reasons. Gardens have a strictly utilitarian function for most farm workers and are hence given over almost entirely to the growth of vegetables and fruit. Growing flowers, unless they are for a show, is regarded as women's work and a small patch is usually rather grudgingly set aside for the wife to look after. The cultivation of fruit and vegetables, however, is often fiercely competitive in a friendly-serious way, institutionalized in a multitude of local societies with their accompanying shows, but also expressed in less formal and more subtle ways among neighbours and workmates. Gardening is rather different in its social connotations for the newcomers, though, for whom the garden is primarily ornamental, or, with row after row of bedding plants, a matter of conspicuous consumption.

Outside the home the main centre of leisure activities is undoubtedly the local pub, and this applies to all age groups. A pub was visited once a week or more often by 58·8 per cent of the respondents in the survey, and it remains, together with the place of work, as one of the most important arenas within which the norms and values of the local social system are reinforced and in which the status of the agricultural worker is evaluated among his peers. Beyond the pub, affiliation becomes more diverse. Like most men, a majority of farm workers were interested in soccer, but mostly in a passive way, following the results of Ipswich Town or Norwich City and watching the matches on television, but only a few making regular trips to Portman Road or Carrow Road. A number of the younger workers also played for local village sides. As far as participation was concerned, however, the most typical sports were angling, bowls and darts and an activity which is half sporting, half artistic – bell ringing. The most widely followed sport after soccer was speedway, which is very popular in Suffolk and which probably attracts more regular spectators among farm workers than soccer. Another significant group of pursuits were centred on farming – Young Farmers Clubs, farm machinery clubs, stockmen's clubs and so on. Here farm workers could rub shoulders socially with farmers and farmers' sons. Religious associations were rather sparsely adhered to – only 9·4 per cent of the sample attended church or chapel more than once a month. Finally political organizations were virtually insignificant, although members of the Conservative Party outnumbered members of the Labour Party by four to one.

It is often alleged that communal village activities have been virtually killed off by television. Certainly nearly all workers watch television regularly, but there is little evidence to suggest that it alone has ruined the quality of village life. This would be to suppose that before the advent of television the village was the centre of a whole series of communal activities. In fact, village life in the nineteenth and early twentieth centuries was probably rather dull and, although increasingly privatized forms of leisure have had an effect, to regard them as having brought about the downfall of 'community' is to exaggerate wildly the extent and variety of locally based entertainment and discussion in the past. Similarly it is easy to exaggerate the effects of the mass media upon the raising of agricultural workers' expectations. Television has undoubtedly contributed to the broadening of the farm worker's horizons but it is merely the latest in a long line of factors which have had this effect since the middle of the nineteenth century. Much of the research on the effects of the mass media elsewhere has concluded that they operate by reinforcing ideas already present rather than creating an entirely new set of values and beliefs. A similar process of self-selection takes place among farm workers, for whom television is a source of entertainment rather than information and whose outlook on life is shaped more by personal contacts with workmates, friends and kin.

As Table 52 shows, in general these networks of friends and kin consisted primarily of agricultural workers or workers employed in industries with somewhat similar work situations. The agricultural worker frequently comes into contact only with workers whose work experiences and ideologies are not radically dissimilar to his own. For example, the great majority of friends and kin worked for small firms (defined, as far as local firms are concerned, as those with less than fifty employees; for firms outside the fieldwork area where it was not always possible to check the number of employees, small firms were those which were not publicly quoted companies). Size of firm is not, of course, always a good guide to the nature of the work situation since many workers in large firms may nevertheless be in work situations not unlike those of many farm workers. Indeed only a minority of those working in large firms were working on a factory floor and many were either working in small branches of national chains (in the case of many service industries) or were not directly employed in production, such as warehousemen, caretakers etc. However, those working for small firms may reasonably be supposed to be in a work situation very similar to that of most agricultural workers and the use of this variable probably underestimates rather than overestimates the absence from the farm worker's immediate social network of individuals whose experiences are different to his own. Thus, in spite of the widespread changes that have occurred in most rural villages, they have operated in such a way that the self-contained social milieu of the farm worker has not been completely broken up. The evidence seems to suggest that the impact of urbanization has been to turn the locals, including the farmers, in upon themselves rather than opening up the social environment of the agricultural worker to new ideas and expectations.

Conclusions

It is difficult to make any generalized conclusions about the status situation of the agricultural worker since, as this chapter has demonstrated, it is an extremely complex and fluid one. It is certainly mistaken to regard it as an entirely homogeneous entity, for not only is it necessary to retain the distinction between attributional and interactional status, but to be aware of the variety of local social systems within which the farm worker is located, according to the extent of urbanization. Because the changes in the composition of most villages have undermined the evaluative consensus upon which status is, by definition, based it has also become difficult to perceive the existence of any unitary status hierarchy in many communities. Hence this chapter has concentrated upon the farm worker's own definition of his status situation and how far the changes referred to have affected this. Thus the portrayal of the changes in the structure of the village community has not been one which newcomers, for example, would instantly recognize.

Taking the notion of an occupational community as a kind of historical bench-mark, an underlying concern has been to assess how far its disintegration has produced a shift in the saliency of status from interactional to attributional criteria. Although farm workers themselves continue to recognize in their own terms the existence of this distinction and of their differing status situations according to which criteria are being employed, one generalization which it is reasonably valid to make is that the emphasis has been moving towards the growing importance of attributional status. Since the latter is much more closely aligned to material factors this has probably made the farm worker more aware of his deprivation compared with other groups of workers and has made this deprivation more important to him. However, there is little *prima facie* evidence to support the view that this has in turn led to an increase in class consciousness. Indeed the class antagonisms which undoubtedly were present beneath the harmonious surface of the occupational community appear to have declined drastically. Here the causes would seem to lie not as much in the undermining of local interactional status as the changed class composition of the interactional status system. For the movement away from the occupational community (together with the diminution of the labour force on most farms) has been accompanied by a change in employer–employee relationships from something akin to pure cash nexus, whatever the ideological gloss that was formerly placed upon it, to a situation in which various aspects of both parties' social lives overlap in a diffuse, multiplex relationship. This has undoubtedly clouded the farm worker's perception of his economic interest as being contrary to that of his employer and with it has disappeared much of the guerrilla class warfare which, although covert, was a prevailing characteristic of the occupational community.

The data on the farm worker's social networks is also a salutary reminder that in spite of the undoubted penetration of many villages by more universal values, the world of the agricultural worker remains a remarkably self-contained one. If the disintegration of the occupational community has resulted in the threatened disappearance of the farm worker's oppositional sub-culture, there appears to have been little scope for forging new forms of collective solidarity with other sections of the working class. Rather, the solidarities of class which characterized the occupational community have given way to the solidarities of localism. Ironically the ideology of common interest based upon common residence which the nineteenth-century forbears of present farmers and landowners tried so hard to cultivate, with only limited success, has now been brought to fruition by the invasion of the village by outsiders and the consequent breaking-up of the community as they once knew it. There are now much fewer opportunities to sustain the animosities of class conflict as a result. Instead the animosity is directed, by farmers and farm workers alike, at the disruptive newcomers. Their arrival has thus diverted from the farmer much of the antagonism that might otherwise have arisen owing to the farm worker's growing awareness of his low pay and low status.

Changes in the village community have therefore generally made the relationship between farmers and farm workers more close, personal, diffuse and pervasive. This is most clearly exemplified in the farm-centred community, where the degree of contact between employer and employee has resorted to something approaching the degree of intimacy that existed before the decline of farm service at the beginning of the nineteenth century. Here the farm worker is presented with few alternative conceptions of what is 'possible, desirable and legitimate'[46] to those values promoted by his employer. With the decline in the agricultural labour force, the continuing urbanization of rural areas and the reluctance of many rural local authorities to build more council housing, the likelihood is that this situation will predominate more and more in the future. Only where farm amalgamations create larger, more bureaucratically organized units will there be any counterveiling tendency towards an increased separation between employer and employee. Otherwise the agricultural worker, socially and geographically isolated from the mainstream of the British working class, is likely to come increasingly under the pervasive social influence of his employer.

---

1. Owing to the multitude of meanings which surround the word 'community' a more precise term would be 'local social system', and these two

terms are used interchangeably in this chapter. In general however, the term 'community' has been used in the interest of parsimonious communication. For a fuller discussion see M. Stacey, 'The Myth of Community Studies', *British Journal of Sociology*, vol. xx, No. 2, 1969, pp. 134–47, and C. Bell and H. Newby, 'The Sources of Variation in Agricultural Workers' Images of Society', *Sociological Review*, vol. 21, No. 2, 1973, pp. 229–53.

2. cf. D. Lockwood, 'Sources of Variation in Working Class Images of Society', *Sociological Review*, vol. 14, No. 3, 1966, p. 254; and 'The New Working Class', *Archives Européennes de Sociologie*, vol. 1, No. 2, 1960, p. 257.

3. F. Parkin, *Class, Inequality and Political Order*, MacGibbon and Kee, 1971, pp. 34–5.

4. J. Littlejohn, *Westrigg*, London: Routledge and Kegan Paul, 1963, pp. 27–36; D. E. G. Plowman, W. E. Minchinton and M. Stacey, 'Local Social Status in England and Wales', *Sociological Review*, vol. 10, No. 2, 1962, pp. 161–202.

5. Parkin, op. cit., p. 35.

6. M. Weber, *The Theory of Social and Economic Organisation*, The Free Press, Glencoe, Ill., 1964, p. 125. Also Parkin, op. cit., p. 33.

7. There are many community studies which have devoted a good deal of attention to describing interactional status systems of this kind, especially in working-class districts. Many are summarized in J. Klein, *Samples from English Cultures*, Routledge and Kegan Paul, 1965, vol. 1. Some of the most relevant to the concerns of this chapter are W. M. Williams, *The Sociology of an English Village*, Routledge and Kegan Paul, 1956; M. Stacey, *Tradition and Change*, OUP, 1960; J. Littlejohn, op. cit.; D. Jenkins, *The Agricultural Community in South West Wales*, University of Wales Press, Cardiff, 1971; R. Roberts, *The Classic Slum*, Penguin Books, 1973; N. Dennis, F. Henriques and C. Slaughter, *Coal Is Our Life*, Tavistock, 1969; R. Hoggart, *The Uses of Literacy*, Penguin Books, 1957. See also the summary in Plowman *et al.* (op. cit.).

8. Parkin, op. cit., pp. 43–4.

9. R. E. Pahl, *Whose City?*, Longman, 1970, p. 23.

10. G. Bourne (Sturt), *Change in the Village*, Duckworth, 1912.

11. cf. N. Dennis, *et al.*, op. cit.; J. Tunstall, *The Fisherman*, MacGibbon and Kee, 1962; R. Brown and P. Brannen, 'Social Relations and Social Perspectives Amongst Shipbuilding Workers – A Preliminary Statement', *Sociology*, vol. 4, Nos. 1, 2, 1970, pp. 71–84, 197–211. More details of the characteristics of the agricultural occupational community, together with the literature from which this summary is drawn, can be found in Chapter I.

12. G. E. Evans, *Where Beards Wag All*, Faber, 1970, pp. 64–5.

13. F. Thompson, *Lark Rise to Candleford*, Penguin Books, 1973, p. 54.

14. This was often how farm workers referred to themselves in a rather jocular fashion in the early trade-union journals, especially *The Labourer*.

15. G. E. Evans, *The Horse in the Furrow*, Faber, 1960, p. 36.

16. R. E. Pahl, 'Newcomers in Town and Country', in *Whose City?*, op. cit.

17. R. E. Pahl, *Urbs in Rure*, Weidenfeld and Nicolson, 1965. Also R. Crichton,

Commuter Village, David and Charles, 1964; Mass-Observation and Hampshire County Planning Dept, *Village Life in Hampshire*, Hampshire C.C., 1966; P. Ambrose, *The Quiet Revolution*, Chatto and Windus for Sussex University Press, 1974. The literature is summarized in J. Connell, 'The Metropolitan Village: Spatial and Social Processes in Discontinuous Suburbs', in J. H. Johnson, (ed.), *The Geography of Suburban Growth*, Wiley, 1974.

18. The phrase is taken from P. Mayer, 'Migrancy and the Study of Africans in Towns', in R. E. Pahl (ed.), *Readings in Urban Sociology*, Pergamon Press, 1968, pp. 306–30. For an early description of this process see E. R. Roper Power, 'The Social Structure of an English County Town', *Sociological Review* (old series), 1937, pp. 391–413. Recently Ambrose (op. cit.) has suggested that this encapsulation is only an initial response to the impact of urbanization.

19. Pahl (1970), op. cit., p. 105.

20. R. E. Pahl, 'The Rural-Urban Continuum', in Pahl (ed.), op. cit., p. 274.

21. See ibid., p. 275; also Stacey, op. cit., and N. Elias and J. L. Scotson, *The Established and the Outsider*, Cass, 1965.

22. C. H. Gardiner, *Your Village and Mine*, Faber, 1944, p. 33.

23. See C. Bell and H. Newby, 'Capitalist Farmers in the British Class Structure', *Sociologia Ruralis*, vol. 14, No. 1/2, 1074, pp. 86–107.

24. See D. E. Thorns, 'The Changing System of Rural Stratification', *Sociologia Ruralis*, vol. XVIII, No. 2, 1968, pp. 161–76.

25. Editorial in the first edition of *The Labourer*, 21 March 1914.

26. *Land Worker*, January 1950, p. 7.

27. ibid. The victim of the writer's wrath was a football correspondent of a national newspaper who, backing a suggestion that football clubs should not buy houses for their players but encourage them to buy their own, had commented that it was 'yet another shackle on the player's freedom. It reduces him to the status of a farm labourer.' In the view of the *Land Worker*, 'It is astonishing that anyone should spoil a perfectly good case by such an insolent and offensive relegation of farm workers to a lower social status than that of footballers.'

28. Pahl (1965), op. cit.; Ambrose, op. cit.

29. R. Blythe, *Akenfield*, Allen Lane, 1968; C. Harris (pseud.), *Hennage: A Social Structure in Miniature*, Holt, Rinehart and Winston, New York, 1974.

30. See Chapter I, n. 7.

31. cf. A. W. Gouldner, *Patterns of Industrial Bureaucracy*, The Free Press, Glencoe, Ill., 1954.

32. These six were Blaxhall, Campsea Ash, Laxfield, Little Glemham, Peasenhall and Sibton. It should be noted that Peasenhall and Sibton (the two parishes form a contiguous settlement) originally grew up around a small agricultural engineering factory which closed in 1967. Peasenhall in particular has as much a manufacturing as an agricultural history, but in 1972 had lapsed into an almost entirely agricultural settlement, with a few of the former engineering workers commuting to a rotovator factory in Halesworth. The village achieved national notoriety after the brutal murder of a local servant girl in 1902 – see R. J. White's novel, *The*

Women of Peasenhall, Macmillan, 1969. It was also the subject of a BBC television documentary in 1970. The village of Blaxhall is the subject of many of George Ewart Evans' early books, especially *Ask the Fellow Who Cut the Hay*, Faber, 1956.

33. Burgh, Debach, Hoo, Letheringham, Monk Soham, Tannington and Ubbeston. In all cases the classification of the villages was based upon familiarization with them gained during fieldwork. Fortunately the life-styles of the newcomers is so different from those of the locals that their presence in the village is easily observable, particularly as far as housing is concerned.

34. A. R. Emerson and R. Crompton, *Suffolk – Some Social Trends*, University of East Anglia, Norwich, School of Social Studies, 1968.

35. ibid., p. 38. Like questions on job satisfaction, most respondents will be predisposed to answer questions about their happiness with the community in the affirmative, so the authors understandably treat this finding with caution.

36. ibid., pp. 44–8. The chief complaints of the immigrants concerned the changing visual aspects of the countryside due to modern farming methods and the siting of new houses.

37. R. J. Green, *County Planning*, Manchester University Press, 1971, p. 19. As noted earlier in this chapter the newcomers' enthusiastic takeover of local associations is often a cause of resentment among the locals rather than a reflection of the newcomers' integration.

38. cf. A. Whitehead, *Social Fields and Social Networks in an English Rural Area, with Special Reference to Stratification*, University College, Swansea, Ph.D. thesis, 1971.

39. Many of these indicators of community attachment are taken from the Royal Commission on Local Government in England, Research Study No. 9, *Community Attitudes Survey: England*, HMSO, 1969.

40. *Guardian*, 11 November 1972 and 9 December 1972.

41. J. Hodgson and K. Richardson, *The Farm Labourer*, Macmillan, 1972.

42. P. Self and H. Storing, *The State and the Farmer*, Allen and Unwin, 1962, p. 176.

43. This figure is depressed slightly by the fact that, unlike the other groups, it includes females.

44. On the road haulage industry, see P. Hollowell, *The Lorry Driver*, Routledge and Kegan Paul, 1968.

45. *Sun*, 16 October 1970.

46. One of the pre-conditions of deference indicated by Lockwood (1966), op. cit., p. 255.

CHAPTER SEVEN

Images of Self and Society

The objective deprivation of the agricultural worker compared with other sections of British society is probably as great today as it has ever been, yet the farm worker displays few outward signs of dissatisfaction: he rarely complains, does not go on strike and does not indulge in absenteeism. It is easy to regard him as 'deferential'. Yet perhaps the most important facet of his overall situation is his relative powerlessness to obtain higher rewards for his labour owing to the still quite rigid constraints that operate in both the labour and housing markets. Therefore a consideration of the agricultural worker's predicament raises in an acute form the nature of the connection between dependence and deference. Does the agricultural worker really endorse his own social subordination or does he merely recognize his own powerlessness and acknowledge that any overt protest would be pointless and self-defeating? To answer this question empirically is fraught with difficulties. Not only is the social situation of the agricultural worker a complex and fast-changing one, but the epistemological problems of actually distinguishing between powerlessness and deference are considerable. Nevertheless this chapter is devoted to an investigation of the alleged deference of the agricultural worker, to try to explain in structural terms the way in which the agricultural worker views the world around him and his own place within it. Only on this basis can the extent of his endorsement of the *status quo* be assessed.

In strictly Marxist terms class consciousness represents a historial process not easily amenable to conventional methods of empirical investigation, although this did not stop Marx himself from attempting to administer a questionnaire on '*enquête ouvrière*' to a sample of contemporaries in order to illuminate the situation further.[1] For Marx, no less than more recent sociological investigators, was anxious to gain some insight into the level of social and political awareness of the contemporary working class rather than rely upon *a priori* assertion or *ex post facto* historical analysis. The epistemological problems are, though, legion. Inquiries in depth among a small number of individuals, whether by interview or by participant observation, raise questions of reliability; survey data collected from large samples of respondents are often statistically reliable but of dubious validity and ignore historical process to boot. In the case of deference, these problems are compounded by a basic confusion over the definition of the term itself. As was pointed out in Chapter 2, the very attractiveness of the deference hypothesis to explain the quiescence of the British working class has been its elasticity of meaning, aided on occasions by tautology (workers are quiescent because they are deferential, which is to say, quiescent). Precisely what counts as deference is by no means clear, even from a detailed reading of the literature on the topic. Both of these problems occurred repeatedly during the investigation of deference among agricultural workers. The validity of the data collected was a recurrent issue because the two research methods employed often provided ostensibly incompatible information, while in addition the insights gained from the research provided a much firmer basis upon which to judge how the issues which underlie the concept of deference can be more usefully understood. The research process was therefore very much an *exploration* of deference and by extension of the agricultural workers' other images of themselves and society, and both this chapter and the one that follows should be read in this light. The original formulation of deference in particular was one that had been superseded by the end.

As explained in Chapter 2, this original formulation was based upon that of Parkin[2] – the subscription to a moral order which endorses the individual's own political, material and social subordination, with the addition that this subordination should be legitimated on traditional grounds. This definition at least overcame the weakness of the most simplistic behavioural definitions of deference which often impute a moral commitment on the basis of mere behavioural observation. From the beginning, however, it was clear that the reputation for deference which farm workers have gained was to a considerable extent based upon such an imputation. Although many farm workers did 'directly experience the social influences and judgements of dominant class members' to which Parkin attributes the occurrence of deference,[3] the variations in work and status situations *within* the agricultural milieu were sufficient to produce a wide range in the social and political outlook of the workers who were interviewed. It then became necessary to relate these variations in ideology to variations in the sociological environment in which the agricultural workers lived out their daily lives. Moreover, as Chapters 5 and 6 demonstrated, fundamental changes have recently occurred in both the farm worker's work and status situations which have had complex but profound effects upon how he has interpreted his own position in society. If one then adds to this the inevitable uniqueness of each farm worker's biographical experience, then the delineation of the agricultural worker's image of society becomes a very complicated exercise. Certainly only a minority of agricultural workers could be unambiguously described as deferential workers, whatever their image among the rest of the population.

The Legitimacy of the Employer

One arena in which the influences and judgements of dominant class members are constantly experienced is place of work. In a minority of cases this even extends to personal knowledge and experience of the aristocratic pinnacle of the British class structure, but even if the employer is not a member of the hereditary landed upper class the agricultural worker is still subject to the values and beliefs which may be said to uphold the legitimacy of the established system of economic and social evaluations. Because the relationship between most farmers and workers is a close personal one, and because most farmers live adjacent to the workplace, the gap in income and life-style between employer and employee is a very visible one. Farmers therefore feel obliged from time to time to justify this inegalitarian distribution of rewards to their workers in terms which can frequently be extended to apply to inequalities in society at large. The work situation may then act as a model of society as a whole in the minds of many workers: inequalities of power, wealth and income in agriculture are a microcosm of general social inequalities; authority relationships at work are the prototype of wider authority relationships; the accepted justifications of subordination at the workplace become normative prescriptions for society as a whole. This influence of work relationships upon the agricultural worker's social consciousness is particularly extensive owing to the relative isolation and self-containment of his social situation.

The data presented in Chapter 5 demonstrated how the vast majority of farm workers tended to view their relationship with their employer as generally a co-operative and harmonious one, but these perceptions mainly concerned the daily transaction of employer–employee relationships at work and did not cover more general issues about the prevailing system of authority and rewards in agriculture in general. On all farms the disparity between farmer and farm worker is obviously enormous. The farmer has the power to hire and fire while he also derives economic rewards in terms of wealth and income that are many times those which accrue to his labour force. There are, then, two issues which arise and which are relevant to the farm worker's class ideology: the legitimacy of the farmer's power over him and the justice of the distribution of rewards which each party draws from the system of agricultural production. Although these two issues are obviously closely linked to each other, it is possible to retain the distinction, for it is one which the farm worker himself often implicitly makes. He often feels dissatisfied with his own level of pay, for example, but does not in general put the blame for this upon his own, or even other, employers[4]: hence he tends not to question the legitimacy of their authority as a consequence. Indeed it is a prevailing characteristic of agriculture that most workers feel economically deprived while remaining on excellent personal relations with their employers.

Any consideration of the agricultural worker's perceptions of his own subordination must begin with a very simple point. Above all the system which has brought about his economic and social subordination is an awesome and apparently irrevocable fact. It is *there* and possesses a reality in comparison with which all alternatives appear abstract and putative. Successive generations of agricultural workers are confronted with a reality which becomes to them self-evident. There have always been bosses and workers, farmers and farm workers, master and man – and there always will be. It is a fact of life as permanent, as tangible and as easily observable as the physical features of the countryside around them. It is, in other words, *natural*, and all suggested alternatives are consequently impractical, unrealistic and doomed to inevitable failure. Farm workers are by no means peculiar in adhering to such a view, but for them it forms an ideological bedrock which reflects their submission to a deep and pervasive cultural hegemony. The worker confronts a system which is there, which works and which even if it works to his own detriment he is incapable of changing, so it seems, by his own efforts, or even those of his workmates. Its very existence then begins to convey its own legitimacy, a legitimacy not consciously arrived at as a result of moral reflection but more or less unthinkingly as a result of continuous involvement in its operations. If it is there, it must work, and it works because it is there.

Some form of inequality is therefore regarded as natural and inevitable, and this is reflected in the agricultural worker's prevailing view of human nature. Time and time again this view would be expressed as follows: 'If you give everyone a thousand pounds today, by tomorrow one half would have two thousand pounds and the other half would have lost it all.' The number of occasions on which this was said was almost uncanny and it seems to reflect the agricultural worker's firm belief in the inevitability of social and economic inequality due to inherent and ineradicable differences in individuals' capabilities. Analogies abound with the world of nature which surrounds the farm worker. He can easily observe the existence of natural inequalities in the animal world: the runt in a litter of pigs, the leader of a pack of hounds, the survival of the fittest at all levels of the evolutionary scale. It becomes easy and plausible to regard the organization of human society in similar terms, to accept existing social and economical inequalities as the inevitable outcome of natural biological differences.[5]

To an inquiring outsider, of course, such a view raises almost as many questions as it answers. In the last analysis the farm worker may regard social inequality as an inevitability, but this need not necessarily result in his regarding the particular system of inequality with which he is confronted as being a legitimate or desirable one. Few workers believe that the process which consigns them to a subordinate role and their employers to a superordinate one is based purely and simply on differences in inate ability, and neither need the distribution of rewards between employer and employee correspond closely to the canons of natural justice. The legitimacy of the farmer's position is therefore based upon other factors than natural inequality, and the implicit belief which almost all farm workers possess in the inevitability of some form of inegalitarianism does not necessarily connote an identification with the particular inequalities between farmer and farm worker as they exist in contemporary agriculture. Upon this latter issue it is much more difficult to make widespread generalizations, for, as previous chapters have shown, the precise nature of the worker's social hierarchy can vary from farm to farm and locality to locality. However, it is possible to discuss some general principles on the basis of which farm workers are prepared to identify with the authority of their employer which can then be examined with the help of the data presented in Table 53.

Table 53 Attitudes to farmers of workers interviewed in Suffolk, 1972

	Agree %	Disagree %	No opinion %
Most farmers have the welfare of their workers at heart	60·1	34·8	5·2
Workers should have more say in the running of their farm	33·9	62·2	3·9
Matters of agricultural policy can be left to farmers to deal with, without workers bothering about them	58·4	32·6	9·0
Farmers know what's best for the farm and workers should do just what they are told	57·5	40·3	2·1
Most farm workers could manage a farm better than farmers	34·8	60·9	4·3
Farmers are getting more than their fair share of farm income	37·8	40·3	21·9
Workers should always be loyal to their farmer, even if this means putting themselves out quite a bit	73·0	23·6	3·4

The farm workers who were interviewed were presented with a series of statements concerning the role of agricultural employers with which they were asked to agree or disagree. In each case they were also asked for their reasons for their answers. One of the most important characteristics that emerged from this was the sanctity of the institution of property. If a fundamental belief in the inevitability of inequality represents one basis of the farm worker's social consciousness, then a hegemony equally profound is reflected in the belief that property confers its own rights upon those fortunate enough to own it. For example, assent to the statement that 'Farmers know what's best for the farm and workers should do just what they are told' was almost entirely expressed in these terms. Even those who disagreed jibbed at the word 'just' and argued that they were entitled to some consultation, but without exception they were prepared to allow the farmer the last word, on the grounds that it was his farm and therefore he had the right to do whatever he wished with it:

'He'll take our advice anyway, but it's the farmer's farm and he's entitled to tell you what he wants you to do.'

'It's the farmer's farm – it's up to him how he runs it.

'It's his money he's spending.'

'The days of bowing and scraping to squires are over, but it's their farm and you've got to have master and man, so the farmer should always have his way in the end, even though you can *suggest* things.'

'We discuss it with our boss but he has the last word. After all, it's his farm.'

This private ownership of the land by the farmer is seen as merely an extension of the ownership by the farm worker himself of his own private possessions, and the farmer is accepted as having similar rights over how this property is to be used or dispensed with. For similar reasons a majority of the workers interviewed (62·2 per cent) did not believe that they should have more say in the running of the farm. Nearly all farm workers would wish to be consulted about day-to-day matters in the running of the farm, and many farmers would acknowledge that many workers have useful ideas to contribute, but most workers recognize that their position is a necessarily inferior one and, in the last analysis, they do not have the right to tamper with someone else's property.

Overlying this, however, there is a recognition that, while farmers have an unarguable right to their own property, their very ownership of the means of production gives them a degree of power which at the very least must be recognized and accommodated to:

'They pay, so you've got to do what they say.'

'If you do it his way you can't be wrong.'

'He pays, he orders. We get some say, but if we wanted any more we would have to put money in as well.'

'If you work for your boss you must do as you're told. We discuss it with our boss but he has the last word so we might as well not bother.'

These comments acknowledge little more than the minimal contractual element in the employer–employee relationship. The farmer pays: you take it or leave it, and mostly you have to take it, so it does not do to make a fuss. But most farm workers extend their identification with their employer beyond this: 73 per cent, for example, felt that farm workers should be loyal, even if this meant putting themselves out quite a bit. Economic interest obviously plays a part in this loyalty, but there is also a kind of functional argument for the farmer's authority – he has the money to keep workers employed and so it is in both parties' interests that profitability should be as high as possible. In the face-to-face situation on most farms this seems more plausible than in large industrial corporations where one could hardly imagine, say, car workers justifying their company's managing director's high salary in terms of the fact that it enabled him personally to employ so many workers. On the farm, however, it is often the farmer's wealth rather than the farm worker's labour which seems to be creating employment. This point was well expressed by Sturt: 'It may be added that most of them are convinced believers in those fallacies which cluster around the phrase "making work". It were strange if they were not. The labourer lives by being employed at work; and, knowing his employer personally – this or that farmer or tradesman or villa resident – he sees the work he lives by actually being 'made'. Only very rarely does it occur to him that when he goes to the shop he, too, makes work. In bad times, perhaps, he gets an inkling of it; and then, when wages are scarce, and the public-house landlord grumbles, old-fashioned villagers will say, "Oh, they misses the poor men, yer see!" But the idea is too abstract to be followed to its logical conclusion. The people do not see the multitudes at work for them in other counties . . . but they do see, and know by name, the well-to-do of the neighbourhood . . . and they naturally infer that labour would perish if there were no well-to-do people to be supplied. Against the rich man, therefore, the labourers have no sort of animosity. If he will spend money freely, the richer he is the better . . . This village looks up to those who control wealth as if they were the source of it.'[6]

A similar train of reasoning is followed by many Suffolk farm

workers today and in the light of this it is easy to see how a substantial
majority of those interviewed believed that most farmers have the
welfare of their workers at heart. Farmers go out of their way to
cultivate such a view among their workers by a variety of means, for
the personal nature of the employer–employee relationship encour-
ages an extension beyond mere cash nexus. Mutual help often dissolves
class barriers in an isolated rural situation when the nearest shops may
be miles away: giving lifts, using telephones, looking after children,
etc. become unavoidable obligations. Sociability also becomes important. Many farm workers interpret their employer's interest in
their welfare in terms of how prepared he is to be sociable, to chat and
gossip and generally pass the time of day discussing matters of mutual
interest. Paradoxically this is a form of familiarity which is only
possible because of the unquestioned fixity of the social divisions
between them, but the prevalence of such human companionship is
often sufficient to ensure the continuing loyalty of the farm worker. In
addition, the notion of welfare also applies to other activities outside
a narrow interpretation of the wage bargain – as noted in Chapter 5
the good employer is one who looks after his workers through numerous acts of appreciation and care. As one worker summed it up,
'That's one thing about the guv'nor, he'll always stop and have a
word with you. You can always talk to him. He doesn't put his money
in a tin, we have a big dinner down there once a year if we've done
well. And every Christmas we get a turkey and ten pounds of tea
and some butter and a £5 voucher to spend in Ipswich. I mean, you
can't turn round to someone like that and say we're going on strike
can you?' In cash terms these gifts may not amount to much, but this
is not the point. The important point is that the farmer has demonstrated in a tangible way his desire to be generous to his workers
beyond what is economically and legally necessary: he has shown that
he *cares*, that his workers are not an impersonal cost of production but
individual human beings capable of being recognized as such. As far
as the farm worker is concerned it is difficult to be antagonistic towards such a nice chap.[7]

The value of these gifts is therefore more symbolic than real. They
help to cement the loyalty of the farm worker. As such, they are
probably cheap at the price, but, even if farm workers were to consider the cash value rather than the 'thought' behind them, he would
have some difficulty in assessing how much his employer could

afford. Most farm workers are very ignorant about the wealth and income of their employer. It is therefore difficult for them to judge whether or not farmers are receiving an equitable return for what they put into the business. During an exceptionally profitable year for East Anglian farmers, a small majority of farm workers still believed that they were receiving a fair share; but a large proportion (21·9 per cent) simply could not judge because they did not know how profitable their farm was. Most farms are not public companies and therefore are not obliged to publish their accounts. In addition the variability from year to year and place to place in farming make estimates hazardous. Farmers, unlike farm workers, do not need to indulge in well-publicized wage negotiations or have their wage rates displayed in local post offices. The only reliable figures are to be found in obscure Ministry publications and even these are only averages of farming income from which individual cases may vary widely – and farm workers do not make a habit of consulting official statistical publications. Moreover farmers are notorious for remaining tight-lipped after a profitable year, while engaging in vociferous and well-organized protest during less renumerative periods. To the onlooker farmers persistently profess their difficulties in making ends meet.

How far does the farm worker believe these protestations of poverty? Certainly there is an element of risk involved in farming, because of the weather and to a lesser extent the state of the market, and farming income does fluctuate considerably from year to year. If the farmer does not volunteer information about the profitability of his farm, the workers are reduced to hunting for clues and making an informed guess. There is often evidence both for and against:

'If they were getting a good screw they wouldn't always be fighting over wages.'

'What with all that capital tied up on the farm, buying tractors and combines and putting up barns and suchlike, there can't be much left over.'

'The boss down there is in a rum position. Everything is controlled. You can't put prices up – their hands are tied. If he could get more money he'd give it to you.'

'You can't blame the employer. It's like if you go to a shop and pay fifteen bob, you've got to pay fifteen bob. So the boss pays as little as he gets away with – you can't blame him.'

'It's a job to know. The farmers say it's the low price of food, but it makes you think when they drive around in their Volvo Estates.'

'They say they can't afford anything but they can buy new Range Rovers, so you can *see* they're not hard up.'

'They always say they can't afford to pay us more, but what else can they say? Those near the towns can do it, 'cos they have to do it or they wouldn't get no workers. Why can't the rest? You see them about in their big cars and their Jaguars. We say, "There he goes; he bought another one out o' his losses." He bought out his neighbour lock, stock and barrel, yet they say there's no money in it. They give themselves away!'

'The government gives 'em enough to live on. They don't need to work. Everything they sell gets a subsidy and they get a grant for any work that wants doing as well. I've been all over the country – on holiday and that – and up in Scotland and Wales and Devon and places like that nothing much grows there, yet they seem to make a living up there. So those in East Anglia must do well!'

'He says he never makes any money but he recently bought a new Volvo and his daughters two Marinas, so someone is conning somebody somewhere. He never covers the rust on his cars. He gets a new one every two years.'

Whichever view is taken few farm workers are sure about their guesswork. For every accusation the farmer has a ready reply: the cars are tax-deductible; the wealth is all on paper; farming gives such a low return that they would be better off with the capital in a building society; costs are always going up; prices are held down, taxation is crippling; the farm is mortgaged to the hilt; the overdraft is enormous; the subsidies go to the consumer not to the farmer – even if the farm worker only half-believes him he does not have the information to dispute it and he gives up, remaining at best agnostic.

This, however, is often sufficient for the employer to retain his legitimacy. A belief in natural inequality, an acceptance of the farmer's property rights, a recognition of the individual employer's personal concern for the worker and an inability to make any definite and conclusive assessment of the farmer's income combine together to give an overwhelming legitimacy to the farmer's authority over his workers. To these can be added one further factor: the farm worker's recognition that he lacks the abilities to operate the system any better than his employer. Of the workers interviewed, 60·9 per cent did not believe that most farm workers could manage a farm better than farmers. Their reasons for this did not relate to the husbandry of the farm (in which a good deal more believed that they *could* do better than most farmers) but to the financial management of the enterprise – the buying and selling, the accounts and so on. Apart from a handful of highly educated supervisory workers, the vast majority of the 34·8 per cent who felt they could do better were thinking solely in terms of husbandry. For much the same reasons a majority of the workers interviewed also believed that agricultural policy matters could be left to farmers to deal with, without farm workers bothering about them. As one worker put it, 'I could do the *work* but not the business side. I could *farm* the farm better than the boss, but I couldn't do the clerical work, let alone draw up all the plans and so forth. There's got to be someone to make the decisions and the workers can't do it.'[8]

So far this account of the agricultural worker's interpretation of his relationship *vis-à-vis* the farmer has treated this relationship in isolation from others which may impinge upon it. In the previous chapter, however, attention was drawn to the fact that, while farmers and farm workers may hold contrary interests according to their respective roles in the means of agricultural production, they also share a similar interest *vis-à-vis* the non-agricultural majority of the population. As Table 54 shows, farm workers show a marked antipathy to industry as a whole, which is usually perceived as an undifferentiated, hostile mass. This antipathy is based partly on a recognition of divergent economic interests, particularly over the price of food, but more particularly because of the low status which, it is believed, urban industrial workers unjustifiably assign to those who work on the land. Urban workers – and particularly car workers, dockers and miners, who represent the urban, industrial stereotype – are perceived to denigrate the agricultural worker when, so the farm worker believes, they are no more skilled or hardworking than himself and his fellow workers. Those working in industry are not only less skilled but they are paid astronomic wages (exaggerated by most agricultural workers) and are constantly on strike for even more money or over trivial and apparently senseless incidents. This results in prices rising for the goods the farm workers buy in the shops, while he in turn has to suffer the consequences of urban demands for cheap food. Consequently the farm worker is aware of being part of a threatened minority who rely upon the production of food for their living, and partaking in a separate and distinctive rural way of life. These feelings are very strongly held, as is indicated by the size of the percentages in the

Table 54 Attitudes to industry of workers interviewed in Suffolk, 1972

	Agree %	Disagree %	No opinion %
Industrial workers are getting more than their fair share in wages	86·3	9·4	4·3
(Industrial) trade unions have too much power in this country	84·1	12·0	3·9
In industry managers know what's best for their firm and workers should do just what they are told	61·8	24·9	13·3
The men who own big business have too much power in this country	77·3	13·3	9·4
Farm workers have more in common with farmers than with workers in other industries	91·8	5·2	3·0

'agree' category in Table 54. This was also reflected in the strength and vehemence of the replies. Some of the comments the respondents made again help to convey this:

'Workers at Garrett's at Leiston [a local engineering factory] used to spit on farm workers if they saw them in leggings and a smock. It was real class distinction. They wouldn't sit with us in a pub. They always classed the farm worker as a nobody. They thought we didn't know nothing, both the farmer and his men. They thought we were the biggest duffers there was.'

'A farm is a small unit with a few people. A factory is a big concern. So the guv'nor in a factory has got to have the whip hand – the workers just don't care. They won't work.'

'Management in industry is altogether different. Farmers and workers work alongside each other, but in industry the boss only walks round the shop floor once a week. A farmer is more like a farm worker – he asks your advice.'

'Tradesmen, electrician people, people like that – they look down on the farm worker. So we never muck in much with other industries because everyone else is in a trade and so they reckon that on the farm there are only ordinary stupid people.'

'A farm worker has a dirty job and no money. In industry they have a clean job, a five-day week and lots of money. So they look down on you because of the job you're in.'

'Factory workers are like bits of clockwork – cogs in a machine. What happens after they've worked their forty hours is immaterial to them. Farm workers live round the farm and live on the job. They work on their own and realize if they don't do the work no one else will. In a factory who's going to miss one in a thousand? So they don't bother. Country people are in a class of their own. Everyone else in the country don't lead the same sort of life.'

As was argued in Chapter 6, recent changes in the social structure of most rural villages has probably exacerbated these feelings of distinctiveness. Together with the closer contact with the employer that has resulted from changes in the work situation, the urbanization of many villages has drawn farmer and worker closer together, so that they share together the faint paranoia against the urban majority of the population, suffer together from the interference of ignorant outsiders, share the sense of achievement from watching the crops and animals grow and share the same sense of chagrin when an unforeseen accident of weather or disease results in setbacks. The farmer even shares his workers' sense of outrage at the social stigma which is attached to working on the land by non-agricultural workers. As one put it, 'When people call farm workers idiots, I feel like they are calling me an idiot too, and I get very annoyed. My men are much more interested because they know I wouldn't ask them to do a job I wouldn't do myself. And I know how they feel. When it's wet I get wet with them and when it's cold I get cold too.' This sharing of experiences, both at the workplace and in leisure hours, tends to obscure the differences in reward which farmers and workers receive for their respective efforts – and of which farm workers are not often capable of making an accurate assessment. Consequently, the proportion of

workers interviewed who believed that they had more in common
with farmers than with workers in other industries was extremely
high – 91·8 per cent. As one worker summed it up, understandably,
though not altogether accurately, 'We both lead the same sort of
life.'

In the light of this, how far may the agricultural worker be said to
defer to his employer? Certainly nearly all farm workers *accept* a
material and social subordination to their employer, but it is by no
means clear that they all *subscribe* to the moral order which endorses
it. Neither is it clear that farm workers legitimate the power of their
employer only on traditional grounds. There is, however, no clear-
cut summary that can be made on either of these issues. Certain aspects
of the farmer's authority which can be regarded as traditional do
contribute to his legitimacy, perhaps the most important of which is
the unquestioned rule of primogeniture which confers upon most of
the employers the right to own and control their own farm. This
traditionalism is also reflected in the fact that most farmers, and
particularly those on the smaller farms, attract a personal attachment
and commitment rather than holding authority solely on the basis of
their role as employer. Nevertheless there are a substantial number of
workers who recognize that the relationship is also fundamentally a
contractual one – 'He pays, he orders' as one worker put it. These two
strands in the relationship overlie one another so that it consists of both
personal loyalty and cash nexus, the latter stemming from the market
situation in which the agricultural worker must sell his labour to his
employer and the former from the identification which the employer
cultivates and which, in many cases, because of the personal, particularistic nature of the relationship, he has achieved to a considerable
degree. There are, however, necessarily certain contradictions between
these two aspects of the relationship which emerge from time to time:
for example, the concern for employees' welfare implies a certain
protection from the worst excesses of market forces, yet at the same
time no employer can afford to ignore the market altogether if he is
to stay in business in the long term. These contradictory strands in the
relationship are often reflected in ambivalence among the workers, so
that they neither reject nor completely endorse the social and economic position of the farmer. They identify with certain aspects of the
relationship but are more detached from others; as a result the best
summary one can make is that farm workers pragmatically accept

what is there, particularly as alternatives are either inconceivable or unrealizable, and for the most part their feelings vary between personal loyalty towards an often kind and thoughtful employer and dissatisfaction with the more instrumental aspects of the relationship.

Deference – An Attitudinal Approach

Before examining in detail the farm worker's general social consciousness, it is necessary to consider briefly a more conventional approach to the study of deference. The collection of studies of deference referred to in Chapter 2 which followed the revival of the deference thesis in the 1960s based their investigations upon opinion survey data. That is, deference was operationalized as the attitudes of members of the British working class towards certain individuals, institutions and symbols deemed representative of traditional values and political culture. The main preoccupation was with working-class Conservative voting behaviour, but a subsidiary theme involved a much broader deference towards institutions connected with the more traditional aspects of the British class structure – the monarchy, the landed aristocracy, the public schools and so on.[9] Although it is rarely stated quite so explicitly, the underlying rationale of these studies is that the affirmation of these institutions is taken as indicating the presence of a 'deferential' ideology which guides the party political choices, the (lack of) political involvement and even the social transactions of the individuals concerned. Deference, then, is taken to be an *attribute* of individual actors guiding their social and political conduct.

Many of the criticisms of the concept of deference, most notably that of Kavanagh,[10] have concentrated on the ambiguities of the term. As Jessop has also pointed out, many of the studies of deference by political scientists have operated with a variety of usages, ranging from a secular 'political deference' (or civility) to the government, whatever its composition, to the most inclusive type of deference, 'socio-cultural deference' (which Jessop also calls 'traditionalism'), which refers to 'the "receptive affirmation" of the legitimacy of established institutions, traditions and values, and the rejection of innovations threatening the order they embody'.[11] Jessop's delineation of the various types of deference helps to clear up a number of the previous ambiguities and also helps to render the term less amorphous and hence more capable of empirical investigation. However, it is noteworthy that both he and Kavanagh, whose criticisms have been in many respects more devastating, share the model of deference as an ideological attribute which individual actors then utilize in order to interpret the world around them. This approach conflicts with another recent theme concerning working-class consciousness (which Jessop also acknowledges), namely the lack of *any* coherent set of beliefs: Horton and Thompson's conclusion that it represents an 'existential guess', Converse's 'proliferation of clusters of ideas' and Mann's 'pragmatic acceptance' of concrete and specific issues.[12] Here the emphasis has been placed upon the absence of *any* all-embracing ideological prescriptions for social and political activity and hence the absence, at least for the majority of those at the bottom of the social scale, of any abstract cultural or political precepts which determine their everyday activities.

This appraisal of working-class beliefs clearly undermines many of the presuppositions upon which the investigation of deference has customarily been based. For example the attitudinal indicators of deference would not represent any cumulative index of deferential ideology, but only a pragmatic and uniquely applied assessment of each statement on its own merits, with perhaps only marginal consequences for future social and political activities and with only an imperfect causal connection to the factors with which they purport to be associated. It therefore has to be admitted that it was with some considerable scepticism that the agricultural workers who were interviewed in Suffolk were presented with a series of statements of the kind which have been traditionally used to indicate the presence of deference. This was carried out partly to discover whether or not agricultural workers could be considered deferential even in the terms in which this word has customarily been understood and investigated, and partly as a piece of participant observation in an attempt to assess how relevant and meaningful this approach was and how these statements are interpreted by the respondent.

Accordingly the farm workers interviewed in the survey were given a number of statements with which to agree or disagree, involving many of the indicators customarily employed in the investigation of deference. Their responses are shown in Table 55. There are two immediate points which can be made about these results. First, even by these measures, the farm worker emerges as being not nearly as deferential as is generally supposed. Unequivocal support for the monarchy and for the upper class is far from being apparent, and the customary image of the obsequious, deferential farm worker is not confirmed from these replies. The second point is that the responses

Table 55 Socio-cultural deference, as measured by attitudinal indicators, of workers interviewed in Suffolk, 1972

	Agree %	Disagree %	No opinion %
There are lots of things wrong with the monarchy that need improving	48·9	31·3	19·7
The aristocracy are born to rule and workers should follow their lead	36·9	48·9	14·2
The ordinary man should have more say in running the country	56·7	41·2	2·1
The House of Lords should be done away with in its present form	26·6	40·3	33·0
The public schools are the best part of our education system	28·6	57·5	12·9
Matters of national policy can be left to the leaders of this country to deal with, without ordinary people bothering about them	57·1	34·3	8·6
The best leaders of the country come from upper-class backgrounds rather than from a more working-class background	47·2	41·6	11·2
A government should do what it thinks right even if the majority of the people disagree	48·1	42·5	9·4

contain a number of apparent contradictions: a majority disagree that the aristocracy is born to rule and workers should follow their lead, but a majority also agree that the best leaders of this country come from upper-class backgrounds rather than from more working–class backgrounds; similarly, a majority believed that ordinary men should have more say in running the country, but a majority also believed that matters of national policy can be left to the leaders of this country to deal with, without ordinary people bothering about them. Although no doubt a number of esoteric and complicated rationalizations *could* be put forward to reconcile these apparent contradictions, the explanation is probably a much more straightforward one. These contradictory replies are indicative of an absence of abstract ideological principles that organize and define responses to specific questions – instead each question is considered separately on its own merits with often little logical consistency between the responses.

They are also indicative of another aspect of this approach – the lack of saliency of the questions. This is much more difficult to demonstrate quantitatively, although it is reflected in the much higher proportion of replies in the 'no opinion' category in Table 55 – an average of 13·9 per cent – compared with Tables 53 and 54, where the averages were 7·1 per cent and 6·8 per cent respectively. Rather it is more a question of using the data-gathering process as data in its own right. Certainly the responses to statements on the legitimacy of farmers and on anti-urbanism usually came quickly, decisively and often vehemently. Most of the workers interviewed were clearly responding to issues which were relevant and meaningful to them and upon which, for the most part, they had definite opinions. This was perhaps not surprising, since most of these opinions concerned aspects of their daily lives which they regularly encountered and even discussed with their friends, family and workmates, in however desultory a fashion. Questions concerning the monarchy, the House of Lords or the public schools hardly fell into the same category. These were not institutions which, most farm workers felt, affected their daily lives to any great extent. Their responses were usually hesitant, tentative and even grudging. Many obviously felt that they *ought* to have an opinion upon such issues and so dutifully searched their minds and came up with one, but the distinct impression was gained that these were concerns which did not regularly exercise their thoughts. It therefore seems unlikely that one can infer much from these responses beyond the nature of the responses themselves – and even these must be considered only weakly adhered to. On many of these questions farm workers simply do not have an attitude in the definitive sense in which this term is usually employed.

The objection to this approach therefore extends beyond the objection to the absence of any Likert-type scaling techniques which help to measure the strength as well as the nature of the beliefs held. The attitudinal approach to the study of deference rests upon an over-

simplified view about the coherence and definitiveness of beliefs held
by supposedly deferential individuals. The emphasis on attitudes leads
to a concentration upon a static and uniform set of purported attributes
of individual actors which is altogether too over-deterministic. In
other words, it is questionable whether, on the basis of the kind of
attitudinal indicators that have been customarily included in studies
of deference, one can then infer the possession of a comprehensive
and ubiquitous ideology which is assumed to direct the behaviour
of deferential individuals towards those superior to them in the
class hierarchy. Such an approach cannot account, for example,
for the sudden explosions of unrest which have characterized the
history of certain allegedly deferential groups, including agricultural
workers. The kind of outbursts of pent-up anger and frustration
which occurred in, say, the Captain Swing revolt, or the 'Revolt of
the Field' under Arch, or the Norfolk strike in 1923 cannot be put
down to mere deviant statistical aberrations from a pervasive and
uniform set of attitudes among farm workers. They were too deeply
rooted to be brushed aside in this manner. As Genovese has argued
concerning the somewhat analogous case of slave rebellions, 'It would
be absurd to argue that a regime could be sufficiently complex to
generate two or more such patterns and yet sufficiently simple to
generate them in mutual isolation.'[13] Analogies can also be drawn
with studies of industrial unrest, such as those by Warner and Low
and Lane and Roberts, which have cast considerable doubt upon the
view that situational factors produce unexpected and apparently
unforeseen aspects of behaviour by generating attitudes which hold
for all workers in all situations.[14] Instead, and the study of agricultural
workers would seem to support this, the beliefs of workers are much
more fragmented and incoherent than has generally been allowed, so
that instead of concentrating upon the attitudinal attributes of
individuals from which their putative behaviour is then inferred, it
becomes more important to study the situational factors which typically confront these individuals and how these affect the nature of the
relationships in which they are engaged.

As far as the study of deference is concerned this implies a movement
away from the study of deferential *people* to a study of deferential
relationships: who defers to whom, under what circumstances and
over which issues. This may appear to be a very simple point, but it is
one which most studies of deference have ignored and for which the

attitudinal approach to deference is inadequate. It is inadequate, not because it is entirely redundant, but because it attempts to encompass too much. It enables a fallacious correspondence to be made between deferential attitudes and deferential people. This point is taken up again in the final chapter.

Images of Society

Instead of exploring the social consciousness of the agricultural worker through a series of attitude questions, therefore, a much more unstructured approach was adopted. Following the method used in *The Affluent Worker* [15] and a number of other studies of working-class social imagery, the farm workers in the survey were asked an open-ended question that was intended to provoke a free-ranging discussion over the issues of class and inequality in British society as perceived by the respondent. The question was: 'People often talk about there being different classes in this country – what do you think?' The conversation which then ensued, in most cases, was as little directed as possible, but there was an *aide mémoire* of points on which data was required: the number of social classes distinguished, the terminology employed, self-rated class, the major factors determining class position, the assessment of mobility and so on. In so far as it was possible this part of the interview was conducted entirely in the terms used by the respondent himself, except for the introduction of the term 'class' in the initial cue question. The responses were taken down in note form, *verbatim* as far as was possible, and later categorized and coded for appropriate analysis. The difficulties involved in this are well known. As Cousins and Brown have pointed out, 'Conventional terms (such as "middle class") may be used for unconventional purposes; the same term may be used to mean different things, and different terms to mean the same thing; self-rankings are meaningless without some understanding of the overall conception of the class structure being used by the respondent; and so on. The problem is not eased when respondents appear to have given many very varied answers to questions about classes and class differences, and when one cannot assume that each respondent has one image of society which provides a point of reference no matter what the question.' [16] All of these problems were encountered in investigating the image of society held by agricultural workers. It would be absurd to make definite pronouncements on the basis of a comparatively short conversation conducted in the middle of a much larger survey questionnaire, but the repetition of many replies and the experience gained from participant observation do allow for most of the responses to be interpreted with a certain degree of validity. While the problems of inter-subjectivity are certainly not completely eradicable, neither are they entirely insuperable, for not only inquiring sociologists but the farm workers themselves seem to be able to overcome them to at least the extent which enables them to conduct their everyday social transactions.

The most immediate impression that stems from the replies of the agricultural workers who were interviewed is of the great diversity of their views. The number of classes distinguished varied between nil and five and there were twenty-four different types of nomenclature applied to the class terminology. Moreover the size of and relationships between these different groups also varied from respondent to respondent, as did the self-ranking within them, the criteria used to differentiate the classes, the assessment of mobility between them and so on. This multiplicity of images suggests immediately that it is an over-simplification to regard agricultural workers as representing a broadly uniform 'traditional deferential' group.[17] However, neither would it be correct to infer that no generalizations are possible or that agricultural workers do not share certain characteristics concerning their social imagery which can in turn be related to their structural location. After all, most agricultural workers share similar work experiences, have been brought up in the same locality and share certain variations in their local community situation. The emphasis in what follows will therefore be to summarize these varied patterns and to investigate how far they can be related to variations in the social milieux of different agricultural workers. Initially, however, some summary descriptions can be made of the images themselves.

One of the problems even with making just summaries of the respondents' images of society is that it tends to confer an entirely spurious air of definitiveness upon them. As has already been argued in this chapter, and as will be further elaborated later in this section, many agricultural workers lacked any single abstract model of society which constituted their entire social consciousness. Instead, many seemed to operate with a multiplicity of images and half-formed beliefs and opinions which did not add up to any single coherent image. Thus it was not always meaningful even to summarize the number of classes which the respondents distinguished, for sometimes they would seem to be using one model and then later refer to another and even to a third. But as a crude and approximate guide the predominant model was taken and used to compute the summary shown in Table 56. Although these severe qualifications must be borne in

Table 56 Number of classes distinguished in predominant image of society, of workers interviewed in Suffolk, 1972

	No.	%
Nil	10	4·4
Two	134	58·8
Three	55	24·1
Four	3	1·3
Five	1	0·4
Pecuniary gradation	25	11·0
	228	100·0

mind, the frequency of two-class models is of some interest. A majority of agricultural workers, 58·8 per cent, tended to operate with this kind of social imagery, a proportion substantially higher, for example, than the 33 per cent of shipbuilding workers reported by Cousins and Brown among an occupational group customarily regarded as corresponding to a more traditional proletarian section of the working class.[18] This 'finding' (and to the extent that it is partly, but only partly, manufactured by the categorization of the responses the term necessitates the inverted commas) is probably a reflection of the very clearly visible and overlapping social divisions which occur between landowners and landless, rich and poor, employers and employees, farmers and farm workers, in a commercial farming area like Suffolk. However, this adherence to a dichotomous model of the class structure does not necessarily connote a conflictual image. Although there could be a consensus on the existence of two classes, and even on the position and criteria of the division between them, the nature of the relationship between the two could be interpreted in diametrically opposite ways, in terms of either conflict or harmony.

The factors that were used to distinguish between classes are shown in Table 57. The emphasis on money as a distinguishing characteristic of class needs to be treated with some caution because it was clearly being used as an idiom in which class differences could be expressed as much as purely a determinant of class differences. However, it is

Table 57 Criteria used to distinguish social classes, of workers interviewed in Suffolk, 1972

	% of replies (N = 365)	% of respondents* (N = 233)
Money	37·6	58·8
Work, job, position	14·0	21·9
Upbringing, social values	12·6	19·8
Employer/employee	10·1	15·9
Education	8·2	12·9
Birth, breeding	7·1	11·2
Life-style	6·8	10·7
Political power	3·6	5·6
	100·0	156·8

*This represents the percentage of respondents citing each criterion. Since more than one reply was often given the total is more than 100 per cent.

doubtful whether the farm workers themselves drew such a fine distinction. Like the workers interviewed in *The Affluent Worker* study, 'it seemed evident during the interviews that respondents answering the class question frequently did not make, or did not grasp, the distinction between *determinants* and *correlates* of class; thus the reference to money could mean only that it was a conveniently observable, and easily conceptualizable, correlate of class differences rather than being seen as their fundamental cause.'[19] Indeed, in so far as the determinants of class were separately ascertainable through further probing, an overwhelmingly ascriptive pattern of class differences seemed to be the one most favoured by the majority of agricultural workers. Inheritance was easily regarded as the most important determinant of class differences, followed by innate ability. More achievement-oriented factors, such as hard work and education, were mentioned by a relatively small minority. These results are shown in Table 58. This predominantly ascriptive view of the class structure is also reflected in the farm workers' assessments of the possibility of

Table 58 Determinants of social class cited by workers interviewed in Suffolk, 1972

	% of replies (N = 253)	% of respondents* (N = 233)
Inheritance	43·9	47·6
Hard work	15·4	16·7
Innate ability	12·6	13·7
Work, job, position	10·7	11·6
Luck	9·1	9·9
Education	6·7	7·3
Solidarity	1·6	1·7
	100·0	108·5

*This represents the percentage of respondents citing each factor. Since more than one reply could be given the total is more than 100 per cent.

individual mobility up and down the social scale. The largest single proportion – 41·9 per cent – thought that there was no possibility of mobility at all and a further 26·1 per cent thought that there was only a little. Only 9·9 per cent thought that there was a lot of mobility in contemporary society. (See Table 59.)

There is, then, at least a fairly general recognition of a dichotomous

Table 59 Assessment of social mobility by workers interviewed in Suffolk, 1972

	No.	%
None	85	41·9
A little	53	26·1
Some	21	10·3
Quite a lot	24	11·8
A lot	20	9·9
	203	100·0

ascriptive class structure, although again it must be emphasized that the categorization of the data imposes a greater definitiveness on the agricultural worker's image of society than he himself possesses. However, there was a general awareness of occupying a position in the lowest class that they distinguished, no matter which images or sets of images of society they were operating with. Although the nomenclature differed according to the idiom used – 'poor', 'lower class', 'working class', 'very low' – 70·3 per cent of the workers interviewed saw the class structure of their society from the bottom upwards in this way. The remainder, including 19·3 per cent who explicitly rated themselves 'middle class', distinguished other groups or individuals below them. Whatever their own assessment of their situation, however, the vast majority of the respondents – 91·2 per cent – regarded class differences as inevitable. As mentioned earlier in this chapter, such social divisions are regarded as an unalterable fact of life by most agricultural workers. Thus, whatever the perceived structure and dynamics of the class system there remained a deeply entrenched belief that some kind of class division was a natural inevitability.

Although nearly all agricultural workers believed class divisions to be inevitable, by no means all thought such a state of affairs to be desirable. In fact only just over half – 52·4 per cent – took this view. Thus while almost all farm workers accepted the existence of some form of class structure, only a much smaller proportion were prepared to endorse it. In most cases those workers who were prepared to endorse a society divided into social classes did so according to the same kind of principles whereby they accepted the legitimacy of their own employer's authority. That is to say that the most common justification of class was based upon an argument akin to functional interdependence:

'Yes, there's always got to be rich and poor. Somebody's got to pay the wages and somebody's got to do the work.'

'You've always got to have a poor man to make a rich man, so there'll always be rich and poor. If the rich had got no money there'd be no work for the poor.'

'It's a good thing. If we didn't have the high class where would we be? They've got to have money so they can pay the poor. If everybody was rich there wouldn't be no work done.'

'There'll always be a boss and there'll always be workers. It's a good thing – if everybody was all the same nobody would say what was to be done. No work would get done. You've got to have someone with money to work for.'

'There must be master and man. It's not worked out in Russia, has it? If everything was shared out equal at seven o'clock in the morning, someone would be on top by one o'clock in the afternoon. There's got to be a master and a worker, otherwise you'd have no workers and everyone would be unemployed.'

'There's always got to be a master and a man or the world wouldn't go round. No one would do the work.'

It is noticeable that those who were prepared to endorse a class system did so on the basis of a class distinction between employers and employees. Those who were hostile towards the notion of class tended to interpret the term in a different way, however. Those who regarded class as an undesirable aspect of society viewed class overwhelmingly in terms of social acceptability or snobbery:

'They're real snobs. The high class always look down on the low class as ignorant types. There's not much good in it really.'

'I could name a few in this village who look on me as down in the lower brackets and that's where they'd like to keep me. If the higher class weren't looking down on the lower class, the lower class would never exist. It's like someone putting someone under their thumb all the time to keep them there and after a while people come to feel they *are* there. But people are now gradually getting to the stage when they say, "Why should I be under him all the time?" They're getting sick of being sat on all the time.'

'I don't think it's a good thing, but it's changing drastically. Lots of wealthy students come here and chase our daughters out – a thing they'd never do years ago!'

'Classes are only what people make them. Some feel they're a little better than everybody else. Some ask you for a basket to pick currants in, but when they see you in the street they don't want to know. If I go and have a drink tonight there's some who'll turn their noses up in the air and won't talk to me – people who haven't got a damn thing but think they've got a little more and treat you as dirt. You notice it more in the country because you know them more. It's terrible.'

Only five respondents were prepared to condemn class in terms of abstract political principles, such as 'Every man should be equal' or 'You've got to be fighting in this country for everything; lower people have got to challenge upper-class people or they won't get anything.' For the most part, however, those who were hostile to the notion of class based their hostility on the social exclusiveness that it often entailed rather than the *principle* of a hierarchical society as such. In fact a status model of the class structure was not necessarily considered in a mutually exclusive fashion from a power or pecuniary model, so that hostility to the status connotations of class need not imply a general condemnation of class *per se*. One or two workers expressed this distinction themselves:

'It's snobbishness more than anything. I don't hold with it, not this. But you've got to have better-off people, you've got to have rich and poor and two kinds of people. There must be some rich people or they'd never pay the workers.'

'Well I think it's a bad thing. Somebody has got to be top and get into business and do well or there'd be no work for anyone, but they might mix with one another a bit more.'

Many farm workers draw a distinction between class, which is acceptable, and class *distinctions*, which are not. Class *per se* is acceptable for much the same reasons that farm workers accept the authority of their employers, with which relationship for many workers it overlaps. Class is acceptable because there is an awareness that society operates economically through the class system, thereby creating employment opportunities and a recognizable, albeit inferior, stake for the workers. The basis of this acceptability therefore tends to be a rather negative one – because the alternatives might be chaos, anarchy, unemployment or worse. Most farm workers are at least willing to put up with their inferior role because, as one worker put it, 'It's inevitable. Let's stick with the one we know and the one we've got.' Anything else would be a leap in the dark, with the risk of even greater deprivation than the current system offers. All that many farm workers demand in return for their acceptance of this inferiority is a degree of

social recognition which does not append a moral and social deprivation to their economic and political subordination. No farm worker's
self-respect will allow him to admit that he is the *moral* inferior of those
higher up the social scale. His role in society may be a necessarily
inferior and humble one but he requires the recognition that he has
his part to play in the successful functioning of society. Hence his
hostility to class distinction, or, in more strictly sociological terms,
the status prerogatives that may accompany class position. Nearly all
agricultural workers are hostile to the idea of social acceptance or
rejection being based upon differences in class. Inevitably some of this
hostility may spill over into their evaluations of class *per se* unless the
separation of the two notions is strictly maintained, so that a professed
hostility to 'class' may mask a general endorsement of broader class
inequalities – class, that is, in sociological terms. Thus the proportion
who regarded class as desirable – 52·4 per cent – probably underestimates the real acceptance of class inequalities.

These complications are not only of an analytical nature. It was
clear from the interviews that many agricultural workers themselves
easily slip backwards and forwards between one notion of class and
another and between status and power models of society according to
the social context. They did not have one image of society which
provided a constant point of reference, but many, a particular model
being utilized when it seemed to best explain the issue in question.
This was compounded by the tendency not to refer to class in terms of
abstract societal models at all but in terms of particular and discrete
situations and occurrences with which they were familiar:

'That's what I mean by class – they go out shooting once a year and
we do the beating for them.'

'Class is the railway carriages – first, second, and third classes. My
family are third class: poor.'

'Class is like the time I saw the boss in an Ipswich hotel and he
didn't want to know me.'

'In the Gardeners' Club one class is here, another there, and so on.
If you're working-class they don't want to listen to you, but if Lord
— says something it's passed.'

'You only want to go to shows and you'll see that. They don't
want to know the likes of you – they're the cream that day . . . They
sort out the wheat from the chaff.'

'People think they are more than they really are. They're the people who try and create a class. People hunting on horses – they think they're really somebody.'

'Like in a pub, you always see the country boys together and the rest won't mix in. If you go into a pub you're not welcome in the lounge but you are in the bar where all the roughs are.'

In some cases these represent metaphors for class, in others the actual social experience of class differences, and in others both types of response. What class *is* to the agricultural worker is therefore not a fixed property – it is an amorphous, nebulous and fluid concept which he feels he recognizes when he is confronted by it, but a clear conception of which is not always necessary for him to engage in his every-day social encounters.

For this reason there tended to be ambiguities in the way in which farm workers perceived the relationships between the different classes that made up society as a whole. The largest proportion, 48·8 per cent, saw the relationships between social classes as being predominantly conflictual, but 21·4 per cent recognized both harmonious and con-flictual aspects. Again it must be emphasized that both of these figures may be exaggerated by the social acceptance basis of class with which many respondents operated. 'Conflict' in many cases therefore repre-sents snobbery rather than the recognition of a conflict of economic interest. When the latter definition is employed, the proportion drops to 19·9 per cent. It is interesting to compare the perceptions of con-flictual relationships between social classes with the farm worker's perception of his own relationship with his employer, in order to assess how far the predominantly co-operative view of employer–employee relationships extends to class relationships in general. As Table 60 shows, there is a correlation, though by no means a strong one, between regarding farmer–worker relationships as teamwork and a harmonious conception of class relations. However, Table 60 also demonstrates how farm workers are capable of distinguishing between general class relationships characteristic of society as a whole and their own particular relationship with their employer. It is also notable that the 'cross-cutting' occurs more among those who have a harmonious view of social class relationships than among those with converse views. This reflects the awareness of the conflict of interest between the agricultural sector of society, consisting of the 'team' of farmers and farm workers, and the non-agricultural sector, including the urban immigrants into rural areas.

Following this descriptive presentation of certain aspects of the agricultural workers' images of society, it is now possible to try to summarize the data according to certain characteristic images of society and to investigate how far these images are structurally located. In his discussion of working-class images of society Lockwood[20]

Table 60 Perception of class relationships against perception of employer–employee relationships of workers interviewed in Suffolk, 1972

	Perception of employer–employee relationships		
	Team (N = 160) %	Opposite sides (N = 50) %	All workers (N = 210) %
Harmony	30·6	22·0	28·6
Conflict	46·9	58·0	49·5
Some harmony/ Some conflict	22·5	20·0	21·9
	100·0	100·0	100·0

distinguished three main types based upon power, status and money which he argued were located respectively among 'traditional proletarian', 'traditional deferential' and 'privatized' workers. These in turn were characterized by certain occupational groups sharing similar work and community situations. Parkin has also emphasized the important role in the stability of the class structure of what he calls 'meaning-systems', a somewhat broader concept than 'images of society', in providing consistent interpretations of the world. Although he employs a rather different typology of 'deferential', 'accommodative' and 'radical' meaning-systems Parkin also emphasizes the ways in which certain work and community situations either expose workers to or isolate them from dominant ideologies in society.[21] Both Lockwood and Parkin are then elaborating Bott's original hypothesis that 'the ingredients, the raw materials, of class ideology are located in the individual's primary social experiences, rather than in his position in a socio-economic category. The hypothesis advanced here is that when an individual talks about class he is trying to say something, in a symbolic form, about his experiences of power and prestige in his actual membership groups and social relationships both past and present.'[22] It is the purpose of the rest of this chapter to explore this approach in the context of the social consciousness of agricultural workers.

The various images of society of the agricultural workers who were interviewed were categorized according to the typology offered by Lockwood; that is, into status, power and pecuniary models typical of deferential, proletarian and privatized workers. The deferential image of society was clearly the type most central to the concerns of this study, but on this Lockwood could only make tentative generalizations based mainly upon political studies of the 'deference voter'. Nevertheless Lockwood concluded that the deferential worker thinks in terms of a four-fold division of society between 'genuine' or 'natural' leaders, their deferential followers, 'spurious' leaders who 'lack the hereditary or quasi-hereditary credentials which the deferential worker recognizes as the true marks of legitimacy' and their 'misguided' working-class counterparts.[23] The evidence from the interviews with agricultural workers who could be clearly identified as deferential in the sense in which that term was defined at the outset suggests that Lockwood's characterization was not too wide of the mark. However, rather than using a four-fold division of society the deferential workers tended to operate with a three-class division. This consisted of 'real' gentlemen, a middle group usually referred to as the 'middle class' who represent the 'spurious' leaders mentioned by Lockwood, and below them the working class, which included the respondents themselves. Although logically one might suppose that the spurious leaders must entail the presence of misguided followers, the latter were not referred to, although on one or two occasions there were suggestions that urban, industrial workers might constitute such a group.

The authentic leaders of society to whom the agricultural worker was willing to defer – the 'real gentlemen' – possessed a number of complex and vaguely defined attributes.[24] Wealth and a certain gracious life-style were important, but they only formed a basis, since those who illegitimately aspire to authority also frequently possess these. They must therefore be overlaid by other factors – a lack of economic instrumentality, especially on the farm; an involvement in local public affairs; benevolence both to the local community and to his own employees; demeanour, particularly the willingness to be sociable to workers, to treat them in fact as moral *equals* as far as everyday social interaction is concerned; and either old age or the possession of a lengthy hereditary pedigree. It is important to emphasize, however, that by no means all of these attributes need be present – a gentleman may compensate for a lack of wealth, for example by his courteous social conduct or his lack of hereditary qualifications by benevolence tempered by a humble demeanour. Indeed 'real gentlemen' are best understood by comparing them with the despised 'middle class', who typically possess the economic basis of upper-class membership but lack the necessary social accoutrements. They do not grant the farm worker the recognition of a moral equal but of an inferior – they look down on the farm worker, but are 'really no better' than he is. The deferential conception of society is therefore an organic one, consisting of an interdependence between the two major social strata of leaders and followers, but in which each has his part to play be it ever so humble and each deserves social recognition on that basis. Those who try to usurp this 'natural' system are condemned for not knowing their 'place' and for trying to appropriate the rights of authority without recognizing their social obligations. It is worth pointing out, therefore, that deference contains a kind of spurious radicalism which can be misleading. Many deferential workers can strongly express radical-sounding views, but these are only directed towards the spurious, 'jumped up', middle class. Meanwhile they firmly endorse the traditional authority of 'real gentlemen'. This suggests again the necessity of regarding deference as a relationship rather than as a cultural attribute of individuals that they bring to bear upon all their social encounters with those high up the social scale.

Deference is considered more fully in the next chapter, but it is worth presenting here some interview material which helps to exemplify these points:

'Well there always has been three classes, hasn't there? There's the real gentlemen, then there's the middle class and then there's the working class. A gentleman has tons of money and never works, but the working man, he works all his life. Then you get the jumped up ones in between. They *think* they've got a lot, but they haven't really. They're more snobs than anything else. The upper crust will talk to you but the middle class feel you shouldn't be there – they'll ignore you.'

'There's the upper class – there's still a few Lord So-and-so's around. Then there's like solicitors and managers. I call them the middle class. Then there's us – the humble man! The top people aren't necessarily the richest but they've spent years learning to be top people. They're born into it. What's happening today is that a lot of workers are trying to put themselves on the same level as the top people. They've lost all sense of proportion. If a working-class man ever got his own business I'd never work for him – he'd be worse than a gentleman with no money at all. A gentleman always recognizes his workmen. You can always tell a gentleman by the way he rubs shoulders with his workmen. He classes them as just one of themselves. Some of the middle class, they're jumped up and happen to be snobby. They think they should have it all.'

'A gentleman is a gentleman. You must have it and you'll never stop it. Over the years they've been born into money and business. I can remember when you had to touch your hat, but that's all gone. Bowing and scraping to squires is all finished. The *real* gentry treat the working man very well. It's the jumped-up man who's got up quick who looks down on him – the two cars, caravan and boat type of people. They're jumped up buggers who've had a bit of money – they're real bastards.'

'Some, like old ex-colonels, expect you to jump to attention when they shout. They think they're it and they've got nothing – jumped-up people. The real high-class fellow is a gentleman and he talks to you different from the jumped-up ones. With them it's all due to breeding. It goes back through the years when the old squire had all the land. It's all tradition and inheritance really – it gets passed on. A gentleman treats you well, but what I call the middle class, those who think they're it, are real bastards. They're mostly people who've moved in, people with plenty of money. I never take any notice of people who buy two or three cottages and make them into one. It's *principles* not money, that's definite. Some of the biggest snobs haven't got any. But titled people, you can talk to them as we talk to ourselves. It's been handed down, generation after generation – it's as simple as that.'

Many agricultural workers possessed what Lockwood characterizes as a 'traditional proletarian' image of society, a dichotomous power model consisting of a contradiction between 'us', the workers, and 'them', the bosses or those in authority generally. This type of social imagery is very familiar from much of the sociological literature on urban working-class occupational groups and has been referred to several times during the course of this book as forming the social imagery typical of East Anglian agricultural workers in the occupational communities that constituted nineteenth-century and early twentieth-century rural villages. Although such imagery is based upon the awareness of a conflict of interest between the two perceived groupings this is reflected not as much in an outright radical opposition as an accommodation to the acknowledged power of the superior class. Again, the agricultural workers' own comments can exemplify this:

'Class? Well, it's farmers and farm workers, isn't it? Take my boss – he's inherited his position and we've inherited the labourers' side of the situation. They don't really want to know us. A lot of that goes on. If you go to a dance or something they keep to one side and we to the other. It's all handed down. They always look down on us as ignorant types. I was born with nothing and so were they. They've robbed the working man in a roundabout way – made us poor buggers work for nothing.'

'There'll always be a high class and a low class. Like this bloke, my boss – he's got money and we're under him. We take the orders and he pays the wages. It's power, too, I think. In this country you've got to keep fighting for anything. The lower people have got to challenge the upper-class people.'

'There's class in this parish for one. There's the tip-top nobs, collar-and-tie people and the under ones like us. They've got the money and I haven't got it and we live our different lives in our own way. I don't expect to go to dinner with my boss. They tell people what they can do and what they can't do. Even in your own yard they tell you what to do. It's been with us for years – the old distinction of "I can do what I like, but he mustn't." The two sides only get together in a concentration camp or a prison or in the middle of the Sahara looking for a drink.'

'There's the workers and then there's the top men who do nothing, the big men who say what the workers should do. They've cheated and robbed, some of these big people have. The employers' class is all in it for their own ends. They'll try and ride on top of you. If they had half a chance they'd run you over.'

A third image of society is a finely graded hierarchy based upon money, job or possessions, with no rigid barriers between the different levels in the hierarchy. Mobility up and down the social scale is quite common and always feasible through hard work, application and educational success. Although many of the agricultural workers living in the farm-centred community situation were highly privatized in a way that corresponded to the home-centred activities described in *The Affluent Worker*[25] study, this image of society was not very prevalent among the sample of workers interviewed. The most plausible reason for this would seem to be the very low degree of geographical mobility among the Suffolk farm workers compared with the workers in Luton interviewed by Goldthorpe *et al.* However, no firm conclusions can be drawn on this point. One equally likely factor is the absence of any extensive gradation of skill or earnings among the hired agricultural labour force compared with that of industrial workers, together with the very clear qualitative break, in East Anglia at least, between farmers and farm workers. Nevertheless, there was a small proportion of agricultural workers whose image of society corresponded to a graded hierarchy in terms of differences in income or material possessions. For example:

'There's quite a range of classes – in work there is. Ordinary labourers, craftsmen, foremen, managers – people like that. It's skill really – what they can do and how they go about it. You get to know how a man can do in his work and this way you know what sort of class he's in. It's a pecking order based on your apparent affluence – house, car, television, washing machine. And the circles they mix in. But I'm indifferent to it all – they're just there.'

'It's all based on money. If you've got money you can make money. It's just a grade from top to bottom – natural and fluid. My age group – we went to one tiny little school in the village. Nowadays it's different. You can get the chance to go to the tip-top. It's education – anyone has the chance to move up today. All the young ones now have much better opportunities for education than we had. You can move up through your work, go to college or night school and get on.'

Although many agricultural workers do hold what appears to be a coherent and easily identifiable image of society, there are many who do not. They either hold a multiplicity of class images from which they will draw upon the one most appropriate to explain a particular situation or define a particular social context, or they hold no overall image of society at all. This has been referred to already as *ambivalence*. It must immediately be admitted that there are certain epistemological problems involved here. The alleged ambivalence of many agricultural workers could be a product of insufficient probing during the interview – in other words, there may be a perfectly justifiable and reasonable rationale for the apparent contradictions and incoherences which the questioning failed to uncover. In retrospect, it has to be regretted that some of the manifest contradictions in many workers' images of society were not put to the respondents themselves to rationalize. However, it is not always an easy matter to engage in a more provocative interviewing style without appearing arrogant and ruining the *rapport* carefully built up with respondents who are not used to the experience and who may feel slightly threatened by it. In any case, a similar argument could be employed to support the contrary case: that the apparent logic and coherence of some workers' images of society is due to the failure to probe deeply enough to uncover the illogicalities that lie beneath them. There is obviously no final answer to these problems, but there are a number of arguments which could be put forward to suggest that the ambivalence of many agricultural workers is not simply an artifact of an inadequate research methodology.

If one accepts a fairly basic sociological premise that an individual's social consciousness is to a large extent influenced by his immediate social context then there is no reason to assume, except in certain limiting cases, that the interpretations provided to and by the individual will always be cumulative or commensurate one with the other. The pattern of most individuals' social relationships is such that they are provided with different, conflicting and often contradictory beliefs about the nature of society at large and their own position within it. From this no single unambiguous image of society is built up. In the case of agricultural workers the single most important factor in providing these alternative interpretations has probably been the impact of urbanization on the rural village, with the resultant co-existence of interactional and attributional prestige systems in the same locality. But there is also the possibility that the interpretations stemming from the work situation and the community situation need not overlap nor need they be based on commensurate definitions of prestige, legitimacy or authority. The normative features that rest upon the patriarchal mode of control at work may not find their counterparts in village society nor in the outside world in general. Such ambivalence is therefore not a very remarkable nor unexpected outcome, given the admixture of work and community situations which most agricultural workers experience.

This ambivalence is, however, of a different order from the more generalized lack of a coherent ideology that has been noted by, in particular, Converse and Mann.[26] Both authors have argued that among lower classes in Britain and the United States there is a dis-crepancy between their adherence to abstract political principles and more concrete references to issues which affect the day-to-day interests of the respondents. Mann has also argued that the working class in general neither possesses nor needs a coherent image of society, since it is not relevant to their conduct of everyday affairs. Instead they are articulated only by those who are concerned with the preser-vation or the change of the *status quo*, principally elite groups in society or working-class political activists. There is a sense in which this could also apply to the situation of agricultural workers. Many of them are placed in highly particularistic social structures where relationships are very diffuse, and above all transacted on a personal basis. Actors therefore confront each other as personally known and evaluated individuals and as such there is little need for abstract ideologies in order to interpret the situation. Most variations in the quality of social relationships are interpreted in terms of personality differences rather than as products of a particular social system. The extent to which agricultural workers *need* a coherent image of society is therefore highly questionable. Nevertheless their close relationship with dominant class members means that they are often *provided* with such images, if only to justify and legitimate the very wide and very visible differences in objective rewards which accrue to farmers and farm workers from the social and economic system in which both are embedded. Similarly, for workers in situations where such contact is lacking, there may be greater opportunities to avail themselves of much more proletarian images of society that arise out of rather different interpersonal relationships.

Empirically it is not very easy or possible to distinguish between these two forms of ambivalence, since the end product, in terms of articulated views, is substantially the same – a hotch-potch of ideas and beliefs without the appearance of any underlying ideological rationale. Such a response has been described by Seabrook as follows: 'Many people opt out of any views at all or, if asked, formulate them on an *ad hoc* basis, arising out of the circumstances of each particular conversation. If people are asked their opinions, they assume that they ought to have some, and obligingly evolve them on the spot ... Conversations generate people's views and not vice versa. People who have known each other for years are quite unaware of each other's religious views, political sympathies or opinions on any socially relevant topic at all. The forces of inertia and conservatism in our society derive less from a conviction that tradition and the existing order represent the best methods of social organization, than from the failure of imagination to be able to conceive of any alternative. This is why people's views are so often encapsulated in received phrases and fixed self-determining ideas ... People are at the mercy of set phrases and received ideas, which determine their view of the world, but it is not an irksome tyranny. They are seldom even aware of it ... and their social philosophy is a random accretion of fragments of belief, often mutually exclusive and contradictory, built up to afford them the consoling illusion that they understand the society in which they live.'[27] Without subscribing to Seabrook's rather misanthropic perspective, many of the interviews with agricultural workers echoed the ambivalent set of attitudes and half-formed beliefs which he found in a more urban setting. It is difficult to convey accurately the precise ambience of these responses, since a great deal depends upon aspects not easily communicated in print – silences, the tone of replies, the lack of responsiveness to prompting. In addition a full illustration would require quite lengthy sections of transcribed conversation. However, a few brief examples may again indicate the nature of this type of response:

'Well, I always say there's two sides to every question, of course the more money you've got the more you can get of anything. If you've got one pound, they'll lend you two, but if you've got nothing they won't let you have any. 'Course, they look after their money, too. If everybody started off with £10,000 each, by the end of the year, one would have £15,000 and the other £5,000. Us workers, we're on a lower basis altogether – money and everything else. We don't get left it like the people who've got money. Mind you, others have built it up – they appreciate their workers more. Round here it's farmers and builders. You know them and went to school with them. But some high people round here the working class never get on with. But others will talk to you – they're not snobbish. The people who were born rich are better than those who've got rich quick.'

'It's a load of rot. Everyone is equal. When you talk of class you remind me of saying, "Yes, sir," "No, sir," "Three bags full, sir." I won't call anyone sir, only mister. But there *is* still some about, some left over from the Victorian era. The employer's class is in it for their own ends. It's more than snobbishness, money's involved. Snobs are bred as one – industrialists, landowners, people like that. They've either made it themselves or got it invested. Still we can't all be equal. If you were all rich, there'd be no workers. As long as they're all right we are. On the farm you see all your mates and the boss and you all work round. It's different in industry – you see different faces and you all hang together all the time.'

'We're more classed as a class on our own as opposed to those in industry. People think it's a job anyone can do, but they can't. Of course, you wouldn't run the country with everyone in the same class – you've got to have somebody really a bit higher than other persons. You've got to have it, but it all depends how things are run. Some are stricter than what the others are. But they all ought to be the same – some bosses aren't strict enough. To them I would be lower, but not by people in the parish. More sort of middle class in this parish. Everybody is matey. There are some people in business who you would think are out of your class but they speak to us and treat us as one of them. I reckon there all ought to be one class.'

These examples illustrate how agricultural workers can operate with combinations of power, status and money models of the class structure according to the context in which they are applying them, producing often contradictory statements in the space of a few

sentences. The apparent illogicalities are never exposed because the
requisite contexts rarely merge to produce contradictory images. This
fragmented form of social consciousness was the most typical of the
images of society among the farm workers who were interviewed. As
Table 61 shows, 43·3 per cent of the workers interviewed possessed no

Table 61 Images of society of workers interviewed in Suffolk, 1972

	No.	%
Ambivalent	101	43·3
Proletarian	52	22·3
Deferential	35	15·0
Graded hierarchy	23	9·9
Classless	9	3·9
Other	8	3·4
Refused/No answer	5	2·1
	233	100·0

single image of society, but gave a variety of ambivalent responses to
questions about the nature of the class structure. It is therefore mistaken on this evidence to regard agricultural workers simply as
deferential traditionalists, since the most typical group retain no
unitary form of social consciousness at all. Indeed, by this measure of
deference, the proportion of the farm workers interviewed who
could be considered 'deferential' was less than the proportion possessing a 'traditional proletarian' image of society. This confirms
evidence presented elsewhere in this study that the deference of the
agricultural worker is more apparent than real and that the image of
the agricultural worker as the deferential worker *par excellence* is due
more to the powerlessness of his situation which hinders any overt
expression of dissatisfaction than to a genuine endorsement of his own
inferior position in society.

Sources of Variation in Images of Society

In the study of the derivation of working-class images of society the structure and content of the individual's network of social relationships both at work and in the local social system have attracted the greatest attention. With regard to the work situation, Lockwood has particularly emphasized the importance of job involvement, interaction and identification with workmates and the extent of interaction and identification with employers.[28] In Chapter 5, it was noted that intrinsic job satisfaction was almost uniformly high among agricultural workers, and it was also explained how the work situation of the agricultural worker is one that, compared with many industrial workers, involves a greater degree of social interaction with the employer and, because they work a great deal on their own, a much lesser degree of interaction with fellow workers. However, it was also pointed out that the major distinguishing characteristic which produces an important qualitative variation in the work situation is the nature of the mode of control operated by the employer. On the patriarchally organized farms, employer–employee relationships are on a face-to-face, 'gaffer-to-man' basis, whereas those farms with a large labour force often have a bureaucratic structure similar to that in many factories with little contact between the owner of the farm and the workers and the control of the labour force left to managers, foremen and charge-hands mediated through a code of formal rules and regulations. On this basis one would expect, other things being equal, the more pervasive interaction between farmers and farm workers on the patriarchally run farms to produce among the workers employed on these farms a set of beliefs similar to, or at least consistent with, the dominant ideology of their employers.

However, the relative proximity at work of the agricultural worker to his employer need not, of its own accord, produce a mechanism whereby 'interaction with' leads to 'identification with' the employer and his ideology. *Prima facie* there is no reason why the proximity of those who are subordinate to those who are superordinate should in itself bring about an identification of the powerless with the powerful. At the end of Chapter 5 it was argued that such identification would pertain only when some degree of totality in the situation hindered access to alternative evaluations of legitimacy which could disrupt the stability of the relationship. For the farm worker this makes it necessary to examine the extent of his exposure to other values off the farm and in the local community. In Chapter 6 a typology of local social situations was offered which was based partly upon variations in the extent to which workplace authority relationships overlapped with the structure of relations in the community. It was argued that the decline of the occupational community had greatly reduced the social distance between employers and employees in the local social system, so that the major social division no longer fell so much along class lines but between locals and newcomers. The extreme situation, where the farm worker is most extensively subjected to the social influences and evaluations of his employer, was in the farm-centred community, where the farm worker leads a somewhat isolated existence cheek-by-jowl with the farmer.

Combining together the typologies of the work situation and the local community situation, then, one can hypothesize that the workers are most likely to possess a deferential image of society when they are located in the most total of these social situations; that is, where members of the dominant class are most omnipresent and where access to alternative or oppositional interpretations of the situation is most difficult. This is most likely to occur when the agricultural worker is in a patriarchal work situation and in a farm-centred community. On the other hand, the farm worker is most likely to possess a proletarian image of society in the converse situation – working on a bureaucratically organized farm and living in an occupational community. In this case contact with dominant class members is perfunctory and comparatively infrequent. In the other combinations of work and community situations one would expect to find ambivalent class images, since farm workers would then be, to a varying extent, subject to both dominant-class and subordinate-class influences. Although the survey data is not entirely appropriate to test this model, since the agricultural workers interviewed are by no means evenly distributed through these various combinations of work and local social situations, the interview material can help to confirm its usefulness in understanding the sources of variations in agricultural workers' images of society.

This was carried out by taking each image of society in turn and plotting the distribution of farm workers possessing this imagery among the different possible combinations of the two typologies. In so doing only data from non-supervisory workers were used, and in addition only material from those workers who had been working on their present farm and been living in their present house for more than five years. This was done in order to allow for the possibilities of 'historical lags' from previous work and community situations producing a somewhat false impression.[29] The distribution of deferential images of society is shown in Table 62. Although the correlation

Table 62 Distribution of deferential images of society by work situation and community situation of workers interviewed in Suffolk, 1972

| Community situation | Work situation | | All workers |
	Patriarchal %	Bureaucratic %	%
Occupational	–	6·7	6·7
Encapsulated	10·0	3·3	13·3
Farm-centred	56·7	23·3	80·0
All workers	66·7	33·3	100·0 (N = 30)

is by no means absolute, most of the deferential workers do appear in the predicted structural location: living in a farm-centred community and working on patriarchally organized farms. Here the nature of the community seems to be more influential than the work situation, although the number of respondents is so small that no firm conclusions can be drawn. However the social isolation of many farm-centred workers, even on the larger farms, probably makes them less likely to be 'deviant' in terms of their ideological stance, whatever their work situation.

The distribution of workers with ambivalent images of society is shown in Table 63. Again the predicted distribution works out reasonably well, with only 17·3 per cent in anomalous situations. The least satisfactory degree of fit, however, was obtained with the proletarian images of society. The distribution of these is shown in Table 64. Here, a (small) majority of 'proletarian' workers are located in occupational communities, but slightly more are also working patriarchal rather than bureaucratic farms. An examination of the characteristics of those workers showed, however, that some of the anomalies were to some extent explicable in terms of factors which do

Table 63 Distribution of ambivalent images of society by work situation and community situation of workers interviewed in Suffolk, 1972

| Community situation | Work situation | | All workers |
	Patriarchal %	Bureaucratic %	%
Occupational	6·7	2·6	9·3
Encapsulated	14·7	21·3	36·0
Farm-centred	14·7	40·0	54·7
All workers	*36·1*	*63·9*	*100·0*
			(N = 75)

not entirely invalidate the model. For example, a number of these workers had had past experience of working on large farms or outside agriculture altogether in industrial employment. The most prevalent

Table 64 Distribution of proletarian images of society by work situation and community situation of workers interviewed in Suffolk, 1972

| Community situation | Work situation | | All workers |
	Patriarchal %	Bureaucratic %	%
Occupational	26·7	26·7	53·4
Encapsulated	16·7	16·7	33·4
Farm-centred	10·0	3·3	13·3
All workers	*53·4*	*46·7*	*100·0*
			(N = 30)

factor, however, was due to the peculiar landholding structure of a number of the parishes categorized as occupational communities. Four of them (out of six) consisted predominantly of large estates split up into small (by Suffolk standards) tenant farms. These were therefore patriarchally run farms in the previously defined sense of this term, but the real local patriarch was absent from the work situation. In some cases the life-style and income of the tenant farmers was not as distinct from that of their employees as was the case with the owner-occupiers. In some cases customary landlord–tenant problems led to expressions of antagonism against local landowners that to some extent was bound to rub off on their employees. For example, the one avowedly Socialist farmer who was interviewed fell into this category. Here, then, the problem is not so much the invalid nature of the model as the lack of appropriate data to test it. One of the important combinations – bureaucratic farm/occupational community – was sufficiently absent to hamper testing of the model. Had the model been derived in advance rather than emerge from the research process, no doubt a better sampling design – presumably matching samples of workers from each combination – could have been constructed.

This approach does have one obvious weakness, however. By taking the agricultural worker at a particular point in time it cannot do full justice to the variations in his own biographical experience which inevitably will affect his present social imagery. Bott, in her original conception, referred to membership groups and social experiences 'both past and present'.[30] While the model outlined above is not entirely static or ahistorical, it clearly cannot account for the trajectory of an individual agricultural worker during his lifetime through the various structural situations it posits. In general, the tendency has been for farms to de-bureaucratize with the continuous decline in the labour force and for farm workers to gravitate from the occupational community towards encapsulated and farm-centred local social structures. Although farm amalgamations have reversed this trend towards greater employer–employee contact in a number of cases the average number of workers per farm continues to fall. Thus in aggregate terms the tendency is for the farm worker to find himself increasingly in the patriarchal farm/farm-centred community situation. However, a substantial number of life-histories will continue to deviate from this trend and it is probably in these terms that many of the anomalies can be understood.

As it stands the data do not suggest that the typology of work and community situations should be completely discarded. Although they do not completely explain the sources of variation in agricultural workers' images of society, few typologies account for each and every empirical case and it seems to work sufficiently well to suggest a conditional acceptance as a basis for future refinement. With the benefit of hindsight there is no doubt that the sensitivity of some of the indicators could be improved. For example the variation *within* the category of 'encapsulated community' is considerable and the term covers a wide range of local social structures with, in particular, variable degrees of mix between locals and newcomers or between agriculturally and non-agriculturally employed locals. Similarly the rather simple and crude division between 'patriarchal' and 'bureaucratic' farms does not do justice to the nuances of employer–employee interaction. The differences between farmers in the extent of their direct involvement in husbandry alongside their workers and the extent to which they are oriented towards profit maximization, to take two variables which are likely to have a considerable effect on employer–employee relationships, cannot be summarized in such a rudimentary dichotomy.[31] All this, however, must await that most banal of conclusions: further research.

1. See Marx's *Enquête Ouvrière* in T. B. Bottomore and M. Rubel (eds.), *Karl Marx: Selected Writings in Sociology and Social Philosophy*, Penguin Books, 1963.

2. F. Parkin, *Class, Inequality and Political Order*, MacGibbon and Kee, 1971, p. 84.

3. ibid., p. 86.

4. See Chapter 3 above.

5. And, it must be added, it is largely in these terms that interpretations of existing inequalities are offered to him by farmers and other locally present dominant class members.

6. G. Bourne (Sturt), *Change in the Village*, Duckworth, 1912, pp. 104–5. In the farm workers' acceptance of property rights there are clearly distant echoes of the 'natural rights' and 'utilitarian' justifications of property that so exercised philosophers, including Locke and Hume, from the eighteenth century onwards.

7. Jessop emphasizes the importance of this appreciation, the 'bestowal of some sort of recognition', in the stability of deferential relationships. See R. D. Jessop, *Traditionalism, Conservatism and British Political Culture*, Allen and Unwin, 1974, p. 33. See also Chapter 8 below.

8. Thereby demonstrating the importance of control of life-chances beyond the farm gate, in this case through access to educational opportunities.

9. See particularly E. A. Nordlinger, *The Working Class Tories*, MacGibbon and Kee, 1967, and R. McKenzie and A. Silver, *Angels in Marble*, Heinemann, 1968.

10. D. Kavanagh, 'The Deferential English: A Comparative Critique', *Government and Opposition*, May 1971, pp. 333–60.

11. R. D. Jessop, op. cit., p. 35.

12. J. E. Horton and W. E. Thompson, 'Powerlessness and Political Negativism: A Study of Defeated Local Referendum', *American Journal of Sociology*, vol. 67, No. 5, 1962, p. 493; P. E. Converse, 'The Nature of Belief Systems in Mass Publics', in D. E. Apter (ed.), *Ideology and Discontent*, The Free Press, Glencoe, Ill., 1964, p. 213; M. Mann, 'The Social Cohesion of Liberal Democracy', *American Sociological Review*, vol. 35, No. 3, 1970, pp. 423–31. Also C. W. Chamberlain and H. F. Moorhouse, 'Lower Class Attitudes Towards the British Political System', *Sociological Review*, vol. 22, No. 4, 1974, pp. 503–26.

13. E. D. Genovese, *In Red and Black*, Allen Lane, 1971, p. 93.

14. W. L. Warner and J. O. Low, *The Modern Factory: The Strike – A Social Analysis*, Yale University Press, 1947; T. Lane and K. Roberts, *Strike at Pilkingtons*, Fontana, 1971.

15. J. K. Goldthorpe, *et al.*, *The Affluent Worker in the Class Structure*, CUP, 1969, Appendix C, pp. 200–202.

16. J. Cousins and R. Brown, 'Patterns of Paradox: Shipbuilding Workers' Images of Society', in M. I. A. Bulmer (ed.), *The Occupational Community of the Traditional Worker*, proceedings of SSRC Conference, Durham, 1972, p. 122.

17. cf. D. Lockwood, 'Sources of Variation in Working Class Images of Society', *Sociological Review*, vol. 14, No. 3, 1966, pp. 248–67.

18. Cousins and Brown, op. cit., p. 123.

19. J. Platt, 'Variations in Answers to Different Questions on Perceptions of Class', *Sociological Review*, vol. 19, No. 3, 1971, p. 417.

20. Lockwood, op. cit.

21. Parkin, op. cit., Ch. 3.

22. E. Bott, *Family and Social Network*, Tavistock, 1957, p. 163. See also the papers presented in Bulmer (ed.), op. cit.

23. Lockwood, op. cit., pp. 252–3.

24. They are the modern successors of those described in Chapter 1. The 'gentlemanly ethic' is discussed further in Chapter 8.

25. Goldthorpe *et al.*, op. cit., Ch. 4.

26. Converse, op. cit., Mann, op. cit.

27. J. Seabrook, *City Close-Up*, Allen Lane, 1971, pp. 42–3, 101.

28. Lockwood, op. cit.

29. This produced a better fit between the actual and expected distribution of the data, thus helping to confirm the relevance of the variables used.

30. Bott, op. cit., p. 163.

31. See C. Bell and H. Newby, 'Capitalist Farmers in the British Class Structure', *Sociologia Ruralis*, vol. 14, No. 1/2, pp. 86–107.

CHAPTER EIGHT
Deference Reconsidered

The evidence presented in Chapter 7 suggests that only a small proportion of agricultural workers can be considered as deferential workers in the sense that they adhere to a reasonably consistent deferential image of society. The deference which is often attributed to the agricultural worker can therefore be seen to rest largely upon a fallacious inference made from his largely quiescent social and political behaviour. This quiescence, however, must be seen to result from the agricultural worker's dependence rather than from his deference. The dependence of the agricultural worker upon the farmer for employment, and in many cases for housing in addition, militates against the overt expression of dissatisfaction, except in the most individualistic and negative ways, like the move to another job. For those who remain by virtue of lack of alternative opportunities for employment and housing, agricultural trade-unionism has not represented a viable means of reducing this dependence or measurably improving the life-chances of the individual agricultural worker. For the most part, therefore, the agricultural worker has acknowledged his powerlessness and decided to make the best of his inferior situation, contriving to take it somewhat for granted while not necessarily endorsing it in terms of social justice. He has simply kept himself to himself, a strategy which his own experiences, and occasionally his observations of the experiences of others, have taught him to be a wise principle to adopt.

This lack of any overt rebelliousness does much to account for the agricultural workers' deferential image. It has also enabled the idyllic view of country life to remain virtually intact among outside observers. The dependence of the agricultural worker has also perforce led him to adopt the rules of social conduct laid down by those in authority over him. In the past it was easy to infer from the sight of a worker touching his forelock that this signified a deeper commitment to the legitimacy of his 'betters'. Often, however, it signified nothing of the kind, but only the conformity to a form of social etiquette whose transgressions could be harshly penalized. However, as Chapters 1 and 4 have shown, the servile appearance of the agricultural worker has often hidden a more covert form of opposition to those in power over him. Today these social rituals have largely disappeared (although they can still be observed, albeit performed somewhat self-consciously, on certain occasions), signifying a change in the rules of social etiquette and rendering the forelock-tugging agricultural worker a mere social caricature. Nevertheless this caricature still tends to determine the public image of him.

If the assumption that agricultural workers are deferential workers rested solely upon these ostensible symbols of social docility then it could be discarded quite easily. Most serious histories of the agricultural worker recognize that, whatever the conventional wisdom of English rural life, the placid exterior obscured sometimes bitter antagonisms, and the history of agricultural trade-unionism contains sufficient angry enmity against farming employers to make the deferential image of the agricultural worker too facile. On the other hand the recent history of the agricultural worker has done little to suggest that such hidden conflict continues to flourish. The rural underworld, whose existence had signified the farm worker's adherence to an alternative set of values to those laid down from above, has now virtually disappeared; likewise it is more than fifty years since agricultural workers were last involved in strike action and there are very few workers who would deny that on a personal level employer-employee relationships have improved immeasurably over this period. These arguments to and fro were rehearsed in Chapter 2 and it was recognized then that, in common with most other studies of working-class deference, it was necessary to go beyond the overt manifestations of what is defined as deferential behaviour and so separate the notion of deference from powerlessness. Hence deference needed to be considered not so much in terms of behaviour that was often habitual, ritualized and even calculative but in terms of a positive, affective identification of the agricultural worker with those who hold power over him.

It was with these considerations in mind that deference was originally defined as the subscription to a traditional moral order which endorses the individual's own political, material and social subordination. However, as has been demonstrated, even in these terms only a minority of agricultural workers – 15 per cent, using the data on images of society – could be considered unequivocally to be deferential workers. Moreover, the data presented in the previous chapter also call into question the utility of this approach to deference, or indeed other class ideologies purported to be held by agricultural workers. It was argued that the general ambivalence and fragmentation of many agricultural workers' images of society does not suggest that they possess a comprehensive and monolithic ideological system which they bring to bear upon the various situations which they find themselves in and which determines their actions accordingly. Indeed the evidence on the sources of variation in images of society suggests the reverse: rather than a coherent ideological system guiding the actor's relationships, deference, or other class ideologies, can be seen as emerging *from* a particular set of relationships. Only where these relationships are overlapping or in some other way structurally homologous does a reasonably coherent belief system emerge – otherwise beliefs are relatively disparate, fragmentary, pragmatic and particularistic. The agricultural worker may therefore enter into deferential *relationships* without being a deferential *person* in the sense that the moral principles which underlie the notion of deference act as precepts which guide all the agricultural worker's social actions.

As far as deference is concerned, this suggests that the concept should be considered not as an ideological attribute of individual workers but as typifying certain relationships which they enter into, and how situational factors affect these. Thus deference is best considered not merely as a particular form of behaviour, since this ignores the problem of its meaning to the actor, nor as a set of attitudes, since this is too over-deterministic, but as a form of social interaction. Specifically deference can best be defined as the form of social interaction which occurs in situations involving the exercise of traditional authority. This also follows Shils' discussion of deference in which he asserts that deference is 'not a substantial property of the person . . . but . . . an element in a relationship between the person deferred to and the deferrent person'.[1] This seems to do less violence to an understanding of how the agricultural worker lives out his daily life than either of the other two approaches to the concept. For example, expressed in this manner the relational aspect of deference is more apparent and account is taken not only of the agricultural worker himself but also of the other individuals who may exercise traditional authority over him – who possesses traditional authority, how it is maintained, how it may change over time, the range of this authority and the extent to which it is accepted by those in subordinate positions. A reconsideration of deference along these lines not only renders the concept more heuristically useful, but can explain much of the data on the social situation of agricultural workers present in this book.

The Deferential Dialectic[2]

By expressing deference as a form[3] of relationship it is possible to divert attention for a moment away from the agricultural worker himself towards the structure of relationships in which he is placed and more specifically to the actions of those who are in positions of power over him. Even on empirical grounds this is quite a legitimate exercise, since the relative powerlessness of the agricultural worker has meant that this structure has not, in general, been one which he has fashioned according to his own needs and values, but rather that he has been acted upon by others who have to a greater or lesser degree controlled this social structure and attempted to run it in their own interests. In the nineteenth and early twentieth centuries this dominant group largely consisted, as Chapter 1 showed, of local oligarchies of landowners and farmers. Although the arrival of middle-class newcomers has brought competitors for positions of local power and the extension of the state has reduced the autonomy of local communities, farmers and landowners still dominate the local social structure, certainly as far as agricultural workers are concerned, with their reliance upon farmers for employment and often housing. The farm worker today, no less than his nineteenth-century counterparts discussed in Chapter 1, is in little doubt as to where this power lies. However, the social structure of the English countryside has not remained static over this period, so that the way in which class relationships have been transacted has altered accordingly.

The power of the farmer today remains, as it always has, fundamentally economically based. It is the power to hire and fire the farm worker as well as to determine his level of rewards in so far as labour market conditions will allow. It is also, in many cases, the power to control housing, either directly through tied accommodation or indirectly through the farmers' control of many rural local councils. Traditionally the economic organization of English agriculture has been based upon relatively small (in terms of the number of employees) family proprietorships, particularly after the break-up of many landed estates shortly after the First World War. Because of the importance of land as a factor of production and because of the necessity, in most branches of agriculture, to perform productive tasks sequentially rather than concurrently, the size of farms has been limited and the number of workers employed, by industrial standards, has been few. With increasing state interference in the control of agriculture since the Second World War the long-standing trend towards the substitution of labour with capital has accelerated, and, although farm amalgamations have also been encouraged, the average number of workers per holding has fallen steadily. As far as the individual farmer is concerned these trends have been dictated to him by market conditions, over which individually he has had little or no control. Whatever his own sentimental feelings about the matter he has been forced to alter his farming practices in order to meet these changing conditions – to adopt new methods of husbandry, to engage in wholesale mechanization, and to shed labour. These have been the basic economic parameters, elaborated elsewhere in this book, upon which the farmer's relationship with his workers has rested.

In Chapter 1 it was noted that under the conditions prevailing in pre-mechanized agriculture there was a wide social division between employers and employees that was reinforced both at work and in the local village community. In both cases relationships between farmers and workers tended to be distant, rigid and authoritarian. Although many employers wished to cultivate deference in their workers, the prevailing social structure of both the workplace and the village made these attempts only partially successful. In both situations contact with dominant class members tended to be somewhat perfunctory while the individual agricultural worker was securely integrated into a rural working-class sub-culture which was reinforced through a dense network of overlapping work and non-work relationships with fellow workers. The stability which farmers and landowners hoped the deference of farm workers would achieve was therefore tenuous and patchy. In the 1870s and again in the period on either side of the First World War there were sharp reminders that this stability owed more to the continuing powerlessness of the agricultural worker than any identification with the authority of their employers, however much this identification was assiduously cultivated.

Farmers today continue to devote considerable effort to obtaining the deference of their workers and it is perhaps ironic that, at a time during which the legitimacy of traditional authority in British society as a whole has declined drastically, the social situation of the agricultural worker has changed in ways that render him more receptive to the traditional authority of his employer than ever before. Now that the contact between farmers and workers is more informal, diffuse and pervasive it is far easier for the farmer to obtain the identification of his employees than it was when farm workers tended to work together in gangs and live in villages which were occupational communities. Nowadays, with most workers working alone or even alongside their employer and living either on the farm itself or in an agricultural enclave in the local village, there are fewer opportunities to sustain the animosities of class conflict than were generated under the old conditions. Because of the increased personal contact between farmers and farm workers there are greater opportunities to stabilize the hierarchical relationship between them by converting the powerlessness of the agricultural worker into his sympathetic agreement with the legitimacy of the farmer's traditional authority. Farmers, almost without exception, desire to achieve this conversion, for not only does it stabilize the relationship and ensure the long-term maintenance of harmonious and peaceful 'industrial relations' in agriculture, but such is the workplace autonomy of the modern agricultural worker that the maximum degree of identification with the employer beyond the size of the pay packet becomes a matter of real financial importance to the farmer.

In view of the general decline of traditional authority in British society it may seem odd that the practical, hard-headed businessmen-farmers of East Anglia should continue to adopt an often paternalistic role *vis-à-vis* their employees. However, this form of authority is partly dictated by the awareness on the part of farmers of the long-term advantages of cultivating a loyalty which involves more than a contractual obligation and is partly determined by the structure of the social situation within which this relationship is located. Legitimation by tradition is, as many farmers instinctively recognize, the most stable form of legitimation, since it is partly granted on the basis of *personal* loyalty to those holding authority positions.[4] It is therefore amenable to personal control and manipulation, and on account of its diffuse nature it tends to be more stable than the more specific criteria of role performance contained in the legitimacy of rational–legal authority. To a certain extent therefore the expertise of the farmer *qua* farmer does not dominate evaluations of his authority. Similarly profitability or efficiency, over which, particularly in agriculture, the farmer may have only marginal control because of the weather and the fertility of the land, becomes less relevant. Instead the evaluation of the farmer is diverted to areas of interpersonal relationships which are more within his control. This is not, of course, peculiar to agriculture, for there are also many industrial employers who are similarly reluctant to treat their workers entirely as impersonal commodities but wish to attract some corporate loyalty over and above that demanded by the vagaries of the labour market. In agriculture, however, with its peculiar structure of a multitude of small employing units, these considerations are amplified by the unavoidably personal nature of the relationship between farmer and worker. Living and working alongside them, it becomes impossible for the farmer to consider his workers merely as so many inputs into the productive process to be dispensed with whenever market conditions demand. Equally, for most workers the employer is not a remote figurehead but someone to whom they can relate personally across a number of roles and in a number of different situations. Under these circumstances traditional authority, whatever the preference of the farmer, becomes almost inescapable unless he takes positive and deliberate steps to behave otherwise.

Traditional authority is also appropriate not only in terms of personal authority but in the second sense in which it was understood by Weber, 'the sanctity of the order and the attendant powers of control as they have been handed down from the past'.[5] This is because most farmers have not achieved the ownership of their land or their position as employers by demonstrating their expertise in agricultural skills but because they have inherited their property and the rights and powers attached to it from their fathers. Their dominant position in the local social structure is therefore based in part upon the almost unquestioned acceptance of the right of the farmer to acquire his farm on the basis of birth. Since the possibility of upward mobility from farm worker to farmer is so remote in East Anglia as to be virtually non-existent, employer and employee roles tend to be ascribed rather than achieved. Thus, while agriculture tends to be a highly rational economic enterprise and certainly not at all backward as far as the acceptance of new innovations in methods of production is concerned, socially the norms and values are of a quite different, traditional order. In this sense, at least, there has been little fundamental change since the nineteenth century, when a similar conjunction could be observed.[6]

As far as farmers are concerned, then, deference relationships represent the desired outcome of their interaction with their workers. Given the close, personal nature of the relationship it is a necessary concomitant of the desire to stabilize existing relations of economic dominance and subordination and so ensure their long-term continuation on the basis of endorsement and consent rather than power and acquiescence. In many industries the most intractable problems would surround this apparent lack of elective affinity between the economic interests of employers to conduct their relations with their workers according to the rationality of market forces and the ideology of traditional authority with which this is overlaid, for occasions arise when employers must necessarily treat their employees in a manner which market conditions demand or otherwise jeopardize the efficiency and even the existence of the business as a competitive concern. For example, they might have to introduce new capital-intensive processes which make large numbers of workers redundant and which, while aimed at preserving the economic viability of the firm, may threaten the stability of the social relationships within it by denying the workers personal protection from market forces which they feel their personal loyalty has deserved. In agriculture, however, this apparent contradiction between the economic interests of farmers and the traditional ideology in which their authority is interpreted to their workers only rarely emerges. This is mainly due to the economic organization of agriculture, where producers do not compete with each other in the accepted industrial sense, and where the falling demand for labour has kept pace with a declining supply. In only one major instance can this contradiction be regularly observed – in the case of threatened tied-cottage evictions. Here the economic demands on the employer – in this case represented by the necessity to free the house in order to accommodate the succeeding worker – conflict with his social obligations which he has promoted over the years through his cultivation of the personal loyalty of the now threatened tenant. The contradiction is particularly acute on small farms, where no alternative accommodation is usually available and where employer–employee relationships have been the most personal. To evict a worker upon retirement or illness is a stark denial of the obligations of traditional authority, but in agriculture, all too often, it occurs only when there is no further need to cultivate the loyalty of the worker in any case, for he has ceased employment. Nevertheless the long-standing bitterness generated by the tied-cottage issue in agriculture can probably be understood in these terms.

The stability given to agriculture by state support (at least as far as East Anglian arable farmers are concerned) has, however, meant that the economic order upon which their dominance rests throws up fewer problems to threaten the stability of employer–employee relationships than in most other industries. Although year-to-year fluctuations in profits due to changing conditions certainly occur, since the war they have not been of such a violent nature as to warrant periodic wholesale redundancies among the agricultural labour force. As far as most farmers are concerned, the problems involved in handling their relations with their workers occur more at the social level, something which is again exacerbated by the fact that they are so personal and diffuse. These problems arise from the inherently dialectical nature of the relationship, since deferential interaction necessarily consists of two opposing and contradictory elements. The first is an element of *differentiation*. This is by definition involved in any hierarchical relationship such as that between a farmer and a farm worker. It is a differentiation fundamentally of power, and it is reflected through the differential control over economic resources in virtually every aspect of the farmer's and farm worker's lives. It is perpetuated as such by the distributive aspects of the contemporary system of economic and social stratification. The second element involved in deferential interaction is an element of *identification*. [7] Any interaction, even of a hierarchical nature, involves at the very least a coming together, but more than this is implied. The stability which deference confers requires more than a simple conjunction but a recognition of commonality which binds the two parties together in an affective relationship.

It is the tension between these opposing elements of differentiation and identification from which contradictions arise which threaten the destruction of the relationship. However, deferential interaction does not occur within a social vacuum – it derives from and is embedded in an inegalitarian system of dominance and rewards. The tensions between differentiation and identification in deference relationships are not, therefore, intractable. They are capable of being managed by the dominant individuals or groups, so that any apparent contradictions which may emerge can be contained or dissipated. Thus the stability which is sought from such forms of interaction will largely depend on what might be called the success of those exercising traditional authority in 'tension-management', in managing the inherent contradictions in the relationship as they become manifest from time to time.[8] Thus, while the structure of deference relationships is inherently dialectical in its nature, the *content*, what is actually acted out and therefore what can be observed, often represents a kind of 'tension-management in action'. Moreover, it may be suggested that the exercise of traditional authority is more successful when such management occurs on a personal, face-to-face basis than when it is mediated through impersonal abstractions or rules. To return to the dictum of Lord Percy, the Northumberland landowner and mine-owner, which was cited in Chapter 1, any landowner great or small 'could manage men with whom he could talk'. Much of the relationship between a farmer and his workers takes this form, with the farmer simultaneously trying to retain the identification of his workers while maintaining the necessary degree of separation from them which his possession of authority also demands.

As was noted in Chapter 1, during the nineteenth century these considerations were embodied in the ethic of the English gentleman, which proved to be such an ambiguous and flexible instrument of authority. They were, indeed, essential in coping with the contradictions inherent in the exercise of traditional authority, since any ethic less rigid than that of the 'gentleman' would have proved itself incapable of coming to terms with the changing social and economic circumstances which continually created new problems of stability and order. Moreover the gentlemanly ethic has not entirely disappeared. Today the word itself is often on the lips of farm workers who wish to distinguish those whom they consider to hold positions of authority in the local community legitimately – 'real gentlemen' – from those who lack the correct social credentials. However, the contemporary version of the gentleman farmer is often a pale imitation of what the Victorian agricultural worker would have understood by that term. Even less than in the countryside of a hundred years ago, the gentleman's reputation does not rest upon his ascribed qualities like birth, wealth or the possession of a large landed estate and a retinue of servants. Gentlemanly behaviour today involves, almost entirely, rules of social conduct, so that the ascriptive criteria of gentility have been greatly diluted. The change has been well summarized by Best: 'The old ruling class of peers and squires had been expected to exercise authority, and themselves expected to do so in order to maintain subordination. The new ruling class of gentlemen had to work more tactfully in a quasi-democratic age and used the gentler sounding words, "responsibility" and "leadership". Nobility and gentry had commanded you to defer to their rank. Gentlemen persuaded you to defer to their quality.'[9]

If the word 'gentleman' today has a rather old-fashioned ring about it, it nonetheless continues to be applied to those possessing high status in rural life. It has though become divested of most of the ascriptive attributes formerly attached to it and today refers almost entirely to the conduct of personal relationships. However, the ethic which prevails on the land today is not so much that of the gentleman as that of the father. The two, of course, overlap – there was a great deal in the notion of the gentlemanly ethic that involved the exercise of paternalism – but, while in the modern economic world, tainted as it is by the ungentlemanly pursuit of 'trade', few farmers would consciously organize their entrepreneurial activities according to the principles of gentlemanly honour, nearly all would wish to look after their workers as though they were members of the same family – indeed family analogies abound in the descriptions of the relationship which they offer. The term 'paternalism', then, more accurately conveys the tenor of these relationships than notions of gentility, for not only, like family relationships, are they conducted on a highly personal basis but they also generate a considerable degree of both dependency and affection. Many of these characteristics are captured in a passage written by John Stuart Mill, which is worth quoting at some length:

'... the lot of the poor, in all things which affect them collectively, should be regulated *for* them, not *by* them. They should not be required or encouraged to think for themselves, or give to their own reflection or forecast an influential voice in the determination of their destiny. It is the duty of the higher classes to think for them, and to take the responsibility of their lot, as the commander and officers of an army take that of the soldiers composing it. This function the higher classes should prepare themselves to perform conscientiously, and their whole demeanour should impress the poor with a reliance on it in order that, while yielding passive and active obedience to the rules prescribed for them, they may resign themselves in all other respects to a trustful *insouciance*, and repose under the shadow of their protectors. The relation between rich and poor should be only partially authoritative; it should be amicable, moral and sentimental; affectionate tutelage on the one side, respectful and grateful deference on the other. The rich should be in *loco parentis* to the poor, guiding and restraining them like children. Of spontaneous action on their part there should be no need. They should be called on for nothing but to do their day's work, and to be moral and religious. Their morality and their religion should be provided for them by their superiors, who should see them properly taught it, and should do all that is necessary to ensure their being, in return for labour and attachment, properly fed, clothed, housed, spiritually edified and innocently amused.'[10]

What Mill is advocating is the construction of an elaborate web of paternalistic relationships which not only consigns its subordinates to a dependent and powerless situation but enables them to endorse the system which achieves this. He is expressing what many agricultural employers instinctively feel and recognize – that the sedative effects of paternalism are of a kind that bring about stability and order and an identification of the workers with their 'betters'. Thus while dependence seems to be embedded in the very idea of paternalism, what is of greater importance in producing a stable system of traditional authority is not so much material dependence as the dependence of subordinates upon certain definitions of their situation. It is because of this that Mill places so much emphasis upon ideological control as well as the fulfilment of material needs. The paternal employer would convey ideologically 'correct' evaluations and moral attitudes, legitimating his own power and defining the worker's role as that of a partner in a co-operative venture. Hence the relationship should only be 'partially authoritative', but rather involve an exchange of 'affectionate tutelage' for 'respectful and grateful deference'. Indeed paternalism involves this dialectic of authority and affection at every level. At one and the same time it may consist of autocracy and obligation, cruelty and kindness, oppression and benevolence, exploitation and protection. Each facet derives from the necessity of maintaining both social differentiation and social identification simultaneously within a hierarchical relationship.

It is tempting, as did Mill, to regard such a system of traditional authority as involving no more than an exchange between such paternalism on the one hand and deference on the other, between the rights and obligations of each of the parties involved. Certainly deference relationships are concerned with some such exchange, but the point that needs to be emphasized is that this exchange is not the coming together of two free agents who then proceed to negotiate the outcome of their interaction of the basis of *a priori* parity.[11] Farmers and farm workers do not confront each other as social equals and deference relationships occur within a context of pre-existing inequality which cannot be ignored. In particular, although deference involves the exchange of certain rights and obligations, this exchange cannot be viewed as 'free', for the dominant party is always capable of defining – and, in the last analysis, imposing – the prevailing 'rate of exchange'. Indeed it is precisely by defining the relationship as a free and fair exchange that it is stabilized, so that the crux of deference relationships is the ability to ensure that the rate of exchange of rights and obligations continues to be regarded as legitimate. It is here that the importance of fostering the required definitions of the relationship become of paramount importance.

The importance of such personally transmitted definitions of the situation also places a premium upon isolating the relationship from the contamination with other interpretations and ideologies which might undermine the legitimacy of the dominant group. The closer that the social structure approximates to a total one then the greater the universality of this ideological hegemony. As was noted in Chapter 1, during the nineteenth century the isolation and self-containment of many rural villages resulted in the creation of relatively total social structures in which the agricultural worker's position was interpreted to him as being entirely natural and immutable. Within the village they were often provided from birth with a coherent world-view which aimed to teach them to know their place and remove them from any subversive ideas to the contrary. Although never completely cut off from the social influences of the outside world, a sufficiently self-contained and total institutional framework was created in some villages to render very extensive the ideological hegemony which the more isolated agricultural workers received. During the twentieth century the total nature of the rural village has gradually been undermined as it has been subject to the penetration of successive social influences and values that have emanated from outside. The autonomy of the local community and the ideology of localism which often accompanied it have therefore become much more attenuated, but it is easy to overestimate the extent to which this has occurred, particularly as far as the agricultural worker is concerned. As Chapter 6 showed, the impact of these general social changes, as mediated through the changing social composition of the rural village, has been to withdraw the agricultural worker into a separate, local agricultural social network which has proved considerably resilient to the inclusion of non-local individuals and the values and beliefs that they represent. If anything these changes have served to emphasize a continuing identification with agricultural employers by underlining a common adherence to agriculture and the 'rural way of life' as well as a common attachment to the local area, a solidarity of place which also functions symbolically to separate the 'locals' from alien outsiders.

With the movement of many farm workers to tied cottages situated on or near the farm, the conditions suitable for the maintenance of such a total social situation have continued. Moreover, in most cases contact between the farmer and the farm worker has remained on a personal basis, so that the characteristically small-scale and total nature of the farm-centred social structure has enabled traditional authority to be successfully maintained. In this sense the farm has become what Coser calls a 'greedy institution'.[12] Such greedy institutions make total claims on their members, seeking exclusive and undivided loyalty and attempting to 'reduce the claims of competing roles and status positions on those they wish to encompass within their boundaries. Their demands on the person are omnivorous.'[13] As Coser points out, there are evident overlaps between such greedy institutions and the more formally designated total institutions, like prisons and mental hospitals, which have been analysed by Goffman.[14] Goffman, however, focuses on the physical arrangements separating the inmates from the outside world, whereas greedy institutions, 'though they may in some cases utilize the device of physical isolation, tend to rely mainly on non-physical mechanisms to separate the insider from the outsider and to erect symbolic boundaries between them ... Nor are greedy institutions marked by external coercion. On the contrary, they tend to rely on voluntary compliance and to evolve means of activating loyalty and commitment.'[15]

While during the nineteenth century there were many large farmers and landowners who attempted to create greedy institutions out of the local village, today the decline of rural social isolation has resulted in a withdrawal of the boundaries of the greedy institution to the farm. Where the agricultural worker both lives and works on the farm there are fewer difficulties to hinder the attempts by farmers to obtain the loyalty and commitment from their workers. The creation of the farm as a greedy institution thus promotes the stabilization of deference relationships by limiting access to alternative definitions of the situation, while constantly promoting on a personal basis those definitions more conducive to reinforcing the legitimacy of the employer. The dominant position of the farmer can thus become 'natural' and inevitable since no alternatives can be readily conceived. Similarly the definitions of equivalence in the exchange of rights and obligations may be completely distorted. Those exercising power instead plead their 'service' to those over whom they rule. While a rigidly hierarchical social relationship such as that between employer and employee becomes an 'organic' relationship of 'mutual dependency'. Only within the confines of a greedy institution is such an ideological alchemy possible, yet the former, and in some cases continuing, adherence to such definitions indicates the degree of endorsement of the existing social order which such institutional arrangements confer.

Attempts by industrial employers to create a greedy institution out of their enterprises are clearly fraught with difficulties, because, no matter how much emphasis is placed upon strategies for obtaining employee commitment within the factory gate, the workers will usually be open to alternative definitions of their situation outside in the locality. For farmers the problems are not quite so great because the frequent overlapping of the work situation with the local community situation enables deferential relationships to become established and stabilized more easily. However, despite the tendency of agricultural workers to gravitate slowly towards the farm-centred community, by no means all workers live on the farm. In other situations therefore the influence of the employer may be more attenuated, as they were in the less isolated villages during the nineteenth century, when much of the informal social activity of the village occupational community was beyond the sight and the control of local farmers. At that time a commonly attempted solution to this problem was to extend the boundaries of the greedy institution beyond the farm gate to encompass the entire village, so that a complete locality could come to represent the spatial framework within which the traditional authority of farmers and landowners operated.[16] This was often reinforced by ideologies of localism and cemented by local elite benevolence in the form of local charitable activity and the gift of 'spiritual edification' and 'innocent amusement', to use Mill's terms. While such generosity continues – farmers may still donate resources towards the provision of village activities – the more typical examples of such benevolence occur much more informally and selectively on the farm as part of cultivating the identification of employees. Now that the village has often been overrun by outsiders, whom local employers have neither the power nor the desire to control in their work situation, the continuation of local benevolence may be regarded as unnecessary and even socially embarrassing. While in a few areas such customs may continue out of habit they are increasingly recognized as being faintly anachronistic.

The importance of gift relationships at the individual level between farmer and farm worker is quite another matter, however. These survive, as has been indicated several times during this book, and indeed flourish. The tension which the opposing elements in deferential relationships create are too critical to be managed in a purely negative way, in terms only of the prevention of the loss of deference. The identification of agricultural workers with their employer often needs to be buttressed in a positive manner by the application of some substantive and/or symbolic form of reinforcement. That is to say that part of the expected obligations upon employers which deference entails is the recognition of duties beyond the minimal level necessary under the agreed terms of the wage contract. Because they go beyond the formal wage bargain any extra rewards are typically regarded as gifts and are attributed to the generosity of the employer. In return they are expected to evoke feelings of gratitude and affection among employees. In monetary terms such gifts – pleasant housing conditions, occasional farm produce, the free use of farm implements and facilities, presents at Christmas, periodic 'treats' of various kinds – may not amount to much, but their symbolic importance is inestimable. First, as has been recognized in anthropological studies of gift relationships in primitive societies, they combine exactly those identificatory and differentiatory elements that characterize deference relationships. Mauss, for example, has noted how gift relationships help to reinforce the social hierarchy in which they occur by prompting feelings of faithfulness and gratitude. 'The great acts of generosity,' he writes, 'are not free from self-interest . . . To give is to show one's superiority, to show that one is something more and higher, that one is *magister*. To accept without returning or repaying more is to face subordination, to become a client and subservient, to become *minister*.'[17] Therefore, whatever the consciously philanthropic motivations which help to stimulate gift relationships, in effect they represent, through their status-enhancing properties, an integral part of the legitimation of traditional authority.

The second area of symbolic importance of such gifts lies in their role in separating the personal conduct of relationships between farmers and farm workers from their hierarchical structure. Although the relationship in terms of its structure is a very inegalitarian one, in terms of content it is suffused with emotions of kindness, affection and generosity. Indeed the mutual recognition of the fixity of the respective social ranks may in itself allow the relationship to be a very close and friendly one – in Mill's words, only 'partially authoritative'. In this manner the exercise of traditional authority directs attention away from the underlying structure of the relationship and diverts evaluations towards such personal judgements. The relationship may be an authoritarian one, but if the dominant person is a 'nice chap' any resentment is immediately disarmed. Paternalism therefore creates through such benevolence a tendency to identify with a particular individual and its strength lies in the fact that as the subordinates come to accept these relationships as legitimate so the prevailing ethos increases in strength.[18] Kindness and affection may develop as the appropriate definitions of mutual obligation are accepted. It thus tends to disguise, however imperfectly, fundamental conflicts of interest and to mediate, however unjustly, between one class and another. The gift, then, enables deference relationships to function in some kind of dynamic equilibrium, in which periodic individual benevolence and generosity help to overcome such tensions and contradictions in the relationship between farmer and farm worker as may arise from time to time.

This amorphous web of personally conducted deference relationships renders the industrial relations of agriculture extremely resistant to outside influence. It can be very difficult for the officials of the NUAAW, for example, to convince the individual agricultural worker that they can better protect his interests than a personally known and trusted employer, let alone convince him that his interests may be at variance with those of a farmer who is clearly concerned about his employees' welfare. Whatever the appallingly low wages that are prevalent in agriculture, how can the individual employer, who is such a kind and considerate person, be held responsible for such exploitation? This is *not* a case of the wicked squire grinding the faces of the poor into the earth – on the contrary it might be easier for both the individual agricultural worker and the NUAAW to come to terms with it if it were. Farmers *individually* do not represent the 'unacceptable face of capitalism', but capitalism at its most considerate and socially responsible: much better to have a quiet word with the boss than involve 'outsiders' in the settlement of any problems that may arise. Paternalism therefore has the consequence of wrong-footing the agricultural worker, for, while most of them recognize their material and economic inferiority compared with workers in general in this country, they find it difficult given the nature of the relationship with the farmer to blame him for their poverty. Given the tendency towards closer farmer–worker relationships it is likely to become easier for this paternalism to be maintained, so that trade-union organization is likely to continue to find it difficult to make rapid headway.

Nevertheless on the farm itself the contradictory nature of deferential relationships will continue to create problems which require constant manipulation and management. For example, the exercise of paternalism grants to the workers certain prerogatives which, while technically in the gift of the employer, tend over time to be appropriated as 'rights'. The farm worker, for example, feels he has a *right* to his tied house after years of faithful service, whatever the legal position may be – indeed in general he may regard the protection from impersonal market forces in whatever form they may take as a right which he can claim on his employer. Custom therefore tends to sanction claims upon those exercising traditional authority which frequently leads to such authority being re-defined from below in a way which may not comply with their original intentions. Much of the conflict that has occurred in the history of rural class relationships in Britain has, indeed, involved a reassertion of the traditional rights of the rural poor rather than a demand for the overthrow of the system of traditional authority itself.[19] By developing a powerful defence of traditional authority those exercising power have from time to time unwittingly invited those beneath them to fashion their own interpretations of the social order by assimilating their own rights, and then later, when changing conditions have threatened them, projecting these rights as demands. This is a particular example of a more general problem which arises in deference relationships: the risk that identification is carried too far, so that the relationship becomes entirely inflexible, making it incapable of surviving changed external circumstances or even resulting in the denial of the hierarchical aspects of the relationship – what may be termed the 'familiarity-breeds-contempt' problem.

This illustrates that the exercise of traditional authority is not solely concerned with cultivating the identification of subordinates; there is also the simultaneous task of maintaining the degree of social differentiation which deferential interaction equally demands. There is therefore a dilemma which reflects the contradictions inherent in the dialectical nature of deferential relationships. In the personal, face-to-face interaction which most successfully consolidates deference certain mechanisms must be employed which maintain social distance. The ritual obeisances often associated with deference – bowing, curtseying, touching the forelock, etc. – are therefore far from being entirely redundant. They are the essential means by which social distance has been maintained in the potentially polluting, closely knit interaction which characterizes traditional authority.[20] While such rituals have all but disappeared with the declining influence of traditionalism in British society as a whole, less observable and more subtle aspects of behaviour remain important in conveying the correct balance between social distance and social intimacy. This crucial mixture of aloofness and conviviality tends to be represented in the most inconspicuous nuances of behaviour; in demeanour rather than overt manifestations of conduct.[21] The precision which is required in conveying exactly the correct mixture of intimacy and distance is of enormous importance and to the discerning can mark out the 'real' gentleman by this 'bearing'. In this most particularistic of areas the norms of demeanour, apparently instinctively understood, remain largely unarticulated and consequently very difficult to communicate in print. Yet they are decisive. If the successful continuation of deferential relationships depends upon the effective handling of the contradictions within them, then in the typically face-to-face situations in which they occur the subtleties of demeanour are crucial.

Apart from the work of Goffman there are few acknowledgements in the sociological literature of the importance of these interactional nuances in setting the correct tone to the relationship. However, there are some good fictional descriptions of this by perceptive novelists. For example, John P. Marquand in *Point of No Return* conveys this admixture rather well: 'He could recognize a particular tone in her voice. It was the gracious, informal tone that she was in the habit of using when she wanted to make a pleasant impression on people who handled her affairs. It kept one at arm's length, though at the same time giving a pretty good picture of her capabilities for universal understanding, democracy and kindliness.'[22] Another, delivered with more satirical intent, is given by Tom Sharpe in his description of the deferential Skullion, the Cambridge college porter in *Porterhouse Blue*: 'The intricate system of social classification in Skullion's mind graded everyone. He could place a man within a hair's breath in the social scale by the tone of his voice or even the look in his eye. Some people thought you could depend on the cut of a man's coat but Skullion knew better. It wasn't externals that mattered, it was something much more indefinable, an inner quality which Skullion couldn't explain but which he recognized immediately. And responded to ... Money didn't count, not in Skullion's eyes anyway. In fact confidence without money was preferable, it indicated real quality and was accordingly revered.'[23] There are many agricultural workers, particularly the older ones, who pride themselves on possessing similar powers of discernment, although it is not necessary for their sensibilities to be quite so finely tuned as this. However, the ability of the farmer to combine an affable sociability with an ineffable superiority often remains the key to his success in man-management.

These considerations serve to emphasize again the importance of pervasive personal contact in the fostering of deferential relationships. However, such is the structure of many farms and community situations that this contact is not always as extensive as it needs to be. On bureaucratically organized farms where such personal interaction between employer and employee is much more abbreviated and in community situations which take the farm worker away from the direct social influences of the farmer, conditions are less favourable to

434   *The Deferential Worker*

the maintenance of deference. While the employer may continue to promote such interaction, the total, 'greedy' nature of the relationship is attenuated by the lack of social closure, the inability to separate the agricultural worker from other social influences and ensure his containment within a network of relationships defined according to the values of traditionalism. Under these circumstances the social influences of the farmer become one among many. The variations in agricultural workers' class ideology can therefore be understood in terms of the extent to which structural conditions allow the inculcation of deference to prosper. During the nineteenth and early twentieth centuries, despite the prevalence of traditionalism in many aspects of English social life as a whole, the prevailing nature of agricultural work and community situations probably made the distribution of deference less ubiquitous than has been generally supposed. However, the changes at work wrought by mechanization and the decline of the village as an occupational community have brought the agricultural worker increasingly under the social influence of his employer. Today most workers are integrated neither into the oppositional rural working-class sub-culture of the occupational community nor into the predominantly traditional, middle-class culture of their employers. In varying proportions they come into contact with a variety of belief systems so that their world-view has become ambivalent and fragmented.

The various strategies that farmers employ in managing their relationships with their workers are therefore only partially successful. They have the effect of producing not so much an unstinting deference as a pragmatic acceptance of his role and a loyalty to him as an individual which is not extended to all farmers or other dominant class members. However, it is as a relationship rather than as a set of attitudinal attributes that the concept of deference seems better to account, not only for the variation in the social consciousness of agricultural workers, but for how their everyday social interaction with the farmer is transacted. Nevertheless the relative powerlessness of the agricultural worker to define how this relationship is structured and conducted suggests that in order to understand the farm worker's actions fully it is necessary not only to concentrate on the worker himself but to understand the motives and values of those who largely control the social structure in which he finds himself – most notably the farmer. This suggests that any work on the social situation of the agricultural worker – and by implication other similarly placed working-class occupational groups – must pay more attention to the variety of inter-class social unfluences to which he is subject. In order to understand fully the important relationship between the farmer and the farm worker, it is necessary to know how the farmer is defining, evaluating and managing this relationship from above, as much as it is to know how it is being interpreted, appraised and manipulated from below. This suggests that in future much more detailed attention should be paid to the precise nature of the values and beliefs of farmers than there has been during the course of this book.

The Farm Worker and the Future

Given the continuing constraints which the agricultural worker is subject to, it seems unlikely that any dramatic improvement in his life-chances will occur in the near future unless there is decisive intervention by external agencies. Despite the shortage of some categories of skilled stockmen that occur from time to time during periods of low unemployment in the economy generally, there seems little prospect of an overall improvement in the farm worker's market situation. Although the severe social stigma which is now attached to working on the land will continue to deter large numbers of school-leavers from seeking permanent employment in agriculture, there is still sufficient slack in the demand for many categories of labour to nullify any comparative improvement that might otherwise occur. There are many farmers who still hoard labour by continuing to employ elderly workers who will not be replaced when they retire, and even if genuine shortages became a real possibility over the majority of rural England there are still enough labour-saving innovations ready to be adopted to reduce the demand still further. In East Anglia, for example, minimum cultivation methods, which obviate the need for ploughing, are the next innovation likely to give a further push to the drift from the land.

Local labour markets in rural areas are therefore unlikely to tighten dramatically unless there is a more vigorous campaign to relocate industry in hitherto predominantly agricultural regions. This has also occurred in East Anglia, providing considerable local stimulus to wage levels, but the effects have been very patchy, with the adoption of relocation schemes in Norfolk and West Suffolk, but their rejection in East Suffolk. The pressures against the further introduction of industry into rural areas are, moreover, likely to increase as local farmers, anxious to fend off threats to their labour supplies, join forces with middle-class newcomers, equally concerned to preserve the 'village in the mind' and retain the countryside as an idyllic and peaceful retreat. Similar considerations are likely to be brought to bear upon the provision of desperately needed local authority housing. Rural preservation societies, consisting largely of urbanite newcomers, will continue to campaign against the erection of council housing estates in their villages, both on amenity grounds and, very often, in order to keep down local rates. Meanwhile the farm worker will be forced either to move to near-by towns for housing and employment or, if he decides to stay on the land, to move into tied accommodation. In this case his dependency upon his employer will increase.

The reduction of this dependency will certainly involve external political action, including legislation, that will emanate from outside rural society itself. The redemption of the Labour Party's long-standing pledge to abolish the tied-cottage system, which at the time of writing appears to be likely in some form, would certainly help to reduce the powerlessness of the farm worker, but much would depend upon the precise way in which such legislation was formulated, and without simultaneously attacking the root of the problem, which is the chronic lack of housing in rural areas, abolition of the tied cottage on its own would not be a panacea and could be unworkable. Nevertheless the removal of the present tied-cottage system would achieve a great deal by way of freeing the farm worker from one of the most potent constraints on his market situation – his inability once in a tied house to consider employment outside agriculture. It would also be a tremendous filip for agricultural trade-unionism and would be justly hailed by the NUAAW as a victory without equal since the establishment of minimum pay legislation and even in its entire history.

Whether the abolition of the tied cottage will suddenly unleash a wave of militancy held back for years by the intimidating prospect of eviction, as is sometimes naïvely expected, is doubtful. However much the agricultural worker may be objectively deprived his relationship with his employer is generally, and increasingly, a close and friendly one. While the diminution in the size of the labour force continues they are, moreover, likely to become even closer and more friendly.

The only counterveiling tendencies to this will occur on those farms which react to market forces by amalgamating and forming very large, bureaucratically run units, occasionally stimulated by the injection of outside capital. On these farms all the prevailing tendencies towards patriarchalism will be reversed and they will provide an opportunity to the NUAAW, which it has already taken in a few cases, to indulge in a degree of plant bargaining and use this as a lever to raise agricultural wage rates in the surrounding area. Much will depend upon the pace at which such amalgamation will take place, but in any event the concentration of labour on such farms is likely to be an extremely slow process.

The only other factor which seems likely to stimulate the dissatisfaction of the agricultural worker is his growing contact, even in his own village, with more universalistic values and in particular the extent to which he can directly observe the standard of living and life-styles of friends and relations who live locally but are employed in higher-paid, non-agricultural occupations. With the increasing urbanization of many rural villages these opportunities to compare directly his own living standards with those of other workers are likely to increase. If the wages gap between agriculture and industry continues to widen and if the expectations of the agricultural worker continue to be raised by his increasing contact with more affluent associates, his dissatisfaction is likely to be expressed in some overt form. Given the continuing powerlessness of most agricultural workers, however, it is likely to be manifested in an increased drift from the land rather than in strikes or other forms of militant action. In any case, under such circumstances the abilities of individual farmers to continue to retain the loyalty and affection of their workers will be considerably tested. They will be fortunate in that, for most farmers, the prevailing trends in the work situation lend themselves to the endurance of the workers' identification.

In view of the prevalence of closer relationships with the employer it is probable that future changes in the values of the agricultural worker will be affected more by changes in the farmers' own values than by any alteration in the situation of the workers themselves. Because the changing structure of his work and community situations have to some extent shielded the farm worker from the decline of traditionalism in Britain as a whole, the declining adherence to traditional values is having less affect on the worker's values than on those of the farmer, who is by no means quite so socially and culturally isolated from the mainstream of society. There are signs that a growing number of farmers, particularly the younger ones, are less inclined to act according to the norms of traditional authority. Often more educated and more aware of contemporary social and economic developments than their fathers, they adopt an ethic which is more professional than gentlemanly. They find the traditional obligations of paternalism irksome, anachronistic and out of place in the modern economic world. They prefer instead to rely upon their expertise and to define their relationships with their employees as far more contractual and instrumental than has customarily been the norm. Since they also tend to offer a better wage bargain than the more traditional employers the short-run consequences of this change may not be very great. However, if their own instrumentality is reflected in an increasing instrumentalism on the part of the workers, particularly the younger workers who are similarly less inclined to accept unquestioningly a state of affairs simply because that is the way it has always been in the past, then the long-run consequences of replacing personal loyalty with cash nexus may be considerable. Certainly the distinctiveness of employer–employee relations in agriculture compared with industry will decline further.

Nevertheless as far as the agricultural worker himself is at present concerned, the chances that his poverty will be relieved in the near future seem hardly less remote than they have ever been. One suspects that the general public will find little reason to change their image of him and that the farm worker will remain alternately ignored and caricatured as he has in the past. Meanwhile he will continue to keep his own counsel. As one farm worker put it, 'How can farm workers make a fuss? Where can farm workers start to fight?'

1. E. Shils, 'Deference', in J. A. Jackson (ed.), *Social Stratification*, CUP, 1968, p. 116. It is a weakness of Shils' analysis, however, that he fails to place deference in any content of power relationships, so that *what* is regarded as conferring status honour is not considered to be problematic, something which is clearly crucial if some degree of stability is going to be conferred on deference relationships. Shils' definition is also adopted by Bob Jessop in *Traditionalism, Conservatism and British Political Culture*, Allen and Unwin, 1974, p. 33. However, Jessop still contrives to reinterpret Shils' approach in terms of the 'supportive culture' thesis. See also C. W. Chamberlain and H. G. Moorhouse, 'Lower Class Attitudes Towards the

British Political System', *Sociological Review*, vol. 22, No. 4, 1974, p. 521, n. 6.

2. Parts of this section repeat arguments put forward in H. Newby, The Deferential Dialectic', *Comparative Studies in Society and History*, vol. 17, No. 2, 1975, pp. 139–64; and Paternalism and Capitalism: A Re-examination of the "Size-Effect"', paper presented to the British Sociological Association Conference on 'Advanced Industrial Societies', Canterbury, 1975.

3. Form, that is, in the sense used by Simmel. Although the exact content of the relationship may vary according to the particularistic concerns of the situation a common (dialectical) structure can be observed which is elaborated below. See K. H. Wolff (ed.), *The Sociology of Georg Simmel*, The Free Press, Glencoe, Ill., 1950, and D. E. Levine (ed.), *Georg Simmel on Individuality and Social Forms*, University of Chicago Press, 1971.

4. cf. M. Weber, *The Theory of Social and Economic Organization*, The Free Press, Glencoe, Ill., 1964, pp. 341–2.

5. ibid., p. 341.

6. cf. R. Williams, *The Country and the City*, Chatto and Windus, 1973, p. 182.

7. These terms are analogous to the concepts of 'fission' and 'fusion' used by Dumont in his analysis of the Indian caste system. See L. Dumont, *Homo Hierarchicus*, Paladin, 1972, especially Ch. 2.

8. The use of 'tension-management' here is not to be understood in the functionalist sense as referring to the integration of sub-systems into the over-arching social system, but as an active strategy by the ruling elite of a society to maintain the stability of the social hierarchy. Although the use of a similar term may be somewhat confusing it seems best to convey what is involved in the relationship.

9. G. Best, *Mid-Victorian Britain, 1851–75*, Panther, 1973, p. 256. See also D. C. Coleman, 'Gentlemen and Players', *Economic History Review*, vol. XXVI, No. 1, 1973, pp. 92–116; and R. H. Wilkinson, 'The Gentlemanly Ideal and the Maintenance of a Political Elite', in P. W. Musgrave (ed.), *Sociology, History and Education*, Methuen, 1970, pp. 126–42.

10. J. S. Mill, *Principles of Political Economy*, vol. II, Beacon Books, Boston, Mass., 1848, pp. 319–20, cited by R. Bendix, *Work and Authority in Industry*, University of California Press, 1956, p. 47.

11. As it is so regarded in much of the literature on deference in small group relations by social exchange theorists – e.g. P. M. Blau, *Exchange and Power in Social Life*, Wiley, New York, 1964, and many of Blau's accompanying papers cited therein.

12. L. Coser, *Greedy Institutions*, The Free Press, New York, 1974.

13. ibid., p. 4.

14. E. Goffman, *Asylums*, Penguin Books, 1968.

15. Coser, op. cit., p. 6.

16. cf. the growth of nineteenth-century company towns promoted by paternalist industrial employers. See, for example, A. H. Birch, *Small Town Politics*, OUP, 1960; T. Lane and K. Roberts, *Strike at Pilkington's*, Fontana, 1971; R. Martin and R. H. Fryer, *Redundancy and Paternalist*

Capitalism, Allen and Unwin, 1963; R. Moore, *Pitmen, Preachers and Politics*, CUP, 1974.

17. M. Mauss, *The Gift*, Cohen and West, 1970, p. 72. See also Simmel's essays on 'Exchange' and 'The Poor' in Levine, op. cit., and on 'Faithfulness and Gratitude' in Wolff, op. cit. For two recent contributions see R. M. Titmuss, *The Gift Relationship*, Allen and Unwin, 1970, and B. Schwartz, 'The Social Psychology of the Gift', *American Journal of Sociology*, vol. 73, No. 1, 1967–8, pp. 1–11.

18. See the interesting discussion by Genovese in *Roll, Jordan Roll*, Pantheon, New York, 1974, Part One and Appendix.

19. See E. J. Hobsbawm and G. Rudé, *Captain Swing*, Lawrence and Wishart, 1970; J. P. D. Dunbabin, *Rural Discontent in Nineteenth Century Britain*, Faber, 1974.

20. See E. Goffman, 'The Nature of Deference and Demeanour', in his *Interaction Ritual*, Penguin University Books, 1972, pp. 47–96; also the studies cited in J. M. Bechers, E. H. Mizruchi and R. Perrucci, 'Social Distance Strategies and Status Symbols: An Approach to the Study of Social Structure', *Sociological Quarterly*, vol. 4, 1963, pp. 311–24.

21. Goffman, op. cit.

22. J. P. Marquand, *Point of No Return*, Little, Brown, Boston, 1947, pp. 31–2.

23. T. Sharpe, *Porterhouse Blue*, Secker and Warburg, 1974, p. 55.

APPENDIX I
The Derivation of the Sample[1]

Obtaining a sample of farm workers to interview is not an easy exercise. One appreciates fully the problems encountered by other interested parties, such as the agricultural trade unions, in contacting such a widely scattered section of the population. Unlike many industrial employees farm workers are not conveniently grouped together in large numbers inside a highly visible factory. They are instead situated mostly in ones and twos in locations which are often hidden away from inquiring outsiders and which makes contact extremely difficult.

There are a number of research strategies which suggest themselves as methods of obtaining some sort of interviewing sample. One would be to establish a sample through trade-union membership records, but in such a lowly unionized industry this is a virtual non-starter. Another strategy would be to descend upon a selected village, establish contacts with local farm workers and proceed by a 'snowball' method to encompass all the workers in an ever-widening area. The problem here is that there is no guarantee that the eventual sample will be in any way representative of even the immediate locality, but, perhaps more important as far as this study was concerned, such a process would be very slow and expensive in terms of time and other resources. The third method is to take a sample of farms and interview the workers on each one. The great disadvantage of this is that in using the farmer as an entrée one might be seen by the workers as an agent of management. The advantage, so it seemed at the beginning, was the availability of a reliable list of farms provided by the Ministry of Agriculture's annual farm census. Although from the outset it was clear that this method of entry might bias some replies towards a more 'official' line on the part of the workers, it was believed to be not too difficult to sensitize oneself to this problem and try to counteract tendencies accordingly. Since selecting a sample in this way seemed easy, quick and reliable it was decided to go ahead on this basis.

The Ministry of Agriculture's Census and Surveys Branch at

Guildford was approached for help in selecting a sample. They refused. In spite of attempts to persuade them to change their minds, their response remained that their hands were tied by the provisions of the Agriculture Act of 1947 which did not allow the divulgence of individual names and addresses unless it was considered to be 'required in the public interest'. The Ministry were quite within their rights, but it was galling, to say the least, to learn subsequently that university research projects are frequently given such assistance under this proviso, although it clearly helps to be employed in a Department of Agriculture or Agricultural Economics. As the Ministry put it, 'there has to be a clear Ministry interest in the results'. (It might also be added that, as so often in these cases, it helps to know whom to approach. A later study of farmers, funded directly by the SSRC, has met with every assistance from the Ministry, the first approach having been made via the newly appointed Academic Liaison Officer. If experience on the workers' study is anything to go by, the establishment of this post will prove to be of considerable use.) An attempt to circumvent Whitehall by approaching the local Ministry office in Bury St Edmunds met with a similar response.

The refusal of the Ministry to co-operate was a severe setback, since it seemed to deny any access to a reliable and comprehensive sampling frame. However, during an interview with the then Suffolk County Secretary of the NFU it emerged that such a list was in the NFU's possession. Permission was sought to use it, but, although it seemed at first that this would be granted, eventually the Finance and General Purposes Committee of the Suffolk County branch declined to help. Although no reasons were given, farmers are usually extremely wary of the dangers of such lists falling into the hands of commercial interests and this probably influenced their decision.

One further source was local-authority rate books. Agricultural land is exempt from rates and it was therefore assumed that there would be a list of such properties in local rate books. However, one local authority denied all knowledge of agricultural derating ('The only things which don't pay rates are church halls') and had no list of agricultural holdings. Another stated that agricultural land was exempt, but they possessed no list and that the rate book was for them a thing of the past – everything was on a computer.

There remained one final source – the reasonably accurate list of farms in the local telephone directory. The Yellow Pages listed (as it turned out) the majority of farmers in the forty-four parishes and this was eventually used as the basis of the sample. By checking the number of farms in each parish obtained from the Yellow Pages against the Ministry's census parish summaries, a rough idea of the coverage could be gauged. In fact 386 addresses out of 487 holdings in the census were obtained, that is, 77 per cent. This seemed a reasonable basis on which to proceed, particularly as the latest available (in 1971) was the 1969 census and so there would have been an annual decrease in holdings over this period of 2 per cent, but mainly because it was surmised that those farmers not in the directory would be likely to be part-time farmers, smallholders and other holdings not employing labour in any case.

Of the 386 addresses it was clear that a number were multiple holdings, that is to say only one farmer was involved in running a single enterprise on different patches of land. On these grounds seventy-four addresses were weeded out and so eventually 312 letters were sent. The letters outlined the nature of the research, guaranteed confidentiality and requested an interview with the farmer concerned. A pre-paid card was enclosed on which a reply could be written and the farmer was also invited to include the number of regular, whole-time male workers on his farm, even if he refused to co-operate, so that some idea could be gained of the non-respondents and the overall reliability of the sample. Of the 312 letters that were sent out 264 replies (84·9 per cent) were returned; of those 105 farmers were willing to be interviewed, 140 were either unwilling or unable to be interviewed and nineteen were further multiple holdings.

Of the 105 willing to be interviewed, four were retired farmers and sixteen employed no labour. These were dropped from the sample, and there now remained eighty-five farmers who were approached. However the final number was further reduced to seventy-one by the uncovering of further multiple holdings even at this stage (owing to lack of communication between fathers and sons or between one partner and another). One farmer who would allow himself to be interviewed proved to be so elusive over the six months' fieldwork period that the attempt was abandoned.

The non-respondents were as follows:

Refused	93
Retired	19
Migrated	12
'Farm' is domestic residence only	9
Deceased	7
	140

Of the ninety-three refusals, seventy-one did not employ labour in any case (having read between the lines of the letter to perceive that the workers were the real centre of interest). Of the remainder, seven farmers employed one man each, seven employed two, five employed three and three farmers employed respectively four, nineteen and forty-four workers. The result of all this was that the medium-sized farmers employing between five and twelve workers must be regarded as being slightly over-represented in the sample.

There were 330 hired men employed on the eventual seventy-one farms where interviews took place. However, ninety-seven of them were not interviewed for the following reasons:

Related to the farmer	23
Unable to contact	21
Under eighteen years of age	10
Mentally retarded	10
Engaged on non-agricultural work (e.g. secretarial staff, etc.)	10
Other (including illness and employment on detached holding outside the fieldwork area)	16
	97

How representative is the sample? This is not easy to answer in any definitive way because no accurate sampling frame was ever available. The Yellow Pages, although useful in their way, were not absolutely representative. During the fieldwork period a check was made in nine out of the forty-four parishes to discover which holdings the Yellow Pages had omitted. These nine parishes contained 100 holdings, from which the Yellow Pages had omitted thirty, sixteen of which turned out to be the multiple holdings of farmers already included in the sample. Out of the remaining fourteen only three employed any labour, with eight full-time workers between them.

The remainder were extremely small holdings which in most cases could not be considered 'farms' in the accepted sense. Many, for example, were ex-farmhouses owned by immigrant commuters who had retained a small paddock for their daughters' ponies.

However, having begun with 497 holdings in the area and ended up with, for whatever reason, seventy-one means that no great claims can be made for representativeness. Nevertheless the counterfactual claim can be made very strongly: there is no reason to believe that the workers interviewed are *un*representative of all the workers in the forty-four parishes, and this claim could even be extended, though necessarily more cautiously, to the remainder of Suffolk and East Anglia, as Table 8 (p. 127) shows. However, the slight bunching towards the middle-size groups must be borne in mind.

1. The concern in this Appendix is only with the derivation of the sample. For overall discussion of the fieldwork methods and experience see the essay in C. Bell and H. Newby, *Doing Sociological Research*, Allen and Unwin, forthcoming.

APPENDIX II
The Questionnaires

Survey of Farmers

Date:

Farm:

1. First of all, could you tell me the acreage of this holding?

2. And what type of farm is it?

1. Specialist dairy	*8. Cropping – mostly cereals*
2. Mainly dairy	*9. General cropping*
3. Rearing – mostly cattle	*10. Predominantly vegetables*
4. Rearing – mostly sheep	*11. Predominantly fruit*
5. Rearing – cattle and sheep	*12. General horticulture*
6. Predominantly poultry	*13. Mixed*
7. Pigs and poultry	

3. Are you the owner of this farm?
   1. *Owner-occupier*
   2. *Tenant*
   3. *Manager*
   4. *Other (specify)*

4A. Now, could you tell me how many workers, including members of your family, you employ on this holding full-time? And how many of them are women?

   B. And what kinds of jobs do they do?

   Probe for hierarchy

   C. How many of them are members of your family?

   D. And how many partners or directors work on the farm full-time?

   E. Now, could I ask you the same question for *regular* part-time workers?

How many regular part-time workers, including members of your family, do you employ?
And how many of these are women?

F. And what kinds of jobs do they do?

Probe for hierarchy

G. How many of these are members of your family?

H. And how many partners or directors work on the farm part-time?

5A. On average over the year, how many hours do you spend in a week on work related to your holding?

B. *If less than 40:* Do you only work on this holding part-time, then?

C. *If part-time:* What is your other occupation?

D. Do you do any agricultural work on any other holding?

E. *If yes:* Where is this?
How often do you work there?

Later on, I want to ask you some more questions about your present work, but first could we fill in some background details of your life up to now? We might as well start at the beginning and work up to the present.

6. So, firstly, where were you born?

7. What year was that?

8. How old were you when you left full-time education?

9. Have you served an apprenticeship or studied for any other qualifications in agriculture?
If yes: Which ones?

Now I'd like to know about the main jobs you have had so far. Let's start with the first job you had and then work up to the present. We'll include any army service you might have had.

10A. What was the first job you had?
If army check whether regular or national service; rank and length of service for both and reasons left for regulars

B. Whereabouts was that?

C. Did you move house *for* the job?

D. How long did you work there?

E. Why did you leave?
Distinguish clearly between a disadvantage of this job and the attraction of another job

F. What were the main jobs you held there?
Report for each job

11A. Casting your mind back on all the jobs you have ever had, *including your present one*, which have you liked the best?

B. What did you like most about this job?

12. Are you married?
If yes: On average over the year how many hours in a week does your wife spend on farm work?

13. Can you give me some details about the types of jobs held by your close relatives. First, I'd like to know about your father. What job does he do?
Take note of don't knows. If anyone is deceased, retired or unemployed, ask of last normal job. Go through persons listed below, asking, in addition, if in farming:
Did you/do you actually work with him?

Repeat for: Eldest brother, Brother No. 2, Brother No. 3, Brother No. 4, Wife's father.

14A. When you have an applicant for a job on your farm, what qualities in him do you look for?

Probe for character v. skill:

B. Do you think that the possession of formal qualifications make a man a better farm worker?

C. Why is this?

D. How much above the minimum wage laid down by the Wages Board would you be willing to pay in order to attract the right man?

Now I'd like to ask you some questions about the availability of labour for your farm. Let's deal with the highly specialized workers like stockmen and so on first.

15A. What is the position over hiring this type of worker at the moment?
Would you say it was
very difficult
fairly difficult
fairly easy
very easy

B. Do you employ this kind of worker on your farm?

C. *If yes:* The last time you hired a man of this kind, how did you go about it?

Probe with list
1. *Use of informal contacts*
2. *Advertise locally (e.g. shop window) (Number?   Duration?)*
3. *Advertise in local press (Number?   Duration?)*
4. *Advertise in national press (Number?   Duration?)*
5. *Employment exchange (Number?   Duration?)*
6. *Other (specify)*
7. *Number of applicants*
8. *Time taken in hiring new worker*

Now, general workers

16A. What is the position over hiring this type of worker at the moment?
Would you say it was
very difficult
fairly difficult
fairly easy
very easy

B. Do you employ this kind of worker on your farm?

C. *If yes:* The last time you hired a man of this kind, how did you go about it?

Probe with list
1. *Use of informal contacts*
2. *Advertise locally (e.g. shop window) (Number?   Duration?)*
3. *Advertise in local press (Number?   Duration?)*
4. *Advertise in national press (Number?   Duration?)*
5. *Employment exchange (Number?   Duration?)*

6. Other (specify)
7. Number of applicants
8. Time taken in hiring new worker

Finally two questions about your full-time labour-force.

17A. Can you tell me how many days were lost altogether last year owing to sickness and absenteeism?

B. Can you tell me how many workers have quit their job on the farm?
   a Over the last year
   b Over the last five years

Thank you very much for your help. Are there any questions you would like to ask me?

Survey of Farm Workers

Date:

Farm:

House: In village: On farm:

1. First of all can you tell me in your own words exactly what it is that you do?

1. Foreman	*6. Shepherd*
2. General farm worker	*7. Pigman*
3. Tractor	*8. Poultryman*
4. Cowman	*9. Horticultural worker*
5. Stockman	*10. Other (specify)*

Later on I want to ask you some more questions about your present work, but first could we fill in some background details of your life up to now? We might as well start at the beginning and work up to the present.

2. So, firstly, where were you born?

3. What year was that?

4. How old were you when you left full-time education?

5. Have you served an apprenticeship or studied for any other qualifications in agriculture?

    If yes: Which one?

    1. *Apprenticeship*
    2. *City and Guilds Stage 1 or exams of the UEI, UCLI or UYI*
    3. *City and Guilds Stage 2 or 3*
    4. *National Certificate*
    5. *National or college diploma*
    6. *University degree*
    7. *None*

    Now I'd like to know about the main jobs you have had so far. Let's start with the first job you had and then work up to the present. We'll include any army service you might have had.

6A. What was the first job you had?

    If army, check whether regular or national service: rank and length of service for both and reasons left for regulars

  B. Whereabouts was that?

  C. Did you move house when you got that job?

    If yes: Did you move house *for* that job?

  D. How long did you work there?

  E. Why did you leave?

    Distinguish clearly between a disadvantage of this job and an attraction of another job

  F. What were the main jobs you held there?

    Repeat for each job

7A. Casting your mind back on all the jobs you have ever had, *including your present one*, which have you liked the best?

    If not present job:

  B. Why did you like this job the most?

8A. Have you ever been unemployed for longer than a few days at a time?

    If yes:

  B. How many times?

  C. About how much time altogether?

  D. How long ago was the last time?

9A. Turning now to your present job, do you find it
interesting all the time
mostly interesting
mostly dull and monotonous
very dull and monotonous

B. Why is this?

C. What do you like most about your job?

D. What do you like least about your job?

E. If you could go back and start life over again would you choose a different trade or occupation?

10A. How do you get on with your farmer? Is it
very well
quite well
not so well
badly

B. Why is it you get on —— with your farmer?

C. Do you work alongside your farmer
regularly
occasionally
rarely
never

11A. How often do you see your farmer? Is it
regularly
occasionally
rarely
never

B. How often is this?

C. Do you think it is a good thing that you see him ——?

D. Why do you say that?

E. Do you ever ask your farmer's advice about personal matters not concerned with the farm?

If yes:
F. What sort of things do you ask him about?

G. And do you usually take his advice?

H. Some people say that nowadays farmers treat their workers more as numbers and not as human beings. Would you say that is true of your farm?

I. Here are two opposing views about farming generally. I'd like you to tell me which you agree with more. Some people say that a farm is like a football side – because good teamwork means success and is to everyone's advantage. Others say that teamwork in agriculture is impossible – because farmers and workers are really on opposite sides. Which view do you agree with more?

12A. In your job do you work on your own
a great deal
now and then
hardly at all

B. How often do you talk to your workmates, then? Would you say it was
a great deal
now and then
hardly at all

C. How often is this? Is it
only at break times
mostly at break times
at any time at all

D. How many people who work on your farm would you call close friends?

E. Do you see him/them off the farm
regularly
occasionally
rarely
never

F. Where do you see him/them?

13A. Now I'd like to ask you how you feel about absence from work. Here are two views on absence – which one comes nearer to your own views?
(a) *A man should not stay away from work in any event, except when it is really necessary as in the case of genuine sickness.*

(b) *It's a free society and a man has the right to take a day off once in a while if he wants to.*

B. Why do you say this?

14A. Do you think your farm is about as good a place as there is to work or do you think there are other places that are better?
   1. *This farm best*
   2. *Others better*
   3. *Don't know*

B. Why do you say this?

15A. Have you ever thought of leaving your present job?
   If yes:

B. Have you done anything about it?

C. Why have you thought of leaving?

D. As you have thought of leaving – what is it that keeps you at your present job?

E. Would you be willing to move house in order to get another job?
   If yes: How far?

F. How far would you be willing to travel each day to another job?

G. If you did leave do you think your farmer would replace you
   with great difficulty
   with some difficulty
   fairly easily
   very easily

16A. Supposing you were offered a job outside farming in this district but at 50p. (10s.) a week more. Would you accept it?
   If no:

B. What if it was £1 a week more?

C. £3?

D. £5?

E. £10?

G. Why would you prefer to stay and lose £(X − 1)?

17A. Do you think that in general farm workers have to worry about getting the sack?

B. Why do you say this?

C. How secure do you think your *own* job is? Would you say it is
   dead safe
   fairly safe
   rather insecure
   very insecure

D. What makes you say that?
   Probe for security via seniority, etc. as opposed to economic prospects

Now I'd like to ask you one or two questions about pay and conditions.

18. On average how many hours do you work each week including overtime?

19A. Not counting overtime, are you paid more than the minimum rate laid down by the Wages Board?

B. And how do you feel about your present level of wages? Are you
   completely satisfied
   quite satisfied
   a little dissatisfied
   very dissatisfied

C. *If dissatisfied:*
   And who do you blame for this state of affairs?

20A. What income do you think is necessary for you in order to maintain a proper standard of living for people like yourself?

B. What sort of people are you thinking of when we talk about 'people like yourself'?

21A. Do you think there are any other sorts of people doing noticeably better at the moment than you and your family?

B. What sort of people do you think are doing noticeably better?

C. What do you feel about this, I mean, do you approve or disapprove of this?
   Why is that?

D. Compared with workers in other industries, would you say that over the last few years you have been improving your financial position, falling behind or doing about the same?
1. *Improving*
2. *Deteriorating*
3. *Same*

Now I'd like to ask you some questions about trade-unionism.

22A. Are you a member of a trade union?
If no: move to (24)

B. Which one?

C. When did you join?

D. Why did you join?

23A. Which branch do you belong to?

B. How often do you go to union branch meetings? Would you say you went
regularly
occasionally
rarely
never

C. When did you last go to one?

D. *If never:* Why is it that you don't go to union branch meetings?

E. Have you ever had any official post in the union?
If yes: Which one?

24. *For non-union men:*

A. Were you ever a union member?

If yes:
B. Which union was that?

C. Why did you leave?

If no:
D. Have you ever seriously thought of joining a union?

If yes:
E. Why didn't you then?

If no:
F. Do you have any serious objections to joining a union?

If yes:

G. Why is this? *Probe for instrumental as against ideological reasons.*

If no:
Is it just that you have never bothered to join then?

25. How often do you talk to your workmates about union affairs?
Would you say
very often
a good deal
now and then
hardly ever

26. *All*

A. If the union called a strike would you come out?

B. Why/Why not?

C. Farm workers do not go on strike though, do they? Why do you think that is?

27. Now I'd like your opinion about some general questions covering agriculture, not just on your own farm but about farming as a whole. I am going to read you some things that people have said. After I read each one would you tell me whether you agree, disagree or have no opinion either way.

A. Most farmers have the welfare of their workers at heart.

B. Workers should have more say in running their farm.

C. Farm workers do not get their fair share of farm income in wages.

D. Farm workers need a stronger trade union to fight for their interests.

E. Matters of agricultural policy can be left to farmers to deal with, without farm workers bothering about them.

F. Workers should follow the lead of farmers rather than trade-unionists in national affairs.

G. Farmers know what's best for the farm and workers should do just what they are told.

H. Most farm workers could manage a farm better than farmers.

I. Farmers are getting more than their fair share of farm income.

458 *The Deferential Worker*

J. Workers should always be loyal to their farm even if this means putting themselves out quite a bit.

Probe: Why do you say this?

28. Now could I ask you a few questions that are not concerned with agriculture so that I can get a more rounded view of how you look at things. First I'd like your opinion on some questions about industry. Just as we did before, I'll read what some people have said. After I've read each one could you tell me whether you agree, disagree or have no opinion either way.

A. Industrial workers these days are getting more than their fair share in wages.

B. The trade unions have too much power in the country.

C. In industry managers know what's best for their firm and workers should do just what they are told.

D. Farm workers have more in common with farmers than with workers in industry.

E. The men who own big business have too much power in this country.

Probe: Why do you say this?

29. People often talk about there being different classes in this country. What do you think?
    Check for:
    1. *No. of social classes*
    2. *Terminology*
    3. *Major factors determining class position*
    4. *Position respondent sees himself as holding*
    5. *Explanations of why individuals hold the class positions they do.*
    6. *Assessment of extent of upward mobility.*
    7. *Views on necessity and desirability of class system.*
    8. *Degree of class harmony or conflict.*

30. Now just like before I'm going to ask your opinion about some statements, only this time about general topics about the society in which we live. Again after I read each one can you tell me whether you agree, disagree or have no opinion either way.

A. There are lots of things wrong with the monarchy that need improving.

B. The aristocracy are born to rule and workers should follow their lead.

C. No one in Britain has ever tried to keep the workers from getting their fair share.

D. The ordinary man should have more say in running the country.

E. The House of Lords should be done away with in its present form.

F. Public schools are the best part of our education system.

G. A few strong leaders would do this country more good than all the laws and ideas being discussed.

H. Matters of national policy can be left to the leaders of this country to deal with without ordinary people bothering about them.

I. The best leaders of this country come from upper-class backgrounds rather than from a more working-class background.

J. A government should do what it thinks right even if the majority of people disagree.

31. We're on the last section now. I'd like to ask you a few questions about life here in the village.

A. First, how long have you lived in ——?

B. Supposing you had to move away from —— how sorry or pleased would you be?
   1. *Very sorry*
   2. *Quite sorry*
   3. *Neither sorry nor pleased*
   4. *Quite pleased*
   5. *Very pleased*
   6. *Don't know*

C. How interested are you to know what goes on in ——?
   1. *Very interested*
   2. *Quite interested*
   3. *Only a little interested*
   4. *Not at all interested*

A. How many people would you say you know who live in —— ?
1. *None*
2. *Only one or two*
3. *A few*
4. *Many*
5. *Very many*
6. *Don't know*

B. Can you think of four men with whom you are friendly and tell me what jobs they have? You can include relations, workmates, neighbours and anyone else with whom you are friendly.
For each one named: Is he a relative? What relative?
If in farming: Does he actually work with you?

C. Thinking of all your friends, about what proportion of them live in —— ?
1. *None of them*
2. *Half or less than half of them*
3. *Most of them*
4. *All of them*
5. *Don't know/No friends*

D. And about how often do you see those in —— to speak to?
1. *Almost every day*
2. *Two or three times a week*
3. *About once a week*
4. *About once a fortnight*
5. *About once a month*
6. *Less often*
7. *Never*
8. *Don't know*

33. Do you belong to any churches, clubs or associations? We'll start with churches:

A. What is your religion, if any?

   If has a religion:
B. About how frequently do you attend?

C. Do you hold any official position in it?

   Now any clubs or associations of which you are a member – any social club, sports clubs, work clubs, anything political, or any organized group?

For each repeat B *and* C *above*

34. Thinking of other social activities, how often do you

    A. Go out visiting relatives or receive visits from relatives?

    B. Go out visiting friends or receive visits from friends?

    C. Go out to the pub for a drink?

35A. What sort of view do you think people in general have of farm workers?

    B. Why do you think they have this view?

    C. What about here in the village? What sort of view do you think other people in the village have of farm workers?

    D. What is it that decides the social standing of different people in the village, do you think?

    Now, just to wind up, can I have a few details about your family?

36A. First, do you live in a service cottage, or tied cottage as it's sometimes called?

    If no:
    B. Are you: buying a house
    renting it from the council
    renting from a private landlord
    living with parents
    other (specify)

    All
    C. Would you like to see any changes in the tied-cottage system?

    If yes:
    D. In what way? Why?

    If no:
    E. Why do you say this?

37A. Are you married?
    1. *Married*
    2. *Single*
    3. *Divorced, widowed, etc.*

If married:
B. Does your wife have a job?

If yes:
C. What type of job is it?

38. Can you give me some details about the types of jobs held by your other close relatives? First I'd like to know about your father. What job does he do?
    Take note of don't knows. If anyone is deceased, retired or unemployed, ask for last normal job. Go through persons listed below, asking in addition: Is he (was he) a trade-union member?
    If in farming: Do you actually work with him?
    Repeat for: Eldest brother, Brother No. 2, Brother No. 3, Brother No. 4, wife's father

39. *If not single*
    A. Do you have any children?

    B. How many?

    C. How many of these are living at home?

    D. How many of your children are working?

    If any working:
    E. What kind of jobs do they do?

    F. How many of those working are living at home?

    If any not working:
    G. Would you recommend a job in farming to your children?

    H. Why/Why not?

40. Now, just one final question: I would be grateful if you could tell me how much on average you earn each week before deductions but including overtime?
    And what is your basic wage?

Well, that's the lot. Thank you very much indeed for your help. Are there any questions you'd like to ask me?

MORE ABOUT PENGUINS
AND PELICANS

Penguinews, which appears every month, contains details of all the new books issued by Penguins as they are published. It is supplemented by our stocklist which includes around 5,000 titles.

A specimen copy of *Penguinews* will be sent to you free on request. Please write to Dept EP, Penguin Books Ltd, Harmondsworth, Middlesex, for your copy.

In the U.S.A.: For a complete list of books available from Penguins in the United States write to Dept CS, Penguin Books, 625 Madison Avenue, New York, New York 10022.

In Canada: For a complete list of books available from Penguins in Canada write to Penguin Books Canada Ltd, 2801 John Street, Markham, Ontario L3R 1B4.